P9-CDG-389

BLACK+DECKER

The Complete Guide to

WIRING

Updated 6th Edition

Current with 2014–2017 Electrical Codes

LIVINGSTON PUBLIC LIBRARY
10 Robert H. Harp Drive
Livingston, NJ 07039

COOL
SPRINGS
PRESS
Home and Garden Experts™

MINNEAPOLIS, MINNESOTA

621.319
COM
6th ED.

1-12-15 dt

COOL
SPRINGS
PRESS

Home and Garden Experts™

© 2014 Cool Springs Press

Sixth Edition first published in 2014 by Cool Springs Press, an imprint of Quarto Publishing Group USA Inc., 400 First Avenue North, Suite 400, Minneapolis, MN 55401. First edition published 1998 by Cowles Creative Publishing, Inc.

All rights reserved. With the exception of quoting brief passages for the purposes of review, no part of this publication may be reproduced without prior written permission from the Publisher.

The information in this book is true and complete to the best of our knowledge. All recommendations are made without any guarantee on the part of the author or Publisher, who also disclaims any liability incurred in connection with the use of this data or specific details.

Cool Springs Press titles are also available at discounts in bulk quantity for industrial or sales-promotional use. For details write to Special Sales Manager at Quarto Publishing Group USA Inc., 400 First Avenue North, Suite 400, Minneapolis, MN 55401 USA. To find out more about our books, visit us online at www.coolspringspress. com.

Library of Congress Cataloging-in-Publication Data

The complete guide to wiring : current with 2014-2017 electrical codes. -- 6th edition.
   pages cm
 At head of title: BLACK+DECKER.
 Summary: "New 6th edition has been revised and updated to be fully compliant with the 2014 National Electrical Code. Full-color photography and step-by-step information covers all of the most common do-it-yourself home wiring skills and projects, including installation and repair."-- Provided by publisher.
 Includes index.
 ISBN 978-1-59186-612-1 (paperback)
 1. Electric wiring, Interior--Amateurs' manuals. 2. Dwellings--Maintenance and repair--Amateurs' manuals. 3. Dwellings--Electric equipment--Amateurs' manuals. I. Black & Decker Corporation (Towson, Md.) II. Title: BLACK+DECKER The complete guide to wiring.

TK3284.C65 2014
621.319'24--dc23

2014000449

Acquisitions Editor: Mark Johanson
Design Manager: Brad Springer
Layout: Laurie Young
Edition Editor: Bruce Barker
Photography: Rau + Barber
Photo Assistance: Adam Esco

Printed in China
10 9 8 7 6 5 4 3 2

The Complete Guide to Wiring
Created by: The Editors of Cool Spring Press, in cooperation with BLACK+DECKER.
BLACK+DECKER and the BLACK+DECKER logo are trademarks of The Black & Decker Corporation and are used under license. All rights reserved.

NOTICE TO READERS

For safety, use caution, care, and good judgment when following the procedures described in this book. The publisher and BLACK+DECKER cannot assume responsibility for any damage to property or injury to persons as a result of misuse of the information provided.

The techniques shown in this book are general techniques for various applications. In some instances, additional techniques not shown in this book may be required. Always follow manufacturers' instructions included with products, since deviating from the directions may void warranties. The projects in this book vary widely as to skill levels required: some may not be appropriate for all do-it-yourselfers, and some may require professional help.

Consult your local building department for information on building permits, codes, and other laws as they apply to your project.

Contents

The Complete Guide to
Wiring 6th Edition

Introduction 7

Working Safely with Wiring 9

How Electricity Works 10

Glossary of Electrical Terms 14

Understanding Electrical Circuits 16

Grounding & Polarization 18

Home Wiring Tools 20

Wiring Safety 22

Wire, Cable & Conduit 25

Wire & Cable 26

NM Cable 34

Conduit 42

Surface-Mounted Wiring 48

Boxes & Panels 59

Electrical Boxes 60

Installing Boxes 66

Electrical Panels 74

Switches 83

Wall Switches 84

Types of Wall Switches 86

Specialty Switches 94

Testing Switches 98

Receptacles 103

Types of Receptacles 104

Receptacle Wiring 110

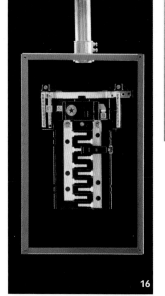

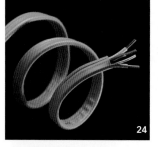

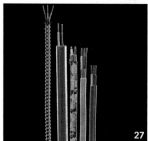

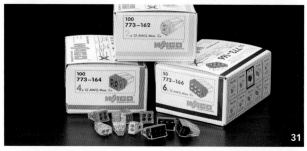

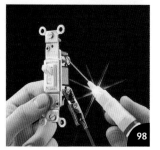

Contents (Cont.)

GFCI Receptacles 114

Testing Receptacles 118

Preliminary Work 121

Planning Your Project 122

Highlights of the National Electrical Code 128

Wiring a Room Addition 140

Wiring a Kitchen 144

Circuit Maps 149

Common Household Circuits 150

Common Wiring Projects 167

GFCI & AFCI Breakers 168

Whole-House Surge Arrestors 170

Service Panels 172

Grounding & Bonding a Wiring System 180

Subpanels 186

120/240-Volt Dryer Receptacles 190

120/240-Volt Range Receptacles 191

Ceilings Lights 192

Recessed Ceiling Lights 196

Track Lights 200

Undercabinet Lights 204

Vanity Lights 208

Low-Voltage Cable Lights 210

Hard-Wired Smoke & CO Alarms 214

Landscape Lights 216

Doorbells 220

Programmable Thermostats 224

Wireless Switches 228

Baseboard Heaters. 232

Wall Heaters. 236

Underfloor Radiant Heat Systems 238

Ceiling Fans 244

Remote-Control Ceiling Fan Retrofit 248

Bathroom Exhaust Fans. 252

Range Hoods 256

Backup Power Supply 260

Installing a Transfer Switch 266

Outbuildings. 272

Motion-Sensing Floodlights 280

Standalone Solar Lighting System 284

Repair Projects. 293

Repairing Light Fixtures 294

Repairing Chandeliers 298

Repairing Ceiling Fans 300

Repairing Fluorescent Lights 304

Replacing Plugs & Cords 310

Replacing a Lamp Socket. 314

Appendix: Common Mistakes. 316

Conversions. 330

Resources. 331

Index 336

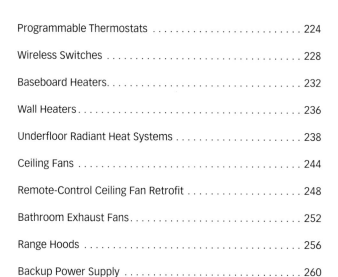
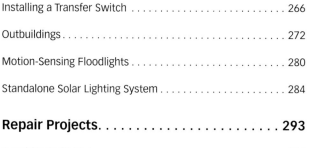

Introduction

This newly updated, 6th edition of BLACK+DECKER *Complete Guide to Wiring* is the most comprehensive and current book on home wiring you'll find anywhere. The information you'll find within conforms to the 2014 edition of the National Electrical Code (NEC) as published by its governing authority, the National Fire Prevention Association. Typically, most simple home wiring projects are unaffected by the changes to the NEC, which is updated every three years. But according to top-notch home inspector Bruce Barker, who helped us update this book for its 6th edition, there are four code alterations that may impact homeowners and their DIY wiring projects soon. Most local governing authorities use the NEC as the basis for their set of codes, although it usually takes a few years before the changes are adopted. And local codes always supersede any national codes.

Here are the changes most likely to affect your wiring project, based on the new 2014 edition of the NEC:

1. **The available neutral at switch boxes.** Some switch wiring methods require that the white wire be used (and labeled) as a hot wire. A single pole switch at the end of the circuit (a switch leg) is one example. Three-way and four-way switches are other examples.

   New computer-controlled and timer switches need power to operate, which means that a neutral wire is required to complete the electrical circuit. To allow easier installation of these new switches, the new NEC requires an available neutral wire in many switch boxes. In most cases, you will just cap the neutral wire and leave it, looking a bit lonely, in the switch box. To provide this neutral wire, you'll need another wire. You may need to substitute 3-wire cable where you formerly used 2-wire cable, or you may need to substitute 2 runs of 2-wire cable where you formerly used 3-wire cable. Our new wiring diagrams will show you how to do this. When it goes into effect, this change will apply only to new construction and expanded circuits.

2. **AFCI protection for most circuits.** Changes to the NEC earlier this century mandated AFCI (Arc Fault Circuit Interrupter) protection on all bedroom circuits. The new NEC expands this requirement to include most 15 and 20 amp, 120 volt, receptacle and lighting circuits. Exceptions include the kitchen and bathroom receptacle circuits and the garage and exterior receptacle circuits. AFCI circuit breakers are required in most cases. AFCI receptacles are available and may be allowed when it is impractical to install AFCI circuit breakers.

   Adding an AFCI device may not be as easy as installing it. Some AFCI devices may not be compatible with shared neutral (multi-wire) branch circuits. Some AFCI devices may not be compatible with dimmers, especially solid-state dimmers. You may want to have an electrician help you when you install AFCI devices.

3. **Garage receptacles may not feed other outlets.** You may no longer tie into a receptacle in your garage to power anything outside of the garage, such as an outdoor security light. Also, you must provide a receptacle for every parking spot in the garage.

4. **AFCI and GFCI (Ground Fault Circuit Interrupter) protection for new receptacles.** When that old receptacle blows you may not replace it with a standard duplex receptacle, even if that's what you had before. If codes require AFCI or GFCI protection for the affected receptacle you need to provide it.

Working Safely with Wiring

The only way you can possibly manage home wiring projects safely is to understand how electricity works and how it is delivered from the street to the outlets in your home.

The most essential quality to appreciate about electricity is that the typical amounts that flow through the wires in your home can be fatal if you contact it directly. Sources estimate that up to 1,000 people are electrocuted accidentally in the U.S. every year. In addition, as many as 500 die in fires from electrical causes. Home wiring can be a very satisfying task for do-it-yourselfers, but if you don't know what you're doing or are in any way uncomfortable with the idea of working around electricity, do not attempt it.

This chapter explains the fundamental principles behind the electrical circuits that run through our homes. It also includes some basic tips for working safely with wiring, and it introduces you to the essential tools you'll need for the job. The beginner should consider it mandatory reading. Even if you have a good grasp of electrical principles, take some time to review the material. A refresher course is always useful.

In this chapter:

- How Electricity Works
- Glossary of Electrical Terms
- Understanding Electrical Circuits
- Grounding & Polarization
- Home Wiring Tools
- Wiring Safety

How Electricity Works

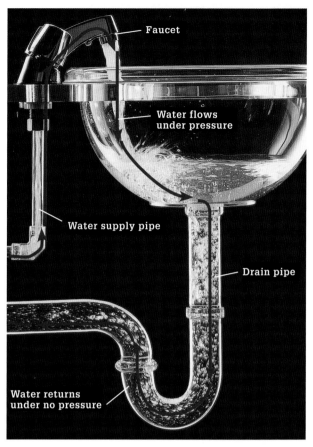

Faucet

Water flows
under pressure

Water supply pipe

Drain pipe

Water returns
under no pressure

A household electrical system can be compared with a home's plumbing system. Electrical current flows in wires in much the same way that water flows inside pipes. Both electricity and water enter the home, are distributed throughout the house, do their "work," and exit.

In plumbing, water first flows through the pressurized water supply system. In electricity, current first flows along hot wires. Current flowing along hot wires also is pressurized. Electrical pressure is called voltage.

Large supply pipes can carry a greater volume of water than small pipes. Likewise, large electrical wires carry more current than small wires. This electrical current-carrying capacity of wires is called ampacity.

Water is made available for use through the faucets, spigots, and showerheads in a home. Electricity is made available through receptacles, switches, and fixtures.

Water finally leaves the home through a drain system, which is not pressurized. Similarly, electrical current flows back through neutral wires. The current in neutral wires is not pressurized and is at zero voltage.

Water and electricity both flow. The main difference is that you can see water (and touching water isn't likely to kill you). Like electricity, water enters a fixture under high pressure and exits under no pressure.

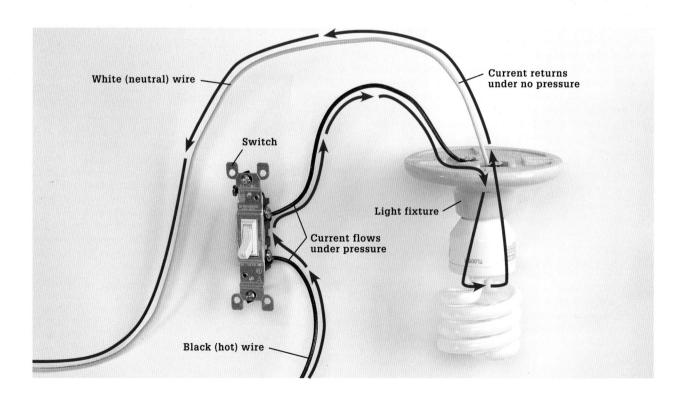

White (neutral) wire

Current returns
under no pressure

Switch

Light fixture

Current flows
under pressure

Black (hot) wire

The Delivery System

Electricity that enters the home is produced by large power plants. Power plants are located in all parts of the country and generate electricity with generators that are turned by water, wind, or steam. From these plants electricity enters large "step-up" transformers that increase voltage to half a million volts or more.

Electricity flows at these high voltages and travels through high-voltage transmission wires to communities that can be hundreds of miles from the power plants. "Step-down" transformers located at substations then reduce the voltage for distribution along street wires. On utility power poles, smaller transformers further reduce the voltage to ordinary 120-volt electricity for household use.

Wires carrying electricity to a house either run underground or are strung overhead and attached to a post called a service mast. Most homes built after 1950 have three wires running to the service head: two power wires, each carrying 120 volts, and a grounded neutral wire. Electricity from the two 120-volt wires may be combined at the service panel to supply electricity to large 240-volt appliances such as clothes dryers or electric water heaters.

Incoming electricity passes through a meter that measures electricity consumption. Electricity then enters the service panel, where it is distributed to circuits that run throughout the house. The service panel also contains fuses or circuit breakers that shut off power to the individual circuits in the event of a short circuit or an overload. Certain high-wattage appliances, such as microwave ovens, are usually plugged into their own individual circuits to prevent overloads.

Voltage ratings determined by power companies and manufacturers have changed over the years. These changes do not affect the performance of new devices connected to older wiring. For making electrical calculations, use a rating of 120 volts or 240 volts for your circuits.

Power plants supply electricity to thousands of homes and businesses. Step-up transformers increase the voltage produced at the plant.

Substations are located near the communities they serve. A typical substation takes electricity from high-voltage transmission wires and reduces it for distribution along street wires.

Electrical transformers reduce the high-voltage electricity that flows through wires along neighborhood streets. A utility pole transformer—or ground transformer—reduces voltage from 10,000 volts to the normal 120-volt electricity used in households.

Parts of the Electrical System

The service mast (metal pole) and the weatherhead create the entry point for electricity into your home. The mast is supplied with three wires, two of which (the insulated wires) each carry 120 volts and originate at the nearest transformer. In some areas electricity enters from below ground as a lateral, instead of the overhead drop shown above.

The meter measures the amount of electricity consumed. It is usually attached to the side of the house and connects to the service mast. The electric meter belongs to your local power utility company. If you suspect the meter is not functioning properly, contact the power company.

Surges in current flow to grounding rod

Current flows back to neutral at service mast

A grounding wire connects the electrical system to the earth through a metal grounding rod driven next to the house.

Light fixtures attach directly to a household electrical system. They are usually controlled with wall switches. The two common types of light fixtures are incandescent and fluorescent.

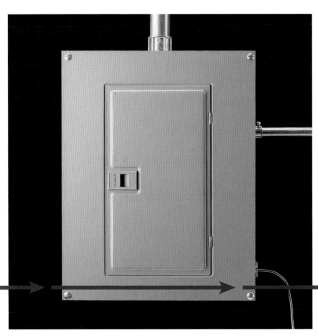

The main service panel, in the form of a fuse box or breaker box, distributes power to individual circuits. Fuses or circuit breakers protect each circuit from short circuits and overloads. Fuses and circuit breakers also are used to shut off power to individual circuits while repairs are made.

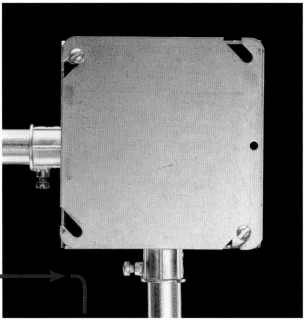

Electrical boxes enclose wire connections. According to the National Electrical Code, all wire splices and connections must be contained entirely in a covered plastic or metal electrical box.

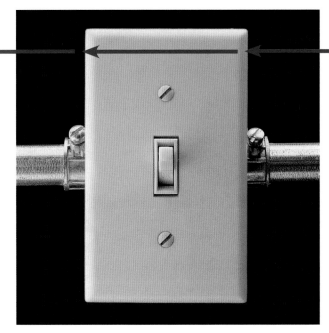

Switches control electricity passing through hot circuit wires. Switches can be wired to control light fixtures, ceiling fans, appliances, and receptacles.

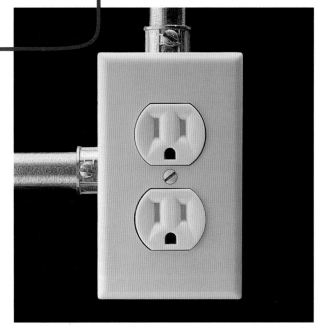

Receptacles, sometimes called outlets, provide plug-in access to electricity. A 120-volt, 15-amp receptacle with a grounding hole is the most typical receptacle in wiring systems installed after 1965. Most receptacles have two plug-in locations and are called duplex receptacles.

Glossary of Electrical Terms ▸

Ampere (or amp): Refers to the rate at which electrical current flows to a light, tool, or appliance.

Armored cable: An assembly of insulated wires enclosed in a flexible, interlocked metallic armor.

Box: A device used to contain wiring connections.

BX: A brand name for an early type of armored cable that is no longer made. The current term is armored cable.

Cable: Two or more wires that are grouped together and protected by a covering or sheath.

Circuit: A continuous loop of electrical current flowing along wires.

Circuit breaker: A safety device that interrupts an electrical circuit in the event of an overload or short circuit.

Conductor: Any material that allows electrical current to flow through it. Copper wire is an especially good conductor.

Conduit: A metal or plastic pipe used to protect wires.

Continuity: An uninterrupted electrical pathway through a circuit or electrical fixture.

Current: The flow of electricity along a conductor.

Duplex receptacle: A receptacle that provides connections for two plugs.

Flexible metal conduit (FMC): Hollow, coiled steel or aluminum tubing that may be filled with wires (similar to Armored Cable, but AC is pre-wired).

Fuse: A safety device, usually found in older homes, that interrupts electrical circuits during an overload or short circuit.

Greenfield: A brand name for an early type of flexible metal conduit. The current term is flexible metal conduit. Note: flexible metal conduit is different from armored cable.

Grounded wire: See neutral wire.

Grounding wire: A wire used in an electrical circuit to conduct current to the service panel in the event of a ground fault. The grounding wire often is a bare copper wire.

Hot wire: Any wire that carries voltage. In an electrical circuit, the hot wire usually is covered with black or red insulation.

Insulator: Any material, such as plastic or rubber, that resists the flow of electrical current. Insulating materials protect wires and cables.

Junction box: See box.

Meter: A device used to measure the amount of electrical power being used.

Neutral wire: A wire that returns current at zero voltage to the source of electrical power. Usually covered with white or light gray insulation. Also called the grounded wire.

Non-metallic sheathed cable: NM cable consists of two or more insulated conductors and, in most cases, a bare ground wire housed in a durable PVC casing.

Outlet: A place where electricity is taken for use. A receptacle is a common type of outlet. A box for a ceiling fan is another type of outlet.

Overload: A demand for more current than the circuit wires or electrical device was designed to carry. This should cause a fuse to blow or a circuit breaker to trip.

Pigtail: A short wire used to connect two or more wires to a single screw terminal.

Polarized receptacle: A receptacle designed to keep hot current flowing along black or red wires and neutral current flowing along white or gray wires.

Power: The work performed by electricity for a period of time. Use of power makes heat, motion, or light.

Receptacle: A device that provides plug-in access to electricity.

Romex: A brand name of plastic-sheathed electrical cable that is commonly used for indoor wiring. Commonly known as NM cable.

Screw terminal: A place where a wire connects to a receptacle, switch, or fixture.

Service panel: A metal box usually near the site where electricity enters the house. In the service panel, electrical current is split into individual circuits. In residences, the service panel has circuit breakers or fuses to protect each circuit.

Short circuit: An accidental and improper contact between two current-carrying wires or between a current-carrying wire and a grounding conductor.

Switch: A device that controls electricity passing through hot circuit wires. Used to turn lights and appliances on and off.

UL: An abbreviation for Underwriters Laboratories, an organization that tests electrical devices and manufactured products for safety.

Voltage (or volts): A measurement of electricity in terms of pressure.

Wattage (or watt): A measurement of electrical power in terms of total work performed. Watts can be calculated by multiplying the voltage times the amps.

Wire connector: A device used to connect two or more wires together. Also called a wire nut.

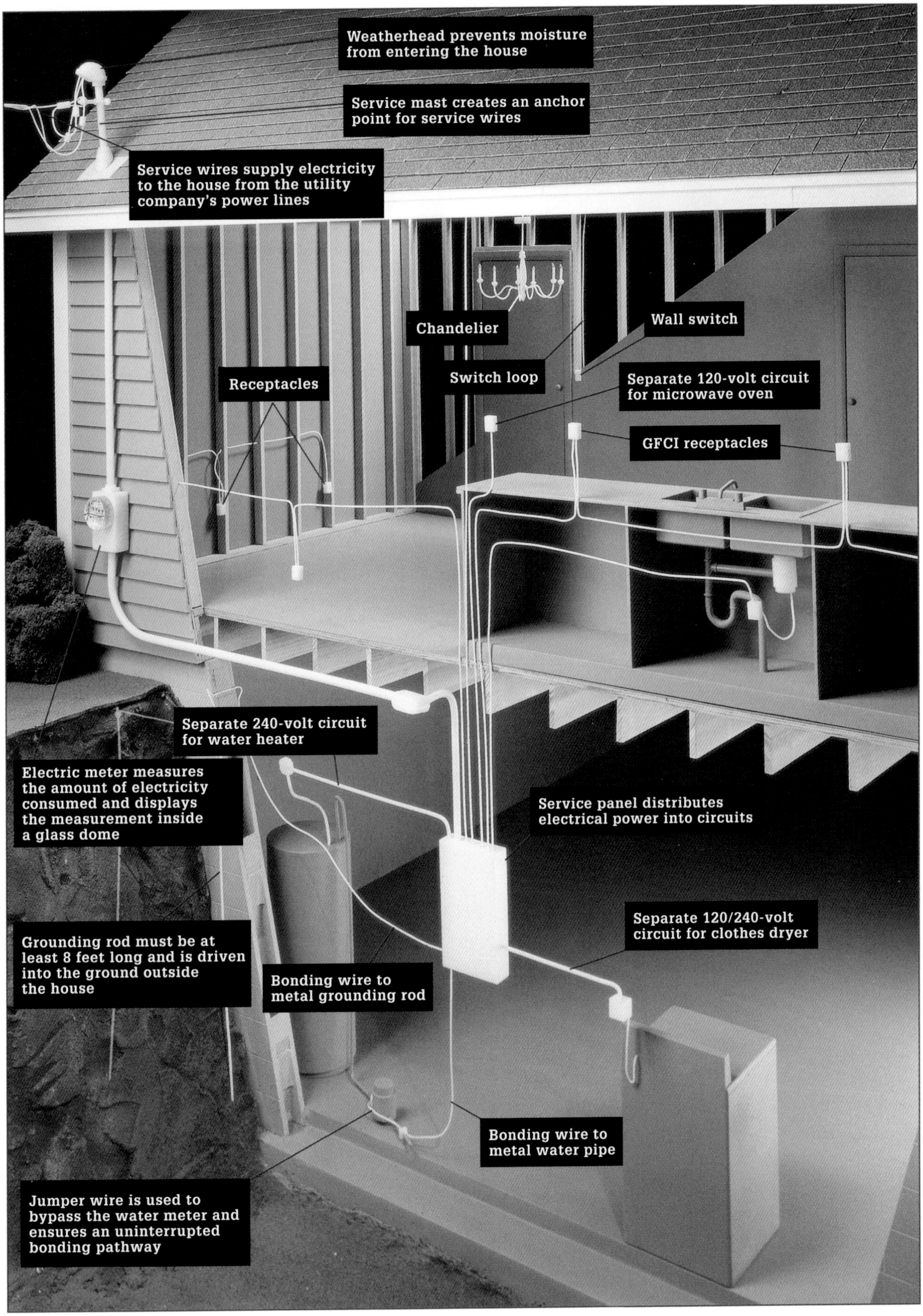

Weatherhead prevents moisture from entering the house

Service mast creates an anchor point for service wires

Service wires supply electricity to the house from the utility company's power lines

Chandelier

Wall switch

Receptacles

Switch loop

Separate 120-volt circuit for microwave oven

GFCI receptacles

Separate 240-volt circuit for water heater

Electric meter measures the amount of electricity consumed and displays the measurement inside a glass dome

Service panel distributes electrical power into circuits

Separate 120/240-volt circuit for clothes dryer

Grounding rod must be at least 8 feet long and is driven into the ground outside the house

Bonding wire to metal grounding rod

Bonding wire to metal water pipe

Jumper wire is used to bypass the water meter and ensures an uninterrupted bonding pathway

Understanding Electrical Circuits

An electrical circuit is a continuous loop. Household circuits carry electricity from the main service panel, throughout the house, and back to the main service panel. Several switches, receptacles, light fixtures, or appliances may be connected to a single circuit.

Current enters a circuit loop on hot wires and returns along neutral wires. These wires are color coded for easy identification. Hot wires are black or red, and neutral wires are white or light gray. For safety, all modern circuits include a bare copper or green insulated grounding wire. The grounding wire conducts current in the event of a ground fault (see page 165) and helps reduce the chance of severe electrical shock. The service panel also has a bonding wire connected to a metal water pipe and a grounding wire connected to a metal grounding rod, buried underground, or to another type of grounding electrode.

If a circuit carries too much current, it can overload. A fuse or a circuit breaker protects each circuit in case of overloads.

Current returns to the service panel along a neutral circuit wire. Current then leaves the house on a large neutral service wire that returns it to the utility transformer.

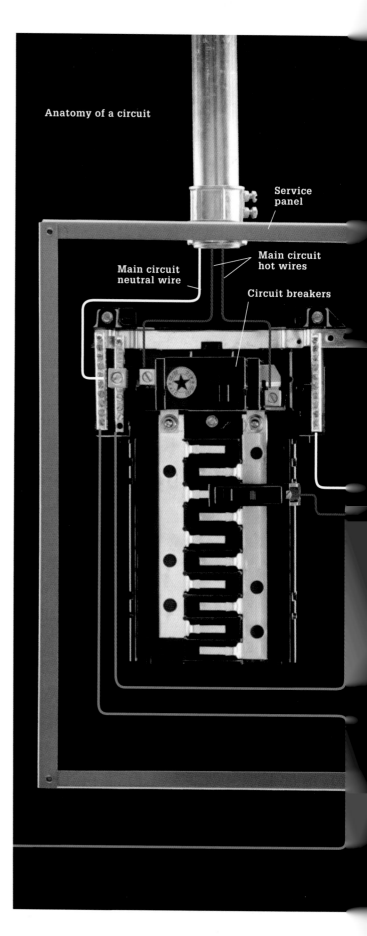

Anatomy of a circuit

Service panel

Main circuit hot wires

Main circuit neutral wire

Circuit breakers

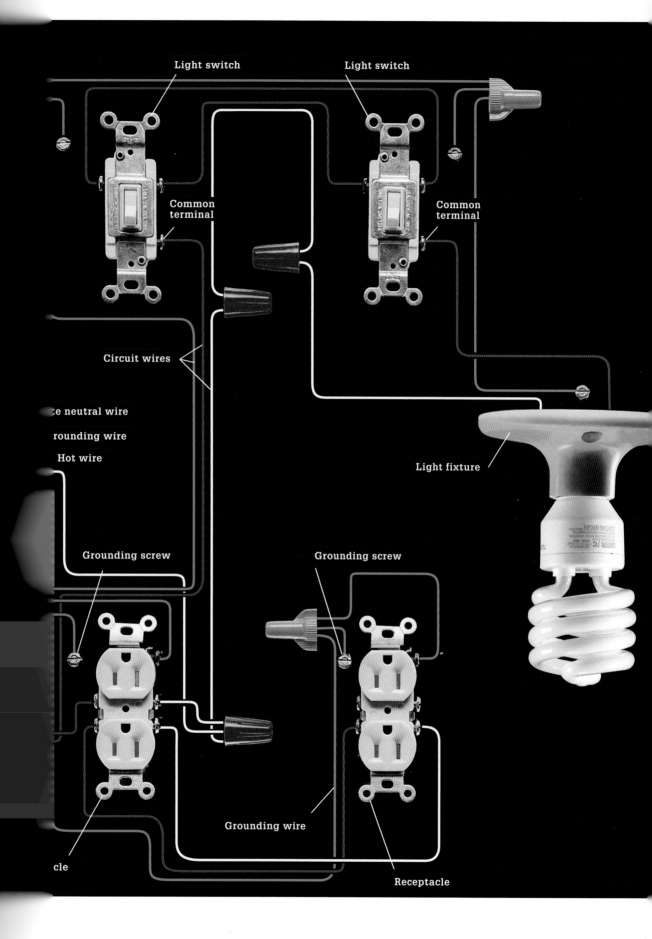

Light switch

Light switch

Common
terminal

Common
terminal

Circuit wires

ce neutral wire

rounding wire

Hot wire

Grounding screw

Grounding screw

Light fixture

Grounding wire

cle

Receptacle

Grounding & Polarization

Electricity always seeks to return to its source and complete a continuous circuit. Contrary to popular belief, electricity will take all available return paths to its source, not just the path of lowest resistance. In a household wiring system, this return path is provided by white neutral wires that return current to the main service panel. From the service panel, current returns along the uninsulated neutral service wire to a power pole transformer.

You will see the terms grounding and bonding used in this and other books about electricity. These terms are often misunderstood. You should understand the difference to safely work on electrical circuits.

Bonding connects the non-current-carrying metal parts of the electrical system, such as metal boxes and metal conduit, in a continuous low-resistance path back to the main service panel. If this metal becomes energized (a ground fault), current travels on the bonded metal and quickly increases to an amount that trips the circuit breaker or blows the fuse. The dead circuit alerts people to a problem.

Other metal that could become energized also must be bonded to the home's electrical system. Metal water and gas pipes are the most common examples. A metal water and gas pipe could become energized by coming in contact with a damaged electrical wire. Metal gas pipe could become energized by a ground fault in a gas appliance such as a furnace.

Bonding is a very important safety system. A person could receive a fatal shock if he or she touches energized metal that is improperly bonded, because that person becomes electricity's return path to its source. Bonding is also a fire safety system that reduces the chance of electrical fires.

Grounding connects the home's electrical system to the earth. Grounding's primary purpose is to help stabilize voltage fluctuations caused by lightning and other problems in the electrical grid. Grounding also provides a secondary return path for electricity in case there is a problem in the normal return path.

Grounding is accomplished by connecting a wire between the main service panel and a grounding electrode. The most common grounding electrode is a buried copper rod. Other grounding electrodes include reinforcing steel in the footing, called a ufer ground.

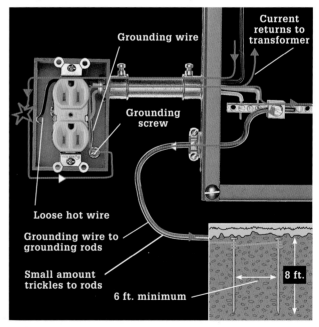

Normal current flow: Current enters the electrical box along a black hot wire and then returns to the service panel along a white neutral wire.

Ground Fault: Current is detoured by a loose wire in contact with the metal box. The grounding wire and bonded metal conduit pick it up and channel it back to the main service panel, where the overcurrent device is tripped, stopping further flow of current. Most current in the bonding and ground system flows back to the transformer; some may trickle out through the copper that leads to the grounding node.

Grounding of the home electrical system is accomplished by wiring the household electrical system to a metal cold water pipe and metal grounding rods that are buried in the earth.

After 1920, most American homes included receptacles that accepted polarized plugs. The two-slot polarized plug and receptacle was designed to keep hot current flowing along black or red wires and neutral current flowing along white or gray wires.

The metal jacket around armored cable and flexible metal conduit, widely installed in homes during the 1940s, provided a bonding path. When connected to metal junction boxes, it provided a metal pathway back to the service panel. Note, however, that deterioration of this older cable may decrease its effectiveness as a bonding conductor.

Modern cable includes a green insulated or bare copper wire that serves as the bonding path. This grounding wire is connected to all three-slot receptacles and metal boxes to provide a continuous pathway for any ground-faulted current. By plugging a three-prong plug into a grounded three-slot receptacle, people are protected from ground faults that occur in appliances, tools, or other electric devices.

Use a receptacle adapter to plug three-prong plugs into two-slot receptacles, but use it only if the receptacle connects to a grounding wire or grounded electrical box. Adapters have short grounding wires or wire loops that attach to the receptacle's coverplate mounting screw. The mounting screw connects the adapter to the grounded metal electrical box.

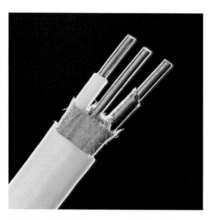

Modern NM (nonmetallic) cable, found in most wiring systems installed after 1965, contains a bare copper wire that provides bonding for receptacle and switch boxes.

Armored cable is sold pre-installed in a flexible metal housing. It contains a green insulated ground wire along with black and white conductors. Flexible metal conduit (not shown) is sold empty.

Polarized receptacles have a long slot and a short slot. Used with a polarized plug, the polarized receptacle keeps electrical current directed for safety.

Tamper resistent three-slot receptacles are required by code for new homes. They are usually connected to a standard two-wire cable with ground.

A receptacle adapter allows three-prong plugs to be inserted into two-slot receptacles. The adapter should only be used with receptacles mounted in a bonded metal box, and the grounding loop or wire of the adapter must be attached to the coverplate mounting screw.

Double-insulated tools have non-conductive plastic bodies to prevent shocks caused by ground faults. Because of these features, double-insulated tools can be used safely with ungrounded receptacles.

Home Wiring Tools

To complete the wiring projects shown in this book, you need a few specialty electrical tools as well as a collection of basic hand tools. As with any tool purchase, invest in quality products when you buy tools for electrical work. Keep your tools clean, and sharpen or replace any cutting tools that have dull edges.

The materials used for electrical wiring have changed dramatically in the last 20 years, making it much easier for homeowners to do their own electrical work. The following pages show how to work with the following components for your projects.

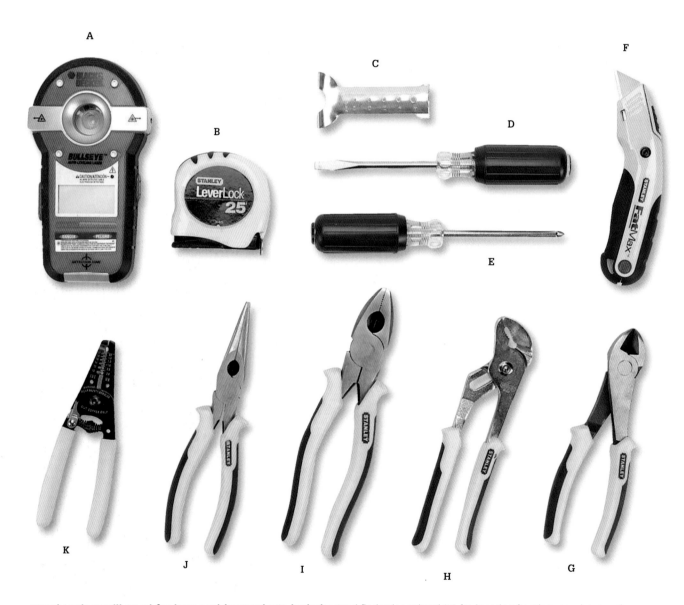

Hand tools you'll need for home wiring projects include: Stud finder/laser level (A) for locating framing members and aligning electrical boxes; tape measure (B); a cable ripper (C) for scoring NM sheathing; standard (D) and Phillips (E) screwdrivers; a utility knife (F); side cutters (G) for cutting wires; channel-type pliers (H) for general gripping and crimping; linesman pliers (I) that combine side cutter and gripping jaws; needlenose pliers (J); wire strippers (K) for removing insulation from conductors.

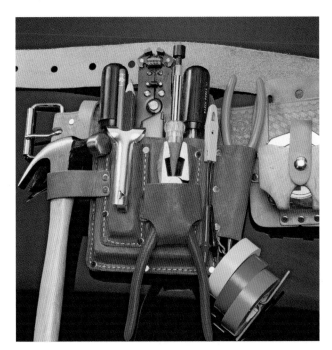

Use a tool belt to keep frequently used tools within easy reach. Electrical tapes in a variety of colors are used for marking wires and for attaching cables to a fish tape.

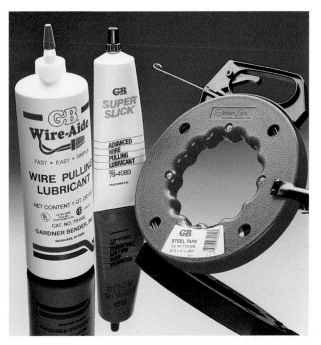

A fish tape is useful for installing cables in finished wall cavities and for pulling wires through conduit. Products designed for lubrication reduce friction and make it easier to pull cables and wires.

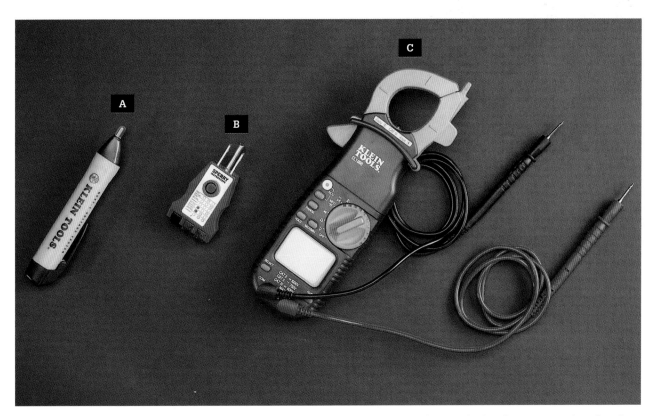

Diagnostic tools for home wiring use include: A touchless circuit tester (A) to safely check wires for current and confirm that circuits are dead; a plug-in tester (B) to check receptacles for correct polarity, grounding, and circuit protection; a multimeter (C) to measure AC/DC voltage, AC/DC current, resistance, capacitance, frequency, and duty cycle (model shown is an auto-ranging digital multimeter with clamp-on jaws that measure through sheathing and wire insulation).

Wiring Safety

Safety should be the primary concern of anyone working with electricity. Although most household electrical repairs are simple and straightforward, always use caution and good judgment when working with electrical wiring or devices. Common sense can prevent accidents.

The basic rule of electrical safety is: Always turn off power to the area or device you are working on. At the main service panel, remove the fuse or shut off the circuit breaker that controls the circuit you are servicing. Then check to make sure the power is off by testing for power with a voltage tester. *Tip: Test a live circuit with the voltage tester to verify that it is working before you rely on it.* Restore power only when the repair or replacement project is complete.

Follow the safety tips shown on these pages. Never attempt an electrical project beyond your skill or confidence level.

Shut power OFF at the main service panel or the main fuse box before beginning any work.

Create a circuit index and affix it to the inside of the door to your main service panel. Update it as needed.

Confirm power is OFF by testing at the outlet, switch, or fixture with a voltage tester.

Use only UL-approved electrical parts or devices. These devices have been tested for safety by Underwriters Laboratories.

Wear rubber-soled shoes while working on electrical projects. On damp floors, stand on a rubber mat or dry wooden boards.

Use fiberglass or wood ladders when making routine household repairs near the service mast.

Extension cords are for temporary use only. Cords must be rated for the intended usage.

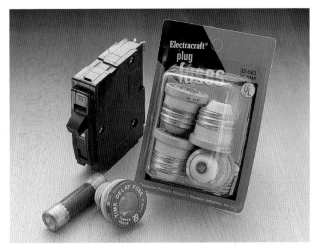

Breakers and fuses must be compatible with the panel manufacturer and match the circuit capacity.

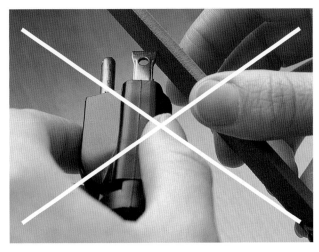

Never alter the prongs of a plug to fit a receptacle. If possible, install a new grounded receptacle.

Do not penetrate walls or ceilings without first shutting off electrical power to the circuits that may be hidden.

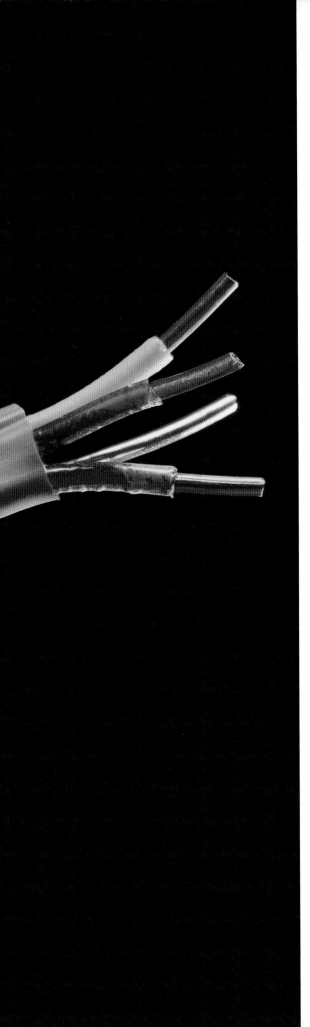

Wire, Cable & Conduit

Wire and cable comprise the electrical infrastructure in your home. Selecting the appropriate size and type and handling it correctly is absolutely necessary to a successful wiring project that will pass inspection.

Copper wire is the primary conductor of electricity in any home. The electricity itself travels on the outer surfaces of the wire, so insulation is normally added to the wires to protect against shock and fires. The insulated wires are frequently grouped together and bound up in rugged plastic sheathing according to gauge and function. Multiple wires housed in shared sheathing form a cable. In some cases, the wires are grouped in metal or plastic tubes known as conduit. Conduit (also known as raceway) is used primarily in situations where the cables or wires are exposed, such as open garage walls.

This chapter introduces some of the many varieties of wire, cable, and conduit used in home construction and explains which types to use where. It also will demonstrate the essential skills used to run new cable, install conduit, strip sheathing, make wire connections, and more.

In this chapter:

- Wire & Cable
- NM Cable
- Conduit
- Surface-Mounted Wiring

Wire & Cable

Wires are made of copper, aluminum, or aluminum covered with a thin layer of copper. Solid copper wires are the best conductors of electricity and are the most widely used. Aluminum and copper-covered aluminum wires require special installation techniques.

A group of two or more wires enclosed in a metal, rubber, or plastic sheath is called a cable (see photo, opposite page). The sheath protects the wires from damage. Conduit also protects wires, but it is not considered a cable.

Individual wires are covered with rubber or plastic vinyl insulation. An exception is a bare copper grounding wire, which does not need an insulation cover. The insulation is color coded (see chart, below left) to identify the wire as a hot wire, a neutral wire, or a grounding wire. New cable sheathing is also color coded to indicate the size of the wires inside. White means #14 wire, yellow means #12 wire, and red means #10 wire.

In most wiring systems installed after 1965, the wires and cables are insulated with plastic vinyl. This type of insulation is very durable and can last as long as the house itself.

Before 1965, wires and cables were insulated with rubber. Rubber insulation has a life expectancy of about 25 years. Old insulation that is cracked or damaged can be reinforced temporarily by wrapping the wire with plastic electrical tape. However, old wiring with cracked or damaged insulation should be inspected by a qualified electrician to make sure it is safe.

Wires must be large enough for the amperage rating of the circuit (see chart, below right). A wire that is too small can become dangerously hot. Wire sizes are categorized according to the American Wire Gauge (AWG) system. To check the size of a wire, use the wire stripper openings of a combination tool (see page 30) as a guide.

Wire Color Chart ▸

WIRE COLOR		FUNCTION
	White or gray	Neutral wire carrying current at zero voltage
	Black	Hot wire carrying current at full voltage
	Red	Hot wire carrying current at full voltage
	White, black markings	Hot wire carrying current at full voltage
	Green	Serves as a bonding pathway
	Bare copper	Serves as a bonding pathway

Individual wires are color-coded to identify their function. In some circuit installations, the white wire serves as a hot wire that carries voltage. If so, this white wire may be labeled with black tape or paint to identify it as a hot wire.

Wire Size Chart ▸

WIRE GAUGE		WIRE CAPACITY & USE
	#6	55 amps, 240 volts; central air conditioner, electric furnace
	#8	40 amps, 240 volts; electric range, central air conditioner
	#10	30 amps, 240 volts; window air conditioner, clothes dryer
	#12	20 amps, 120 volts; light fixtures, receptacles, microwave oven
	#14	15 amps, 120 volts; light fixtures, receptacles
	#16	Light-duty extension cords
	#18 to 22	Thermostats, doorbells, security systems

Wire sizes (shown actual size) are categorized by the American Wire Gauge system. The larger the wire size, the smaller the AWG number. The ampacities in this table are for copper wires in NM cable. The ampacity for the same wire in conduit is usually more. The ampacity for aluminum wire is less.

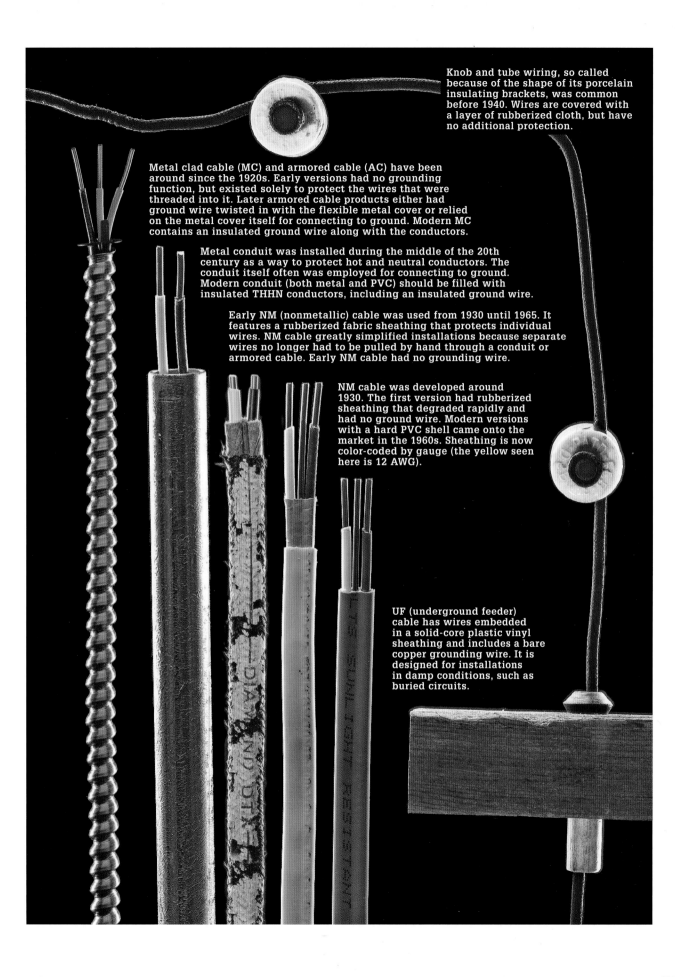

Knob and tube wiring, so called because of the shape of its porcelain insulating brackets, was common before 1940. Wires are covered with a layer of rubberized cloth, but have no additional protection.

Metal clad cable (MC) and armored cable (AC) have been around since the 1920s. Early versions had no grounding function, but existed solely to protect the wires that were threaded into it. Later armored cable products either had ground wire twisted in with the flexible metal cover or relied on the metal cover itself for connecting to ground. Modern MC contains an insulated ground wire along with the conductors.

Metal conduit was installed during the middle of the 20th century as a way to protect hot and neutral conductors. The conduit itself often was employed for connecting to ground. Modern conduit (both metal and PVC) should be filled with insulated THHN conductors, including an insulated ground wire.

Early NM (nonmetallic) cable was used from 1930 until 1965. It features a rubberized fabric sheathing that protects individual wires. NM cable greatly simplified installations because separate wires no longer had to be pulled by hand through a conduit or armored cable. Early NM cable had no grounding wire.

NM cable was developed around 1930. The first version had rubberized sheathing that degraded rapidly and had no ground wire. Modern versions with a hard PVC shell came onto the market in the 1960s. Sheathing is now color-coded by gauge (the yellow seen here is 12 AWG).

UF (underground feeder) cable has wires embedded in a solid-core plastic vinyl sheathing and includes a bare copper grounding wire. It is designed for installations in damp conditions, such as buried circuits.

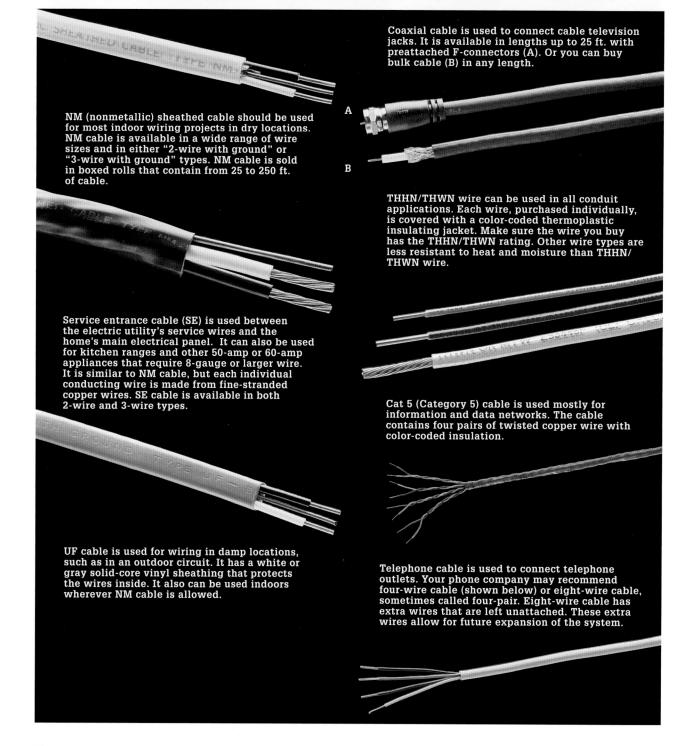

NM (nonmetallic) sheathed cable should be used for most indoor wiring projects in dry locations. NM cable is available in a wide range of wire sizes and in either "2-wire with ground" or "3-wire with ground" types. NM cable is sold in boxed rolls that contain from 25 to 250 ft. of cable.

Service entrance cable (SE) is used between the electric utility's service wires and the home's main electrical panel. It can also be used for kitchen ranges and other 50-amp or 60-amp appliances that require 8-gauge or larger wire. It is similar to NM cable, but each individual conducting wire is made from fine-stranded copper wires. SE cable is available in both 2-wire and 3-wire types.

UF cable is used for wiring in damp locations, such as in an outdoor circuit. It has a white or gray solid-core vinyl sheathing that protects the wires inside. It also can be used indoors wherever NM cable is allowed.

Coaxial cable is used to connect cable television jacks. It is available in lengths up to 25 ft. with preattached F-connectors (A). Or you can buy bulk cable (B) in any length.

THHN/THWN wire can be used in all conduit applications. Each wire, purchased individually, is covered with a color-coded thermoplastic insulating jacket. Make sure the wire you buy has the THHN/THWN rating. Other wire types are less resistant to heat and moisture than THHN/THWN wire.

Cat 5 (Category 5) cable is used mostly for information and data networks. The cable contains four pairs of twisted copper wire with color-coded insulation.

Telephone cable is used to connect telephone outlets. Your phone company may recommend four-wire cable (shown below) or eight-wire cable, sometimes called four-pair. Eight-wire cable has extra wires that are left unattached. These extra wires allow for future expansion of the system.

NM Sheathing Colors

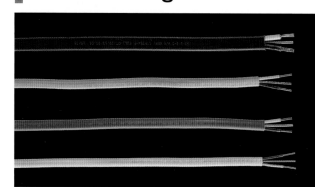

The PVC sheathing for NM cable is coded by color so wiring inspectors can tell what the capacity of the cable is at a glance.

- Black = 6 or 8 AWG conductors
- Yellow = 12 AWG conductors
- Orange = 10 AWG conductors
- White = 14 AWG conductors
- Gray = UF cable (see photo above)

Reading NM (Nonmetallic) Cable

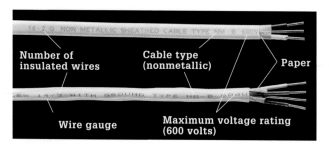

Number of insulated wires

Cable type (nonmetallic)

Paper

Wire gauge

Maximum voltage rating (600 volts)

NM cable is labeled with the number of insulated wires it contains. The bare grounding wire is not counted. For example, a cable marked 14/2 G (or 14/2 WITH GROUND) contains two insulated 14-gauge wires, plus a bare copper grounding wire. Cable marked 14/3 WITH GROUND has three 14-gauge wires plus a grounding wire. NM cable also is stamped with a maximum voltage rating, as determined by Underwriters Laboratories (UL).

Reading Unsheathed, Individual Wire

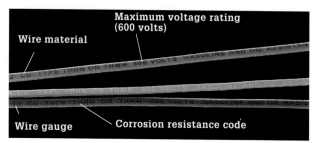

Wire material

Maximum voltage rating (600 volts)

Wire gauge

Corrosion resistance code

Unsheathed, individual wires are used for conduit and raceway installations. Wire insulation is coded with letters to indicate resistance to moisture, heat, and gas or oil. Code requires certain letter combinations for certain applications. T indicates thermoplastic insulation. H stands for heat resistance, and two Hs indicate high resistance (up to 194° F). W denotes wire suitable for wet locations. Wire coded with an N is impervious to damage from oil or gas.

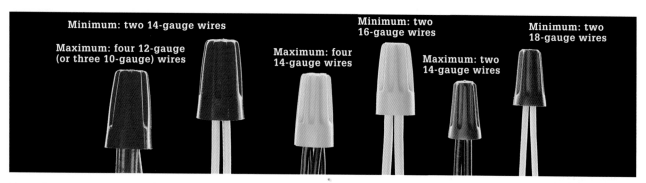

Maximum: four 12-gauge (or three 10-gauge) wires

Minimum: two 14-gauge wires

Maximum: four 14-gauge wires

Minimum: two 16-gauge wires

Maximum: two 14-gauge wires

Minimum: two 18-gauge wires

Use wire connectors rated for the wires you are connecting. Wire connectors are color-coded by size, but the coding scheme varies according to manufacturer. The wire connectors shown above come from one major manufacturer. To ensure safe connections, each connector is rated for both minimum and maximum wire capacity. These connectors can be used to connect both conducting wires and grounding wires. Green wire connectors are used only for grounding wires.

Tips for Working with Wire ▸

WIRE GAUGE		AMPACITY	MAXIMUM WATTAGE LOAD
	14-gauge	15 amps	1,440 watts (120 volts)
	12-gauge	20 amps	1,920 watts (120 volts) 3,840 watts (240 volts)
	10-gauge	30 amps	2,880 watts (120 volts) 5760 watts (240 volts)
	8-gauge	40 amps	7,680 watts (240 volts)
	6-gauge	55 amps	10,560 watts (240 volts)

Wire "ampacity" is a measurement of how much current a wire can carry safely. Ampacity varies by the size of the wires. When installing a new circuit, choose wire with an ampacity rating matching the circuit size. For dedicated appliance circuits, check the wattage rating of the appliance and make sure it does not exceed the maximum wattage load of the circuit. The ampacities in this table are for copper wires in NM cable. The ampacity for the same wire in conduit is usually more. The ampacity for aluminum wire is less.

How to Strip NM Sheathing & Insulation

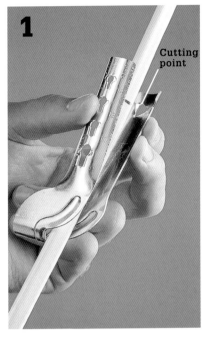

1

Measure and mark the cable 8 to 10" from the end. Slide the cable ripper onto the cable, and squeeze tool firmly to force the cutting point through the plastic sheathing.

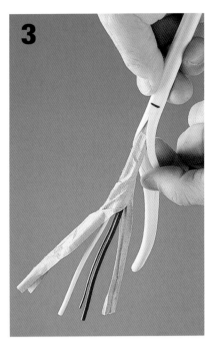

2

Grip the cable tightly with one hand, and pull the cable ripper toward the end of the cable to cut open the plastic sheathing.

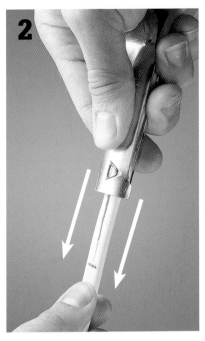

3

Peel back the plastic sheathing and the paper wrapping from the individual wires.

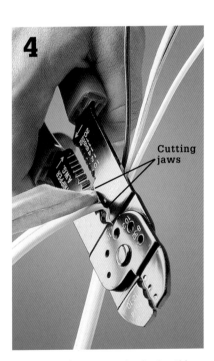

4

Cut away the excess plastic sheathing and paper wrapping using the cutting jaws of a combination tool.

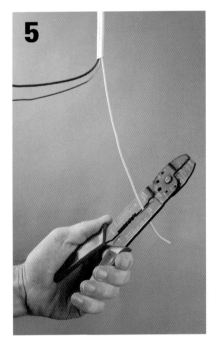

5

Cut individual wires as needed using the cutting jaws of the combination tool. Leave a minimum of 3" of wire running past the edge of the box.

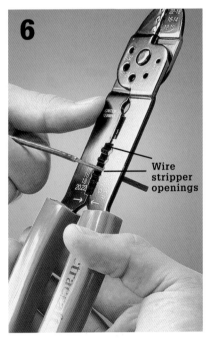

6

Strip insulation for each wire using the stripper openings. Choose the opening that matches the gauge of the wire, and take care not to nick or scratch the ends of the wires.

How to Connect Wires to Screw Terminals

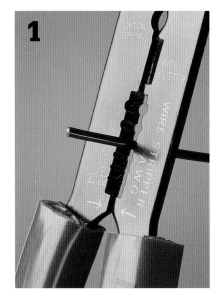

1

Strip about ¾" of insulation from each wire using a combination tool. Choose the stripper opening that matches the gauge of the wire, and then clamp the wire in the tool. Pull the wire firmly to remove plastic insulation.

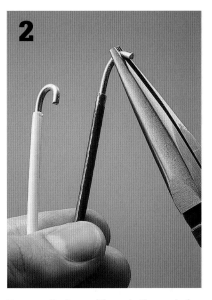

2

Form a C-shaped loop in the end of each wire using a needlenose pliers or the hole of the correct gauge in a pair of wire strippers. The wire should have no scratches or nicks.

3

Hook each wire around the screw terminal so it forms a clockwise loop. Tighten the screw firmly. Insulation should just touch head of screw. Never place the ends of two wires under a single screw terminal. Instead, use a pigtail wire (see page 35).

Cable Staples ▸

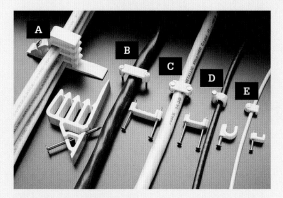

Use plastic cable staples to fasten cables. Choose staples sized to match the cables. Stack-It® staples (A) hold up to four 2-wire cables; ¾" staples (B) for 12/2, 12/3, and all 10-gauge cables; ½" staples (C) for 14/2, 14/3, or 12/2 cables; coaxial staples (D) for anchoring television cables; bell wire staples (E) for attaching telephone cables.

Push-in connectors ▸

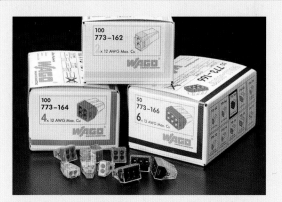

Push-in connectors are a relatively new product for joining wires. Instead of twisting the bare wire ends together, you strip off about ¾" of insulation and insert them into a hole in the connector. The connectors come with two to four holes sized for various gauge wires. These connectors are perfect for inexperienced DIYers, because they do not pull apart like a sloppy twisted connection can.

How to Join Wires with a Wire Connector

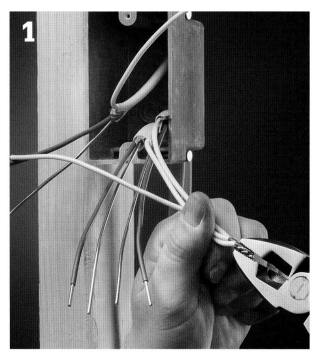

Ensure power is off and test for power. Grasp the wires to be joined in the jaws of a pair of linesman's pliers. The ends of the wires should be flush and they should be parallel and touching. Rotate the pliers clockwise two or three turns to twist the wire ends together.

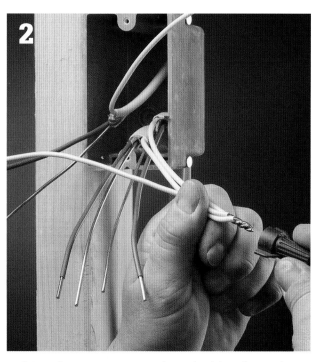

Twist a wire connector over the ends of the wires. Make sure the connector is the right size (see page 29). Hand-twist the connector as far onto the wires as you can. There should be no bare wire exposed beneath the collar of the connector.

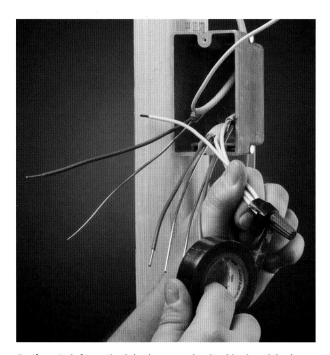

Option: Reinforce the joint by wrapping it with electrician's tape. By code, you cannot bind the wire joint with tape only, but it can be used as insurance. Few professional electricians use tape for purposes other than tagging wires for identification.

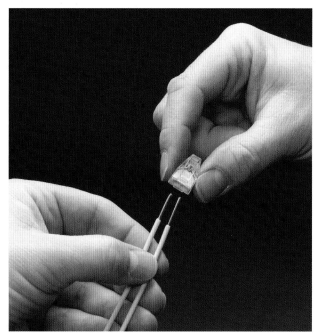

Option: Strip ¾" of insulation off the ends of the wires to be joined, and insert each wire into a push-in connector. Gently tug on each wire to make sure it is secure.

How to Pigtail Wires

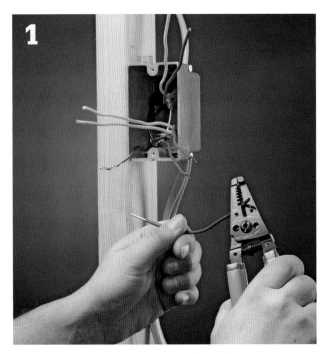

Cut a 6" length from a piece of insulated wire the same gauge and color as the wires it will be joining. Strip ¾" of insulation from each end of the insulated wire. *Note: Pigtailing is done mainly to avoid connecting multiple wires to one terminal, which is a code violation.*

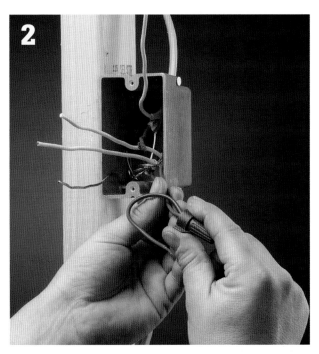

Join one end of the pigtail to the wires that will share the connection using a wire nut.

Alternative: If you are pigtailing to a grounding screw or grounding clip in a metal box, you may find it easier to attach one end of the wire to the grounding screw before you attach the other end to the other wires.

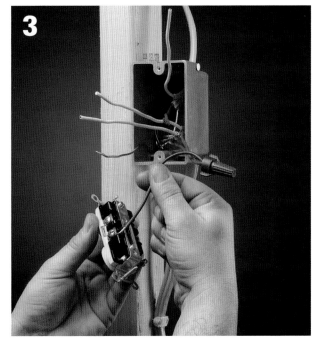

Connect the pigtail to the appropriate terminal on the receptacle or switch. Fold the wires neatly and press the fitting into the box.

NM Cable

Non-metallic (NM) cable is used for most indoor wiring projects except those requiring conduit and those in damp areas such as against concrete or masonry walls with dirt on the other side. Cut and install the cable after all electrical boxes have been mounted. Refer to your wiring plan to make sure each length of cable is correct for the circuit size and configuration.

Cable runs are difficult to measure exactly, so leave plenty of extra wire when cutting each length. Cable splices inside walls are not allowed by code. When inserting cables into a circuit breaker panel, make sure the power is shut off.

After all cables are installed and all the ground wires spliced, call your electrical inspector to arrange for the rough-in inspection. Do not install wallboard or attach light fixtures and other devices until this inspection is done. Check with your building inspector before using NM cable. Some areas, such as the Chicago area, do not allow NM cable.

Pulling cables through studs is easier if you drill smooth, straight holes at the same height. Prevent kinks by straightening the cable before pulling it through the studs. Use plastic grommets to protect cables on steel studs (inset).

Tools & Materials ▸

Drill and bits	NM cable
Tape measure	Cable clamps
Cable ripper	Cable staples
Combination tool	Masking tape
Screwdrivers	Electrical tape
Needlenose pliers	Grounding pigtails
Hammer	Wire connectors
Fish tape	Eye and ear protection

FRAMING MEMBER	MAXIMUM HOLE SIZE	MAXIMUM NOTCH SIZE
2 × 4 loadbearing stud	1⁷⁄₁₆" diameter	⅞" deep
2 × 4 non-loadbearing stud	2⅛" diameter	1⁷⁄₁₆" deep
2 × 6 loadbearing stud	2³⁄₁₆" diameter	1⅜" deep
2 × 6 non-loadbearing stud	3⁵⁄₁₆" diameter	2³⁄₁₆" deep
2 × 6 joists	1¹³⁄₁₆" diameter	¹⁵⁄₁₆" deep
2 × 8 joists	2½" diameter	1¼" deep
2 × 10 joists	3¹⁄₁₆" diameter	1⁹⁄₁₆" deep
2 × 12 joists	3¾" diameter	1⅞" deep

This framing member chart shows the maximum sizes for holes and notches that can be cut into studs and joists when running cables. When boring holes, there must be at least ⅝" of wood between the edge of a stud and the hole and at least 2" between the edge of a joist and the hole. Joists can be notched only in the end third of the overall span; never in the middle third of the joist. If 1¼" clearance cannot possibly be maintained, you may be able to satisfy code by installing a metal nail plate over the point of penetration in the stud or joist. Different rules apply to wood I-joists, metal-plate-connected trusses, engineered beams, and beams assembled from lumber. In general, you may not drill and notch trusses and assembled beams. Manufacturers of I-joists and engineered beams have limits about the size and location of holes.

How to Install NM Cable

Drill ⅝" holes in framing members for the cable runs. This is done easily with a right-angle drill, available at rental centers. Holes should be set back at least 1¼" from the front face of the framing members.

Where cables will turn corners (step 6, page 36), drill intersecting holes in adjoining faces of studs. Measure and cut all cables, allowing 2 ft. extra at ends entering the breaker panel and 1 foot for ends entering the electrical box.

Shut off power to the circuit breaker panel. Use a cable ripper to strip the cable, leaving at least ¼" of sheathing to enter the circuit breaker panel. Clip away the excess sheathing.

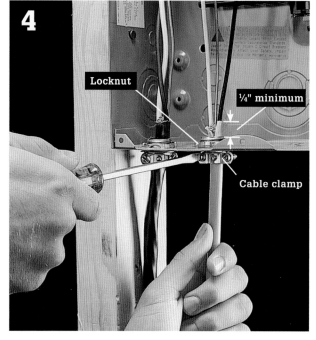

Locknut

¼" minimum

Cable clamp

Open a knockout in the circuit breaker panel using a hammer and screwdriver. Insert a cable clamp into the knockout, and secure it with a locknut. Insert the cable through the clamp so that at least ¼" of sheathing extends inside the circuit breaker panel. Tighten the mounting screws on the clamp so the cable is gripped securely but not so tightly that the sheathing is crushed.

(continued)

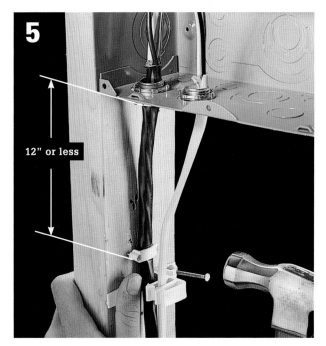

5

12" or less

Anchor the cable to the center of a framing member within 12" of the circuit breaker panel using a cable staple. Stack-It® staples work well where two or more cables must be anchored to the same side of a stud. Run the cable to the first electrical box. Where the cable runs along the sides of framing members, anchor it with cable staples no more than 4 ft. 6 in. apart.

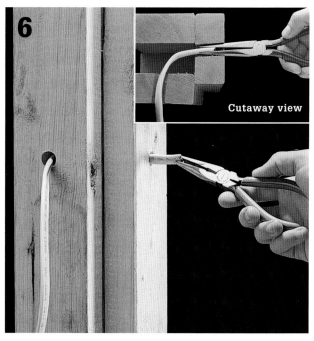

6

Cutaway view

At corners, form a slight L-shaped bend in the end of the cable and insert it into one hole. Retrieve the cable through the other hole using needlenose pliers (inset).

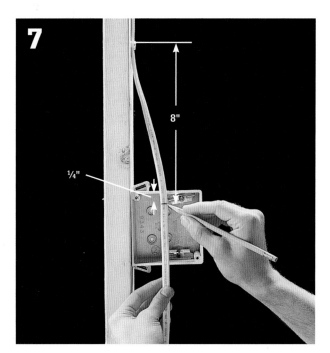

7

8"

¼"

Staple the cable to a framing member within 8" from where the sheathing ends in the box. Hold the cable taut against the front of the box, and mark a point on the sheathing ¼" past the box edge. Remove sheathing from the marked line to the end using a cable ripper, and clip away excess sheathing with a combination tool. Insert the cable through the knockout in the box.

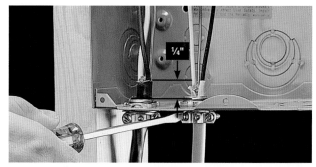

¼"

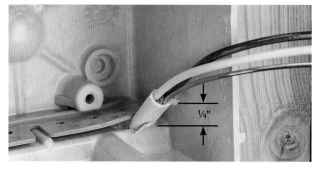

¼"

Variation: Different types of boxes have different clamping devices. Make sure cable sheathing extends ¼" past the edge of the clamp to ensure that the cable is secure and that the wire won't be damaged by the edges of the clamp. Clamp cable inside all boxes except single gang (2¼ x 4") boxes.

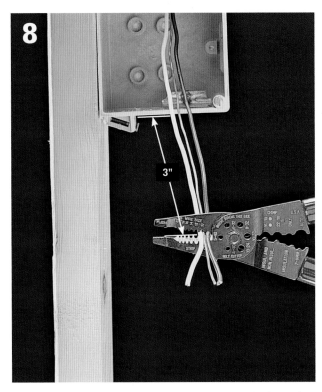

8

As each cable is installed in a box, clip back each wire so that at least 3" of workable wire extends past the front edge of the box.

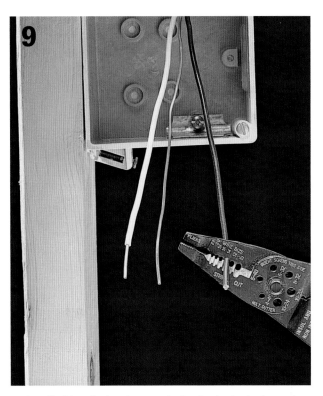

9

Strip ¾" of insulation from each circuit wire in the box using a combination tool. Take care not to nick the copper.

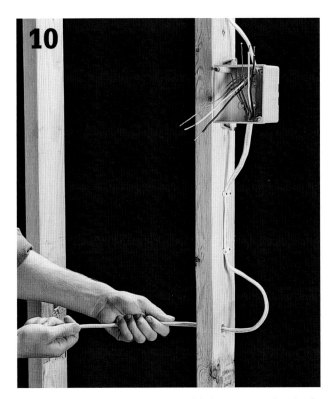

10

Continue the circuit by running cable between each pair of electrical boxes, leaving an extra 1 ft. of cable at each end.

11

At metal boxes and recessed fixtures, open knockouts, and attach cables with cable clamps. From inside the fixture, strip away all but ¼" of sheathing. Clip back wires so there is 8" of workable length, and then strip ¾" of insulation from each wire.

(continued)

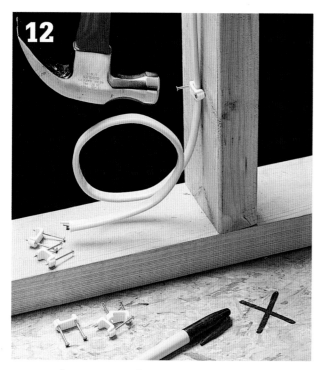

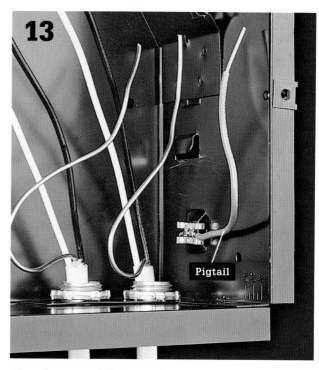

For a surface-mounted fixture such as a baseboard heater or fluorescent light fixture, staple the cable to a stud near the fixture location, leaving plenty of excess cable. Mark the floor so the cable will be easy to find after the walls are finished.

At each recessed fixture and metal electrical box, connect one end of a grounding pigtail to the metal frame using a grounding clip attached to the frame (shown above) or a green grounding screw.

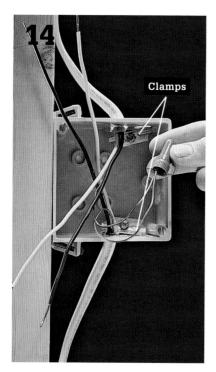

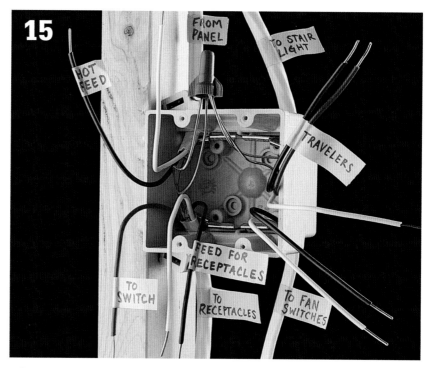

At each electrical box and recessed fixture, join grounding wires together with a wire connector. If the box has internal clamps, tighten the clamps over the cables.

Label the cables entering each box to indicate their destinations. In boxes with complex wiring configurations, also tag the individual wires to make final hookups easier. After all cables are installed, your rough-in work is ready to be reviewed by the electrical inspector.

How to Run NM Cable inside a Finished Wall

1

From the unfinished space below the finished wall, look for a reference point, such as a soil stack, plumbing pipes, or electrical cables, that indicates the location of the wall above. Choose a location for the new cable that does not interfere with existing utilities. Drill a 1" hole up into the stud cavity.

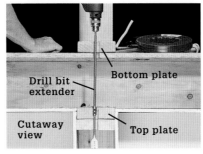

2

From the unfinished space above the finished wall, find the top of the stud cavity by measuring from the same fixed reference point used in step 1. Drill a 1" hole down through the top plate and into the stud cavity using a drill bit extender.

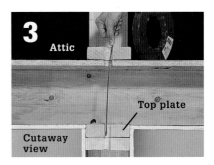

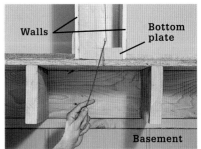

3

Extend a fish tape down through the top plate, twisting the tape until it reaches the bottom of the stud cavity. From the unfinished space below the wall, use a piece of stiff wire with a hook on one end to retrieve the fish tape through the drilled hole in the bottom plate.

4

Trim back 2" of sheathing from the end of the NM cable, and then insert the wires through the loop at the tip of the fish tape.

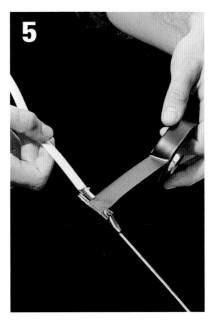

5

Bend the wires against the cable, and then use electrical tape to bind them tightly. Apply cable-pulling lubricant to the taped end of the fish tape.

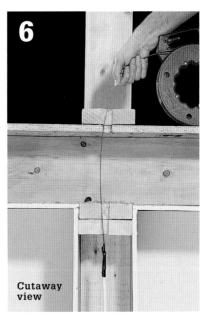

6

From above the finished wall, pull steadily on the fish tape to draw the cable up through the stud cavity. This job will be easier if you have a helper feed the cable from below as you pull.

Running Cable inside Finished Walls

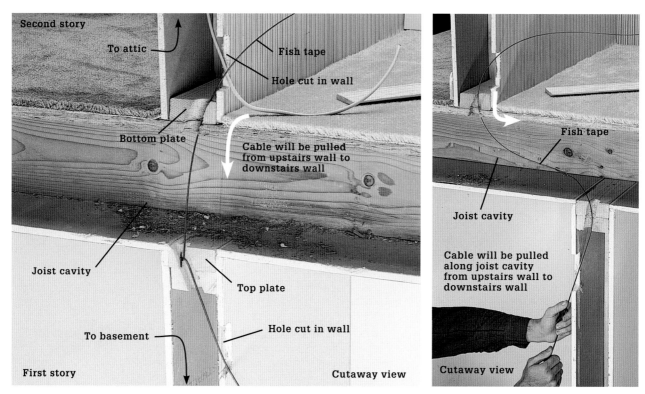

Second story

To attic

Fish tape

Hole cut in wall

Bottom plate

Cable will be pulled from upstairs wall to downstairs wall

Joist cavity

Top plate

To basement

Hole cut in wall

First story

Cutaway view

Fish tape

Joist cavity

Cable will be pulled along joist cavity from upstairs wall to downstairs wall

Cutaway view

If there is no access space above and below a wall, cut openings in the finished walls to run a cable. This often occurs in two-story homes when a cable is extended from an upstairs wall to a downstairs wall. Cut small openings in the wall near the top and bottom plates, then drill an angled 1" hole through each plate. Extend a fish tape into the joist cavity between the walls and use it to pull the cable from one wall to the next. If the walls line up one over the other (left), you can retrieve the fish tape using a piece of stiff wire. If walls do not line up (right), use a second fish tape. After running the cable, repair the holes in the walls with patching plaster or wallboard scraps and taping compound.

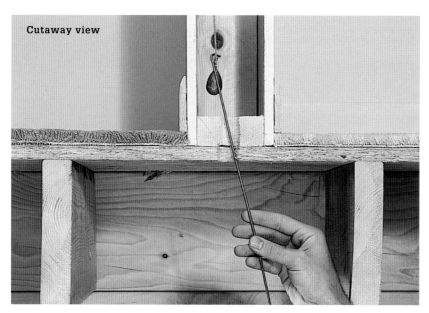

Cutaway view

If you don't have a fish tape, use a length of sturdy string and a lead weight or heavy washer. Drop the line into the stud cavity from above, and then use a piece of stiff wire to hook the line from below.

Use a flexible drill bit, also called a bell-hanger's bit, to bore holes through framing in finished walls.

How to Install NM Cable in Finished Ceilings

If you don't have access to a ceiling from above, you can run cable for a new ceiling fixture from an existing receptacle in the room up the wall and into the ceiling without disturbing much of the ceiling. Be sure not to tap into a restricted circuit such as the kitchen counter top and bathroom receptacles. To begin, run cable from the receptacle to the stud channel that aligns with the ceiling joists on which you want to install a fixture. Be sure to plan a location for the new switch. Remove short strips of drywall from the wall and ceiling. Make a notch in the center of the top. Use a fish tape to pull the new cable up through the wall cavity and the notch in top plates. Next use the fish tape to pull the cable through the ceiling to the fixture hole. When you are finished pulling the cable, protect the notch with metal nail guards. After having your work inspected, replace the drywall and install the fixture and switch.

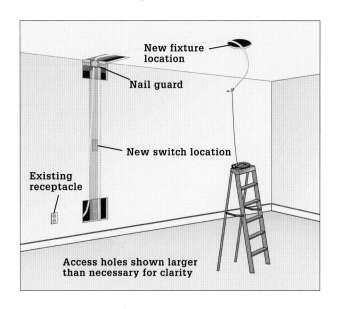

New fixture location

Nail guard

New switch location

Existing receptacle

Access holes shown larger than necessary for clarity

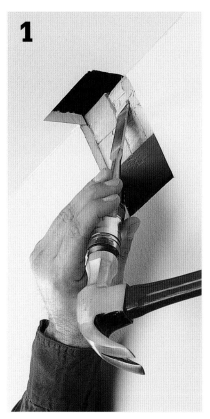

1

Plan a route for running cable between electrical boxes (see illustration above). Remove drywall on the wall and ceiling surface. Where cable must cross framing members, cut a small access opening in the wall and ceiling surface; then cut a notch into the framing with a wood chisel.

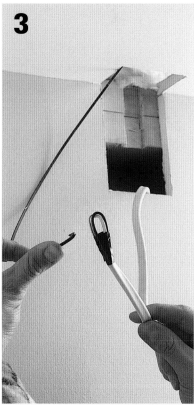

2

Fish a cable from the existing receptacle location up to the notch at the top of the wall. Protect the notch with a metal nail stop.

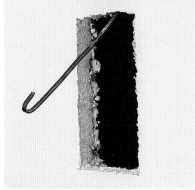

3

Fish the cable through the ceiling to the location of the new ceiling fixture.

Conduit

Electrical Bonding of Metal Conduit

All individual wires (such as THHN/THWN) must be installed in conduit or in thinner material called tubing. Cables and wires that are subject to physical damage must be installed in conduit or some types of tubing to protect them. Whether a location is subject to physical damage depends on the judgment of the electrical inspector. Cables that are exposed and are within the reach of an adult and most cables installed outside are often considered subject to physical damage. Other exposed locations may also qualify.

The interior of conduit and tubing installed outside is considered a wet area. Don't install NM cable inside conduit installed outside. Use UF cable instead or pull individual wires rated for wet area use. Conduit and tubing installed outdoors must be rated for exterior use.

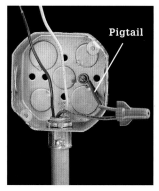
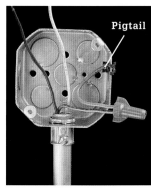

Install a green insulated grounding wire for any circuit that runs through metal conduit. Although code allows the metal conduit to serve as the grounding conductor, most electricians install a green insulated wire as a more dependable means of grounding the system. The grounding wires must be connected to metal boxes with a pigtail and grounding screw (left) or grounding clip (right).

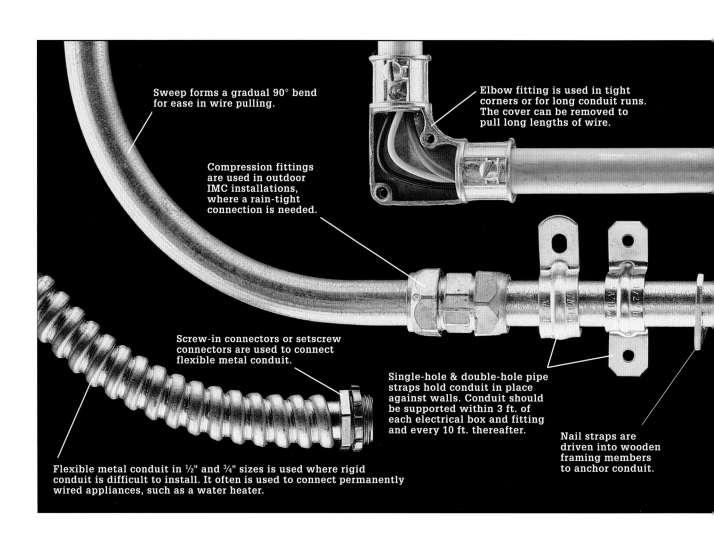

Sweep forms a gradual 90° bend for ease in wire pulling.

Elbow fitting is used in tight corners or for long conduit runs. The cover can be removed to pull long lengths of wire.

Compression fittings are used in outdoor IMC installations, where a rain-tight connection is needed.

Screw-in connectors or setscrew connectors are used to connect flexible metal conduit.

Single-hole & double-hole pipe straps hold conduit in place against walls. Conduit should be supported within 3 ft. of each electrical box and fitting and every 10 ft. thereafter.

Nail straps are driven into wooden framing members to anchor conduit.

Flexible metal conduit in ½" and ¾" sizes is used where rigid conduit is difficult to install. It often is used to connect permanently wired appliances, such as a water heater.

Metal Conduit

EMT ½" in diameter can hold up to twelve 14-gauge or nine 12-gauge THHN/THWN wires (A), five 10-gauge wires (B), or three 8-gauge wires (C). Use ¾" conduit for greater fill capacity.

Fill Capacity

EMT

IMC

Rigid metal conduit

EMT is lightweight and easy to install. IMC has thicker galvanized walls and is a good choice for exposed outdoor use. Rigid metal conduit provides the greatest protection for wires, but it is more expensive and requires threaded fittings. EMT is the preferred metal material for home use.

Plastic Conduit

Plastic PVC conduit and tubing are allowed by many local codes. It is assembled with solvent glue and PVC fittings that resemble those for metal conduit. When wiring with PVC conduit and tubing, always run a green grounding wire. Use material approved for use in electrical applications. Do not use PVC plumbing pipes.

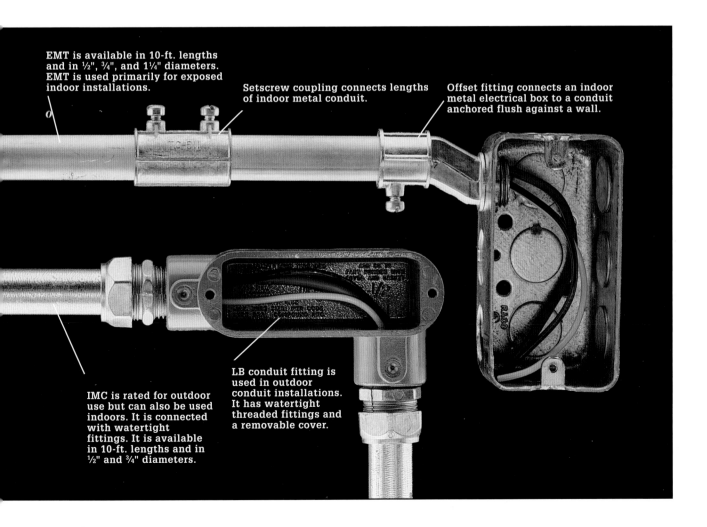

EMT is available in 10-ft. lengths and in ½", ¾", and 1¼" diameters. EMT is used primarily for exposed indoor installations.

Setscrew coupling connects lengths of indoor metal conduit.

Offset fitting connects an indoor metal electrical box to a conduit anchored flush against a wall.

IMC is rated for outdoor use but can also be used indoors. It is connected with watertight fittings. It is available in 10-ft. lengths and in ½" and ¾" diameters.

LB conduit fitting is used in outdoor conduit installations. It has watertight threaded fittings and a removable cover.

Working with Conduit

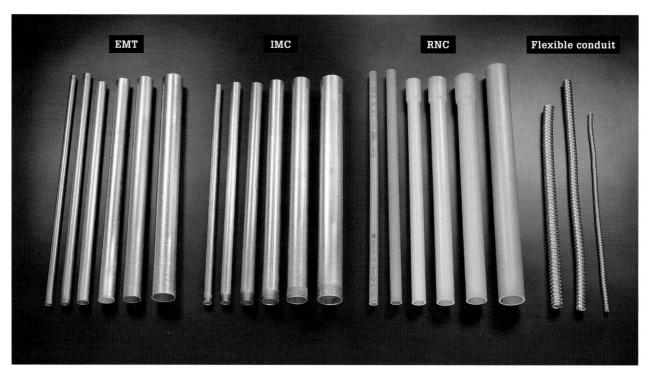

Conduit types used most in homes are EMT (electrical metallic tubing), IMC (intermediate metallic conduit), RNC (rigid nonmetallic conduit), and flexible metal conduit. The most common diameters by far are ½" and ¾", but larger sizes are stocked at most building centers.

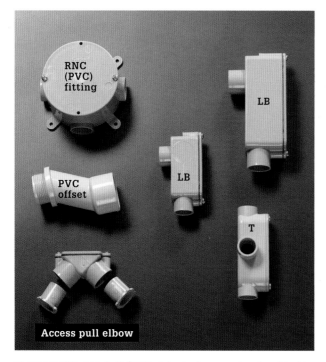

Nonmetallic conduit fittings typically are solvent-welded to nonmetallic conduit, as opposed to metal conduit, which can be threaded and screwed into threaded fittings or attached with setscrews or compression fittings.

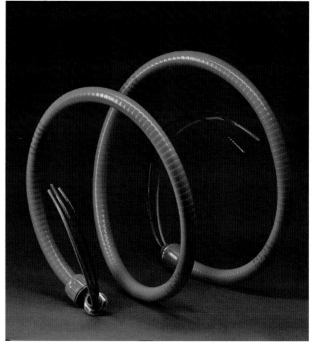

Liquid-tight flexible conduit (LFC) is used in outdoor applications, especially around pools and water features and at irrigation controllers.

How to Make Nonmetallic Conduit Connections

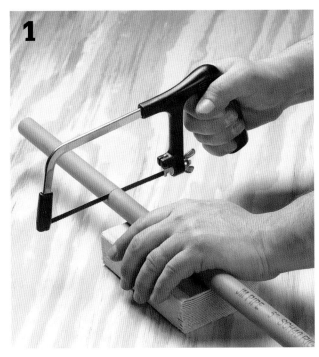

Cut the rigid nonmetallic conduit (RNC) to length with a fine-tooth saw, such as a hacksaw. For larger diameter (1½" and above), use a power miter box with a fine-tooth or plastic cutting blade.

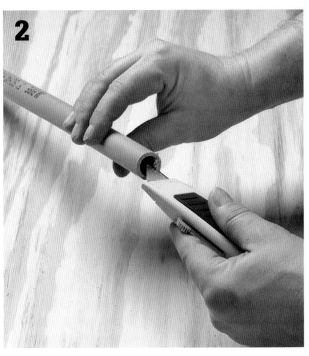

Deburr the cut edges with a utility knife or fine sandpaper such as emery paper. Wipe the cut ends with a dry rag. Also wipe the coupling or fitting to clean it.

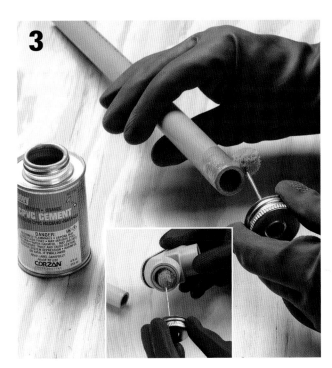

Apply a coat of PVC cement to the end of the conduit and to the inside walls of the coupling (inset). Wear latex gloves to protect your hands. The cement should be applied past the point on the conduit where it enters the fitting or coupling.

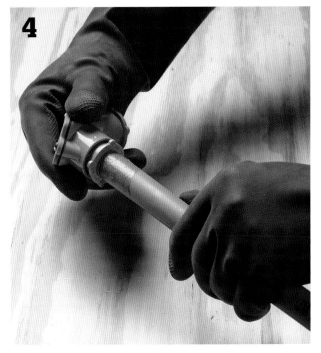

Insert the conduit into the fitting or coupling and spin it a quarter turn to help spread the cement. Allow the joint to set undisturbed for 10 minutes.

How to Install Conduit & Wires on a Concrete Wall

1

Measure from the floor to position electrical boxes on the wall, and mark location for mounting screws. Boxes for receptacles in an unfinished basement or other damp areas are mounted at least 2 ft. from the floor. Laundry receptacles usually are mounted at 48".

2

Drill pilot holes with a masonry bit, then mount the box against a masonry wall with masonry anchors, or use masonry anchors and panhead screws.

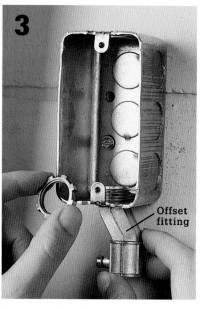

3

Offset fitting

Open one knockout for each length of conduit that will be attached to the box. Attach an offset fitting to each knockout using a locknut.

4

Measure the first length of conduit and cut it with a hacksaw. Remove any rough inside edges with a pipe reamer or a round file. Attach the conduit to the offset fitting on the box, and tighten the setscrew.

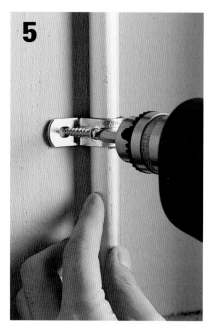

5

Anchor the conduit against the wall with pipe straps and masonry anchors. Conduit should be anchored within 3 ft. of each box and fitting and every 10 ft. thereafter.

6

Make conduit bends by attaching a sweep fitting using a setscrew fitting or compression fitting. Continue attaching additional lengths. You can also use a conduit bender (inset) to make your own sweeps and bends.

7 **Use an elbow fitting** in conduit runs that have many bends or in runs that require very long wires. The cover on the elbow fitting can be removed to make it easier to extend a fish tape and pull wires.

8 **At the panel,** turn the power off, and then remove the cover and test for power. Open a knockout in the panel, attach a setscrew fitting, and install the last length of conduit.

9 **Unwind the fish tape** and extend it through the conduit from the circuit breaker panel outward. Remove the cover on an elbow fitting when extending the fish tape around tight corners.

10 **Trim back 2" of outer insulation** from the end of the wires, and then insert the wires through the loop at the tip of the fish tape.

11 **Retrieve the wires** through the conduit by pulling on the fish tape with steady pressure. *Note: Use extreme care when using a metal fish tape inside a circuit breaker panel, even when the power is turned off.*

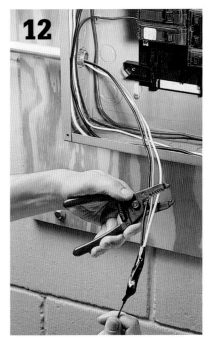

12 **Clip off the taped ends** of the wires. Leave at least 2 ft. of wire at the service panel and 3" extending beyond the front edges at each electrical box.

Surface-Mounted Wiring

Surface-mounted wiring is a network of electrical circuits that run through small, decorative tubes that function much like conduit. The systems include matching elbows, T-connectors, and various other fittings and boxes that are also surface-mounted. The main advantage to a surface-mounted wiring system is that you can add a new fixture onto a circuit without cutting into your walls.

Although they are extremely convenient and can even contribute to a room's decor when used thoughtfully, surface-mounted wiring systems do have some limitations. They are not allowed for some specific applications (damp areas such as bathrooms, for example) in many areas, so check with the local building authorities before beginning a project. And

the boxes that house the switches and receptacles tend to be very shallow and more difficult to work with than ordinary boxes.

In some cases, you may choose to run an entirely new circuit with surface-mounted wiring components (at least starting at the point where the branch circuit wire reaches the room from the service panel). But more often, a surface-mounted wiring circuit ties into an existing receptacle or switch. If you are tying into a standard switch box for power, make sure the load wire for the new surface-mounted wiring circuit is connected to the hot wire in the switch box before it is connected to the switch (otherwise, the surface-mounted wiring circuit will be off whenever the switch is off).

After

Before

Surface-mounted wiring circuits are networks of cable channels and electrical boxes that allow you to run new wiring without cutting into walls. If you have a room with too much demand on a single receptacle (inset), installing a surface-mounted circuit with one or more new outlets is a good solution.

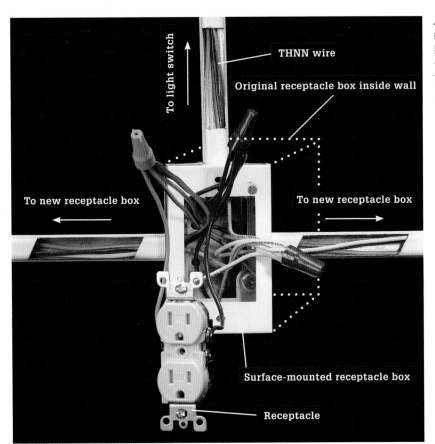

To light switch

THNN wire

Original receptacle box inside wall

To new receptacle box

To new receptacle box

Surface-mounted receptacle box

Receptacle

A surface-mounted receptacle box is mounted directly to the original electrical box (usually for a receptacle) and raceway tracks are attached to it. The tracks house THNN wires that run from the new box to new receptacles and light switches.

Parts of a Surface-Mounted System

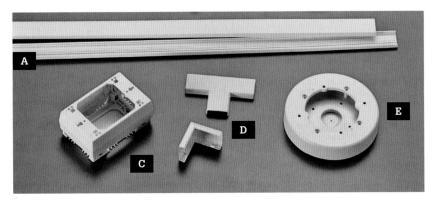

A

C

D

E

Surface-mounted wiring systems employ two-part tracks that are mounted directly to the wall surface to house cable. Lighter-duty plastic raceways (A), used frequently in office buildings, are made of snap-together plastic components. For home wiring, look for a heavier metal-component system (B). Both systems include box extenders for tying in to a receptacle (C), elbows, T-connectors, and couplings (D), and boxes for fixtures (E).

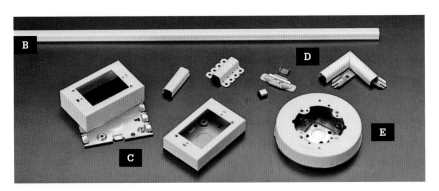

B

D

C

E

How to Install Surface-Mounted Wiring

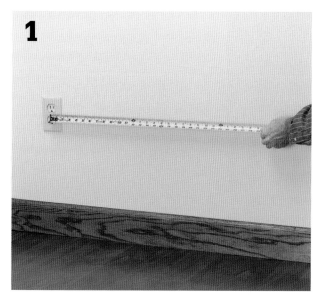

1

Confirm that the circuit you want to expand will support a new receptacle or light (see pages 136 to 141). Measure from the power source to the new receptacle or switch. Purchase enough raceway to cover this distance plus about 10 percent extra. Buy a surface-mounted starter box, new receptacle box, and fittings for your project (the raceway product packaging usually provides guidance for shopping).

2

Shut off the power to the outlet. Remove the cover plate from the receptacle by unscrewing the screw that holds the plate to the electrical box. Set the screws and the plate aside. With the cover plate off, you will be able to see the receptacle and the electrical box it is attached to. If your existing receptacle is not a tamper-resistant model replace it with one (see page 109).

3

Before you remove the old receptacle, use a touchless circuit tester to double-check that the circuit is dead. Hold your voltage sensor's probe within ½" of the wires on each side of the receptacle. If the sensor beeps or lights up, then the receptacle is still live, and you'll need to trip the correct breaker to disconnect power to the receptacle. If the sensor does not beep or light up, the receptacle is dead and you can proceed safely.

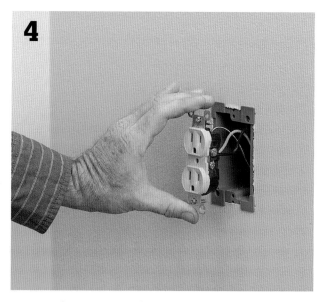

4

Remove the receptacle from the box by unscrewing the two long screws that hold it to the box. Once the screws are out, gently pull the receptacle away from the box. Depending on how your receptacle has been wired, you may find two insulated wires and a bare copper wire or four insulated wires and a bare wire. Detach these wires and set the receptacle aside.

5

Your starter box includes a box and a mounting plate with an open back. Pull all the wires you just disconnected through the opening. Screw the mounting plate to the existing receptacle box with the included mounting screws. The predrilled ground screw hole should contain a #10/32 grounding screw.

6

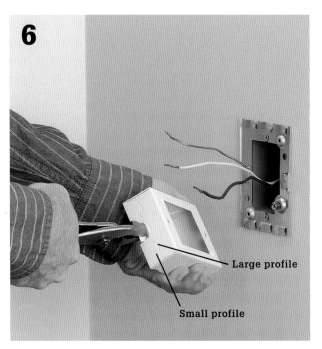

Large profile

Small profile

Remove a knockout from the starter box to create an opening for the track using pliers. Often the prepunched knockouts have two profile options—make sure the knockout you remove matches the profile of your track.

7

Hold the box portion of the starter box over the mounting plate on the existing receptacle. Drive the mounting screws through the holes in the box and into the threaded openings in the mounting plate.

8

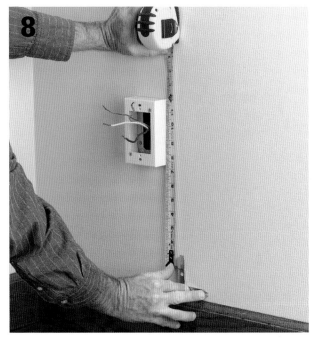

Set the mounting bracket for an elbow connector ¼" above the baseboard (having the track run along the baseboard edge looks better than running it in a straight line out of the starter box). Measure from the knockout in the starter box to the top of the bracket and cut a piece of track ½" longer than this measurement.

(continued)

Tool Tip ▸

Metal raceway can be cut like metal conduit. Secure the track or conduit in a vise or clamping work support, and cut with a hacksaw. For best results, use long, slow strokes and don't bear down too hard on the saw. Once the cut is made, file the metal burrs smooth with a metal file.

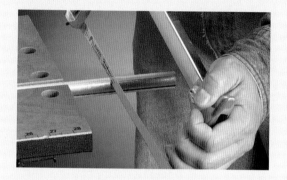

9

At the new receptacle location, transfer the height of the top of the starter box and mark a reference line. If possible, locate the box so at least one screw hole in the mounting plate falls over a wall stud. Position the mounting plate for the receptacle box up against the reference line and secure it with screws driven through the mounting plate holes. If the plate is not located over a wall stud, use wall anchors (see below right).

10

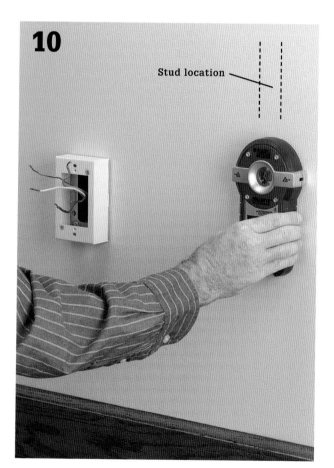

Stud location

Use a stud finder to locate and mark all of the wall framing members between the old receptacle and the new one. There is usually a 1½"-wide stud every 16" behind the wall.

Wall Anchors ▸

Here's how to install wall anchors. Mark screw locations on the wall, and then drill a narrow guide hole for the screw anchor. Drive the anchor into the guide holes until the flange is flush with the wall surface.

Ideally anything you attach to a drywall wall should be anchored at a wall stud location. Of course, in the real world this often is not possible. You'll find many kinds of wall anchors for sale at the local hardware store. Some work better than others. The common tapered plastic sleeves that are driven into guide holes will work for lighter duty, but they don't grip the wall well enough to secure surface mounted wiring components. For this, use coarse-threaded, screw-in anchors. You simply mark the location for your mounting screws and drive the sleeve directly into the wall with a drill/driver: no pilot hole required.

11

Mounting clip

At stud locations mark a reference line ¼" above the top of the baseboard. Attach mounting clips for the track at these marks.

12

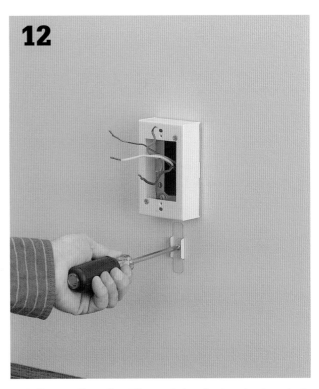

Install mounting clips ½" or so below the knockouts on both the starter box and the new receptacle box. The clips should line up with the knockouts.

13

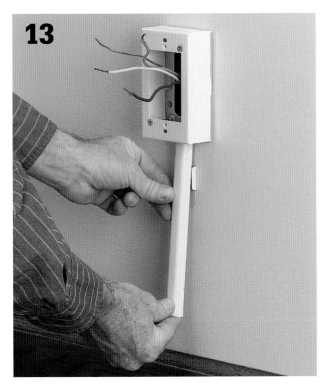

At the starter box slide one end of the short piece of raceway into the knockout so that about ⅛" extends into the box. Snap the raceway into the clip below the knockout. Repeat this same procedure at the new receptacle box.

14

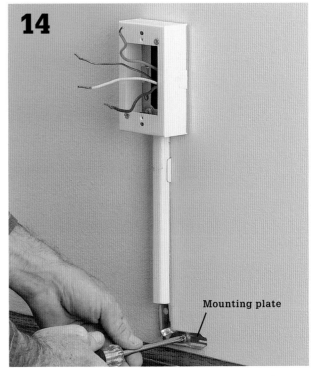

Mounting plate

The elbow piece will have two parts, a mounting plate and a cap. Install the mounting plates directly below the pieces of track entering the receptacle boxes.

(continued)

Measure and cut the long piece of track that fits between the two receptacles. Measure the distance between the ends of the horizontal parts of the elbows, and cut a length of raceway to that length. Be sure to measure all the way to the base of the clip, not just to the tips of the connector points.

Snap the long piece of track into the mounting clips. Line up one end of the track with the end of an elbow and tap the track with a rubber mallet until it is snapped into all of the clips. At the new receptacle location, snake the ends of the wires up through the vertical piece of track and into the new receptacle box. There should be about 3" of wire coming out at each box.

Tip: Making corners with raceway ▸

What if I need to go around a corner? Use corner pieces to guide around corners. Corners are available for inside or outside corners and consist of a mounting plate and a cap piece. Inside corners may be used at wall/ceiling junctures.

Wall meets wall

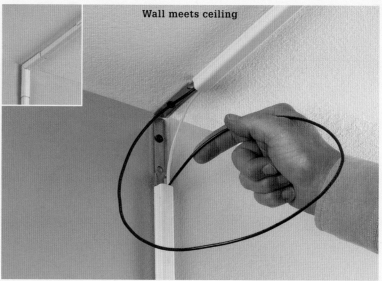

Wall meets ceiling

Tip: Splicing raceway ▸

What if I need a piece of track that's longer than the longest piece available at the hardware store (usually 5 ft.)? You can use straight connector pieces to join two lengths of track. Much like an elbow piece, they have a mounting plate and a cover that snaps over the wiring.

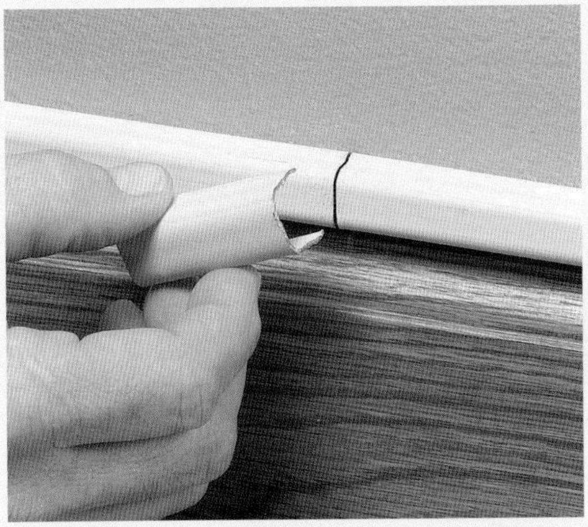

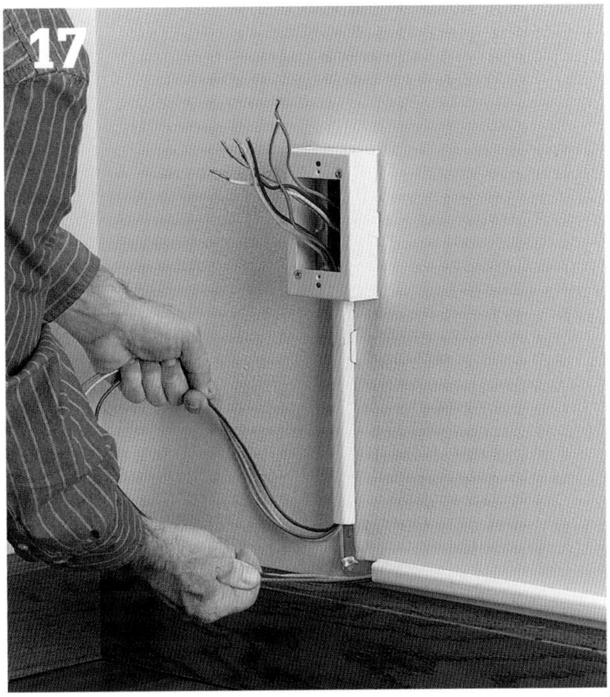

Cut black, white, and green THNN wire about 2 ft. longer than the length of each wiring run. Snake the end of each wire into the starter box, through the knockout, and into the vertical track. Then snake the wire all the way through the long piece of track so about 12 to 16" comes out on each end.

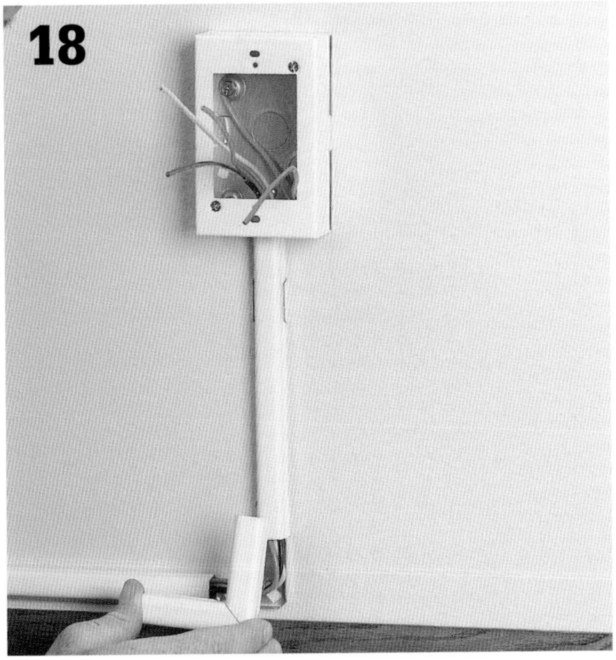

Finish the track installation by snapping the elbow cover pieces into place over the mounting plates, one at the starter box and another at the new receptacle location. You may need to rap the plate with a rubber mallet to get enough force to snap it on. Make sure all of the wire fits completely within the cover pieces.

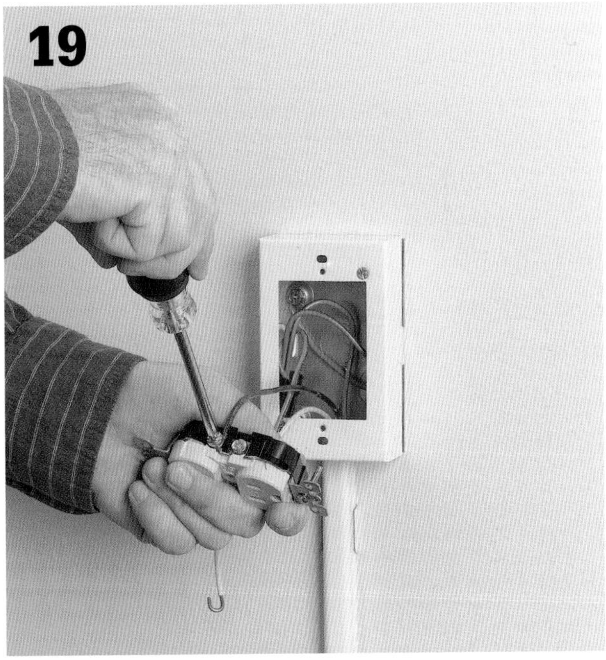

Now you can wire the receptacles. Begin at the new receptacle location. Wrap the end of the black wire around the bottom gold screw on the side of the receptacle. Tighten the screw so it's snug.

(continued)

20

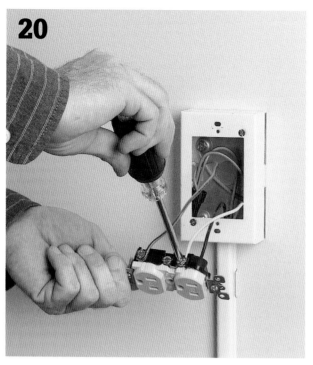

Wrap the end of the white wire around the silver screw opposite the gold one you just used. Tighten the screw so it's snug. Connect the green wire to the green-colored screw on the bottom of the receptacle.

21

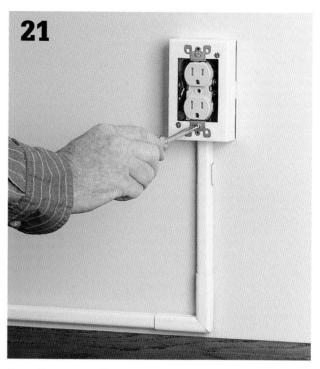

Once the connections are made, gently tuck the wires and the receptacle into the box so the holes in the top and bottom of the receptacle align with the holes in the box. Use a screwdriver to drive the two long mounting screws that hold the receptacle to the box. Attach the cover plate.

22

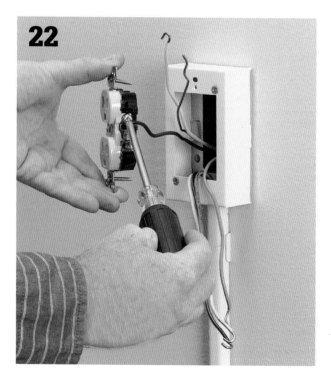

Now you can install the new receptacle at the starter box. First make sure the power is still off with your touchless circuit tester. Wrap the end of the black wire around the top gold screw on the side of the receptacle. Tighten the screw.

23

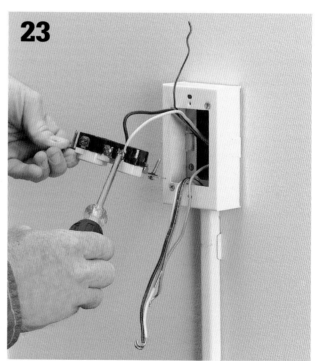

Wrap the end of the white wire around the silver screw opposite the gold one you just used. Tighten the screw.

24

Original receptacle

Black wire lead to new receptacle

Connect the old receptacle to the new one. Take the black wire that goes into the raceway and wrap the end of the wire around the bottom gold screw on the side of the receptacle. Tighten the screw.

25

Black wire lead to new receptacle

White wire lead to new receptacle

Wrap the end of the old white wire around the silver screw opposite the copper one you just used. Tighten the screw.

26

Finally, cut a piece of green wire at least 6" long and strip ¾" from both ends (this is called a pigtail wire). Join one end of the pigtail with the ends of the bare and green wires in the box using a wire connector. Wrap the other end of the pigtail around the green screw on the receptacle.

27

Once the connections are made, tuck the wires and the receptacle into the box so the holes in the top and bottom of the receptacle align with the holes in the box. Use a screwdriver to drive the two long mounting screws that hold the receptacle to the box. Install the cover plate. You can now restore the power and test your new receptacle.

Boxes & Panels

All wiring connections must be housed within a box that is accessible. The box may be as simple as a small handy box for making a splice or as complex as a 200-amp main service panel. It is typically rectangular, square, round, or octagonal, but be aware that the boxes are shaped as they are for specific reasons, so make sure you are using the right one for the job.

Installing a box that is too small is an extremely common wiring mistake that is easy to understand: small boxes cost less. But they are not one-size fits all. The smallest common boxes, called handy boxes, may be used only for a single device (such as a switch or receptacle) with no more than three conductors. Be sure to refer to a box fill chart (see page 60) to learn which size and shape box is required for your job.

Electrical panels function like other electrical boxes insofar as they house connections, but they also house breakers or fuses and other parts that transmit power from the service entry to the individual circuits. Subpanels are smaller electrical panels that perform the same function but are supplied by the main service panel so they can distribute power into multiple circuits in a remote spot.

In this chapter:

- Electrical Boxes
- Installing Boxes
- Electrical Panels

Electrical Boxes

The National Electrical Code requires that wire connections and cable splices be contained inside an approved metal or plastic box. The box shields framing members and other flammable materials from electrical sparks and protects people from being shocked.

Electrical boxes come in several shapes. Rectangular and square boxes are used for switches and receptacles. Rectangular (2 × 3") boxes are used for single switches or duplex receptacles. Square (4 × 4") boxes are used any time it is convenient for two switches or receptacles to be wired, or "ganged," in one box. Octagonal electrical boxes contain wire connections for ceiling fixtures.

Electrical boxes are available in different depths. A box must be deep enough so a switch or receptacle can be removed or installed easily without crimping and damaging the circuit wires. The box must also be large enough to safely dissipate the heat from wires, switches, and receptacles. This is an important fire safety rule. Replace an undersized box with a larger box using the Electrical Box Fill Chart (right) as a guide. In addition to the maximum box fill allowed by the chart, the area of all wires, taps, and splices should not exceed 75% of the box area. The NEC also says that all electrical boxes must remain accessible. Never cover an electrical box with drywall, paneling, or wallcoverings.

Electrical Box Fill Chart ▸

BOX SIZE AND SHAPE	MAXIMUM NUMBER OF CONDUCTORS PERMITTED (SEE NOTES BELOW)			
Wire Size	10 AWG	8 AWG	14 AWG	12 AWG
Junction Boxes				
4 × 1¼" R or O	5	5	6	5
4 × 1½" R or O	6	5	7	6
4 × 2⅛" R or O	8	7	10	9
4 × 1¼" S	7	6	9	8
4 × 1½" S	8	7	10	9
4 × 2⅛" S	12	10	15	13
4¹¹⁄₁₆ × 1¼" S	10	8	12	11
4¹¹⁄₁₆ × 1½" S	11	9	14	13
4¹¹⁄₁₆ × 2⅛" S	16	14	21	18
Device Boxes				
3 × 2 × 1½"	3	2	3	3
3 × 2 × 2"	4	3	5	4
3 × 2 × 2¼"	4	3	5	4
3 × 2 × 2½"	5	4	6	5
3 × 2 × 2¾"	5	4	7	6
3 × 2 × 3½"	7	6	9	8
4 × 2⅛ × 1½"	4	3	5	4
4 × 2⅛ × 1⅞"	5	4	6	5
4 × 2⅛ × 2⅛"	5	4	7	6

Notes:
- *R = Round; O = Octagonal; S = Square or rectangular*
- *Each hot or neutral wire entering the box is counted as one conductor.*
- *Grounding wires are counted as one conductor in total—do not count each one individually.*
- *Raceway fittings and external cable clamps do not count. Internal cable connectors and straps count as either half or one conductor, depending on type.*
- *Devices (switches and receptacles mainly) each count as two conductors.*
- *When calculating total conductors, any nonwire components should be assigned the gauge of the largest wire in the box.*
- *For wire gauges not shown here, contact your local electrical inspections office.*

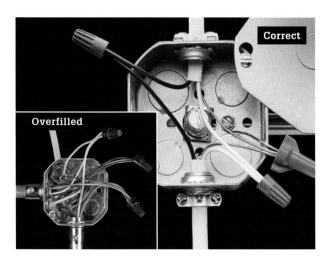

Octagonal boxes usually contain wire connections for ceiling fixtures. Because the ceiling fixture attaches directly to the box, the box should be anchored firmly to a framing member. A properly installed octagonal box can support a ceiling fixture weighing up to 35 pounds. Any box must be covered with a tightly fitting cover plate, and the box must not have open knockouts. Do not overfill the box (inset).

Common Electrical Boxes

Detachable side

Rectangular boxes are used with wall switches and duplex receptacles. Single-size rectangular boxes (shown above) may have detachable sides that allow them to be ganged together to form double-size boxes.

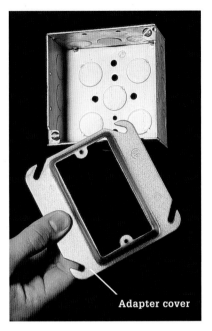

Adapter cover

Square 4" × 4" boxes are large enough for most wiring applications. They are used for cable splices and ganged receptacles or switches. To install one switch or receptacle in a square box, use an adapter cover.

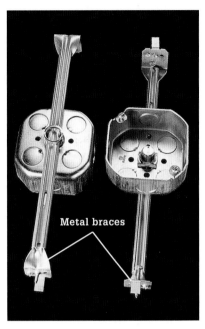

Metal braces

Braced octagonal boxes fit between ceiling joists. The metal braces extend to fit any joist spacing and are nailed or screwed to framing members.

Foam gasket

Outdoor boxes have sealed seams and foam gaskets to guard a switch or receptacle against moisture. Corrosion-resistant coatings protect all metal parts. Code compliant models include a watertight hood that protects even when the outlet is in use.

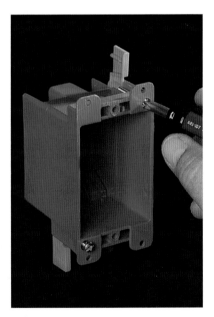

Old work boxes can be installed to upgrade older boxes or to allow you to add new additional receptacles and switches. One type (above) has built-in clamps that tighten against the inside of a wall and hold the box in place.

Plastic boxes are common in new construction. The box may include preattached nails for anchoring it to framing members. Wall switches must have grounding screws if installed in plastic boxes.

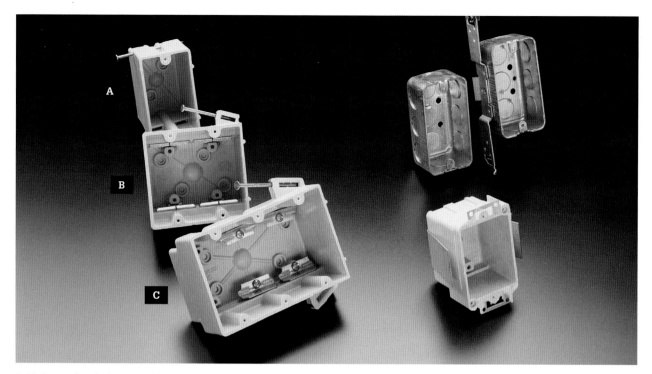

3½"-deep plastic boxes with preattached mounting nails are used for any wiring project protected by finished walls. Common styles include single-gang (A), double-gang (B), and triple-gang (C). Double-gang and triple-gang boxes require internal cable clamps. Metal boxes should be used for exposed indoor wiring, such as conduit installations in an unfinished basement. Metal boxes also can be used for wiring that will be covered by finished walls. Plastic retrofit boxes are used when a new switch or receptacle must fit inside a finished wall. Use internal cable clamps.

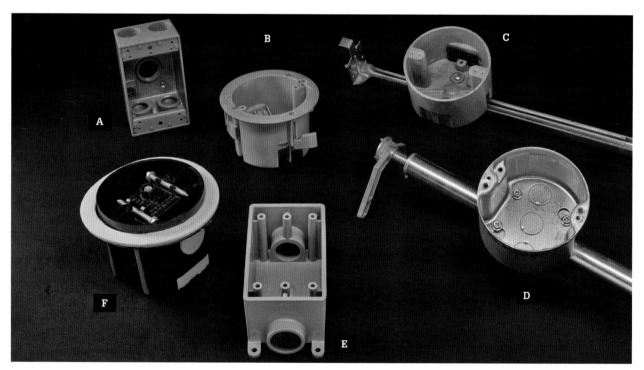

Additional electrical boxes include, cast aluminum box (A) for use with outdoor fixtures, including receptacles that are wired through metal conduit (these must have in-use covers if they house receptacles); old work ceiling box (B) used for light fixtures; light-duty ceiling fan box (C) with brace that spans ceiling joists; heavy-duty retrofit ceiling fan box (D) designed for retrofit; PVC box (E) for use with PVC conduit in indoor or outdoor setting; vapor-proof ceiling box with foam gasket (F).

Box Specifications ▸

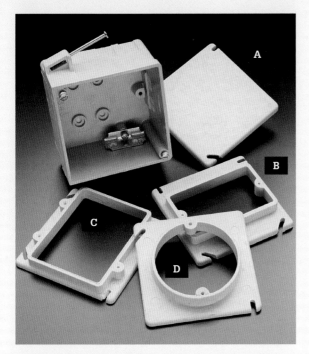

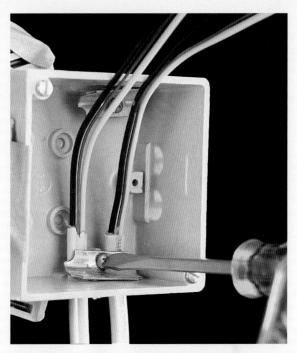

High-quality nonmetallic boxes are rigid and don't contort easily. A variety of adapter plates are available, including junction box cover plate (A), single-gang (B), double-gang (C), and light fixture (D). Adapter plates come in several thicknesses to match different wall constructions.

Boxes larger than 2 × 4" and all retrofit boxes must have internal cable clamps. After installing cables in the box, tighten the cable clamps over the cables so they are gripped firmly, but not so tightly that the cable sheathing is crushed.

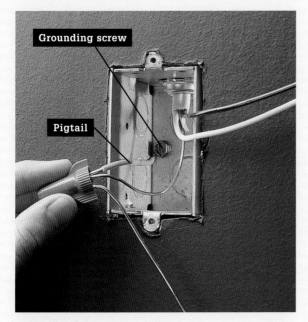

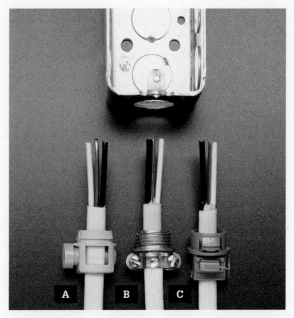

Metal boxes must be bonded to the circuit grounding system. Connect the circuit grounding wires to the box with a green insulated pigtail wire and wire connector (as shown) or with a grounding clip (page 38).

Cables entering a metal box must be clamped. A variety of clamps are available, including plastic clamps (A, C) and threaded metal clamps (B).

Nonmetallic Boxes

Nonmetallic electrical boxes have taken over much of the do-it-yourself market. Most are sold prefitted with installation hardware—from metal wings to 10d common nails attached at the perfect angle for a nail-in box. The bulk of the nonmetallic boxes sold today are inexpensive blue PVC. You can also purchase heavier-duty fiberglass or thermoset plastic models that provide a nonmetallic option for installing heavier fixtures such as ceiling fans and chandeliers.

In addition to cost and availability, nonmetallic boxes hold a big advantage over metal boxes in that their resistance to conducting electricity will prevent a sparking short circuit if a hot wire contacts the box. Nonmetallic boxes generally are not approved for exposed areas, where they may be susceptible to damage. Their lack of rigidity also allows them to compress or distort, which can reduce the interior capacity beyond code minimums or make outlets difficult to attach.

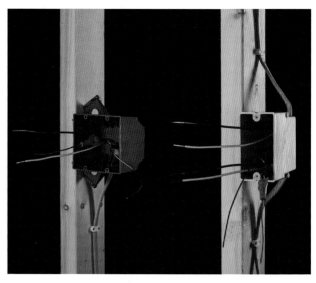

Low cost is the primary reason that blue PVC nail-in boxes are so popular. Not only are they inexpensive, they also feature built-in cable clamps so you may not need to buy extra hardware to install them. The standard PVC nail-in box is prefitted with a pair of 10d common nails for attaching to exposed wall studs. These boxes, often called handy boxes, are too small to be of much use (see fill chart, page 62).

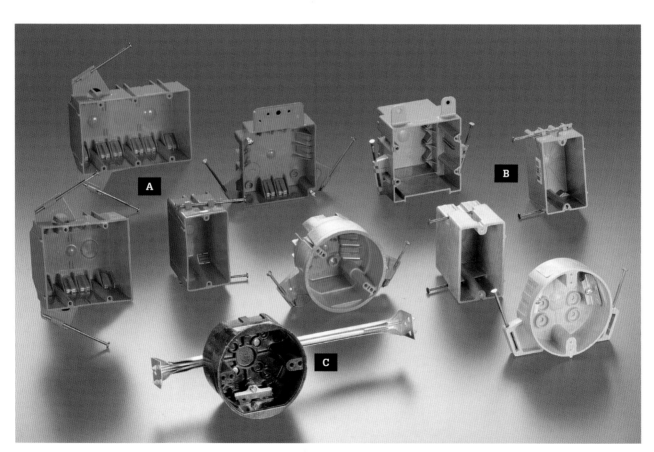

Nonmetallic boxes for home use include: Single-gang, double-gang, triple gang, and quad boxes (A); thermoset and fiberglass boxes for heavier duty (B); and round fixture boxes (C) for ceiling installation (nail-in and with integral metal bracket).

Working With Nonmetallic Boxes

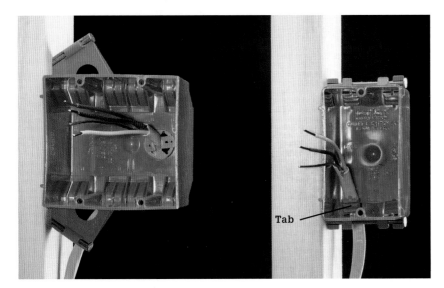

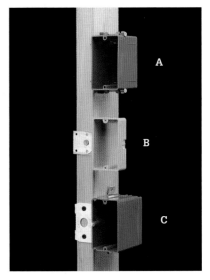

Do not break off the tabs that cover cable entry holes in plastic boxes. These are not knockouts as you would find in metal boxes. In single-gang boxes (right), the pressure from the tab is sufficient to secure the cable as long as it enters with sheathing intact and is stapled no more than 8" from the box. On larger boxes (left), you will find traditional knockouts intended to be used with plastic cable clamps that resemble metal cable clamps. Use these for heavier gauge cable and cable with more than three wires.

Nail-in boxes (A) are prefitted with 10d nails that are attached perpendicular to the face of single-gang boxes and at an inward angle for better gripping power on larger boxes. Side-mount boxes (B) feature a nailing plate that is attached to the front of the stud to automatically create the correct setback; adjustable side-mount boxes (C) are installed the same way but can be moved on the bracket.

Distortion can occur in nonmetallic boxes when nails or other fasteners are overdriven or installed at improper angles, or when the semiflexible boxes are compressed into improperly sized or shaped openings. This can reduce the box capacity and prevent devices and faceplates from fitting.

Integral ribs cast into many nonmetallic boxes are used to register the box against the wall studs so the front edges of the box will be flush with the wall surface after drywall is installed. Most are set for ½" drywall, but if your wall will be a different thickness you may be able to find a box with corresponding ribs. Otherwise, use a piece of the wallcovering material as a reference.

Installing Boxes

Install electrical boxes for receptacles, switches, and fixtures only after your wiring project plan has been approved by your inspector. Use your wiring plan as a guide, and follow electrical code height and spacing guidelines when laying out box positions.

Always use the deepest electrical boxes that are practical for your installation. Using deep boxes ensures that you will meet code regulations regarding box volume and makes it easier to make the wire connections.

Some electrical fixtures, such as recessed light fixtures, electric heaters, and exhaust fans, have built-in wire connection boxes. Install the frames for these fixtures at the same time you are installing the other electrical boxes. The box heights recommended on the following pages are for most situations. Boxes heights for handicap accessible situations are different.

Electrical boxes in adjacent rooms should be positioned close together when they share a common wall and are controlled by the same circuit. This simplifies the cable installations and also reduces the amount of cable needed.

Fixtures That Do Not Need Electrical Boxes

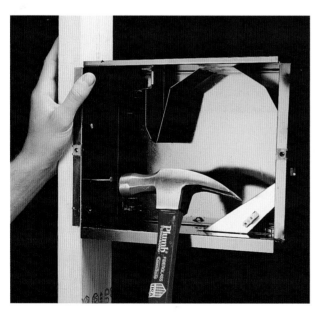 

Wire connection box

Recessed fixtures that fit inside wall cavities have built-in wire connection boxes and require no additional electrical boxes. Common recessed fixtures include electric blower-heaters (left), bathroom vent fans (right), and recessed light fixtures. Install the frames for these fixtures at the same time you are installing the other electrical boxes along the circuit. Surface-mounted fixtures such as electric baseboard heaters (pages 232 to 235) and under-cabinet fluorescent lights (pages 204 to 207) also have built-in wire connection boxes. These fixtures are not installed until it is time to make the final hookups.

How to Install Electrical Boxes for Receptacles

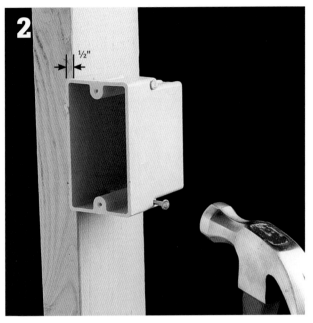

Mark the location of each box on studs. Standard receptacle boxes should be centered 12" above floor level. GFCI receptacle boxes in a bathroom should be mounted so they will be about 10" above the finished countertop.

Position each box against a stud so the front face will be flush with the finished wall. For example, if you will be installing ½" drywall, position the box so it extends ½" past the face of the stud, plus the thickness of any additional material, such as tile. Anchor the box by driving the mounting nails into the stud.

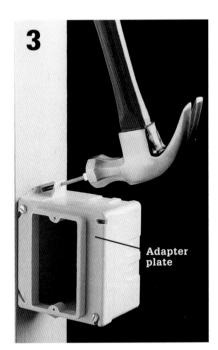

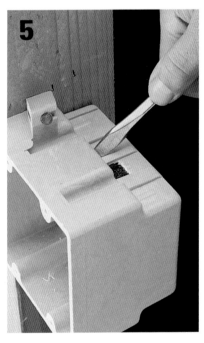

If installing square boxes, attach the adapter plates before positioning the boxes. Use adapter plates that match the thickness of the finished wall. Anchor the box by driving the mounting nails into the stud.

Open one knockout for each cable that will enter the box using a hammer and screwdriver. Always introduce the new cable through the knockout that is farthest way from the wall stud.

Break off any sharp edges that might damage vinyl cable sheathing by rotating a screwdriver in the knockout.

How to Install Boxes for Light Fixtures

1

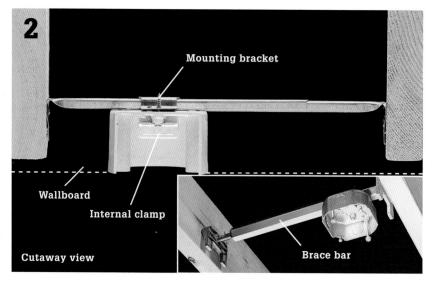

2

Position the light fixture box for a vanity light above the frame opening for a mirror or medicine cabinet. Place the box for a ceiling light fixture in the center of the room. Position each box against a framing member so the front face will be flush with the finished wall or ceiling, and then anchor the box by driving the mounting nails into the framing.

To position a light fixture between joists, attach an electrical box to an adjustable brace bar. Nail the ends of the brace bar to joists so the face of the box will be flush with the finished ceiling surface. Slide the box along the brace bar to the desired position, and then tighten the mounting screws. Use internal cable clamps when using a box with a brace bar. *Note: For ceiling fans and heavy fixtures, use a metal box and a heavy-duty brace bar rated for heavy loads (inset photo).*

How to Install Boxes for Switches

1

48"

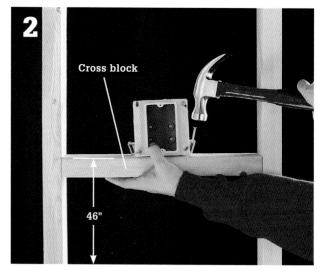

2

Cross block

46"

Install switch boxes at accessible locations, usually on the latch side of a door, with the center of the box 48" from the floor. The box for a thermostat is mounted at 48" to 60". Position each box against the side of a stud so the front face will be flush with the finished wall, and drive the mounting nails into the stud.

To install a switch box between studs, first install a cross block between studs, with the top edge 46" above the floor. Position the box on the cross block so the front face will be flush with the finished wall, and drive the mounting nails into the cross block.

How to Locate Electrical Boxes

Heights of electrical boxes vary depending on use. In the kitchen shown here, boxes above the countertop are 45" above the floor, in the center of 18" backsplashes that extend from the countertop to the cabinets. All boxes for wall switches also are installed at this height. The center of the box for the microwave receptacle is 72" off the floor. The centers of the boxes for the range and food disposer receptacles are 12" off the floor, but the center of the box for the dishwasher receptacle is 6" off the floor.

Typical Wallcovering Thickness

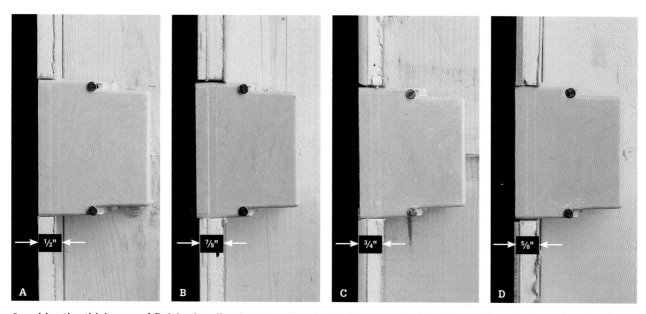

Consider the thickness of finished walls when mounting electrical boxes against framing members. Code requires that the front face of boxes be flush with the finished wall surface, so how you install boxes will vary depending on the type of wall finish that will be used. For example, if the walls will be finished with ½" wallboard (A), attach the boxes so the front faces extend ½" past the front of the framing members. With ceramic tile and wall board (B), extend the boxes ⅞" past the framing members. With ¼" Corian® over wallboard (C), boxes should extend ¾"; and with wallboard and laminate (D), boxes extend ⅝".

Ceiling Boxes

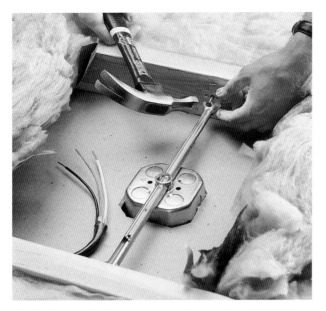

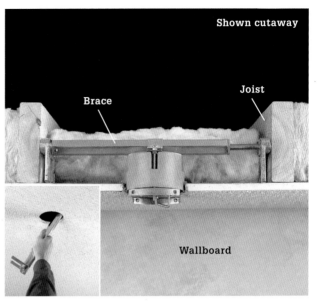

Shown cutaway

Brace

Joist

Wallboard

Ceiling boxes for lights are generally round or octagonal in shape to fit typical lamp mounting plates. The easiest way to install one is by nailing the brace to open ceiling joists from above. If the ceiling is insulated, pull the insulation away from the box if the fixture you're installing is not rated IC for insulation contact.

A heavy-duty brace is required for anchoring boxes that will support heavy chandeliers and ceiling fans. A remodeling brace such as the one seen here is designed to install through a small cutout in the ceiling (inset photo).

How to Install a Junction Box

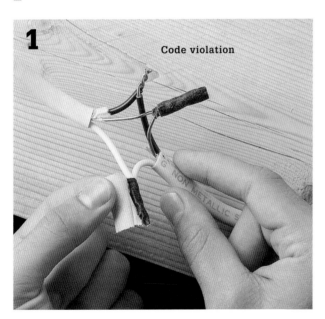

1

Code violation

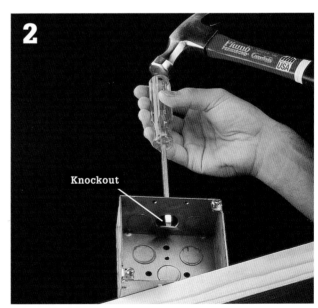

2

Knockout

Turn off power to circuit wires at the main service panel. Test for power. Carefully remove any tape or wire connectors from the exposed slice. Disconnect the illegally spliced wires.

Open one knockout for each cable that will enter the box using a hammer and screwdriver. Any unopened knockouts should remain sealed.

3

Anchor the electrical box to a wooden framing member using screws or nails.

4

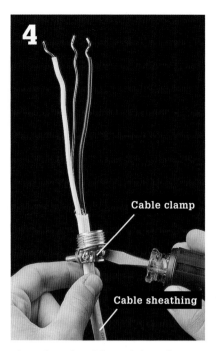

Cable clamp

Cable sheathing

Thread each cable end through a cable clamp. Tighten the clamp with a screwdriver. See if there is any slack in the cables so you can gain a little extra cable to work with.

5

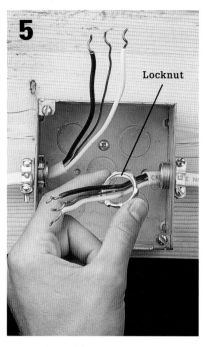

Locknut

Insert the cables into the electrical box, and screw a locknut onto each cable clamp.

6

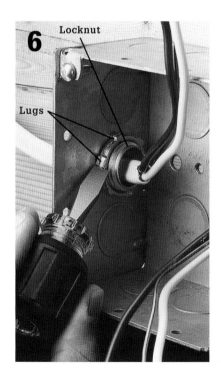

Locknut

Lugs

Tighten the locknuts by pushing against the lugs with the blade of a screwdriver.

7

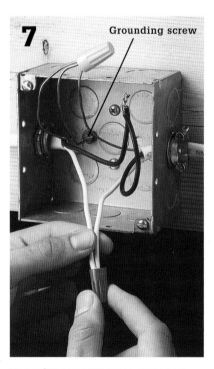

Grounding screw

Use wire connectors to reconnect the wires. Pigtail the copper grounding wires to the green grounding screw in the back of the box.

8

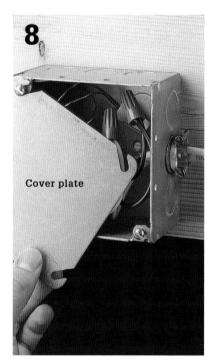

Cover plate

Carefully tuck the wires into the box, and attach the cover plate. Turn on the power to the circuit at the main service panel. Make sure the box remains accessible and is not concealed by finished walls or ceilings.

Installing Pop-in Retrofit Boxes

Attaching an electrical box to a wall stud during new construction is relatively easy (pages 66 to 69). The task becomes complicated, however, when you're working in finished walls during remodeling or repair. In most cases, it's best to use an electronic stud finder, make a large cutout in the wall, and attach a new box directly to a framing member or bracing (and then replace and refinish the wall materials). But there are occasions when this isn't possible or practical and you just need to retrofit an electrical box without making a large hole in the wall. You also may find that an older switch or receptacle box is too shallow to accommodate a new dimmer or GFCI safely. These situations call for a pop-in retrofit box (sometimes called an "old work" box).

A pop-in box typically has wings, tabs, or brackets that are drawn tight against the wall surface on the wall cavity side, holding the box in place. It can be made either of metal or plastic.

Pop-in boxes for remodeling come in a variety of styles. For walls, they include plastic retrofit boxes with flip-out wings (A), metal or plastic boxes with compression tabs or brackets (B), metal retrofit boxes with flip-out wings (C), and metal boxes with bendable brackets, also known as F-straps, (D). For ceilings, plastic fixture boxes with flip-out wings (E) are available.

Tools & Materials ▸

Screwdriver
Pencil
String
Electrical tape

Wallboard saw
Template (if provided)
Plastic or metal pop-in box
Eye protection

How to Replace an Electrical Box

1

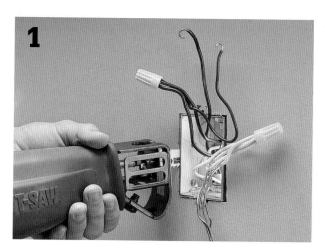

To install a dimmer switch or GFCI receptacle, you may have to replace an old, overcrowded box. Shut off power and remove the old switch or receptacle. Identify the location of nails holding the box to the framing member and cut the nails with a hacksaw or reciprocating saw with a metal blade inserted between the box and the stud.

2

Bind the cable ends together and attach string in case they fall into the wall cavity when the old box is removed. Disconnect the cable clamps and slide the old box out. Install a new pop-in box (see next page).

How to Install a Pop-in Box

Use a template to trace a cutout for the box at the intended location. If no template is provided, press the pop-in box against the wall surface and trace its front edges (but not the tabs on the top and bottom).

Puncture the wallboard with the tip of a wallboard saw or by drilling a small hole inside the lines, and make the cutout for the box.

Pull NM cable through a knockout in the box (no cable clamp is required with a plastic box; just be sure not to break the pressure tab that holds the cable in place).

Flip-out wings

Back of wall

Insert the box into the cutout so the tabs are flush against the wall surface. Tighten the screws that cause the flip-out wings to pivot (right) until the box is held firmly in place. Connect the switch or receptacle that the box will house.

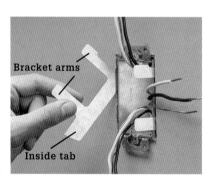

Bracket arms

Inside tab

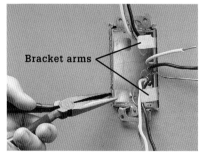

Bracket arms

Variation: Feed cable into the new box and secure it in the opening after clamping the cables. With this pop-in box, bracket arms are inserted at the sides of the box (top) and then bent around the front edges to secure the box in the opening (bottom).

Electrical Panels

Every home has a main panel that distributes electrical current to the individual circuits. The main panel may be found in the basement, garage, utility area, or on an exterior wall and can be identified by its metal casing. Before making any repair to your electrical system, you must shut off power to the correct circuit at the main panel or at the subpanel where the circuit begins. Every circuit in every panel should be labeled (see page 22) so circuits can be identified easily.

Panels vary in appearance, depending on the age of the system. Very old wiring may operate on 30-amp service that has only two circuits. New homes can have up to 400-amp service with 30 or more circuits. Find the size of the service by reading the amperage rating printed on the main fuse block or main circuit breakers.

Regardless of age, all panels have fuses or circuit breakers (see pages 78 to 81) that protect each circuit from overloads. In general, older service panels use fuses, while newer panels use circuit breakers.

In addition to the main panel, your electrical system may have one or more subpanels that protect some of the circuits in the home. A subpanel has its own circuit breakers or fuses.

The subpanel resembles the main service panel but is usually smaller. It may be located near the main panel, or it may be found near the areas served by the new circuits. Garages and basements that have been updated often have their own subpanels. If your home has subpanels, make sure that their circuits are indexed correctly.

When handling fuses or circuit breakers, make sure the area around the panel is dry. Never remove the protective cover on the panel. After turning off a circuit to make electrical repairs, remember to always test the circuit for power before touching any wires.

200-amp Service Panel

The main panel is the heart of your wiring system. As our demand for household energy has increased, the panels have also grown in capacity. Today, a 200-amp panel is often installed in new construction. Many homebuilders are installing dual 200-amp panels to deliver 400 amps to larger houses. A pair of 200-amp panels is much cheaper than one 400-amp panel.

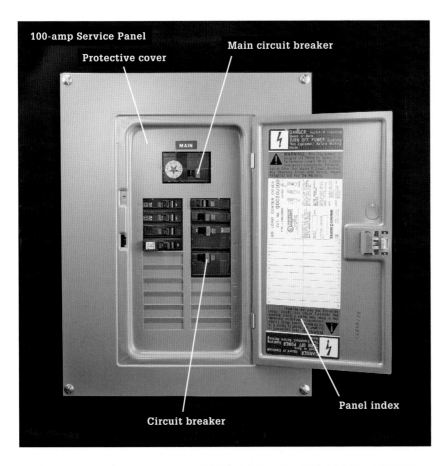

100-amp Service Panel

Protective cover

Main circuit breaker

Panel index

Circuit breaker

A circuit breaker panel providing 100 amps or more of current is common in wiring systems installed during the 1960s and later. A circuit breaker panel is housed in a gray metal cabinet that contains two rows of individual circuit breakers. You can determine service size by reading the amperage rating of the main circuit breakers. In systems rated 200 amps and below, the main breaker is often located in the main panel, but it may be in a separate cabinet located elsewhere.

Larger new homes may have 300- or 400-amp service. These systems usually have two main circuit breakers in the main panel and at least one subpanel.

A 100-amp service panel is now the minimum standard for all new housing. It is adequate for a medium-sized house with no more than three major electric appliances. However, larger houses with more electrical appliances require a service panel that provides 150 amps or more.

To shut off power to individual circuits in a circuit breaker panel, flip the lever on the appropriate circuit breaker to the OFF position. To shut off the power to the entire house, turn the main circuit breakers to the OFF position.

Some older homes may still have a 60-amp fuse panel. It usually is housed in a gray metal cabinet that contains four individual plug fuses, plus one or two pull-out fuse blocks that hold cartridge fuses. A 60-amp panel is considered undersized by current standards. The system should be upgraded for both convenience and safety. Insurance companies and mortgage lenders may require a complete electrical system upgrade before issuing a homeowner insurance policy or approving mortgage financing.

To shut off power to a circuit, carefully unscrew the plug fuse, touching only its insulated rim. To shut off power to the entire house, hold the handle of the main fuse block and pull sharply to remove it. Major appliance circuits are controlled with another cartridge fuse block. Shut off the appliance circuit by pulling out this fuse block.

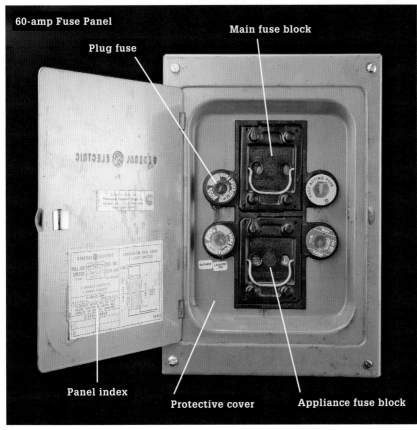

60-amp Fuse Panel

Plug fuse

Main fuse block

Panel index

Protective cover

Appliance fuse block

Circuit Breaker Panels

The circuit breaker panel is the electrical distribution center for your home. It divides the current into branch circuits that are carried throughout the house. Each branch circuit is protected by a circuit breaker that protects the wires from dangerous current overloads. When installing new circuits, the last step is to connect the wires to new circuit breakers at the panel. Follow basic safety procedures and always shut off the main circuit breaker and test for power before touching any parts inside the panel. Never touch the service wire lugs. If unsure of your own skills, hire an electrician to make the final circuit connections. (If you have an older electrical service with fuses instead of circuit breakers, always have an electrician make these final hookups.)

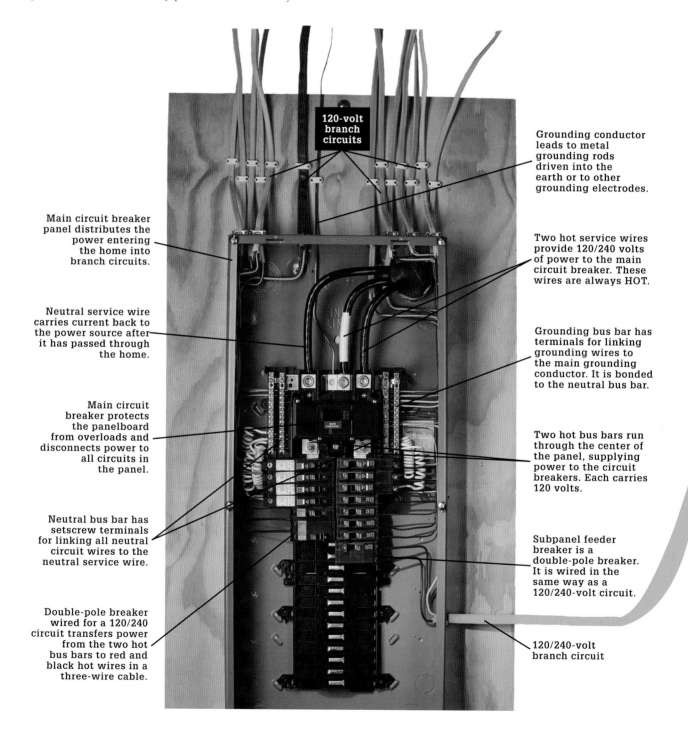

120-volt branch circuits

Grounding conductor leads to metal grounding rods driven into the earth or to other grounding electrodes.

Main circuit breaker panel distributes the power entering the home into branch circuits.

Neutral service wire carries current back to the power source after it has passed through the home.

Main circuit breaker protects the panelboard from overloads and disconnects power to all circuits in the panel.

Neutral bus bar has setscrew terminals for linking all neutral circuit wires to the neutral service wire.

Double-pole breaker wired for a 120/240 circuit transfers power from the two hot bus bars to red and black hot wires in a three-wire cable.

Two hot service wires provide 120/240 volts of power to the main circuit breaker. These wires are always HOT.

Grounding bus bar has terminals for linking grounding wires to the main grounding conductor. It is bonded to the neutral bus bar.

Two hot bus bars run through the center of the panel, supplying power to the circuit breakers. Each carries 120 volts.

Subpanel feeder breaker is a double-pole breaker. It is wired in the same way as a 120/240-volt circuit.

120/240-volt branch circuit

If a circuit breaker panel does not have enough open slots for new full-size circuit breakers, you may be able to install ½-height (slimline) circuit breakers. Otherwise, you will need to install a subpanel.

Before installing any new wiring, evaluate your electrical service to make sure it provides enough current to support both the existing wiring and any new circuits. If your service does not provide enough current, you will need to upgrade to a higher amp rating panel with enough extra breaker slots for the new circuits you want to install.

Safety Warning ▶

Never touch any parts inside a circuit breaker panel until you have checked for power (see page 80). Circuit breaker panels differ in appearance, depending on the manufacturer. Never begin work in a circuit breaker panel until you understand its layout and can identify the parts.

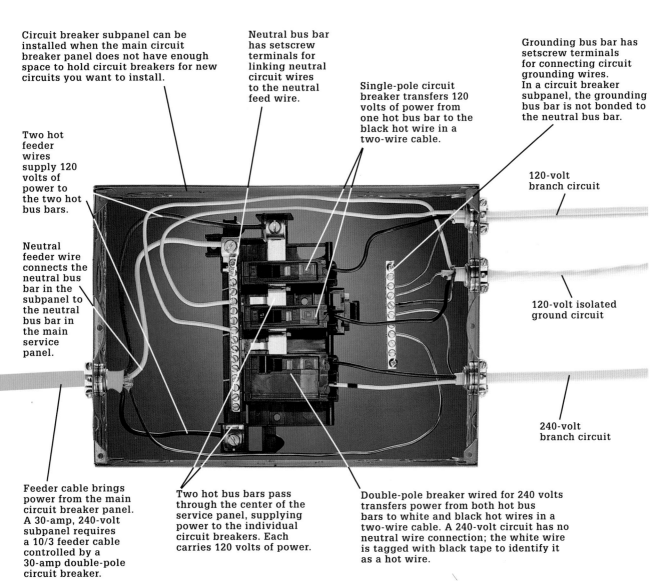

Circuit breaker subpanel can be installed when the main circuit breaker panel does not have enough space to hold circuit breakers for new circuits you want to install.

Two hot feeder wires supply 120 volts of power to the two hot bus bars.

Neutral feeder wire connects the neutral bus bar in the subpanel to the neutral bus bar in the main service panel.

Neutral bus bar has setscrew terminals for linking neutral circuit wires to the neutral feed wire.

Single-pole circuit breaker transfers 120 volts of power from one hot bus bar to the black hot wire in a two-wire cable.

Grounding bus bar has setscrew terminals for connecting circuit grounding wires. In a circuit breaker subpanel, the grounding bus bar is not bonded to the neutral bus bar.

120-volt branch circuit

120-volt isolated ground circuit

240-volt branch circuit

Feeder cable brings power from the main circuit breaker panel. A 30-amp, 240-volt subpanel requires a 10/3 feeder cable controlled by a 30-amp double-pole circuit breaker.

Two hot bus bars pass through the center of the service panel, supplying power to the individual circuit breakers. Each carries 120 volts of power.

Double-pole breaker wired for 240 volts transfers power from both hot bus bars to white and black hot wires in a two-wire cable. A 240-volt circuit has no neutral wire connection; the white wire is tagged with black tape to identify it as a hot wire.

Fuses & Circuit Breakers

Fuses and circuit breakers are safety devices designed to protect the electrical system from short circuits and overloads. Fuses and circuit breakers are located in the main service panel and in subpanels.

Most service panels installed before 1965 rely on fuses to protect individual circuits. Screw-in plug fuses protect 120-volt circuits that power lights and receptacles. Cartridge fuses protect 240-volt appliance circuits and the main shutoff of the service panel.

Inside each fuse is a current-carrying metal alloy ribbon. If a circuit is overloaded, the metal ribbon melts and stops the current flow. A fuse must match the amperage rating of the circuit. Never replace a fuse with one that has a larger amperage rating.

In most service panels installed after 1965, circuit breakers protect individual circuits. Single-pole circuit breakers protect 120-volt circuits, and double-pole circuit breakers protect 240-volt circuits. Amperage ratings for circuit breakers range from 15 to 100 amps.

Each circuit breaker has a permanent metal strip that heats up and bends when current passes through it. If a circuit is overloaded, the metal strip inside the breaker bends enough to "trip" the switch and stop the flow of power. Circuit breakers are listed to trip twice. After the second trip they weaken and tend to nuisance trip at lower currents. Replace breakers that have tripped more than twice—they may fail.

When a fuse blows or a circuit breaker trips, it is usually because there are too many light fixtures and plug-in appliances drawing power through the circuit. Move some of the plug-in appliances to another circuit, and then replace the fuse or reset the breaker. If the fuse blows or the breaker trips again immediately, there may be a short circuit in the system. Call a licensed electrician if you suspect a short circuit.

Circuit breakers are found in the majority of panels installed since the 1960s. Single-pole breakers control 120-volt circuits. Double-pole breakers rated for 20 to 60 amps control 240-volt circuits. Ground-fault circuit interrupter (GFCI) provides protection from shocks. Arc-fault circuit interrupter (AFCI) breakers provide protection from fire-causing arcs for the entire circuit.

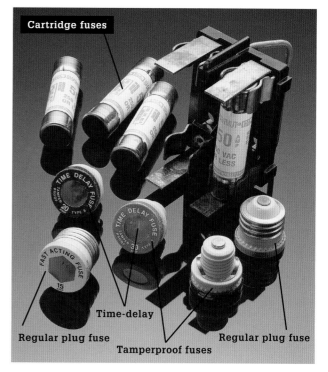

Fuses are used in older panels. Plug fuses usually control 120-volt circuits rated for 15, 20, or 30 amps. Tamper-proof plug fuses have threads that fit only matching sockets, making it impossible to install a wrong-sized fuse. Time-delay fuses absorb temporary heavy power loads without blowing. Cartridge fuses control 240-volt circuits and range from 30 to 100 amps.

Old-style fuse boxes can accept modern "s" type fuses if you use an Edison adapter. Be sure to screw the fuse into the adapter first, and then screw the assembly into the socket.

How to Identify & Replace a Blown Plug Fuse

Locate the blown fuse at the panel. If the metal ribbon inside is cleanly melted (left), the circuit was overloaded. If window is discolored (right), there was a short circuit.

Unscrew the fuse, being careful to touch only the insulated rim of the fuse. Replace it with a fuse that has the same amperage rating.

How to Remove, Test & Replace a Cartridge Fuse

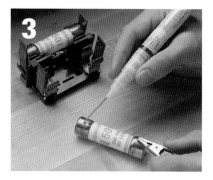

Remove cartridge fuses by gripping the handle of the fuse block and pulling sharply.

Remove the individual cartridge fuses from the block using a fuse puller.

Test each fuse using a continuity tester. If the tester glows, the fuse is good. If not, install a new fuse with the same amperage rating.

How to Reset a Circuit Breaker

Open the service panel and locate the tripped breaker. The lever on the tripped breaker will be either in the OFF position or in a position between ON and OFF.

Reset the tripped circuit breaker by pressing the circuit breaker lever all the way to the OFF position and then pressing it to the ON position.

Test AFCI and GFCI circuit breakers by pushing the TEST button. The breaker should trip to the OFF position. If not, the breaker is faulty and must be replaced.

Connecting Circuit Breakers

The last step in a wiring project is connecting circuits at the breaker panel. After this is done, the work is ready for the final inspection.

Circuits are connected at the main panel, if it has enough open slots, or at a circuit breaker subpanel (see pages 74–77). When working at a subpanel, make sure the feeder breaker at the main panel has been turned off, and test for power (see photo, right) before touching any parts in the subpanel.

Make sure the circuit breaker amperage does not exceed the ampacity of the circuit wires you are connecting to it. Also be aware that circuit breaker styles and installation techniques vary according to manufacturer. Use breakers made by the panel manufacturer. You should install AFCI circuit breakers for most 15- and 20-amp, 120-volt circuits inside the home.

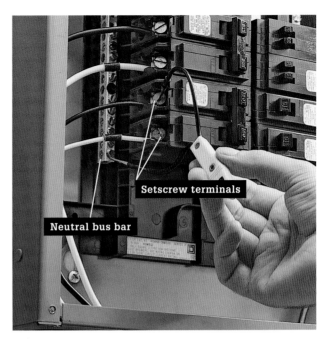

Setscrew terminals

Neutral bus bar

Test for current before touching any parts inside a circuit breaker panel. With the main breaker turned off but all other breakers turned on, touch one probe of a neon tester to the neutral bus bar, and touch the other probe to each setscrew on one of the double-pole breakers (not the main breaker). If the tester does not light for either setscrew, it is safe to work in the panel. *Note: Touchless circuit testers are preferred in most situations where you are testing for current because they're safer. But in some instances you'll need a tester with individual probes to properly check for current.*

Tools & Materials ▸

Screwdriver
Hammer
Pencil
Combination tool
Cable ripper

Circuit tester
Pliers
Cable clamps
Single- and double-pole
   AFCI circuit breakers

How to Connect Circuit Breakers

Shut off the main circuit breaker in the main circuit breaker panel (if you are working in a subpanel, shut off the feeder breaker in the main panel). Remove the panel cover plate, taking care not to touch the parts inside the panel. Test for power (photo, top).

Open a knockout in the side of the circuit breaker panel using a screwdriver and hammer. Attach a cable clamp to the knockout.

Hold the cable across the front of the panel near the knockout, and mark the sheathing about ½" inside the edge of the panel. Strip the cable from the marked line to the end using a cable ripper. (There should be 18" to 24" of excess cable.) Insert the cable through the clamp and into the service panel, and then tighten the clamp.

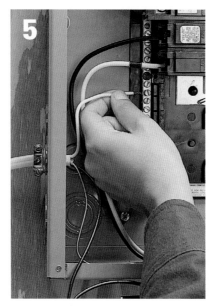

Bend the bare copper grounding wire around the inside edge of the panel to an open setscrew terminal on the grounding bus bar. Insert the wire into the opening on the bus bar, and tighten the setscrew. Fold excess wire around the inside edge of the panel.

For 120-volt circuits, bend the white circuit wire around the outside of the panel to an open setscrew terminal on the neutral bus bar. Clip away excess wire, and then strip ½" of insulation from the wire using a combination tool. Insert the wire into the terminal opening, and tighten the setscrew.

Strip ½" of insulation from the end of the black circuit wire. Insert the wire into the setscrew terminal on a new single-pole circuit breaker, and tighten the setscrew.

Slide one end of the circuit breaker onto the guide hook, and then press it firmly against the bus bar until it snaps into place. (Breaker installation may vary, depending on the manufacturer.) Fold excess black wire around the inside edge of the panel.

120/240-volt circuits (top): Connect red and black wires to the double-pole breaker. Connect white wire to the neutral bus bar, and the grounding wire to grounding bus bar. For 240-volt circuits (bottom), attach white and black wires to the double-pole breaker, tagging white wire with black tape. There is no neutral bus bar connection on this circuit.

Remove the appropriate breaker tab on the panel cover plate to make room for the new circuit breaker. A single-pole breaker requires one tab, while a double-pole breaker requires two tabs. Reattach the cover plate, and label the new circuit on the panel index.

Switches

Among wiring devices, switches fail with surprising frequency. If you've carefully wired a new circuit or a fixture and you know you got it right, but when you turn on the power it doesn't work, you should direct your attention to any switches in the line. Even brand-new switches can fail to function correctly. This is why most professional electricians will pay the extra couple of dollars to buy a quality switch out of the gate. It is also why most of them routinely test each switch for continuity before installing it (see pages 98 to 101).

The most basic switches for home wiring are single-pole switches, which control only one fixture and have only two screw (or push-in) terminals (not counting the grounding screw). Next, three-way switches and four-way switches have more installation possibilities and control circuits that are more complicated to wire. Dimmer switches, isolated ground switches, and motion-sensor switches are some of the other switch options.

Use caution when you handle switches. The wires are usually attached to screw terminals on the sides of the fitting, which makes them very easy to contact if you grab the switch. Always shut off the power to the switch before removing the switch cover plate. Also shut off the power at the service panel if you will be working downline from the switch—never count on a switch that is open to function as a breaker.

In this chapter:

- Wall Switches
- Types of Wall Switches
- Specialty Switches
- Testing Switches

Wall Switches

An average wall switch is turned on and off more than 1,000 times each year. Because switches receive constant use, wire connections can loosen and switch parts gradually wear out. If a switch no longer operates smoothly, it must be replaced.

The methods for replacing a switch vary slightly, depending on the switch type and its location along an electrical circuit. When working on a switch, use the photographs on pages 86 to 100 to identify your switch type and its wiring configuration. Individual switch styles may vary from manufacturer to manufacturer, but the basic switch types are universal.

It is possible to replace most ordinary wall switches with a specialty switch, such as a timer switch or an electronic switch. When installing a specialty switch, make sure it is compatible with the wiring configuration and size of the switch box. Notice: Two changes in the NEC affect how new switch wiring should be installed. These changes do not affect existing switch wiring. The pictures and instructions in this book about replacing

existing switches show wiring that does not comply with these new requirements. This is because you will probably see non-compliant wiring for many years to come. Pictures and instructions about installing new switch wiring show wiring that complies with these new requirements.

One change requires that a wire with white insulation should not supply current to a light or receptacle, even when the wire is marked as hot. A black or red colored wire should supply current to the device. A white colored wire, marked as hot, may supply current to the switch.

The other change requires that a neutral wire be available at switch boxes. An exception allows you to ignore this requirement if the switch box is accessible from above or below, such as from a basement, crawlspace, or attic. This new requirement is intended to allow easier installation of devices, such as intelligent switch controllers, that need power for controller operation.

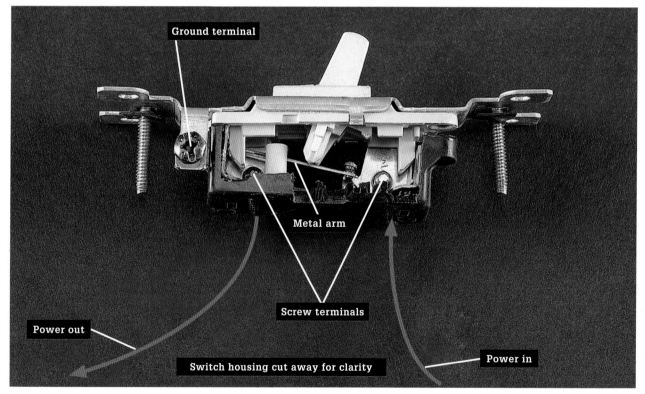

A typical wall switch has a movable metal arm that opens and closes the electrical circuit. When the switch is ON, the arm completes the circuit and power flows between the screw terminals and through the black hot wire to the light fixture. When the switch is OFF, the arm lifts away to interrupt the circuit, and no power flows. Switch problems can occur if the screw terminals are not tight or if the metal arm inside the switch wears out. *Note: The switch above has had part of its housing removed so the interior workings can be seen. Switches or fixtures that are not in original condition should never be installed.*

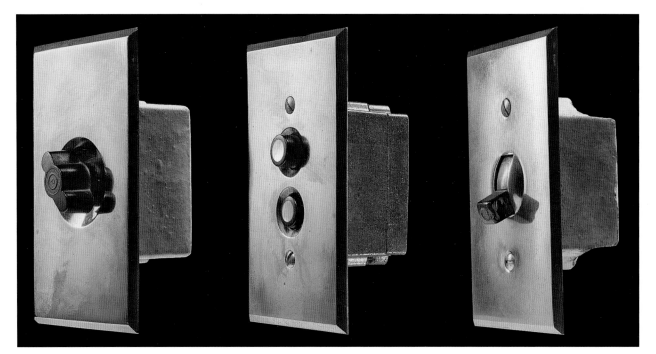

Rotary snap switches are found in many installations completed between 1900 and 1920. The handle is twisted clockwise to turn light on and off. The switch is enclosed in a ceramic housing.

Push-button switches were widely used from 1920 until about 1940. Many switches of this type are still in operation. Reproductions of this switch type are available for restoration projects.

Toggle switches were introduced in the 1930s. This early design has a switch mechanism that is mounted in a ceramic housing sealed with a layer of insulating paper.

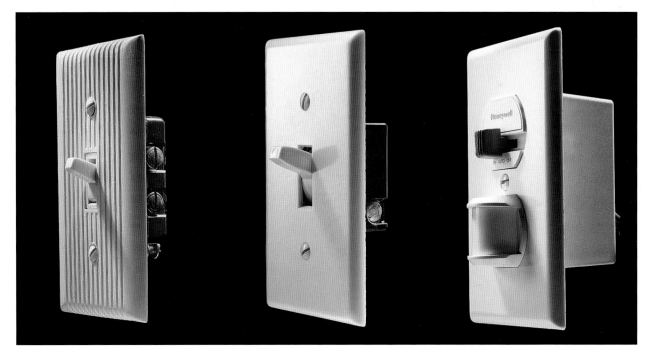

Toggle switches were improved during the 1950s and are now the most commonly used type. This switch type was the first to use a sealed plastic housing that protects the inner switch mechanism from dust and moisture.

Mercury switches became common in the early 1960s. They conduct electrical current by means of a sealed vial of mercury. No longer manufactured for home use, old mercury switches are considered a hazardous waste.

Electronic motion-sensor switches have an infrared eye that senses movement and automatically turns on lights when a person enters a room. Motion-sensor switches can provide added security against intruders.

Types of Wall Switches

Wall switches are available in three general types. To re-connect or replace a switch, it is important to identify its type.

Single-pole switches are used to control a set of lights from one location. Three-way switches are used to control a set of lights from two different locations and are always installed in pairs. Four-way switches are used in combination with a pair of three-way switches to control a set of lights from three or more locations.

Identify switch types by counting the screw terminals. Single-pole switches have two screw terminals, three-way switches have three screw terminals, and four-way switches have four. Most switches include a grounding screw terminal, which is identified by its green color.

When replacing a switch, choose a new switch that has the same number of screw terminals as the old one. The location of the screws on the switch body varies depending on the manufacturer, but these differences will not affect the switch operation.

Whenever possible, connect switches using the screw terminals rather than push-in fittings. Some specialty switches (pages 94 to 97) have wire leads instead of screw terminals. They are connected to circuit wires with wire connectors.

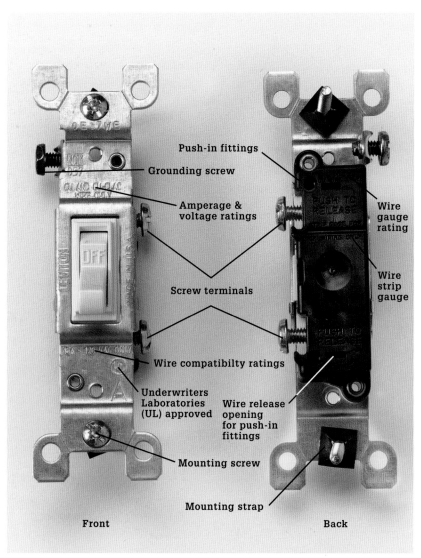

Front   **Back**

Push-in fittings
Grounding screw
Amperage & voltage ratings
Wire gauge rating
Screw terminals
Wire strip gauge
Wire compatibilty ratings
Underwriters Laboratories (UL) approved
Wire release opening for push-in fittings
Mounting screw
Mounting strap

A wall switch is connected to circuit wires with screw terminals or with push-in fittings on the back of the switch. A switch may have a stamped strip gauge that indicates how much insulation must be stripped from the circuit wires to make the connections.

The switch body is attached to a metal mounting strap that allows it to be mounted in an electrical box. Several rating stamps are found on the strap and on the back of the switch. The abbreviation UL or UND. LAB. INC. LIST means that the switch meets the safety standards of the Underwriters Laboratories. Switches also are stamped with maximum voltage and amperage ratings. Standard wall switches are rated 15A or 125V. Voltage ratings of 110, 120, and 125 are considered to be identical for purposes of identification.

For standard wall switch installations, choose a switch that has a wire gauge rating of #12 or #14. For wire systems with solid-core copper wiring, use only switches marked COPPER, CU, or CO/ALR. For aluminum wiring, use only switches marked CO/ALR. Note that while CO/ALR switches and receptacles are approved by the National Electrical Code for use with aluminum wiring, the Consumer Products Safety Commission does not recommend using these. Switches and receptacles marked AL/CU can no longer be used with aluminum wiring, according to the National Electrical Code.

Single-Pole Wall Switches

A single-pole switch is the most common type of wall switch. It has ON-OFF markings on the switch lever and is used to control a set of lights, an appliance, or a receptacle from a single location. A single-pole switch has two screw terminals and a grounding screw. When installing a single-pole switch, check to make sure the ON marking shows when the switch lever is in the up position.

In a correctly wired single-pole switch, a hot circuit wire is attached to each screw terminal. However, the color and number of wires inside the switch box will vary, depending on the location of the switch along the electrical circuit.

If two cables enter the box, then the switch lies in the middle of the circuit. In this installation, both of the hot wires attached to the switch are black.

If only one cable enters the box, then the switch lies at the end of the circuit. In this installation (sometimes called a switch loop), one of the hot wires is black, but the other hot wire usually is white. A white hot wire should be coded with black tape or paint.

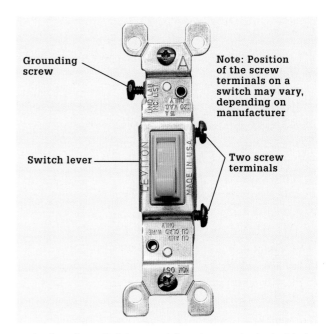

A single-pole switch is essentially an interruption in the black power supply wire that is opened or closed with the toggle. Single-pole switches are the simplest of all home wiring switches.

Typical Single-Pole Switch Installations

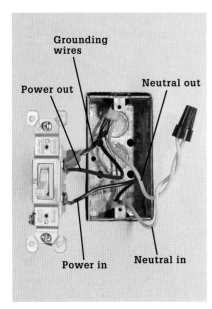

Two cables enter the box when a switch is located in the middle of a circuit. Each cable has a white and a black insulated wire, plus a bare copper grounding wire. The black wires are hot and are connected to the screw terminals on the switch. The white wires are neutral and are joined together with a wire connector. Grounding wires are pigtailed to the switch.

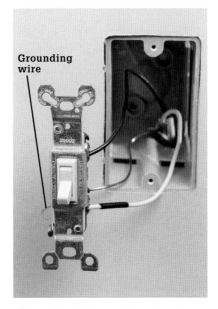

Old method: One cable enters the box when a switch is located at the end of a circuit. In this installation, both of the insulated wires are hot. The white wire should be labeled with black tape or paint to identify it as a hot wire. The grounding wire is connected to the switch grounding screw.

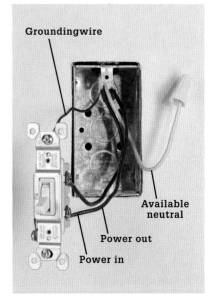

Code change: In new switch wiring, the white wire should not supply current to the switched device and a separate neutral wire should be available in the switch box.

Three-Way Wall Switches

Three-way switches have three screw terminals and do not have ON-OFF markings. Three-way switches are always installed in pairs and are used to control a set of lights from two locations.

One of the screw terminals on a three-way switch is darker than the others. This screw is the common screw terminal. The position of the common screw terminal on the switch body may vary, depending on the manufacturer. Before disconnecting a three-way switch, always label the wire that is connected to the common screw terminal. It must be reconnected to the common screw terminal on the new switch.

The two lighter-colored screw terminals on a three-way switch are called the traveler screw terminals. The traveler terminals are interchangeable, so there is no need to label the wires attached to them.

Because three-way switches are installed in pairs, it sometimes is difficult to determine which of the switches is causing a problem. The switch that receives greater use is more likely to fail, but you may need to inspect both switches to find the source of the problem.

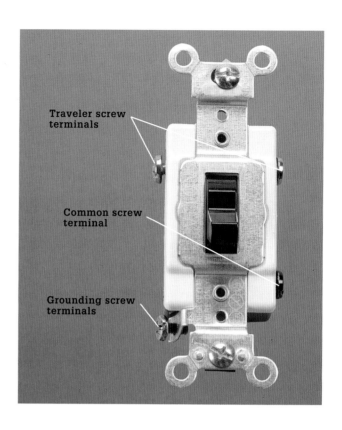

Traveler screw terminals

Common screw terminal

Grounding screw terminals

Typical Three-Way Switch Installation

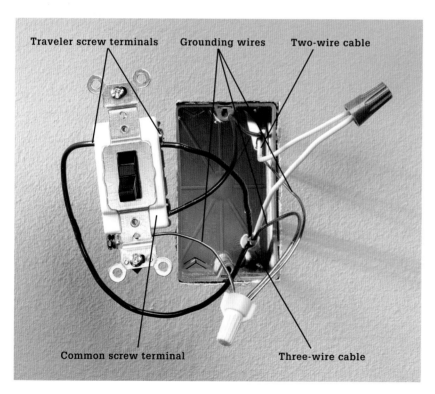

Traveler screw terminals   Grounding wires   Two-wire cable

Common screw terminal   Three-wire cable

Two cables enter the box: one cable has two wires, plus a bare copper grounding wire; the other cable has three wires, plus a ground. The black wire from the two-wire cable is connected to the dark common screw terminal. The red and black wires from the three-wire cable are connected to the traveler screw terminals. The white neutral wires are joined together with a wire connector, and the grounding wires are pigtailed to the grounded metal box.

How to Replace a Three-Way Wall Switch

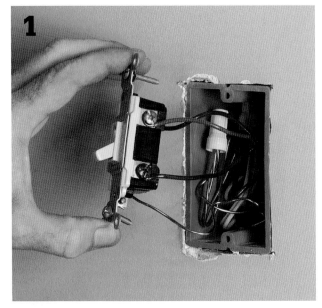

1

Turn off the power to the switch at the panel, and then remove the switch cover plate and mounting screws. Holding the mounting strap carefully, pull the switch from the box. Be careful not to touch the bare wires or screw terminals until they have been tested for power. *Note: If you are installing a new switch circuit, you must provide a neutral conductor at the switch.*

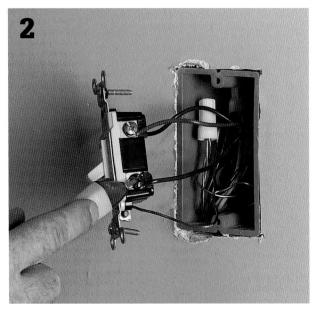

2

Test for power by touching one probe of the circuit tester to the grounded metal box or to the bare copper grounding wire and touching the other probe to each screw terminal. Tester should not glow. If it does, there is still power entering the box. Return to the panel, and turn off the correct circuit.

3

Common screw terminal

Locate the dark common screw terminal, and use masking tape to label the "common" wire attached to it. Disconnect wires and remove switch. Test the switch for continuity. If it tests faulty, buy a replacement. Inspect wires for nicks and scratches. If necessary, clip damaged wires and strip them.

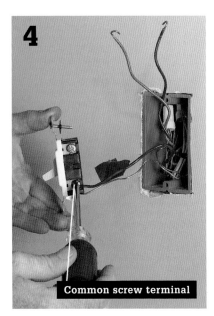

4

Common screw terminal

Connect the common wire to the dark common screw terminal on the switch. On most three-way switches, the common screw terminal is black. Or it may be labeled with the word COMMON stamped on the back of the switch. Reconnect the grounding screw, and connect it to the circuit grounding wires with a pigtail.

5

Connect the remaining two circuit wires to the screw terminals. These wires are interchangeable and can be connected to either screw terminal. Carefully tuck the wires into the box. Remount the switch, and attach the cover plate. Turn on the power at the panel.

Four-Way Wall Switches

Four-way switches have four screw terminals and do not have ON-OFF markings. Four-way switches are always installed between a pair of three-way switches. This switch combination makes it possible to control a set of lights from three or more locations. Four-way switches are common in homes where large rooms contain multiple living areas, such as a kitchen opening into a dining room. Switch problems in a four-way installation can be caused by loose connections or worn parts in a four-way switch or in one of the three-way switches (facing page).

In a typical installation, there will be a pair of three-wire cables that enter the box for the four-way switch. With most switches, the white and red wires from one cable should be attached to the bottom or top pair of screw terminals, and the white and red wires from the other cable should be attached to the remaining pair of screw terminals. However, not all switches are configured the same way, and wiring configurations in the box may vary, so always study the wiring diagram that comes with the switch.

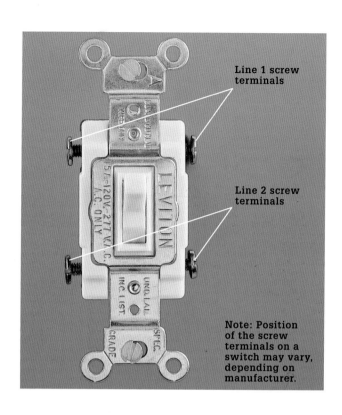

Line 1 screw terminals

Line 2 screw terminals

Note: Position of the screw terminals on a switch may vary, depending on manufacturer.

Typical Four-Way Switch Installation

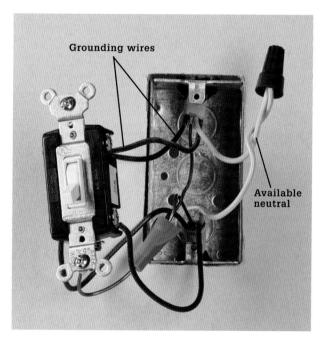

Grounding wires

Available neutral

Four wires are connected to a four-way switch. The red and white wires from one cable are attached to the top pair of screw terminals, while the red and white wires from the other cable are attached to the bottom screw terminals. In new switch wiring, the white wire should not supply current to the switched device, and a separate neutral wire should be available in the switch box.

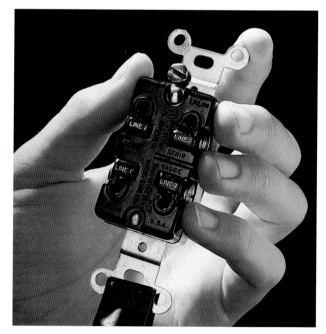

Switch variation: Some four-way switches have a wiring guide stamped on the back to help simplify installation. For the switch shown above, one pair of color-matched circuit wires will be connected to the screw terminals marked LINE 1, while the other pair of wires will be attached to the screw terminals marked LINE 2.

How to Replace a Four-Way Wall Switch

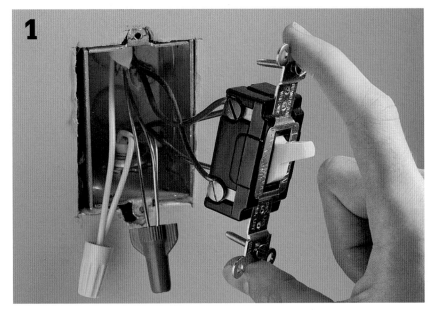

1

Turn off the power to the switch at the panel, and then remove the switch cover plate and mounting screws. Holding the mounting strap carefully, pull the switch from the box. Be careful not to touch any bare wires or screw terminals until they have been tested for power. Test for power by touching one probe of the neon circuit tester to the grounded metal box or bare copper grounding wire and touching the other probe to each of the screw terminals. The tester should not glow. If it does, there is still power entering the box. Return to the panel, and turn off the correct circuit.

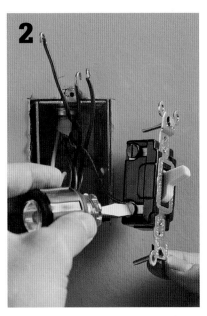

2

Disconnect the wires and inspect them for nicks and scratches. If necessary, clip damaged wires and strip them. Test the switch for continuity (pages 98 to 101). Buy a replacement if the switch tests faulty.

3

Connect two wires from one incoming cable to the top set of screw terminals.

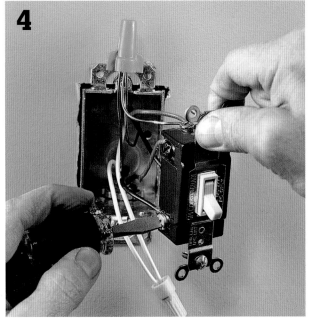

4

Attach remaining wires to the other set of screw terminals. Pigtail the grounding wires to the grounding screw. Carefully tuck the wires inside the switch box, and then remount the switch and cover plate. Turn on power at the panel.

Double Switches

A double switch has two switch levers in a single housing. It is used to control two light fixtures or appliances from the same switch box.

In most installations, both halves of the switch are powered by the same circuit. In these single-circuit installations, three wires are connected to the double switch. One wire, called the feed wire (which is hot), supplies power to both halves of the switch. The other wires, called the switch leg, carry power out to the individual light fixtures or appliances.

In rare installations, each half of the switch is powered by a separate circuit. In these separate-circuit installations, four wires are connected to the switch, and the metal connecting tab joining two of the screw terminals is removed (see photo below).

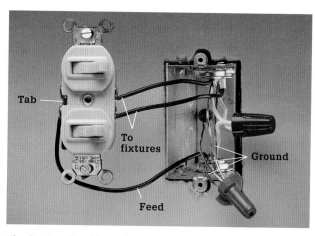

Single-circuit wiring: Three black wires are attached to the switch. The black feed wire bringing power into the box is connected to the side of the switch that has a connecting tab. The wires carrying power out to the light fixtures or appliances are connected to the side of the switch that does not have a connecting tab. The white neutral wires are connected together with a wire connector.

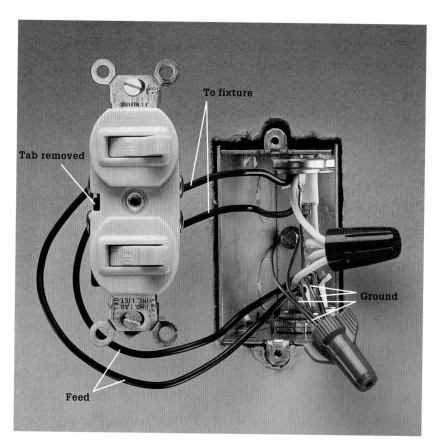

Separate-circuit wiring: Four black wires are attached to the switch. Feed wires from the power source are attached to the side of the switch that has a connecting tab, and the connecting tab is removed (photo, right). Wires carrying power from the switch to light fixtures or appliances are connected to the side of the switch that does not have a connecting tab. White neutral wires are connected together with a wire connector.

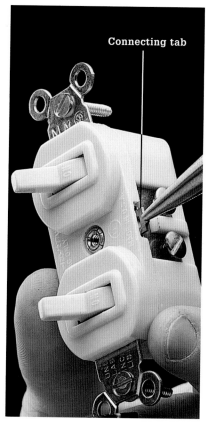

Remove the connecting tab on a double switch when wired in a separate-circuit installation. The tab can be removed with needlenose pliers or a screwdriver.

Pilot-Light Switches

A pilot-light switch has a built-in bulb that glows when power flows through the switch to a light fixture or appliance. Pilot-light switches often are installed for convenience if a light fixture or appliance cannot be seen from the switch location. Basement lights, garage lights, and attic exhaust fans frequently are controlled by pilot-light switches.

A pilot-light switch requires a neutral wire connection. A switch box that contains a single two-wire cable has only hot wires and cannot be fitted with a pilot-light switch.

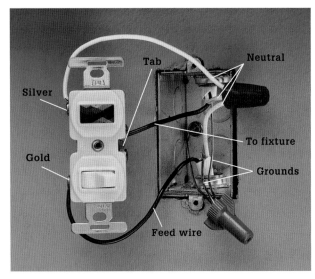

Pilot-light switch wiring: Three wires are connected to the switch. One black wire is the feed wire that brings power into the box. It is connected to the brass (gold) screw terminal on the side of the switch that does not have a connecting tab. The white neutral wires are pigtailed to the silver screw terminal. The black wire carrying power out to a light fixture or appliance is connected to the screw terminal on the side of the switch that has a connecting tab.

Switch/Receptacles

A switch/receptacle combines a grounded receptacle with a single-pole wall switch. In a room that does not have enough wall receptacles, electrical service can be improved by replacing a single-pole switch with a switch/receptacle.

A switch/receptacle requires a neutral wire connection. A switch box that contains a single two-wire cable has only hot wires and cannot be fitted with a switch/receptacle.

A switch/receptacle can be installed in one of two ways. In the most common installations, the receptacle is hot even when the switch is off (photo, right).

In rare installations, a switch/receptacle is wired so the receptacle is hot only when the switch is on. In this installation, the hot wires are reversed, so that the feed wire is attached to the brass screw terminal on the side of the switch that does not have a connecting tab.

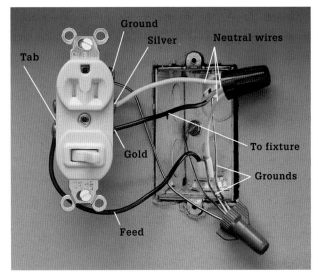

Switch/receptacle wiring: Three wires are connected to the switch/receptacle. One of the hot wires is the feed wire that brings power into the box. It is connected to the side of the switch that has a connecting tab. The other hot wire carries power out to the light fixture or appliance. It is connected to the brass screw terminal on the side that does not have a connecting tab. The white neutral wire is pigtailed to the silver screw terminal. The grounding wires must be pigtailed to the green grounding screw on the switch/receptacle and to the grounded metal box.

Specialty Switches

Your house may have several types of specialty switches. Dimmer switches (pages 96 to 97) are used frequently to control light intensity in dining and recreation areas. Timer switches and time-delay switches (below) are used to control light fixtures and exhaust fans automatically. Electronic switches provide added convenience and home security, and they are easy to install. Electronic switches are durable, and they rarely need replacement.

Most specialty switches have preattached wire leads instead of screw terminals and are connected to circuit wires with wire connectors. Some motor-driven timer switches require a neutral wire connection and

cannot be installed in switch boxes that have only one cable with two hot wires. It is precisely due to the rise in popularity of "smart" switches that the NEC Code was changed in 2014 to require an available neutral wire in newly-installed switch boxes.

If a specialty switch is not operating correctly, you may be able to test it with a continuity tester. Timer switches and time-delay switches can be tested for continuity, but dimmer switches cannot be tested. With electronic switches, the manual switch can be tested for continuity, but the automatic features cannot be tested.

Timer Switches

Countdown timer switches can be set to turn lights or fans on and off automatically once each day. They are commonly used to control outdoor light fixtures.

Timer switches have three preattached wire leads. The black wire lead is connected to the hot feed wire that brings power into the box, and the red lead is connected to the wire carrying power out

to the light fixture. The remaining wire lead is the neutral lead. It must be connected to any neutral circuit wires. A switch box that contains only one cable has no neutral wires, so it cannot be fitted with a timer switch.

After a power failure, the dial on a timer switch must be reset to the proper time.

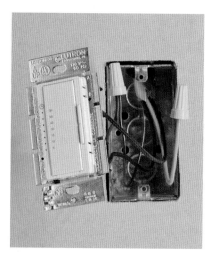

Countdown timer switch. This rocker-type switch gives you the option to easily program the switch to shut off after a specified time: from 5 to 60 minutes. Garage lights or basement lights are good applications: anywhere you want the light to stay on long enough to allow you to exit, but not to stay on indefinitely. These switches often are used to control vent fans.

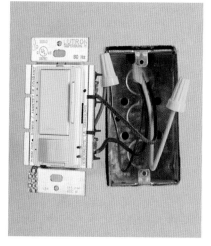

Occupancy sensor. Many smart switches incorporate a motion detector that will switch the lights on if they sense movement in the room and will also shut them off when no movement is detected for a period of time. The model shown above also has a dimmer function for further energy savings.

Programmable timer switch. A dial-type timer allows you to program the switch to turn on for specific time periods at designated times of day within a 24-hour cycle. Security lights, space heaters, towel warmers, and radiant floors are typical applications.

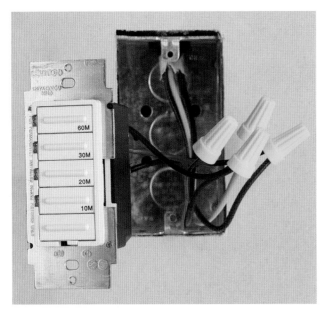

Preset timer switch. This lets you turn on lights, heat lamps, and other loads for a designated amount of time (10 to 60 minutes) with one easy push of a button. The green LED at the bottom of this unit provides a readout of how much time is left before the switch shuts off. The model shown is not compatible with fluorescent ballasts.

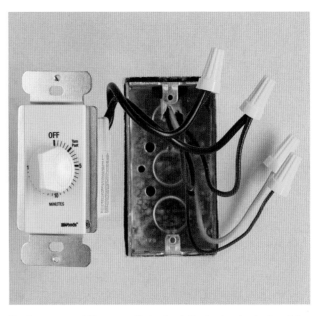

Spring-wound timer switch. A relatively simple device, this timer switch functions exactly like a kitchen timer, employing a hand-turned dial to and spring mechanism to shut the switch off in increments up to 15 minutes.

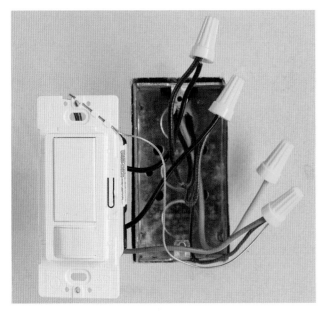

Daylight sensor switch. This switch automatically turns on when light levels drop below a proscribed level. It can also be programmed as an occupancy sensor to shut off when the room is vacant and turn on when the room is entered.

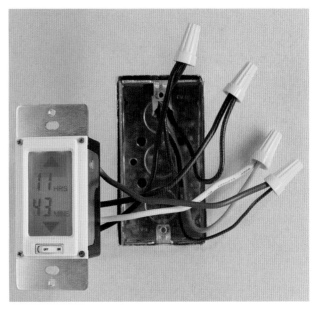

Backlit countdown timer. This digital switch lets you program lights or other devices to stay on for up to 24 hours and then shut off automatically. The backlit, LED readout gives a countdown, in minutes, of the amount of time left in the "on" cycle. Up and down buttons let you raise or lower the remaining time easily, and a manual override button will shut off the switch until it is turned back on.

Dimmer Switches

A dimmer switch makes it possible to vary the brightness of a light fixture. Dimmers are often installed in dining rooms, recreation areas, or bedrooms.

Any standard single-pole switch can be replaced with a dimmer, as long as the switch box is of adequate size. Dimmer switches have larger bodies than standard switches. They also generate a small amount of heat that must dissipate. For these reasons, dimmers should not be installed in undersized electrical boxes or in boxes that are crowded with circuit wires. Always follow the manufacturer's specifications for installation.

In lighting configurations that use three-way switches (pages 88 to 89), buy a packaged pair of three-way dimmers designed to work together.

Dimmer switches are available in several styles (see photo, right). All types have wire leads instead of screw terminals, and they are connected to circuit wires using wire connectors. Some types have a green grounding lead that should be connected to the grounded metal box or to the bare copper grounding wires. Until very recently, dimmers were designed to work only with incandescent lamps. They may not work well, or may not work at all, with CFL and LED lamps. When replacing incandescent lamps with CFL and LED lamps, make sure the new lamps are designed to work with older dimmers. When replacing dimmers, make sure the new dimmers are designed to work with CFL and LED lamps.

Tools & Materials ▸

Screwdriver
Circuit tester
Needlenose pliers

Wire connectors
Masking tape

Tip: Automatic dimmers ▸

An automatic dimmer has an electronic sensor that adjusts the light fixture to compensate for the changing levels of natural light. An automatic dimmer also can be operated manually. For another example, see page 95, lower left.

Switch Action Options

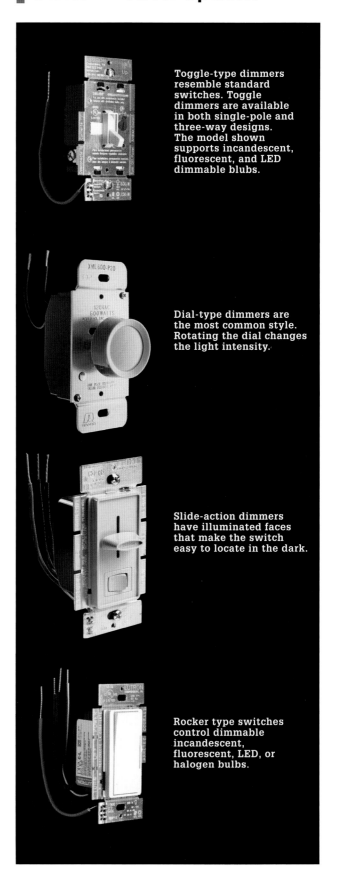

Toggle-type dimmers resemble standard switches. Toggle dimmers are available in both single-pole and three-way designs. The model shown supports incandescent, fluorescent, and LED dimmable blubs.

Dial-type dimmers are the most common style. Rotating the dial changes the light intensity.

Slide-action dimmers have illuminated faces that make the switch easy to locate in the dark.

Rocker type switches control dimmable incandescent, fluorescent, LED, or halogen bulbs.

How to Install a Dimmer Switch

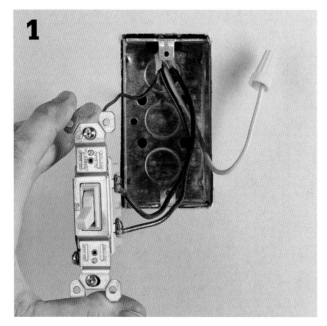

Turn off power to the switch at the panel, and then remove the cover plate and mounting screws. Holding the mounting straps carefully, pull the switch from the box. Be careful not to touch bare wires or screw terminals until they have been tested for power. In new switch wiring, the white wire should not supply current to the switched device, and a separate neutral wire should be available in the switch box.

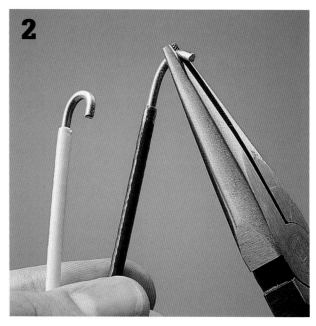

Disconnect the circuit wires and remove the switch. Straighten the circuit wires, and clip the ends, leaving about ½" of the bare wire end exposed.

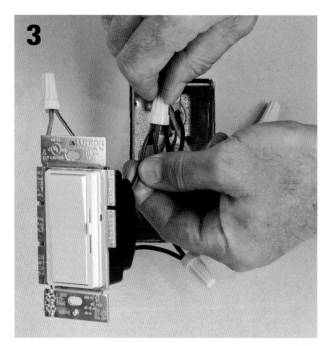

Connect the wire leads on the dimmer switch to the circuit wires using wire connectors. The switch leads are interchangeable and can be attached to either of the two circuit wires.

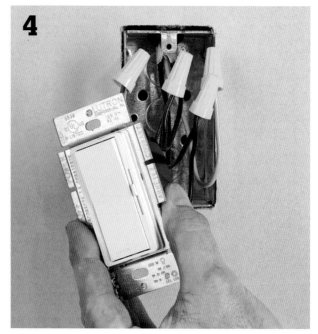

A three-way dimmer has an additional wire lead. This "common" lead is connected to the common circuit wire. When replacing a standard three-way switch with a dimmer, the common circuit wire is attached to the darkest screw terminal on the old switch. In new switch wiring, the white wire should not supply current to the switched device, and a separate neutral wire should be available in the switch box.

Testing Switches

A switch that does not work properly may have worn or broken internal parts. Test switches with a battery-operated continuity tester. The continuity tester detects any break in the metal pathway inside the switch. Replace the switch if the continuity tester shows the switch to be faulty.

Never use a continuity tester on wires that might carry live current. Always shut off the power and disconnect the switch before testing for continuity.

Some specialty switches, such as dimmers, cannot be tested for continuity. Electronic switches can be tested for manual operation using a continuity tester, but the automatic operation of these switches cannot be tested.

How to Test a Single-Pole Wall Switch

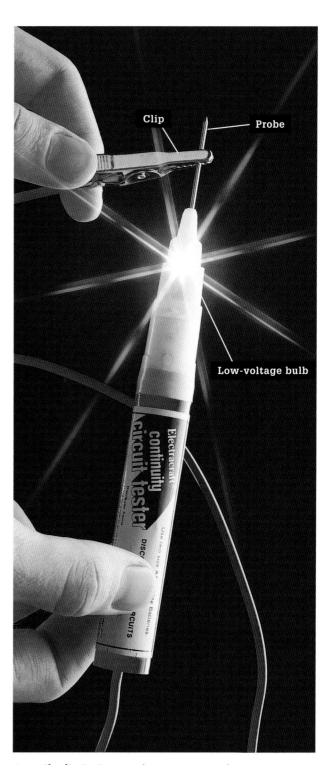

Clip | Probe

Low-voltage bulb

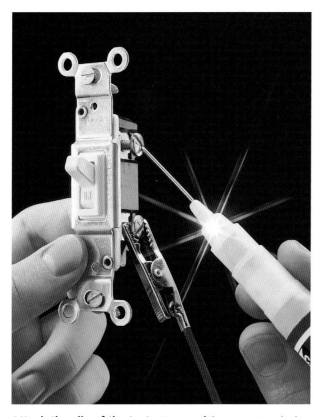

Attach the clip of the tester to one of the screw terminals. Touch the tester probe to the other screw terminal. Flip the switch lever from ON to OFF. If the switch is good, the tester glows when the lever is ON but not when it's OFF.

A continuity tester uses battery-generated current to test the metal pathways running through switches and other electrical fixtures. Always "test" the tester before use. Touch the tester clip to the metal probe. The tester should glow. If not, then the battery or lightbulb is dead and must be replaced.

How to Test a Three-Way Wall Switch

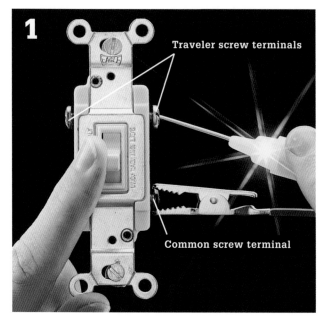

Traveler screw terminals

Common screw terminal

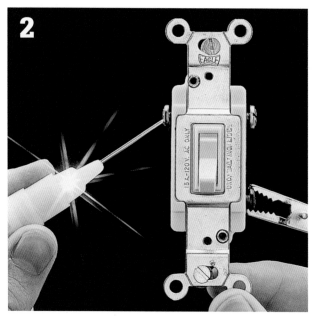

Attach the tester clip to the dark common screw terminal. Touch the tester probe to one of the traveler screw terminals, and flip the switch lever back and forth. If the switch is good, the tester should glow when the lever is in one position, but not both.

Touch the probe to the other traveler screw terminal, and flip the switch lever back and forth. If the switch is good, the tester will glow only when the switch lever is in the position opposite from the positive test in step 1.

How to Test a Four-Way Wall Switch

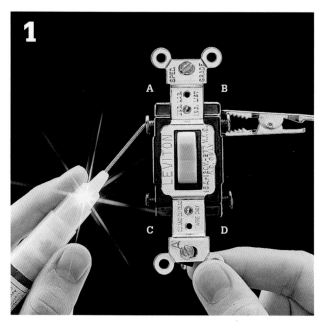

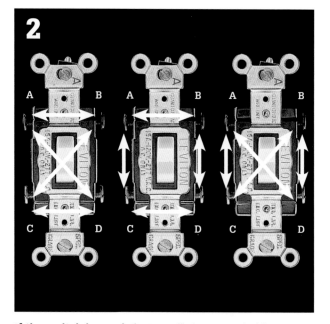

Test the switch by touching the probe and clip of the continuity tester to each pair of screw terminals (A-B, C-D, A-D, B-C, A-C, B-D). The test should show continuous pathways between the two different pairs of screw terminals. Flip the lever to the opposite position, and repeat the test. It should show continuous pathways between two different pairs of screw terminals.

If the switch is good, the test will show a total of four continuous pathways between screw terminals—two pathways for each lever position. If not, then the switch is faulty and must be replaced. (The arrangement of the pathways may differ, depending on the switch manufacturer. The photo above shows the three possible pathway arrangements.)

How to Test a Pilot-Light Switch

Test the pilot light by flipping the switch lever to the ON position. Check to see if the light fixture or appliance is working. If the pilot light does not glow even though the switch operates the light fixture or appliance, then the pilot light is defective and the unit must be replaced.

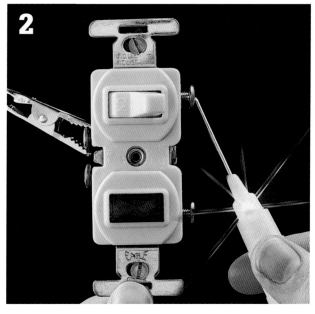

Test the switch by disconnecting the unit. With the switch lever in the ON position, attach the tester clip to the top screw terminal on one side of the switch. Touch the tester probe to the top screw terminal on the opposite side of the switch. If the switch is good, the tester will glow when switch is ON but not when OFF.

How to Test a Timer Switch

Attach the tester clip to the red wire lead on the timer switch, and touch the tester probe to the black hot lead. Rotate the timer dial clockwise until the ON tab passes the arrow marker. The tester should glow. If it does not, the switch is faulty and must be replaced.

Rotate the dial clockwise until the OFF tab passes the arrow marker. The tester should not glow. If it does, the switch is faulty and must be replaced.

How to Test a Switch/Receptacle

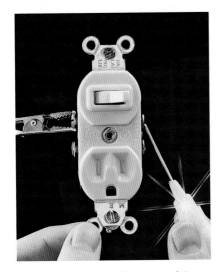

Attach the tester clip to one of the top screw terminals. Touch the tester probe to the top screw terminal on the opposite side. Flip the switch lever from ON to OFF position. If the switch is working correctly, the tester will glow when the switch lever is ON but not when it's OFF.

How to Test a Double Switch

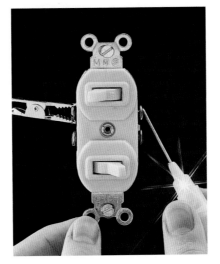

Test each half of the switch by attaching the tester clip to one screw terminal and touching the probe to the opposite side. Flip the switch lever from ON to OFF position. If the switch is good, the tester glows when the switch lever is ON but not when it's OFF. Repeat the test with the remaining pair of screw terminals. If either half tests faulty, replace the unit.

How to Test a Time-Delay Switch

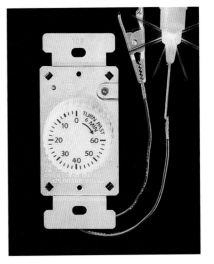

Attach the tester clip to one of the wire leads, and touch the tester probe to the other lead. Set the timer for a few minutes. If the switch is working correctly, the tester will glow until the time expires.

How to Test Manual Operation of Electronic Switches

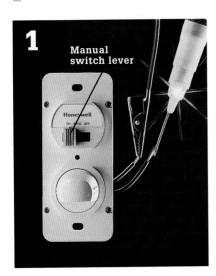

1 Manual switch lever

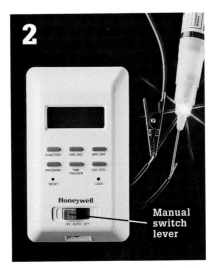

2

Manual switch lever

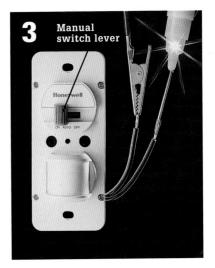

3 Manual switch lever

Automatic switch: Attach the tester clip to a black wire lead, and touch the tester probe to the other black lead. Flip the manual switch lever from ON to OFF position. If the switch is working correctly, the tester will glow when the switch lever is ON but not when it's OFF.

Programmable switch: Attach the tester clip to a wire lead, and touch the tester probe to the other lead. Flip the manual switch lever from ON to OFF position. If the switch is working correctly, the tester will glow when the switch lever is ON but not when it's OFF.

Motion-sensor switch: Attach the tester clip to a wire lead, and touch the tester probe to the other lead. Flip the manual switch lever from ON to OFF position. If the switch is working correctly, the tester will glow when the switch lever is ON but not when it's OFF.

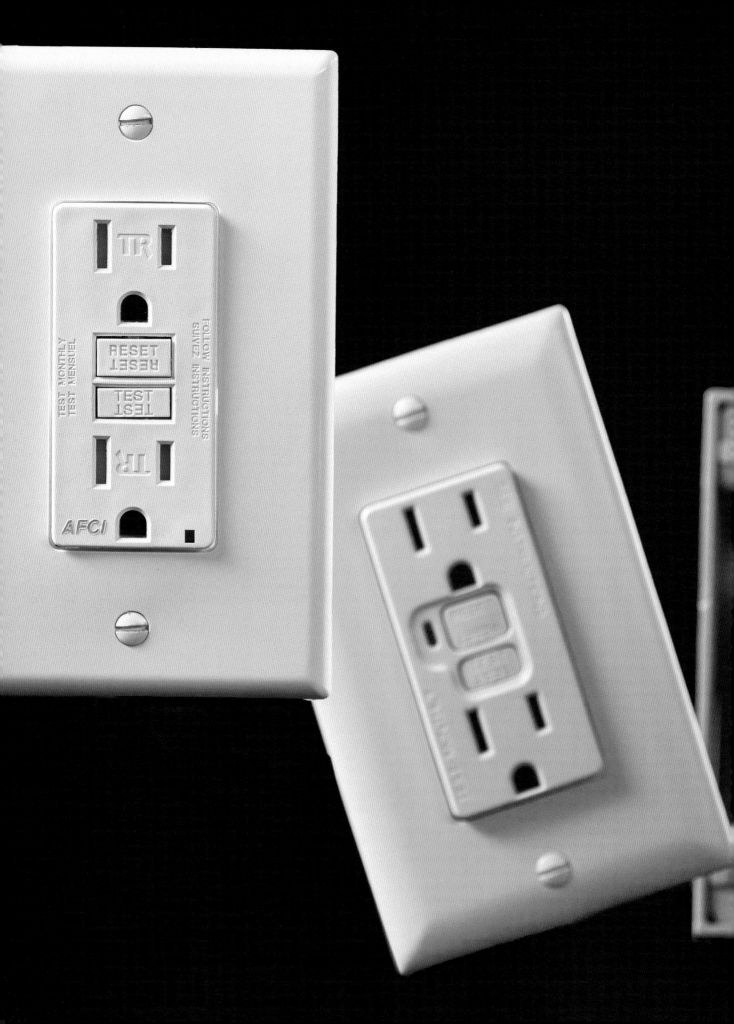

Receptacles

Whether you call them outlets, plug-ins, or receptacles, these important devices represent the point where the rubber meets the road in your home wiring system. From the basic 15-amp, 120-volt duplex receptacle to the burly 50-amp, 240-volt appliance receptacle, the many receptacles in your home do pretty much the same thing: transmit power to a load.

Learning the differences between receptacles does not take long. You need to know the amperage, voltage, and the number of devices on the circuit to select the correct receptacle. For circuits with one receptacle, match the circuit and receptacle amperage and voltage. A duplex receptacle (with a space for two plugs) counts as two receptacles. Use 15-amp receptacles on 15-amp circuits with multiple receptacles. Use either 15- or 20-amp receptacles on 20-amp circuits with multiple receptacles. Twenty-amp receptacles have the horizontal slot that forms a T with the large slot. Receptacles for 240-volt service have unique slot configurations so you can't accidentally plug in an appliance that's not rated for the amperage in the circuit. Though some receptacles can be wired using the push-in wire holes, this method is not recommended. If you use this method, use only 15-amp receptacles with #14 wire and 20-amp receptacles with #12 wire. Some receptacles provide built-in, ground-fault circuit protection, tripping the receptacle if there is a ground fault or power surge. These are easy to identify by reset and test buttons.

One last bit of information about receptacles: like switches, they vary quite a bit in quality. Paying the extra couple of dollars for a well made, durable device is worth the money.

In this chapter:

- Types of Receptacles
- Receptacle Wiring
- GFCI Receptacles
- Testing Receptacles

Types of Receptacles

Several different types of receptacles are found in the typical home. Each has a unique arrangement of slots that accepts only a certain kind of plug, and each is designed for a specific job.

Household receptacles provide two types of voltage: normal and high. Although voltage ratings have changed slightly over the years, normal receptacles should be rated for 110, 115, 120, or 125 volts. For purposes of replacement, these ratings are considered identical. High-voltage receptacles are rated at 220, 240, or 250 volts. These ratings are considered identical.

When replacing a receptacle, check the amperage rating of the circuit at the main service panel, and buy a receptacle with the correct amperage rating.

15 amps, 120 volts. Polarized two-slot receptacles are common in homes built before 1960. Slots are different sizes to accept polarized plugs.

15 amps, 120 volts. Three-slot grounded receptacles have two different-sized slots and a U-shaped hole for grounding which is required in all new wiring installations.

20 amps, 120 volts. This three-slot grounded receptacle features a special T-shaped slot. It is installed for use with large appliances or portable tools that require 20 amps of current.

15 amps, 240 volts. This receptacle is used primarily for window air conditioners. It is available as a single unit or as half of a duplex receptacle, with the other half wired for 120 volts.

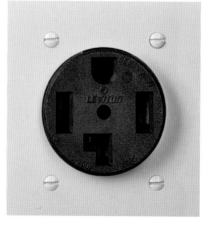

30 amps, 120/240 volts. This grounded receptacle is used for clothes dryers. It provides high-voltage current for heating coils and 120-volts to run lights and timers.

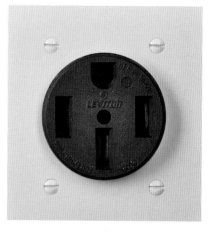

50 amps, 120/240 volts. This new, grounded receptacle is used for ranges. The high voltage powers heating coils, and the 120-volts run clocks and lights.

Older Receptacles

Older receptacles may look different from more modern types, but most will stay in good working order. Follow these simple guidelines for evaluating or replacing older receptacles:

- Never replace a receptacle with one of a different voltage or higher amperage rating.

- Do not replace a two-slot receptacle with a three-slot receptacle. Replace the two-slot receptacle with a polarized two-slot receptacle or with a GFCI receptacle.
- If in doubt, contact an electrician.
- Never alter the prongs of a plug to fit an older receptacle. Altering the prongs may remove the grounding or polarizing features of the plug.

The earliest receptacles were modifications of the screw-in light bulb. This receptacle was used in the early 1900s.

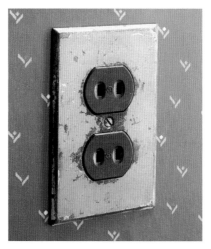

Unpolarized receptacles have same-length slots. Modern plugs may not fit these receptacles. Never modify the prongs of a polarized plug to fit the slots of an unpolarized receptacle.

Surface-mounted receptacles were popular in the 1940s and 1950s for their ease of installation. Wiring ran behind hollowed-out base moldings. These receptacles are usually ungrounded.

Ceramic duplex receptacles were manufactured in the 1930s. They are polarized but ungrounded, and they are wired for 120 volts.

Twist-lock receptacles are designed to be used with plugs that are inserted and rotated. A small tab on the end of one of the prongs prevents the plug from being pulled from the receptacle.

This ceramic duplex receptacle has a unique hourglass shape. It is rated for 250 volts but only 5 amps and would not be allowed by today's electrical codes.

High-Voltage Receptacles

High-voltage receptacles provide current to large appliances such as clothes dryers, ranges, and air conditioners. The slot configuration of a high-voltage receptacle (page 104) will not accept a plug rated for 120 volts.

A high-voltage receptacle can be wired in one of two ways. In one type of high-voltage receptacle, voltage is brought to the receptacle with two hot wires, each carrying a maximum of 120 volts. No white neutral wire is necessary, but a grounding wire should be attached to the receptacle and to the metal receptacle box. Conduit may also act as a grounding conductor from the metal receptacle box back to the panel in old circuits without a grounding wire. This method is not allowed today.

A clothes dryer or range also may require 120 volts to run lights, timers, and clocks. If so, a white neutral wire will be attached to the receptacle. The appliance itself will split the incoming electricity into a 120-volt circuit and a 240-volt circuit.

It is important to identify and tag all wires on the existing receptacle so that the new receptacle will be properly wired.

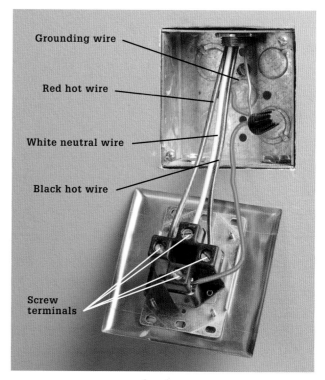

A receptacle rated for 120/240 volts has two incoming hot wires, each carrying 120 volts, a white neutral wire, and a copper grounding wire. Connections are made with setscrew terminals at the back of the receptacle.

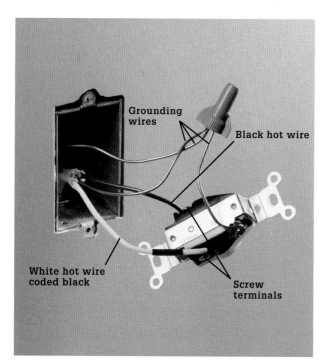

One type of receptacle rated for 240 volts has two incoming hot wires and no neutral wire. A grounding wire is pigtailed to the receptacle and to the metal receptacle box.

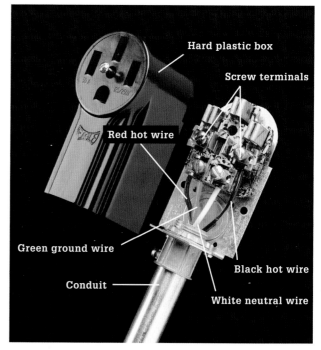

This surface-mounted receptacle rated for 240 volts has a hard plastic box that can be installed on concrete or block walls. Surface-mounted receptacles are often found in basements and utility rooms.

Childproofing

Childproof your receptacles or adapt them for special uses by adding receptacle accessories. Before installing an accessory, be sure to read the manufacturer's instructions.

Homeowners with small children should add inexpensive caps or covers to guard against accidental electric shocks.

Plastic caps do not conduct electricity and are virtually impossible for small children to remove. A receptacle cover attaches directly to the receptacle and fits over plugs, preventing the cords from being removed. Tamper-resistant receptacles are now required in all new residential installations.

Standard receptacles present a real shock hazard to small children. Fortunately there are many products that make receptacles safer without making them less convenient.

Protect electronic equipment, such as a home computer or stereo, with a surge protector. The surge protector reduces the chance of any damage to sensitive equipment caused by sudden drops or surges in power.

A recessed wall receptacle permits a plug-in clock to be hung flush against a wall surface.

Snap protective caps over sockets to prevent children from having access to the slots.

Duplex Receptacles

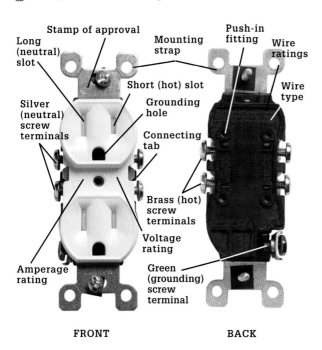

Stamp of approval
Long (neutral) slot
Mounting strap
Push-in fitting
Wire ratings
Short (hot) slot
Wire type
Silver (neutral) screw terminals
Grounding hole
Connecting tab
Brass (hot) screw terminals
Voltage rating
Amperage rating
Green (grounding) screw terminal

FRONT   BACK

The standard duplex receptacle has two halves for receiving plugs. Each half has a long (neutral) slot, a short (hot) slot, and a U-shaped grounding hole. The slots fit the wide prong, narrow prong, and grounding prong of a three-prong plug. This ensures that the connection between receptacle and plug will be polarized and grounded for safety.

Wires are attached to the receptacle at screw terminals or push-in fittings. A connecting tab between the screw terminals allows a variety of different wiring configurations. Receptacles also include mounting straps for attaching to electrical boxes.

Stamps of approval from testing agencies are found on the front and back of the receptacle. Look for the symbol UL or UND. LAB. INC. LIST to make sure the receptacle meets the strict standards of Underwriters Laboratories.

The receptacle is marked with ratings for maximum volts and amps. The common receptacle is marked 15A, 125V. Receptacles marked CU or COPPER are used with solid copper wire. Those marked CU-CLAD ONLY are used with copper-coated aluminum wire. Only receptacles marked CO/ALR may be used with solid aluminum wiring. Receptacles marked AL/CU no longer may be used with aluminum wire, according to code.

AFCI receptacles have integral protection against arc faults and may be required in some remodeling situations where AFCI protection cannot be provided at the service panel.

The ground-fault circuit-interrupter, or GFCI, receptacle is a modern safety device. When it detects slight changes in current, it instantly shuts off power. The larger picture shows a modern GFCI with an alert bulb that lights when the device is tripped. The older but more familiar style is seen in the inset photo.

Common Receptacle Problems ▸

Household receptacles, also called outlets, have no moving parts to wear out and usually last for many years without servicing. Most problems associated with receptacles are actually caused by faulty lamps and appliances or their plugs and cords. However, the constant plugging in and removal of appliance cords can wear out the metal contacts inside a receptacle. Any receptacle that does not hold plugs firmly should be replaced. In addition, older receptacles made of hard plastic may harden and crack with age. They must be replaced when this happens.

A loose wire connection with the receptacle box is another possible problem. A loose connection can spark (called arcing), trip a circuit breaker, or cause heat to build up in the receptacle box, creating a potential fire hazard.

Wires can come loose for a number of reasons. Everyday vibrations caused by walking across floors, or from nearby street traffic, may cause a connection to shake loose. In addition, because wires heat and cool with normal use, the ends of the wires will expand and contract slightly. This movement also may cause the wires to come loose from the screw terminal connections.

Not all receptacles are created equally. When replacing, make sure to buy one with the same amp rating as the old one. Inadvertently installing a 20-amp receptacle in replacement of a 15-amp receptacle is a very common error.

PROBLEM	REPAIR
Circuit breaker trips repeatedly, or fuse burns out immediately after being replaced.	1. Repair or replace worn or damaged lamp or appliance cord. 2. Move lamps or appliances to other circuits to prevent overloads. 3. Tighten any loose wire connections. 4. Clean dirty or oxidized wire ends.
Lamp or appliance does not work.	1. Make sure the lamp or appliance is plugged in. 2. Replace burned-out bulbs. 3. Repair or replace a worn or damaged lamp or appliance cord. 4. Tighten any loose wire connections. 5. Clean dirty or oxidized wire ends. 6. Replace any faulty receptacle.
Receptacle does not hold plugs firmly.	1. Repair or replace worn or damaged plugs. 2. Replace the faulty receptacle.
Receptacle is warm to the touch, buzzes, or sparks when plugs are inserted or removed.	1. Move lamps or appliances to other circuits to prevent overloads. 2. Tighten any loose wire connections. 3. Clean dirty or oxidized wire ends. 4. Replace the faulty receptacle.

Receptacle Wiring

A 120-volt duplex receptacle can be wired to the electrical system in several ways. The most common are shown on these pages.

Wiring configurations may vary slightly from these photographs, depending on the kind of receptacles used, the type of cable, or the technique of the electrician who installed the wiring. To make dependable repairs or replacements, use masking tape and label each wire according to its location on the terminals of the existing receptacle.

Receptacles are wired as either end-of-run or middle-of-run. These two basic configurations are easily identified by counting the number of cables entering the receptacle box. End-of-run wiring has only one cable, indicating that the circuit ends. Middle-of-run wiring has two cables, indicating that the circuit continues on to other receptacles, switches, or fixtures.

A split-circuit receptacle is shown on the next page. Each half of a split-circuit receptacle is wired to a separate circuit. This allows two appliances of high wattage to be plugged into the same receptacle without blowing a fuse or tripping a breaker. This wiring configuration is similar to a receptacle that is controlled by a wall switch. Code requires a switch-controlled receptacle in most rooms that do not have a built-in light fixture operated by a wall switch.

Split-circuit and switch-controlled receptacles are connected to two hot wires, so use caution during repairs or replacements. Make sure the connecting tab between the hot screw terminals is removed.

Two-slot receptacles are common in older homes. There is no grounding wire attached to the receptacle, but the metal box may be grounded with armored cable or metal conduit. Tamper-resistant receptacles are now required in all new residential installations.

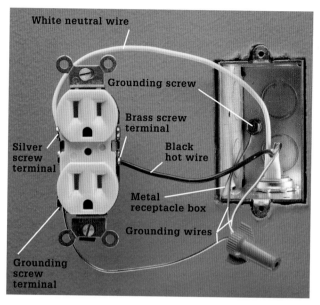

A single cable entering the box indicates end-of-run wiring. The black hot wire is attached to a brass screw terminal, and the white neutral wire is connected to a silver screw terminal. If the box is metal, the grounding wire is pigtailed to the grounding screws of the receptacle and the box. In a plastic box, the grounding wire is attached directly to the grounding screw terminal of the receptacle.

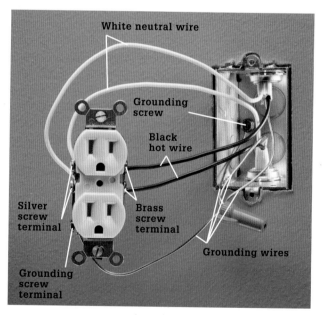

Two cables entering the box indicate middle-of-run wiring. Black hot wires are connected to brass screw terminals and white neutral wires to silver screw terminals. The grounding wire is pigtailed to the grounding screws of the receptacle and the box.

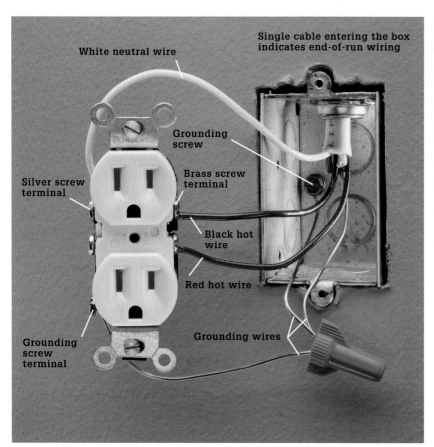

White neutral wire

Single cable entering the box
indicates end-of-run wiring

Grounding
screw

Brass screw
terminal

Silver screw
terminal

Black hot
wire

Red hot wire

Grounding
screw
terminal

Grounding wires

A split-circuit receptacle (technically a multi-wire branch circuit) is attached to a black hot wire, a red hot wire, a white neutral wire, and a bare grounding wire. The wiring is similar to a switch-controlled receptacle. The hot wires are attached to the brass screw terminals, and the connecting tab or fin between the brass terminals is removed. The white wire is attached to a silver screw terminal, and the connecting tab on the neutral side remains intact. The grounding wire is pigtailed to the grounding screw terminal of the receptacle and to the grounding screw attached to the box.

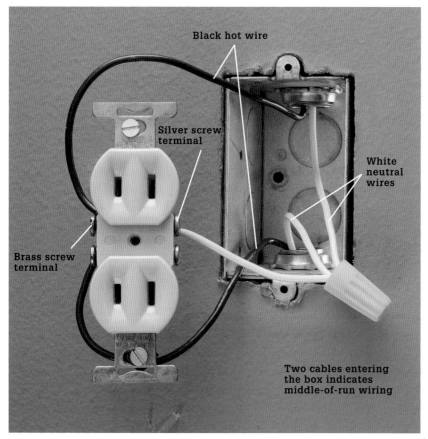

Black hot wire

Silver screw
terminal

White
neutral
wires

Brass screw
terminal

Two cables entering
the box indicates
middle-of-run wiring

A two-slot receptacle is often found in older homes. The black hot wires are connected to the brass screw terminals, and the white neutral wires are pigtailed to a silver screw terminal. Two-slot receptacles may be replaced with three-slot types, but only if a means of grounding exists at the receptacle box. In some municipalities, you may replace a two-slot receptacle with a GFCI receptacle as long as the receptacle has a sticker that reads "No equipment ground."

How to Install a New Receptacle

1

Position the new old work box on the wall and trace around it. Consider the location of hidden utilities within the wall before you cut.

2

Remove baseboard between the new and existing receptacle. Cut away the drywall about 1" below the baseboard with a jigsaw, wallboard saw, or utility knife.

3

Drill a ⅝" hole in the center of each stud along the opening between the two receptacles. A drill bit extender or a flexible drill bit will allow you a better angle and make drilling the holes easier.

4

Run the branch cable through the holes from the new location to the existing receptacle. Staple the cable to the stud below the box. Install a metal nail plate on the front edge of each stud that the cable routes through.

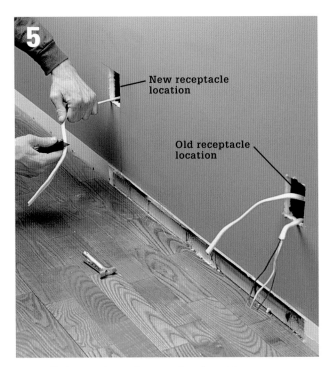

Turn off the power at the panel and test for power. Remove the old receptacle and its box, and pull the new branch cable up through the hole. Remove sheathing and insulation from both ends of the new cable.

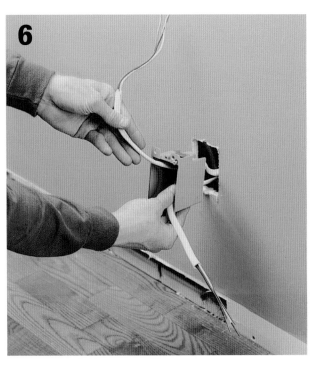

Thread the new and old cables into an old work box large enough to contain the added wires and clamp the cables. Fit the box into the old hole and attach it.

Reconnect the old receptacle by connecting its neutral, hot, and grounding screws to the new branch cable and the old cable from the panel with pigtails.

Pull the cable through another old work box for the new receptacle. Secure the cable and install the box. Connect the new receptacle to the new branch cable. Insert the receptacle into the box and attach the receptacle and cover plate with screws. Patch the opening with ½"-thick wood strips or drywall. Reattach the baseboard to the studs.

GFCI Receptacles

The ground-fault circuit interrupter (GFCI) protects against electrical shock caused by a faulty appliance or a worn cord or plug. It senses small changes in current flow and can shut off power in as little as $\frac{1}{40}$ of a second. GFCIs can be a circuit breaker and protect the circuit from the panel. Often, however, they are receptacles that protect one receptacle and may protect other receptacles and light fixtures downstream.

GFCIs are now required in bathrooms, kitchens, garages, crawl spaces, unfinished basements, and outdoor receptacle locations. Consult your local codes for any requirements regarding the installation of GFCIs. Most GFCI receptacles use standard screw terminal connections, but some have wire leads and are attached with wire connectors. Because the body of a GFCI receptacle is larger than a standard receptacle, small, crowded electrical boxes may need to be replaced with more spacious boxes.

Because the GFCI is so sensitive, it is most effective when wired to protect a single location. The more receptacles any one GFCI protects, the more susceptible it is to "phantom tripping," shutting off power because of tiny, normal fluctuations in current flow. GFCI receptacles installed in outdoor locations must be rated for outdoor use and weather resistance (WR) along with ground fault protection.

Tools & Materials ▸

Circuit tester
Screwdriver

Wire connectors
Masking tape

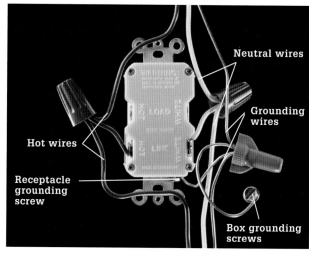

A GFCI wired for single-location protection (shown from the back) has hot and neutral wires connected only to the screw terminals marked LINE. A GFCI connected for single-location protection may be wired as either an end-of-run or middle-of-run configuration.

Modern GFCI receptacles have tamper-resistant slots. Look for a model that's rated "WR" (for weather resistance) if you'll be installing it outdoors or in a wet location.

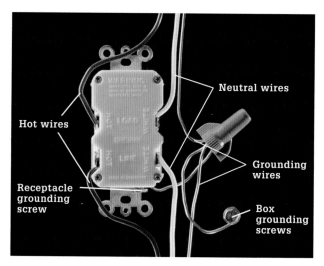

A GFCI wired for multiple-location protection (shown from the back) has one set of hot and neutral wires connected to the LINE pair of screw terminals and the other set connected to the LOAD pair of screw terminals. A GFCI receptacle connected for multiple-location protection may be wired only as a middle-of-run configuration.

How to Install a GFCI for Single-Location Protection

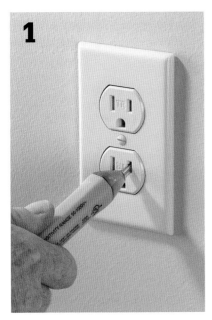

1

Shut off power to the receptacle at the panel. Test for power with a neon circuit tester. Be sure to check both halves of the receptacle.

2

Remove the cover plate. Loosen mounting screws, and gently pull the receptacle from the box. Do not touch wires. Confirm power is off with a circuit tester.

3

Disconnect all white neutral wires from the silver screw terminals of the old receptacle.

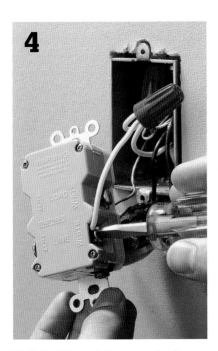

4

Pigtail all the white neutral wires together, and connect the pigtail to the terminal marked WHITE LINE on the GFCI (see photo on opposite page).

5

Disconnect all black hot wires from the brass screw terminals of the old receptacle. Pigtail these wires together, and connect them to the terminal marked HOT LINE on the GFCI.

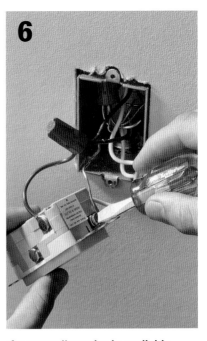

6

If a grounding wire is available, connect it to the green grounding screw terminal of the GFCI. Mount the GFCI in the receptacle box, and reattach the cover plate. Restore power, and test the GFCI according to the manufacturer's instructions. If a grounding wire is not available, label the receptacle cover plate: "NO EQUIPMENT GROUND".

How to Install a GFCI for Multiple-Location Protection

Use a map of your house circuits to determine a location for your GFCI. Indicate all receptacles that will be protected by the GFCI installation.

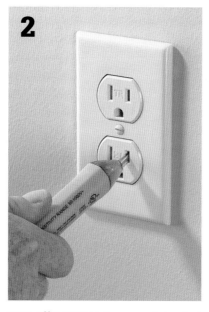

Turn off power to the correct circuit at the panel. Test all the receptacles in the circuit with a neon circuit tester to make sure the power is off. Always check both halves of each duplex receptacle.

Remove the cover plate from the receptacle that will be replaced with the GFCI. Loosen the mounting screws and gently pull the receptacle from its box. Take care not to touch any bare wires. Confirm the power is off with a neon circuit tester.

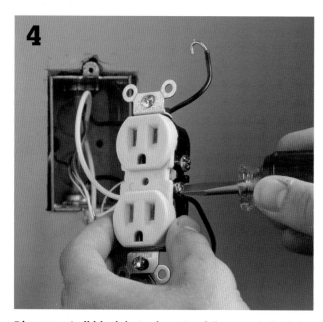

Disconnect all black hot wires. Carefully separate the hot wires and position them so that the bare ends do not touch anything. Restore power to the circuit at the panel. Determine which black wire is the feed wire by testing for hot wires. The feed wire brings power to the receptacle from the service panel. Use caution: This is a live wire test, during which the power is turned on temporarily.

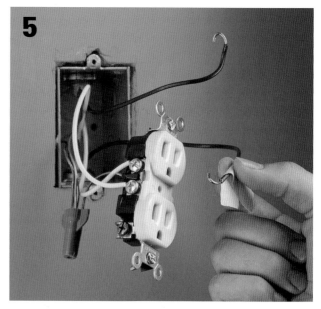

When you have found the hot feed wire, turn off power at the panel. Identify the feed wire by marking it with masking tape.

6

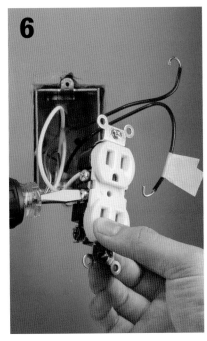

Disconnect the white neutral wires from the old receptacle. Identify the white feed wire and label it with masking tape. The white feed wire will be the one that shares the same cable as the black feed wire.

7

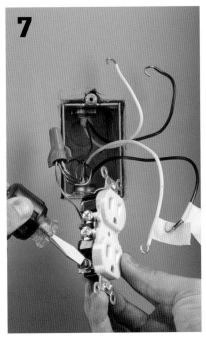

Disconnect the grounding wire from the grounding screw terminal of the old receptacle. Remove the old receptacle. Connect the grounding wire to the grounding screw terminal of the GFCI.

8

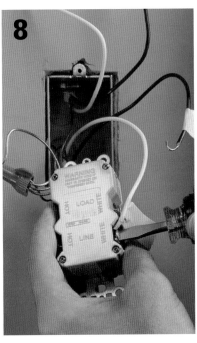

Connect the white feed wire to the terminal marked WHITE LINE on the GFCI. Connect the black feed wire to the terminal marked HOT LINE on the GFCI.

9

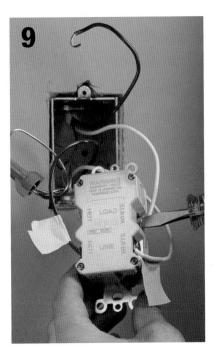

Connect the other white neutral wire to the terminal marked WHITE LOAD on the GFCI.

10

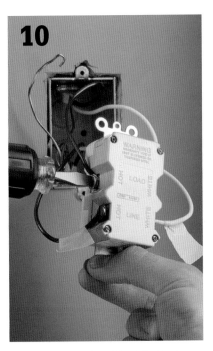

Connect the other black hot wire to the terminal marked HOT LOAD on the GFCI.

11

Carefully tuck all wires into the receptacle box. Mount the GFCI in the box and attach the cover plate. Turn on power to the circuit at the panel. Test the GFCI according to the manufacturer's instructions.

Testing Receptacles

For testing receptacles and other devices for power, grounding, and polarity, neon circuit testers are inexpensive and easy to use. But they are less sensitive than auto-ranging multimeters. In some cases, neon testers won't detect the presence of lower voltage in a circuit. This can lead you to believe that a circuit is shut off when it is not—a dangerous mistake. The small probes on a neon circuit tester also force you to get too close to live terminals and wires. For a quick check and confirmation, a neon circuit tester (or a plug-in tester) is adequate. But for the most reliable readings, buy and learn to use a multimeter.

The best multimeters are auto-ranging models with a digital readout. Unlike manual multimeters, auto-ranging models do not require you to preset the voltage range to get an accurate reading. Unlike neon testers, multimeters may be used for a host of additional diagnostic functions such as testing fuses, measuring battery voltage, testing internal wiring in appliances, and checking light fixtures to determine if they're functional.

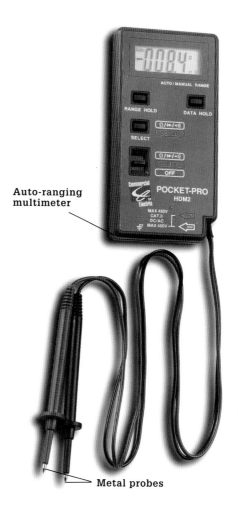

Auto-ranging multimeter

Metal probes

Tools & Materials ▸

Multimeter
Touchless circuit tester

Plug-in tester
Screwdriver

How to Use a Plug-in Tester

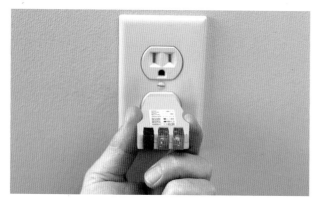

Use a plug-in tester to test a three-slot receptacle. With the power on, insert the tester into the suspect outlet. The face of the tester has three colored lights that will light up in different combinations, according to the outlet's problem. A reference chart is provided with the tester, and there may be a chart on the tester itself. These testers are useful, but they do not test for all wiring errors.

How to Test Quickly for Power

Use a touchless circuit tester to verify that power is not flowing to a receptacle. Using either a no-touch sensor or a probe-style circuit tester, test the receptacle for current before you remove the cover plate. Once the plate is removed, double-check at the terminals to make sure there is no current.

How to Test a Receptacle with a Multimeter

1

Set the selector dial for alternating-current voltage. Plug the black probe lead into the common jack (labeled COM) on the multimeter. Plug the red probe lead into the V-labeled jack.

2

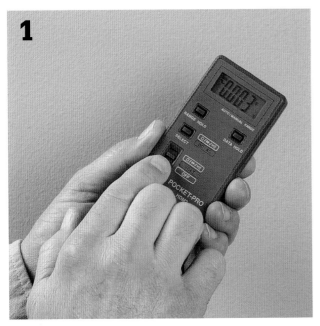

Insert the test ends of the probe into the receptacle slots. It does not make a difference which probe goes into which slot as long as they're in the same receptacle. If power is present and flowing normally, you will see a voltage reading on the readout screen.

3

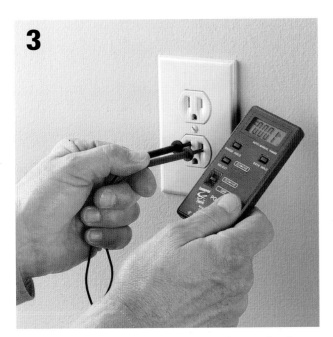

If the multimeter reads 0 or gives a very low reading (less than 1 or 2 volts), power is not present in the receptacle and it is safe to remove the cover plate and work on the fixture (although it's always a good idea to confirm your reading by touching the probes directly to the screw terminals on the receptacles).

Option: When a receptacle or switch is in the middle of a circuit, it is difficult to tell which wires are carrying current. Use a multimeter to check. With power off, remove the receptacle and separate the wires. Restore power. Touch one probe to the bare ground or the grounded metal box and touch the other probe to the end of each wire. The wire that shows current on the meter is hot.

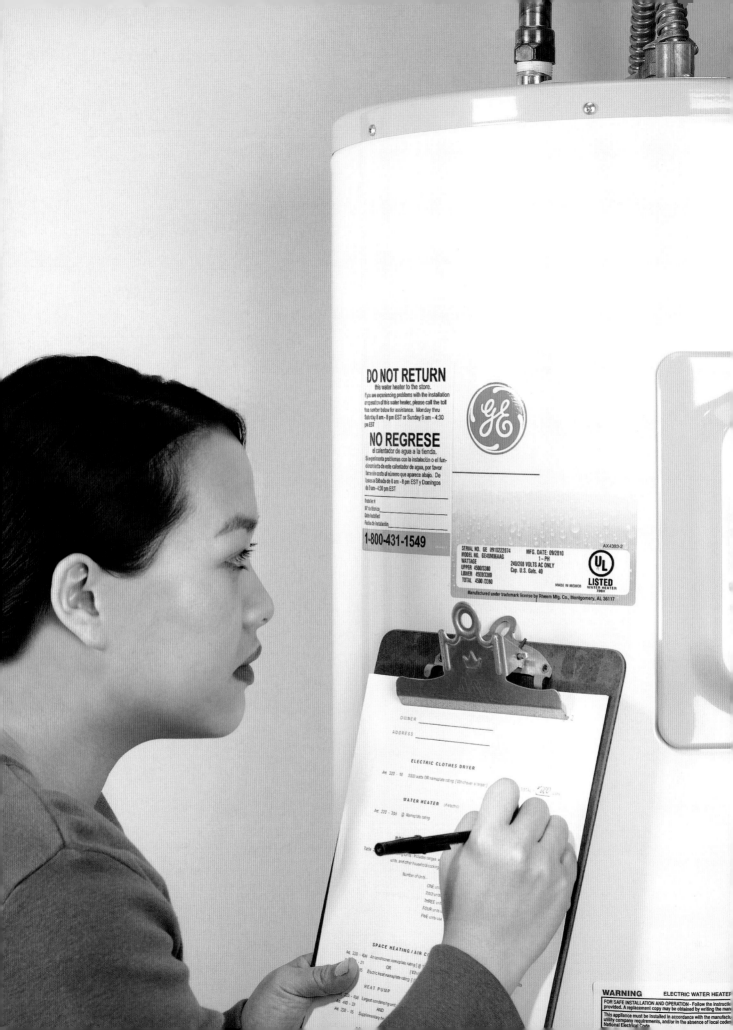

Preliminary Work

Some very important parts of any electrical project occur well before you ever make a box cutout or strip a wire. In addition to the most elementary tasks of figuring out what needs to happen and how it's done, there are required procedural steps you'll need to take as well as some basic household planning.

To form an overview of what you want to accomplish and how to get it done, you'll need to begin by assessing the condition of your wiring system as it exists. This involves a little investigative work and a little math. You'll find plenty of information on both in this chapter.

Once you've made an evaluation of what you have to work with, it's time to start the planning in earnest. Naturally the amount of planning required depends largely on the scale of the project. If you are wiring a room addition or an extensive remodel, the wiring plan should be established and approved well in advance of the start of the project. In fact, without an approved wiring plan you will be unable to obtain a valid building permit. Even for small-scale projects, such as adding a new light circuit, you need a permit, and to get the permit you need a plan. You typically do not need a permit for simple one-for-one replacements of devices such as switches and receptacles, but it still pays to plan. For example, if you are replacing a light switch, you should plan ahead and do the job during the daytime to take advantage of the natural light.

In this chapter:

- Planning Your Project
- Wiring a Room Addition
- Wiring a Kitchen

Planning Your Project

Careful planning of a wiring project ensures you will have plenty of power for present and future needs. Whether you are adding circuits in a room addition, wiring a remodeled kitchen, or adding an outdoor circuit, consider all possible ways the space might be used, and plan for enough electrical service to meet peak needs.

For example, when wiring a room addition, remember that the way a room is used can change. In a room used as a spare bedroom, a single 15-amp circuit provides plenty of power, but if you ever choose to convert the same room to a family recreation space, you will need additional circuits.

When wiring a remodeled kitchen, it is a good idea to install circuits for an electric oven and countertop range, even if you do not have these electric appliances. Installing these circuits now makes it easy to convert from gas to electric appliances at a later date.

A large wiring project adds a considerable load to your main electrical service. In about 25 percent of all homes, some type of service upgrade is needed before new wiring can be installed. For example, many homeowners will need to replace an older 60-amp electrical service with a new service rated for 100 amps or more. This is a job for a licensed electrician but is well worth the investment. In other cases, the existing main service provides adequate power, but the main circuit breaker panel is too full to hold any new circuit breakers. In this case it is necessary to install a circuit breaker subpanel to provide room for hooking up added circuits. Installing a subpanel is a job most homeowners can do themselves (see pages 187 to 189).

This chapter gives an easy five-step method for determining your electrical needs and planning new circuits.

Five Steps for Planning a Wiring Project

Examine your main service panel (see page 124). The amp rating of the electrical service and the size of the circuit breaker panel will help you determine if a service upgrade is needed.

Learn about codes (see pages 125 to 129). The National Electrical Code (NEC), and local electrical codes and building codes, provide guidelines for determining how much power and how many circuits your home needs. Your local electrical inspector can tell you which regulations apply to your job.

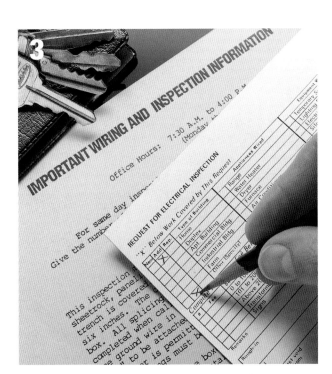

Prepare for inspections (see pages 130 to 131). Remember that your work must be reviewed by your local electrical inspector. When planning your wiring project, always follow the inspector's guidelines for quality workmanship.

Evaluate electrical loads (see pages 132 to 137). New circuits put an added load on your electrical service. Make sure that the total load of the existing wiring and the planned new circuits does not exceed the service capacity or the capacity of the panel.

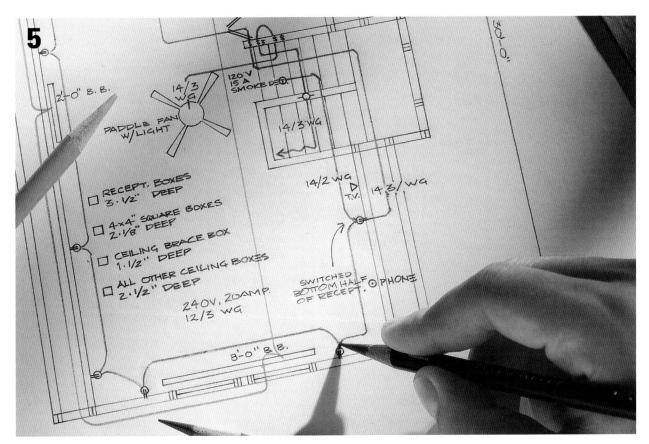

Draw a wiring diagram and get a permit (see pages 138 to 139). This wiring plan will help you organize your work.

Examine Your Main Service Panel

The first step in planning a new wiring project is to look in your main circuit breaker panel and find the size of the service by reading the amperage rating on the main circuit breaker. As you plan new circuits and evaluate electrical loads, knowing the size of the main service helps you determine if you need a service upgrade.

Also look for open circuit breaker slots in the panel. The number of open slots will determine if you need to add a circuit breaker subpanel.

Find the service size by opening the main service panel and reading the amp rating printed on the main circuit breaker. In most cases, 100-amp service provides enough power to handle the added loads of projects such as the ones shown in this book. A service rated for 60 amps or less should be upgraded. Note: In some homes the main circuit breaker is located in a separate box.

Older service panels use fuses instead of circuit breakers. Have an electrician replace this type of panel with a circuit breaker panel that provides enough power and enough open breaker slots for the new circuits you are planning.

Look for open circuit breaker slots in the main circuit breaker panel or in a circuit breaker subpanel, if your home already has one. You will need one open slot for each 120-volt circuit you plan to install and two slots for each 240-volt circuit. If your main circuit breaker panel has no open breaker slots, install a subpanel (see pages 187 to 189) to provide room for connecting new circuits.

Learn About Codes

To ensure public safety, your community requires that you get a permit to install new wiring and have the work reviewed by an inspector. Electrical inspectors use the National Electrical Code (NEC) as the primary authority for evaluating wiring, but they also follow the local building code and electrical code standards.

Most communities use a version of the NEC that is not the most current version. Also, many communities make amendments to the NEC, and these amendments may affect your work.

As you begin planning new circuits, call or visit your local electrical inspector and discuss the project with him or her. The inspector can tell you which of the national and local code requirements apply to your job and may give you a packet of information summarizing these regulations. Later, when you apply to the inspector for a work permit, he or she will expect you to understand the local guidelines as well as a few basic NEC requirements.

The NEC is a set of standards that provides minimum safety requirements for wiring installations. It is revised every three years. The national code requirements for the projects shown in this book are thoroughly explained on the following pages. For more information, you can find copies of the current NEC, as well as a number of excellent handbooks based on the NEC, at libraries and bookstores.

In addition to being the final authority of code requirements, inspectors are electrical professionals with years of experience. Although they have busy schedules, most inspectors are happy to answer questions and help you design well-planned circuits.

Basic Electrical Code Requirements

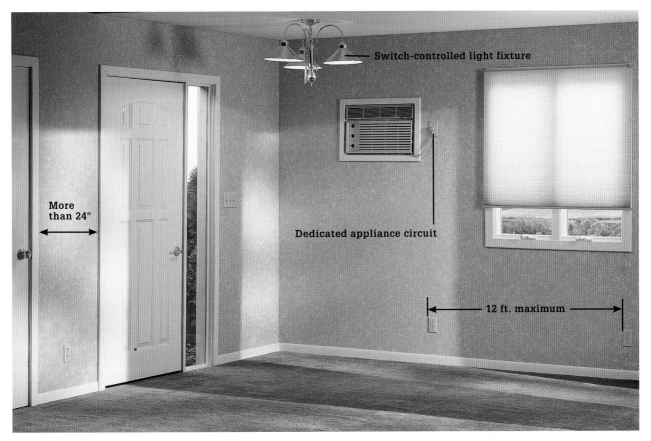

Switch-controlled light fixture

Dedicated appliance circuit

More than 24"

12 ft. maximum

Electrical code requirements for living areas: Living areas need at least one 15-amp or 20-amp basic lighting/receptacle circuit for each 600 sq. ft. of living space and should have a dedicated circuit for each type of permanent appliance, such as an air conditioner, or a group of baseboard heaters. Receptacles on basic lighting/receptacle circuits should be spaced no more than 12 ft. apart. Many electricians and electrical inspectors recommend even closer spacing. Any wall more than 24" wide also needs a receptacle. Every room should have a wall switch at the point of entry to control either a ceiling or wall-mounted light or plug-in lamp. Kitchens and bathrooms must have a ceiling or wall-mounted light fixture.

Selected NEC Standards & Tips

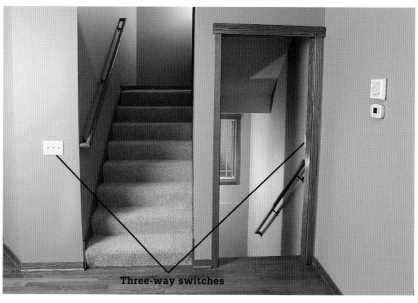

Three-way switches

Measure the living areas of your home, excluding unconditioned spaces. A sonic measuring tool gives room dimensions quickly and contains a built-in calculator for figuring floor area. You will need a minimum of one basic lighting/receptacle circuit for every 600 sq. ft. of living space. The total square footage also helps you estimate heating and cooling needs for new room additions.

Stairways must have a light fixture near each landing, including the top and bottom landings, or must have a light fixture above each flight of stairs. The light fixture must be controlled by three-way switches at the top and bottom landings.

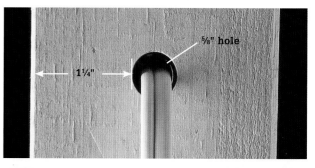

⅝" hole

1¼"

Nail guard

Furring strip

Cutaway view

Kitchen and bathroom receptacles must be protected by a ground-fault circuit-interrupter (GFCI). Also, all outdoor receptacles and general-use receptacles in an unfinished basement or crawl space and garages must be protected by a GFCI.

Cables must be protected against damage by nails and screws by at least 1¼" of wood (top). When cables pass through 2" × 2" furring strips (bottom), protect the cables with metal nail guards. Nail guards also may be used to protect cable that cannot meet the 1¼" of wood protection standard.

Closets and other storage spaces should have at least one light fixture that is controlled by a wall switch near the entrance. Prevent fire hazards by positioning the light fixtures so the outer globes are at least 12" away from all shelf areas. Note: This suggestion is primarily for homeowner convenience and is not required by most codes.

Hallways more than 10 ft. long need at least one receptacle. All hallways should have a switch-controlled light fixture.

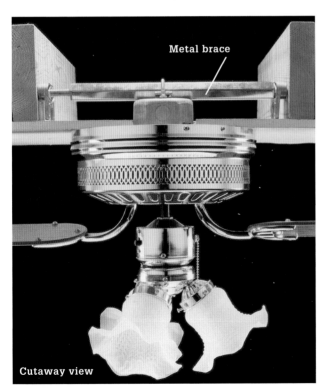

Metal brace

Cutaway view

A metal brace attached to framing members is required for ceiling fans and large light fixtures that are too heavy to be supported by an electrical box. All ceiling fans must be installed in a box that is fan-rated.

Label new circuits on an index attached to the circuit breaker panel. List the rooms and appliances controlled by each circuit. Make sure the area around the panel is clean, well lighted, and accessible.

Highlights of the National Electrical Code ▶

BY MATERIAL
Panels
- Maintain a minimum 30" wide by 36" deep of clearance in front of the panel.
- Match the amperage rating of the circuit when replacing fuses.
- Use handle ties on all 240-volt breakers and on 120-volt breakers protecting multi-wire branch circuits.
- Close all unused panel openings.
- Label each fuse and breaker clearly on the panel.

Electrical Boxes
- Use boxes that are large enough to accommodate the number of wires and devices in the box.
- Install all junction boxes so they remain accessible.
- Leave no gaps greater than ⅛" between wallboard and the front of electrical boxes.
- Place receptacle boxes flush with combustible surfaces.
- Leave a minimum of 3" of usable cable or wire extending past the front of the electrical box.

Wires & Cables
- Use wires that are large enough for the amperage rating of the circuit (see Wire Size Chart, page 26).
- Drill holes at least 2" from the edges of joists. Do not attach cables to the bottom edge of joists.
- Do not run cables diagonally between framing members.
- Use nail plates to protect cable that is run through holes drilled or cut into studs less than 1¼" from the front edge of a stud.
- Do not crimp cables sharply.
- Contain spliced wires or connections entirely in a plastic or metal electrical box.
- Use wire connectors to join wires.
- Use staples to fasten cables within 8" of an electrical box and every 54" along its run.
- Leave a minimum ¼" (maximum 1") of sheathing where cables enter an electrical box.
- Clamp cables and wires to electrical boxes with approved clamps. No clamp is necessary for one-gang plastic boxes if cables are stapled within 8".
- Connect only a single wire to a single screw terminal. Use pigtails to join more than one wire to a screw terminal.

Switches
- Use a switch-controlled receptacle in rooms without a built-in light fixture operated by a wall switch.
- Use three-way switches at the top and bottom on stairways with six risers or more.
- Use switches with grounding screws with plastic electrical boxes.
- Locate all wall switches within easy reach of the room entrance and not behind the door.
- Install a neutral wire in switch boxes.
- Use black or red wires to supply power to switched devices.

Receptacles
- Install receptacles on all walls 24" wide or greater.
- Install receptacles so a 6-ft. cord can be plugged in from any point along a wall or every 12 ft. along a wall.
- Include receptacles in any hallway that is 10 ft. long or longer.
- Use three-slot, grounded receptacles for all 15- or 20-amp, 120-volt branch circuits.
- Include a switch-controlled receptacle in rooms without a built-in light fixture operated by a wall switch.
- Install GFCI-protected circuits in bathrooms, kitchens, garages, crawl spaces, unfinished basements, and outdoor receptacle locations.

Light Fixtures
- Use mounting straps that are anchored to the electrical boxes to mount ceiling fixtures.
- Keep non-IC-rated recessed light fixtures 3" from insulation and ½" from combustibles.
- Include at least one switch-operated lighting outlet in every room.

Grounding (page 20)
- Ground receptacles by connecting receptacle grounding screws to the circuit grounding wires.
- Use switches with grounding screws whenever possible. Always ground switches installed in plastic electrical boxes and all switches in kitchens, bathrooms, and basements.

BY ROOM
Kitchens/Dining Rooms

- Install at least two 20-amp small appliance receptacle circuits.
- Install dedicated 15-amp, 120-volt circuits for dishwashers and food disposals (required by many local codes).
- Install GFCI protection for all countertop receptacles; receptacles behind fixed appliances do not need to be GFCI protected.
- Position receptacles for appliances that will be installed within cabinets, such as microwaves or food disposals, according to the manufacturer's instructions.
- Include receptacles on all counters wider than 12".
- Space receptacles a maximum of 48" apart above countertops and closer together in areas where many appliances will be used.
- Locate receptacles on the wall above the countertop not more than 20" above the countertop.
- Install at least one receptacle not more than 12" below the countertop on islands and peninsulas that are 12" × 24" or greater.
- Do not connect lights to the small appliance receptacle circuits.
- Install at least one wall or ceiling-mounted light fixture.

Bathrooms

- Install a separate 20-amp GFCI-protected circuit only for bathroom receptacles.
- Ground switches in bathrooms.
- Install at least one receptacle not more than 36" from each sink.
- Install at least one ceiling- or wall-mounted light fixture.

Utility/Laundry Rooms

- Install a separate 20-amp circuit for a washing machine.
- Install approved conduit for wiring in unfinished rooms.
- Use GFCI-protected circuits for 120-volt receptacles within 6 feet from a sink (including the washing machine receptacle).

Living, Entertainment, Bedrooms

- Install at least one 15- or 20-amp lighting/receptacle circuit for each 600 sq. ft. of living space.
- Install a dedicated circuit for each permanent appliance, such as an air conditioner or group of electric baseboard heaters.
- Use electrical boxes listed and labeled to support ceiling fans.
- Include receptacles on walls 24" wide or more.
- Space receptacles on walls in living and sleeping rooms a maximum of 12 ft. apart.
- Check with your local electrical inspector about requirements for installing smoke and carbon monoxide alarms during remodeling.

Outdoors

- Check for underground utilities before digging.
- Use UF cable or other wiring approved for wet locations for outdoor wiring.
- Run cable and wires in schedule 80 PVC plastic and other approved conduit, as required by local code.
- Install in-use rated weatherproof receptacle covers.
- Bury cables and wires run in conduit at least 18" deep; cable not in conduit must be buried at least 24" deep.
- Use weatherproof electrical boxes with watertight covers.
- Install GFCI-protected circuits for receptacles.
- Support boxes that are not attached to a building and that contain switches or receptacles using at least two pieces of conduit. Secure the conduit not more than 18 feet from the box. Locate the box at least 12" above the ground.

Stairs/Hallways

- Use three-way switches at the top and bottom on stairways with six risers or more.
- Include receptacles in any hallway that is 10 ft. long or longer.
- Position stairway lights so each step and landing is illuminated.

Prepare for Inspections

Electrical inspectors who issue the work permit for your wiring project will also visit your home to review the work. Make sure to allow time for these inspections as you plan the project. For most projects, inspectors make two visits.

The first inspection, called the rough-in, is done after the cables are run between the boxes but before the insulation, wallboard, switches, and fixtures are installed. The second inspection, called the final, is done after the walls and ceilings are finished and all electrical connections are made.

When preparing for the rough-in inspection, make sure the area is neat. Sweep up sawdust and clean up any pieces of scrap wire or cable insulation. Before inspecting the boxes and cables, inspectors will check to make sure all plumbing and other mechanical work is completed. Some electrical inspectors will ask to see your building and plumbing permits.

At the final inspection, inspectors check random boxes to make sure the wire connections are correct. If they see good workmanship at the selected boxes, the inspection will be over quickly. However, if they spot a problem, inspectors may choose to inspect every connection.

Inspectors have busy schedules, so it is a good idea to arrange for an inspection several days in advance. In addition to basic compliance with code, inspectors expect your work to meet their own standards for quality. When you apply for a work permit, make sure you understand what the inspectors will look for during inspections.

You cannot put new circuits into use legally until an inspector approves them at the final inspection. If you have planned carefully and done your work well, electrical inspections are routine visits that give you confidence in your own skills.

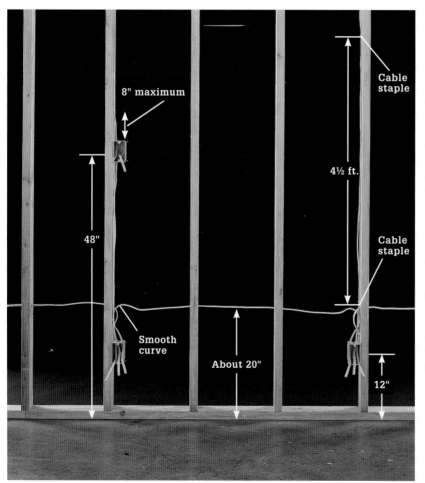

Inspectors may measure to see that electrical boxes are mounted at consistent heights. Height may not be dictated by code, but consistency is a sign of good workmanship. Measured from the center of the boxes, receptacles in living areas typically are located 12" above the finished floor and switches at 48". For special circumstances, inspectors allow you to alter these measurements. For example, you can install switches at 36" above the floor in a child's bedroom, or set receptacles at 24" to make them more convenient for someone using a wheelchair.

Inspectors will check cables to see that they are anchored by cable staples driven within 8" of each box and every 4½ ft. thereafter when they run along studs. When bending cables, form the wire in a smooth curve. Do not crimp cables sharply or install them diagonally between framing members. Some inspectors specify that cables running between receptacle boxes should be about 20" above the floor.

What Inspectors Look for

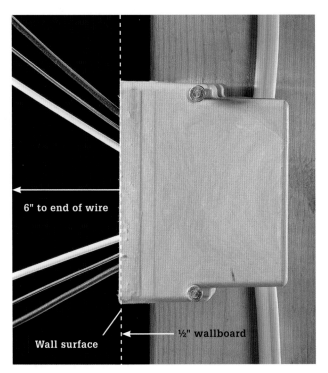

6" to end of wire

Wall surface   ½" wallboard

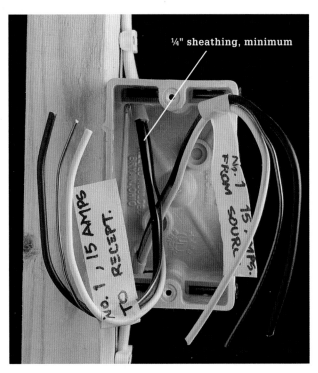

¼" sheathing, minimum

Electrical box faces should extend past the front of framing members so the boxes will be flush with finished walls (left). Inspectors will check to see that all boxes are large enough for the wires they contain. Cables should be cut and stripped back so that at least 3" of usable length extends past the front of the box and so that at least ¼" of sheathing reaches into the box (right). Label all cables to show which circuits they serve: inspectors recognize this as a mark of careful work. The labels also simplify the final hookups after the wallboard is installed.

Is your Receptacle Spacing Correct? ▸

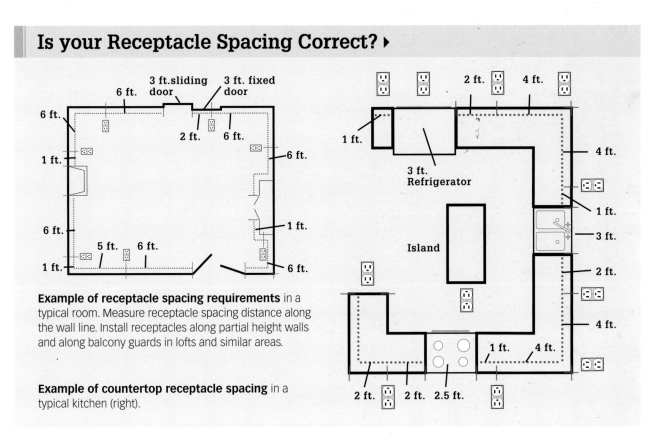

Example of receptacle spacing requirements in a typical room. Measure receptacle spacing distance along the wall line. Install receptacles along partial height walls and along balcony guards in lofts and similar areas.

Example of countertop receptacle spacing in a typical kitchen (right).

Evaluate Electrical Loads

Before drawing a plan and applying for a work permit, make sure your home's electrical service provides enough power to handle the added load of the new circuits. In a safe wiring system, the current drawn by fixtures and appliances never exceeds the main service capacity.

To evaluate electrical loads, use the work sheet on page 137 or whatever evaluation method is recommended by your electrical inspector. Include the load for all existing wiring as well as that for proposed new wiring when making your evaluation.

Most of the light fixtures and plug-in appliances in your home are evaluated as part of general allowances for basic lighting/receptacle circuits and small-appliance circuits. However, appliances that are permanently installed require their own dedicated circuits. The electrical loads for these appliances are added in separately when evaluating wiring.

If your evaluation shows that the load exceeds the main service capacity, you must have an electrician upgrade the main service before you can install new wiring. An electrical service upgrade is a worthwhile investment that improves the value of your home and provides plenty of power for present and future wiring projects.

Amperage ▶

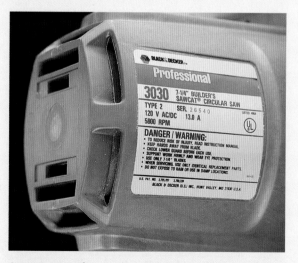

Amperage rating can be used to find the wattage of an appliance. Multiply the amperage by the voltage of the circuit. For example, a 13-amp, 120-volt circular saw is rated for 1,560 watts.

AMPS × VOLTS	TOTAL CAPACITY	SAFE CAPACITY
15 A × 120 V =	1,800 watts	1,440 watts
20 A × 120 V =	2,400 watts	1,920 watts
25 A × 120 V =	3,000 watts	2,400 watts
30 A × 120 V =	3,600 watts	2,880 watts
20 A × 240 V =	4,800 watts	3,840 watts
30 A × 240 V =	7,200 watts	5,760 watts

Calculating Loads

Add 1,500 watts for each small appliance circuit required by the local electrical code. In most communities, three such circuits are required—two in the kitchen and one for the laundry—for a total of 4,500 watts. No further calculations are needed for appliances that plug into small-appliance or basic lighting/receptacle circuits.

If the nameplate gives the rating in kilowatts, find the watts by multiplying kilowatts times 1,000. If an appliance lists only amps, find watts by multiplying the amps times the voltage—either 120 or 240 volts.

Air-conditioning and heating appliances are not used at the same time, so figure in only the larger of these two numbers when evaluating your home's electrical load.

Fixed Devices ▸

Do not connect one or more fixed devices that in total exceed 50 percent of a multiple outlet branch circuit's amperage rating. Fixed devices do not include light fixtures. This means that that all fixed devices (such as a permanently wired disposal or hot water circulating pump) on a multiple outlet branch circuit may not exceed 7.5 amps (about 900 watts) on a 15-amp multiple outlet branch circuit and may not exceed 10 amps (about 1,200 watts) on a 20-amp multiple outlet branch circuit.

Locating Wattage

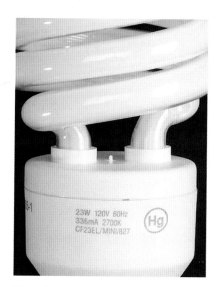

Light bulb wattage ratings are printed on the top of the bulb. If a light fixture has more than one bulb, remember to add the wattages of all the bulbs to find the total wattage of the fixture.

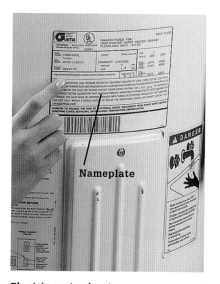

Electric water heaters are permanent appliances that require their own dedicated 30-amp, 240-volt circuits. Most water heaters are rated between 3,500 and 4,500 watts. If the nameplate lists several wattage ratings, use the one labeled "Total Connected Wattage" when figuring electrical loads.

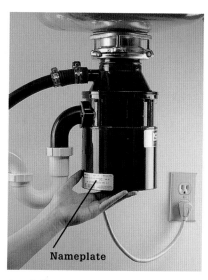

Food disposers are considered permanent appliances and may require their own dedicated 15-amp, 120-volt circuits. Most disposers are rated between 500 and 900 watts.

Dishwashers installed permanently under a countertop may need a dedicated 15-amp, 120-volt circuits. Dishwasher ratings are usually between 1,000 and 1,500 watts. Portable dishwashers are regarded as part of small appliance circuits and are not added in when figuring loads.

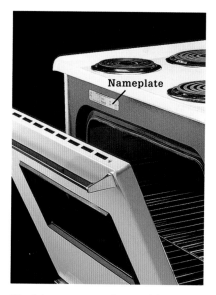

Electric ranges can be rated for as little as 3,000 watts or as much as 12,000 watts. They require dedicated 120/240-volt circuits. Find the exact wattage rating by reading the nameplate found inside the oven door or on the back of the unit.

Microwave ovens are regarded as permanent appliances. Add in its wattage rating when calculating loads. The nameplate is found on the back of the cabinet or inside the front door. Most microwave ovens are rated between 500 and 1,200 watts.

Freezers are permanent appliances that may need a dedicated 15- or 20-amp, 120-volt circuits. Freezer ratings are usually between 240 and 480 watts. But combination refrigerator-freezers rated for 1,000 watts or less are plugged into small appliance circuits and do not need their own dedicated circuits. The nameplate for a freezer is found inside the door or on the back of the unit, just below the door seal.

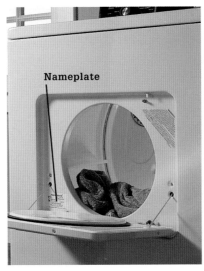

Electric clothes dryers are permanent appliances that need dedicated 30-amp, 120/240-volt circuits. The wattage rating is printed on the nameplate inside the dryer door. Use 5,000 watts as a minimum, regardless of the printed rating. Washing machines and gas-heat clothes dryers with electric tumbler motors do not need dedicated circuits. They plug into the 20-amp small-appliance circuit in the laundry room.

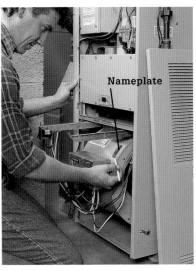

Forced-air furnaces and heat pump air handlers have electric fans and are considered permanent appliances. They require dedicated 15-amp, 120-volt circuits. Include the fan wattage rating, printed on a nameplate inside the control panel, when figuring wattage loads for heating. You should also include the wattage rating for heat pump backup heating coils.

A central air conditioner requires a dedicated 240-volt circuit. Estimate its wattage rating by adding the numbers labeled RLA and FLA on the air conditioner's metal plate. Multiply the RLA+FLA by 240.

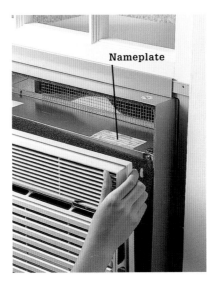

Window air conditioners, both 120-volt and 240-volt types, are permanent appliances that require dedicated circuits. The wattage rating, which can range from 500 to 2,000 watts, is found on the nameplate located inside the front grill. Make sure to include all window air conditioners in your evaluation.

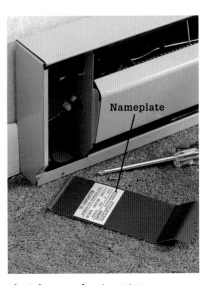

Electric room heaters that are permanently installed require a dedicated circuit and must be figured into the load calculations. Use the maximum wattage rating printed inside the cover. In general, 240-volt baseboard-type heaters are rated for 180 to 250 watts for each linear foot.

Sample Circuit Evaluation

Circuit # __6__ Amps __20__ Volts __120__ Total capacity __2,400__ (watts) Safe capacity __1,920__ (watts)

Appliance or fixture	Notes	Wattage rating
REFRIGERATOR	CONSTANT USE	480
CEILING LIGHT	3 - 60 WATT BULBS	180
MICROWAVE OVEN		625
ELECTRIC CAN OPENER	OCCASIONAL USE	144
STEREO	PORTABLE BOOM BOX	300
CEILING LIGHT (HALLWAY)	2 60 WATT BULBS	120
Total demand:		1,849 (watts)

Photocopy this sample circuit evaluation to keep a record of the power demand of each circuit. The words and numbers printed in blue will not reproduce on photocopies. In this sample kitchen circuit, the demand on the circuit is very close to the safe capacity. Adding another appliance, such as an electric frying pan, could overload the circuit and cause a fuse to blow or a circuit breaker to trip.

Typical Wattage Ratings (120-volt Circuit Except Where Noted) ▸

APPLIANCE	AMPS	WATTS	APPLIANCE	AMPS	WATTS
Air conditioner (central)	13 to 36 (240-v)	3,120 to 8,640	Garbage disposer	3.5 to 7.5	420 to 900
Air conditioner (window)	6 to 13	720 to 1,560	Hair dryer	5 to 10	600 to 1,200
Blender	2 to 4	240 to 480	Heater (portable)	7 to 12	840 to 1,440
Broiler	12.5	1,500	Microwave oven	4 to 10	480 to 1,200
Can opener	1.2	144	Range (oven/stove)	5.5 to 10.8 (240-v)	1,320 to 2,600
Circular saw	10 to 12	1,200 to 1,440	Refrigerator	2 to 4	240 to 600
Clothes dryer	16.5 to 34 (240-v)	3,960 to 8,160	Router	8	960
Clothes iron	9	1,080	Sander (portable)	2 to 5	240 to 600
Coffeemaker	4 to 8	480 to 960	Saw (table)	7 to 10	840 to 1,200
Computer	4 to 7	480 to 840	Sewing machine	1	120
Dishwasher	8.5 to 12.5	1,020 to 1,500	Stereo	2.5 to 4	300 to 480
Drill (portable)	2 to 4	240 to 480	Television	2.5	300
DVD player	2.5 to 4	300 to 480	Toaster	9	1,080
Fan (ceiling)	3.5	420	Trash compactor	4 to 8	480 to 960
Fan (portable)	2	240	Vacuum cleaner	6 to 11	720 to 1,320
Freezer	2 to 4	240 to 600	Waffle iron	7.5	900
Frying pan	9	1,080	Washing machine	12.5	1,500
Furnace, forced-air gas	6.5 to 13	780 to 1,560	Water heater (elec.)	15.8 to 21 (240-v)	3,800 to 5,040

How to Estimate Electrical Loads—with sample numbers

1.	Find the basic lighting/receptacle load by multiplying the square footage of all living areas (including any room additions) times 3 watts.	Existing space: _____ *1,100* _____ sq. ft. New additions: _____ *400* _____ sq. ft. _____ *1,500* _____ total sq. ft. × 3 watts =	*4,500* watts
2.	Add 1,500 watts for each kitchen small-appliance circuit and for the laundry circuit.	_____ *3* _____ circuits × 1,500 watts =	*4,500* watts
3.	Add ratings for permanent electrical appliances, including range, food disposer, dishwasher, freezer, water heater, and clothes dryer.	RANGE 12.3 K.W.=12,300 watts	*12,300* watts
		DRYER 5,000	*5,000* watts
		DISHWASHER 1,200	*1,200* watts
		FREEZER 550	*550* watts
		DISPOSER 800	*800* watts
	Find total wattages for the furnace and heating units, and for air conditioners. Add in only the larger of these numbers.	Furnace heat: _____ *1,200* _____ watts Space heaters: _____ *5,450* _____ watts Total heating = _____ *6,650* _____ watts Central air conditioner: _____ *3,500* _____ watts Window air conditioners: _____ *1,100* _____ watts Total cooling = _____ *4,600* _____ watts	*6,650* watts
4.	Total the wattages to find the gross load.		*36,690* watts
5.	Figure the first 8,000 watts of the gross load at 100%.	100% × 8,000 = 8,000	8,000 watts
6.	Subtract 8,000 watts from the gross load, and then figure the remaining load at 40%.	*28,690* watts − 8,000 = *20,690* watts *20,690* watts × .40 =	*8,276* watts
7.	Add steps 5 and 6 plus total heating load (in step 3) to estimate the true electrical load.		*22,926* watts
8.	Convert the estimated true electrical load to amps by dividing by 230.	*22,926* watts ÷ 230 =	*99.7* amps
9.	Compare the load with the amp rating of your home's electrical service, printed on the main circuit breaker. If the load is less than the main circuit breaker rating, the system is safe. If the load exceeds the main circuit breaker rating, your service should be upgraded.	OK ☒ Upgrade ☐	

Notice: This worksheet is for rough estimates only. For more precise evaluation, contact your electrical inspector for a copy of the worksheet they use.

Draw a Diagram & Obtain a Permit

Drawing a wiring diagram is the last step in planning a circuit installation. A detailed wiring diagram helps you get a work permit, makes it easy to create a list of materials, and serves as a guide for laying out circuits and installing cables and fixtures. Use the circuit maps on pages 148 to 165 as a guide for planning wiring configurations and cable runs. Bring the diagram and materials list when you visit electrical inspectors to apply for a work permit.

Never install new wiring without following your community's permit and inspection procedure. A work permit is not expensive, and it ensures that your work will be reviewed by a qualified inspector. If you install new wiring without the proper permit, an accident or fire traced to faulty wiring could cause your insurance company to discontinue your policy and can hurt the resale value of your home.

When electrical inspectors look over your wiring diagram, they will ask questions to see if you have

a basic understanding of the electrical code and fundamental wiring skills. Some inspectors ask these questions informally, while others give a short written test. Inspectors may allow you to do some, but not all, of the work. For example, they may ask that all final circuit connections at the circuit breaker panel be made by a licensed electrician, while allowing you to do all other work.

A few communities allow you to install wiring only when supervised by an electrician. This means you can still install your own wiring but must hire an electrician to apply for the work permit and to check your work before inspectors review it. The electrician is held responsible for the quality of the job.

Remember that it is the inspectors' responsibility to help you do a safe and professional job. Feel free to call them with questions about wiring techniques or materials.

A detailed wiring diagram and a list of materials is required before electrical inspectors will issue a work permit. If blueprints exist for the space you are remodeling, start your electrical diagram by tracing the wall outlines from the blueprint. Use standard electrical symbols (next page) to clearly show all the receptacles, switches, light fixtures, and permanent appliances. Make a copy of the symbol key and attach it to the wiring diagram for the inspectors' convenience. Show each cable run, and label its wire size and circuit amperage.

How to Draw a Wiring Plan

Draw a scaled diagram of the space you will be wiring, showing walls, doors, windows, plumbing pipes and fixtures, and heating and cooling ducts. Find the floor space by multiplying room length by width, and indicate this on the diagram.

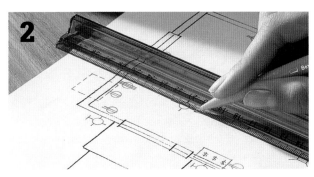

Mark the location of all switches, receptacles, light fixtures, and permanent appliances, using the electrical symbols shown below. Where you locate these devices along the cable run determines how they are wired. Use the circuit maps on pages 148 to 165 as a guide for drawing wiring diagrams.

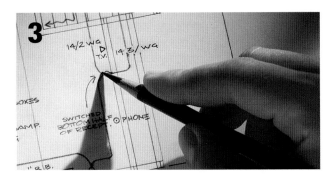

Draw in cable runs between devices. Indicate cable size and type and the amperage of the circuits. Use a different-colored pencil for each circuit.

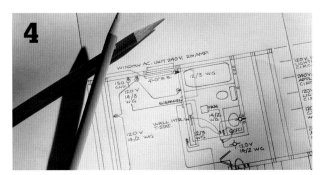

Identify the wattages for light fixtures and permanent appliances and the type and size of each electrical box. On another sheet of paper, make a detailed list of all materials you will use.

Electrical Symbol Key ▶
(copy this key and attach it to your wiring plan)

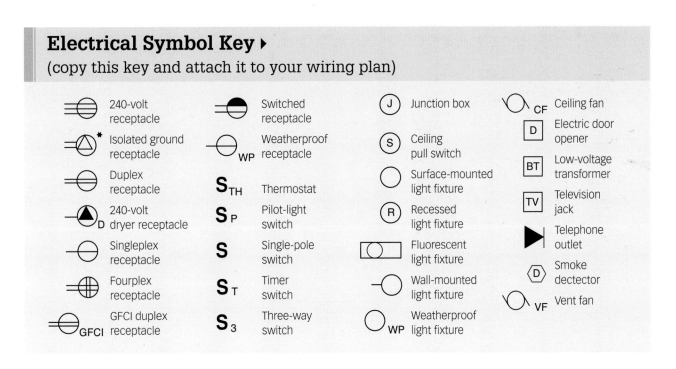

240-volt receptacle	Switched receptacle	Junction box · Ceiling fan
Isolated ground receptacle	Weatherproof receptacle WP	Ceiling pull switch · Electric door opener
Duplex receptacle	S TH Thermostat	Surface-mounted light fixture · Low-voltage transformer BT
240-volt dryer receptacle	S P Pilot-light switch	R Recessed light fixture · Television jack TV
Singleplex receptacle	S Single-pole switch	Fluorescent light fixture · Telephone outlet
Fourplex receptacle	S T Timer switch	Wall-mounted light fixture · Smoke detector
GFCI duplex receptacle	S 3 Three-way switch	Weatherproof WP light fixture · Vent fan VF

Wiring a Room Addition

The photo below shows the circuits you would likely want to install in a large room addition. This example shows the framing and wiring of an unfinished attic converted to an office or entertainment room with a bathroom. This room includes a subpanel and five new circuits plus telephone and cable-TV lines.

A wiring project of this sort is a potentially complicated undertaking that can be made simpler by breaking the project into convenient steps, and finishing one step before moving on to the next. Turn to pages 142 to 143 to see this project represented as a wiring diagram.

Individual Circuits

#1: Bathroom circuit. This 20-amp dedicated circuit supplies power to bathroom lights and fans, as well as receptacles that must be GFCI-protected at the box or at the receptacle. As with small appliance circuits in the kitchen, you may not tap into this circuit to feed any additional loads.

#2: Computer circuit. A 15-amp dedicated circuit with isolated ground is recommended, but an individual branch circuit is all that is required by most codes.

Circuit breaker subpanel receives power through a 10-gauge, three-wire feeder cable connected to a 30-amp,

14/2 cable

Vent fan

Vanity light fixture

GFCI receptac

Circuit breaker subpanel

12/2 cable

12/2 cable

Time & light fixture switch

14/3 cable

Blower heater

10/3 cable

240-volt circuit breaker at the main circuit breaker panel. Larger room additions may require a 60-or 100-amp feeder circuit breaker.

#3: Air-conditioner circuit. This is a 20-amp, 240-volt dedicated circuit. In cooler climates, or in a smaller room, you may need an air conditioner and circuit rated for only 120 volts.

#4: Basic lighting/receptacle circuit. This 15-amp, 120-volt circuit supplies power to most of the fixtures in the bedroom and study areas.

#5: Heater circuit. This 20-amp, 240-volt circuit supplies power to the bathroom blower-heater and to the baseboard heaters. Depending on the size of your room and the wattage rating of the baseboard heaters, you may need a 30-amp, 240-volt heating circuit.

Telephone outlet is wired with 22-gauge four-wire phone cable. If your home phone system has two or more separate lines, you may need to run a cable with eight wires, commonly called four-pair cable.

Cable television jack is wired with coaxial cable running from an existing television junction in the utility area.

14/3 cable

14/3 cable

Phone cable

Coaxial cable

These cables continue through the foreground wall to complete the circuits. This wall has been removed for clarity.

12/2 cable

14/2 cable

Diagram View

The diagram below shows the layout of the five circuits and the locations of their receptacles, switches, fixtures, and devices as shown in the photo on the previous pages. The circuits and receptacles are based on the needs of a 400-sq.-ft. space. An inspector will want to see a diagram like this one before issuing a permit. After you've received approval for your addition, the wiring diagram will serve as your guide as you complete your project.

■ **Circuit #1:** A 20-amp, 120-volt circuit serving the bathroom and closet area. Includes: 12/2 NM cable, double-gang box, timer switch, single-pole switch, 4" × 4" box with single-gang adapter plate, two plastic light fixture boxes, vanity light fixture, closet light fixture, 15-amp single-pole circuit breaker.

■ **Circuit #2:** A 15-amp, 120-volt computer circuit. Includes: 14/2 NM cable, single-gang box, 15-amp receptacle, 15-amp single-pole circuit breaker.

□ **Circuit #3:** A 20-amp, 240-volt air-conditioner circuit. Includes: 12/2 NM cable; single-gang box;

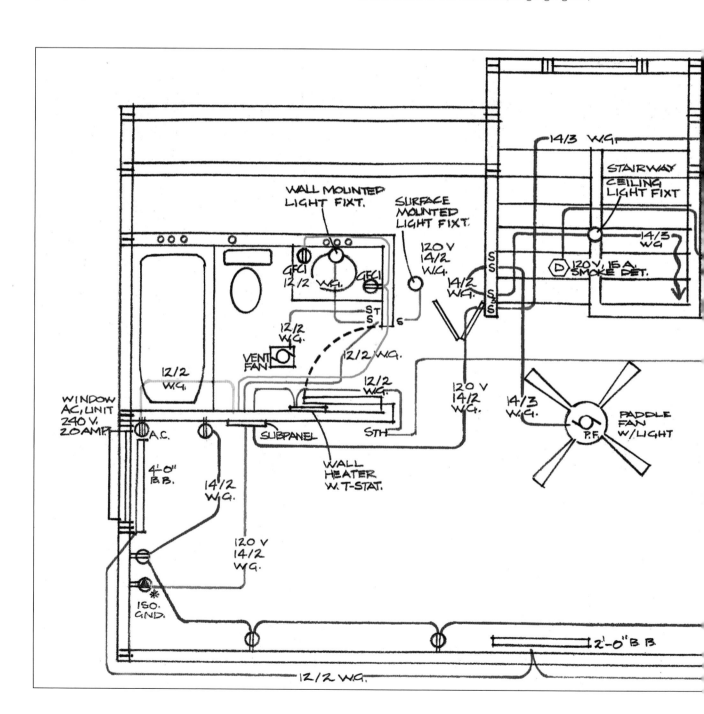

20-amp, 240-volt receptacle (singleplex style); 20-amp double-pole circuit.

■ **Circuit #4:** A 15-amp, 120-volt basic lighting/receptacle circuit serving most of the fixtures in the bedroom and study areas. Includes: 14/2 and 14/3 NM cable, two double-gang boxes, fan speed-control switch, dimmer switch, single-pole switch, two three-way switches, two plastic light fixture boxes, light fixture for stairway, smoke detector, metal light fixture box with brace bar, ceiling fan with light fixture, 10 single-gang boxes, 4" × 4" box with single-gang adapter plate, 10 duplex receptacles (15-amp), 15-amp single-pole circuit breaker.

■ **Circuit #5:** A 20-amp, 240-volt circuit that supplies power to three baseboard heaters controlled by a wall thermostat and to a bathroom blower-heater controlled by a built-in thermostat. Includes: 12/2 NM cable, 750-watt blower heater, single-gang box, line-voltage thermostat, three baseboard heaters, 20-amp double-pole circuit breaker.

TV **Cable television jack:** Coaxial cable with F-connectors, signal splitter, cable television outlet with mounting brackets.

■ **Circuit #6:** A 20-amp, 120-volt, GFCI-protected bathroom receptacle circuit for the bathroom. Includes GFCI breaker, 12/2 NM cable, boxes, and 20-amp receptacles.

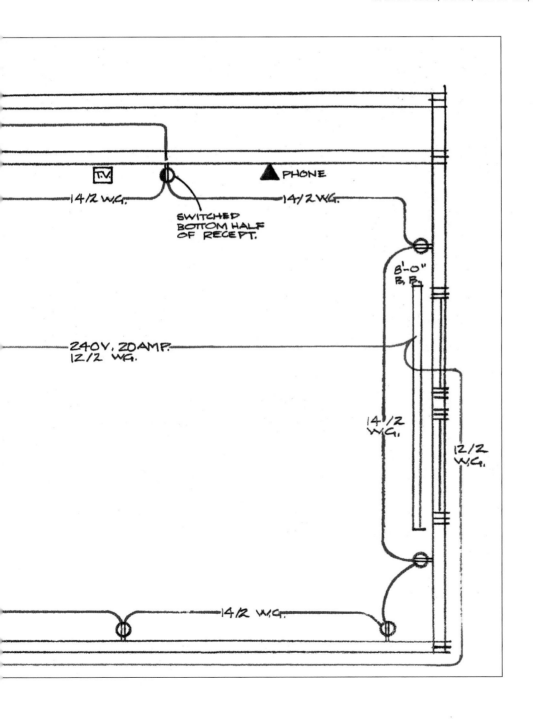

Wiring a Kitchen

14/2 cable

14/2 cable

12/3 cable

12/2 cable

6/3 cable

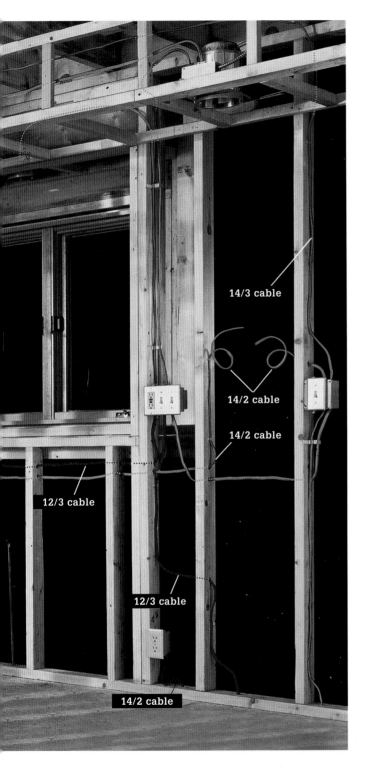

14/3 cable

14/2 cable

14/2 cable

12/3 cable

12/3 cable

14/2 cable

The photo at left shows the circuits you would probably want to install in a total kitchen remodel. Kitchens require a wide range of electrical services, from simple 15-amp lighting circuits to 120/240, 50-amp appliance circuits. This kitchen example has seven circuits, including separate dedicated circuits for a dishwasher and food disposer. Some codes allow the disposer and dishwasher to share a single circuit.

All rough carpentry and plumbing should be in place before beginning any electrical work. As always, divide a project of this scale into manageable steps, and finish one step before moving on. Turn to pages 146 to 147 to see this project represented as a wiring diagram.

Individual Circuits

■ **#1 & #2: Small-appliance circuits.** Two 20-amp, 120-volt circuits supply power to countertop and eating areas for small appliances. All general-use receptacles must be on these circuits. One 12/3 cable fed by a 20-amp double-pole breaker wires both circuits. These circuits share one electrical box with the disposer circuit (#5) and another with the basic lighting circuit (#7). Other circuits may also service the area, as with a dedicated refrigerator circuit.

■ **#3: Range circuit.** A 40- or 50-amp, 120/240-volt dedicated circuit supplies power to the range/ oven appliance. It is wired with 6/3 copper cable.

■ **#4: Microwave circuit.** It is wired with 12/2 cable. Microwaves that use less than 300 watts can be installed on a 15-amp circuit or plugged into the small-appliance circuits.

■ **#5: Food disposer/dishwasher circuit.** A dedicated 15-amp, 120-volt circuit supplies power to the disposer. It is wired with 14/2 cable. Some local codes may allow the disposer to be on the same circuit as the dishwasher if it is a 20-amp circuit.

■ **#6: Basic lighting circuit.** A 15-amp, 120-volt circuit powers the ceiling fixture, recessed fixtures, and undercabinet task lights. 14/2 and 14/3 cables connect the fixtures and switches in the circuit. Each task light has a self-contained switch.

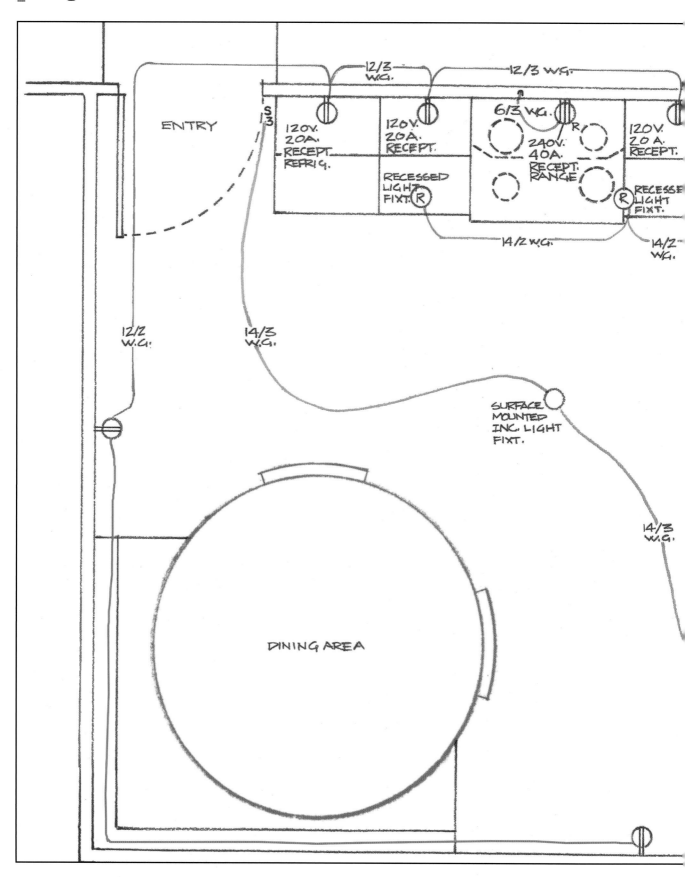

ENTRY

S
3

12/3
W.G.

12/3 W.G.

120V.
20A.
RECEPT.
REFRIG.

120V.
20A.
RECEPT.

6/3 W.G.

R

120V.
20 A.
RECEPT.

240V.
40A.
RECEPT.
RANGE

RECESSED
LIGHT
FIXT. R

R RECESSE
LIGHT
FIXT.

14/2 W.G.

14/2
W.G.

12/2
W.G.

14/3
W.G.

SURFACE
MOUNTED
INC. LIGHT
FIXT.

14/3
W.G.

DINING AREA

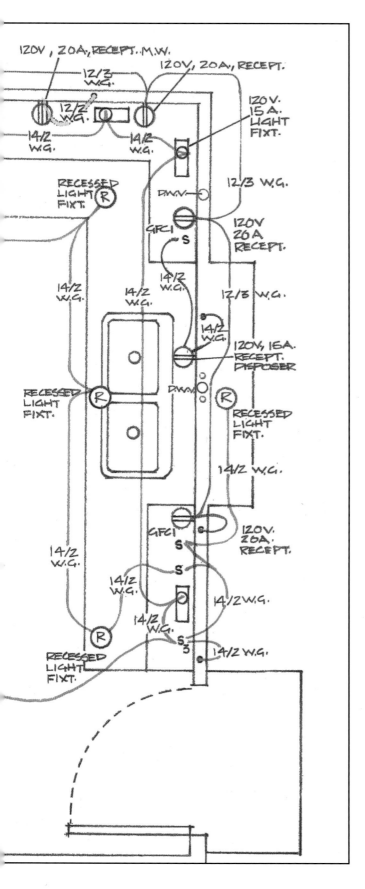

The diagram at left shows the layout of the seven circuits and the locations of their receptacles, switches, fixtures, and devices as shown in the photo on the previous pages. The circuits and receptacles are based on the needs of a 175-sq.-ft. space kitchen. An inspector will want to see a diagram like this one before issuing a permit. After you've received approval for your addition, the wiring diagram will serve as your guide as you complete your project.

▓ **Circuits #1 & #2:** Two 20-amp, 120-volt small-appliance circuits wired with one cable. All general-use receptacles must be on these circuits, and they must be GFCI units. Includes: two GFCI receptacles rated for 20 amps, five electrical boxes that are 4" × 4", and 12/3 cable.

▓ **Circuit #3:** A 50-amp, 120/240-volt dedicated circuit for the range. Includes: a 4" × 4" box; a 120/240-volt, 50-amp range receptacle; and 6/3 NM copper cable.

▓ **Circuit #4:** A 20-amp, 120-volt dedicated circuit for the microwave. Includes: a 20-amp duplex receptacle, a single-gang box, and 12/2 NM cable.

▓ **Circuit #5:** A 15-amp, 120-volt dedicated circuit for the food disposer. Includes: a 15-amp duplex receptacle, a single-pole switch (installed in a double-gang box with a GFCI receptacle from the small-appliance circuits), one single-gang box, and 14/2 cable.

▓ **Circuit #6:** A 15-amp, 120-volt basic lighting circuit serving all of the lighting needs in the kitchen. Includes: two single-pole switches, two three-way switches, single-gang box, 4" × 4" box, triple-gang box (shared with one of the GFCI receptacles from the small-appliance circuits), plastic light fixture box with brace, ceiling light fixture, four fluorescent undercabinet light fixtures, six recessed light fixtures, 14/2 and 14/3 cables.

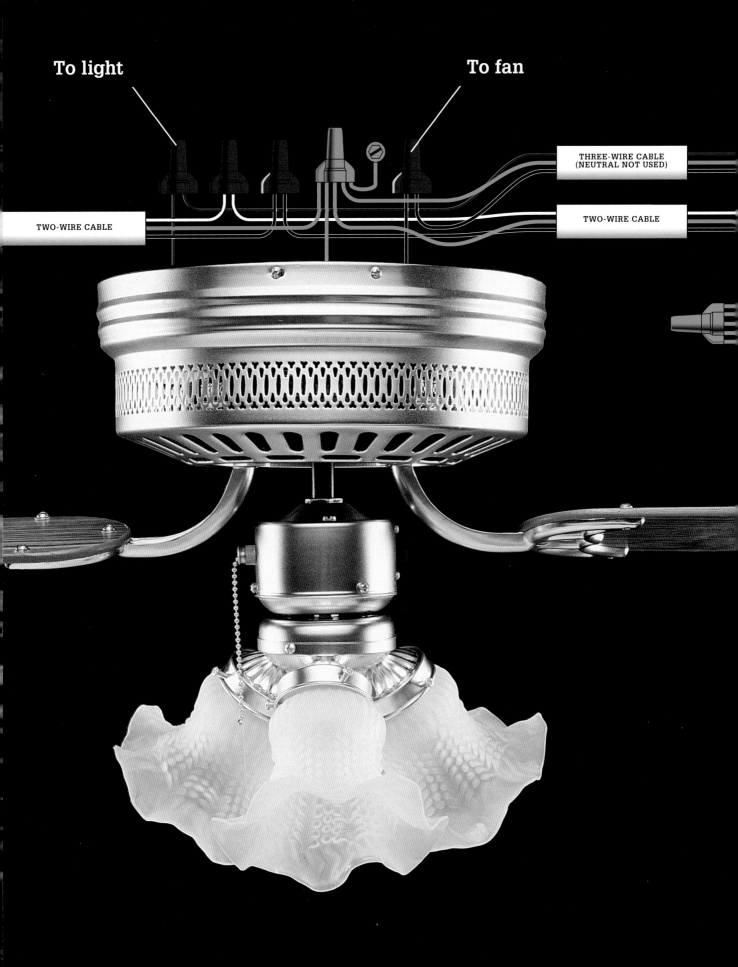

To light

To fan

THREE-WIRE CABLE
(NEUTRAL NOT USED)

TWO-WIRE CABLE

TWO-WIRE CABLE

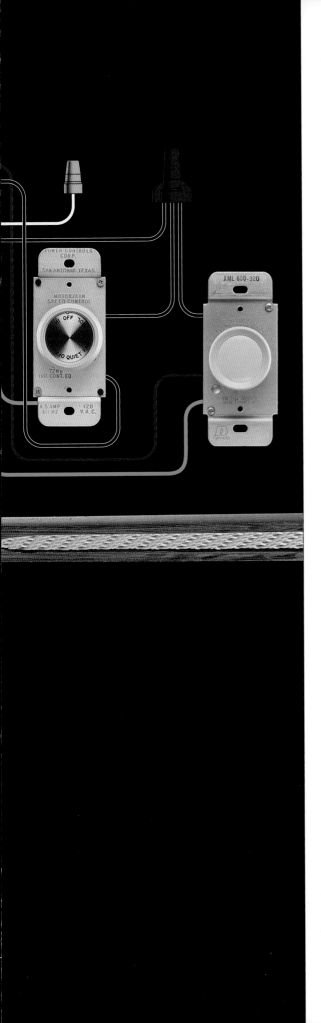

Circuit Maps

The circuit maps on the following pages show the most common wiring variations for typical electrical devices. Most new wiring you install will match one or more of the maps shown. Find the maps that match your situation and use them to plan your circuit layouts.

The 120-volt circuits shown on the following pages are wired for 15 amps using 14-gauge wire and receptacles rated at 15 amps. If you are installing a 20-amp circuit, substitute 12-gauge cables and use receptacles rated for 15 or 20 amps.

In configurations where a white wire serves as a hot wire instead of a neutral, both ends of the wire are coded with black tape to identify it as hot. In addition, each of the circuit maps shows a box grounding screw. This grounding screw is required in all metal boxes, but plastic electrical boxes do not need to be grounded.

You should remember two new code requirements when wiring switches. (1) Provide a neutral wire at every switch box. This may require using 3-wire cable or two 2-wire cables where you may have used one 2-wire cable in the past. (2) Use a black or red wire to supply power from a switch to a light or switched receptacle.

Note: For clarity, all grounding conductors in the circuit maps are colored green. In practice, the grounding wires inside sheathed cables usually are bare copper.

In this chapter:

- Common Household Circuits

Common Household Circuits

1. 120-VOLT DUPLEX RECEPTACLES WIRED IN SEQUENCE

Use this layout to link any number of duplex receptacles in a basic lighting/receptacle circuit. The last receptacle in the cable run is connected like the receptacle shown at the right side of the circuit map below. All other receptacles are wired like the receptacle shown on the left side. This configuration or layout requires two-wire cables.

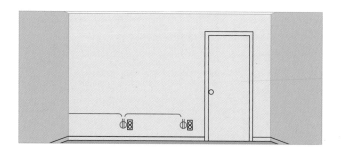

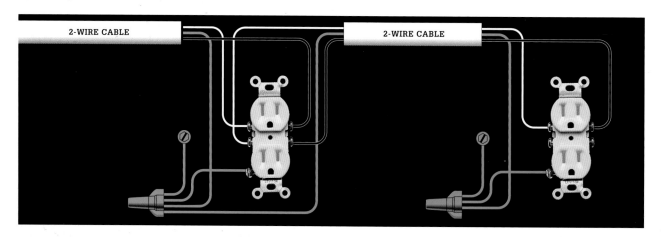

2-WIRE CABLE

2-WIRE CABLE

2. GFCI RECEPTACLES (SINGLE-LOCATION PROTECTION)

Use this layout when receptacles are within 6 ft. of a water source, such as those in kitchens and bathrooms. To prevent nuisance tripping caused by normal power surges, GFCIs should be connected only at the line screw terminal so they protect a single location, not the fixtures on the load side of the circuit. Requires two-wire cables. Where a GFCI must protect other fixtures, use circuit map 3. Remember that bathroom receptacles should usually be on a dedicated 20-amp circuit and that all bathroom receptacles must be GFCI-protected.

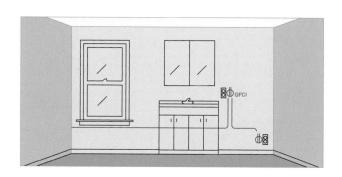

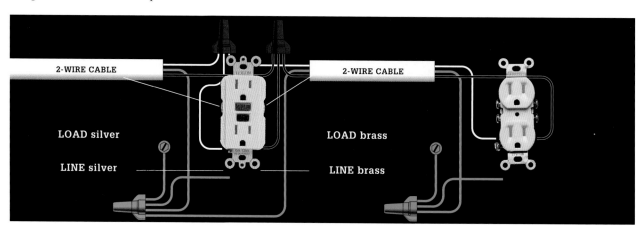

2-WIRE CABLE

2-WIRE CABLE

LOAD silver

LOAD brass

LINE silver

LINE brass

3. GFCI RECEPTACLE, SWITCH & LIGHT FIXTURE (WIRED FOR MULTIPLE-LOCATION PROTECTION)

In some locations, such as an outdoor circuit, it is a good idea to connect a GFCI receptacle so it also provides shock protection to the wires and fixtures that continue to the end of the circuit. Wires from the power source are connected to the line screw terminals; outgoing wires are connected to load screws. Requires two-wire cables.

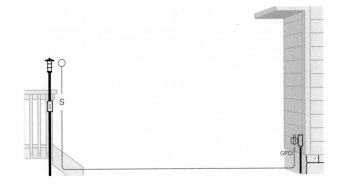

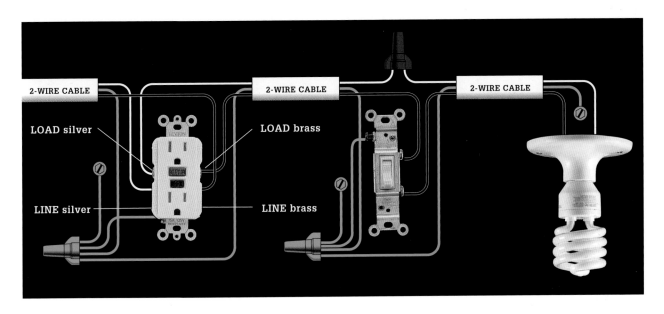

2-WIRE CABLE

2-WIRE CABLE

2-WIRE CABLE

LOAD silver

LOAD brass

LINE silver

LINE brass

4. SINGLE-POLE SWITCH & LIGHT FIXTURE (LIGHT FIXTURE AT END OF CABLE RUN)

Use this layout for light fixtures in basic lighting/receptacle circuits throughout the home. It is often used as an extension to a series of receptacles (circuit map 1). Requires two-wire cables.

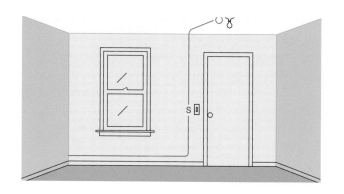

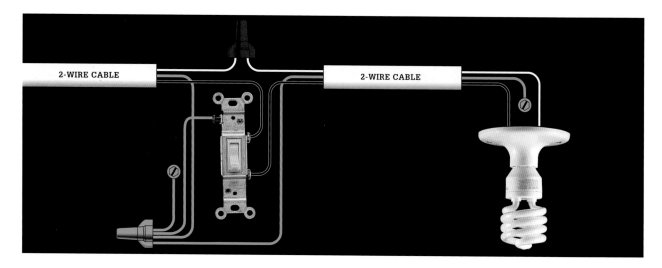

2-WIRE CABLE   2-WIRE CABLE

5. SINGLE-POLE SWITCH & LIGHT FIXTURE (SWITCH AT END OF CABLE RUN)

Use this layout, sometimes called a switch loop, where it is more practical to locate a switch at the end of the cable run. In the last length 3-wire cable is used to make a hot conductor available in each direction. Requires two-wire and three-wire cables.

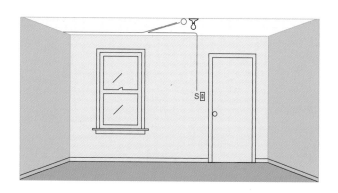

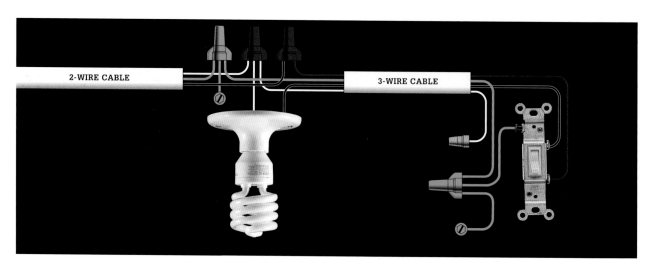

2-WIRE CABLE   3-WIRE CABLE

6. SINGLE-POLE SWITCH & TWO LIGHT FIXTURES (SWITCH BETWEEN LIGHT FIXTURES, LIGHT AT START OF CABLE RUN)

Use this layout when you need to control two fixtures from one single-pole switch and the switch is between the two lights in the cable run. Power feeds to one of the lights. Requires two-wire and three-wire cables.

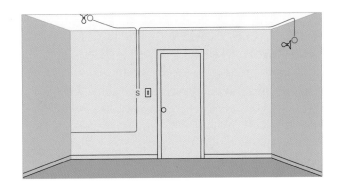

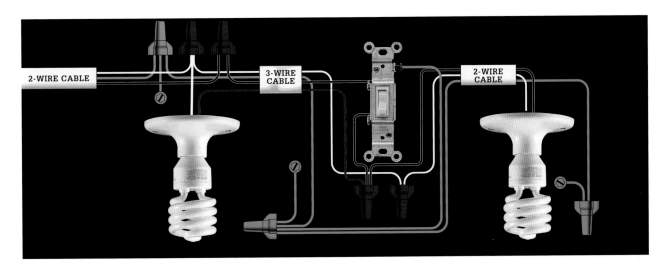

7. SINGLE-POLE SWITCH & LIGHT FIXTURE, DUPLEX RECEPTACLE (SWITCH AT START OF CABLE RUN)

Use this layout to continue a circuit past a switched light fixture to one or more duplex receptacles. To add multiple receptacles to the circuit, see circuit map 1. Requires two-wire and three-wire cables.

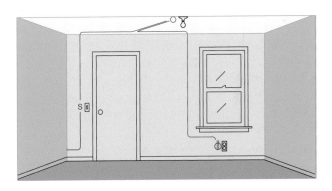

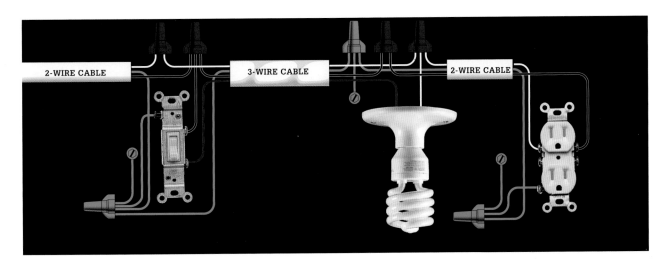

8. SWITCH-CONTROLLED SPLIT RECEPTACLE, DUPLEX RECEPTACLE (SWITCH AT START OF CABLE RUN)

This layout lets you use a wall switch to control a lamp plugged into a wall receptacle. This configuration is required by code for any room that does not have a switch-controlled wall or ceiling fixture. Only the bottom half of the first receptacle is controlled by the wall switch; the top half of the receptacle and all additional receptacles on the circuit are always hot. Requires two-wire and three-wire cables. Some electricians help people identify switched receptacles by installing them upside down.

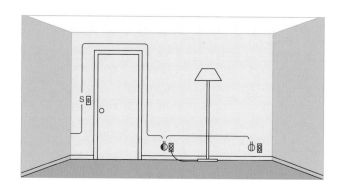

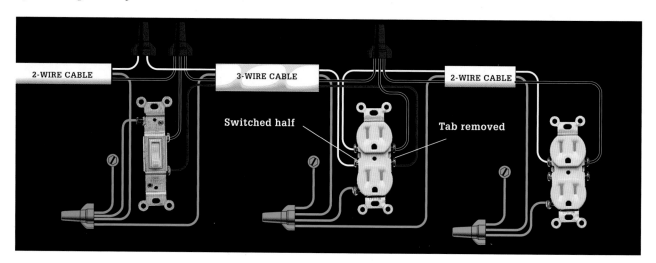

2-WIRE CABLE   3-WIRE CABLE   2-WIRE CABLE

Switched half   Tab removed

9. SWITCH-CONTROLLED SPLIT RECEPTACLE (SWITCH AT END OF CABLE RUN)

Use this switch loop layout to control a split receptacle (see circuit map 7) from an end-of-run circuit location. The bottom half of the receptacle is controlled by the wall switch, while the top half is always hot. Requires two-wire and three-wire cable. Some electricians help people identify switched receptacles by installing them upside down.

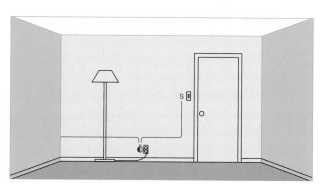

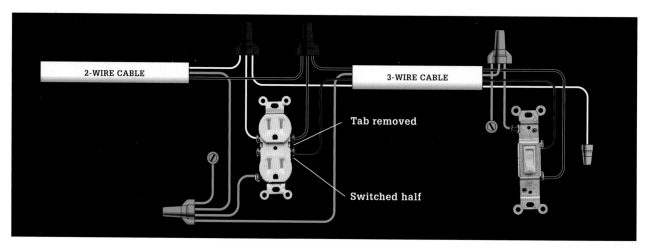

2-WIRE CABLE   3-WIRE CABLE

Tab removed

Switched half

10. SWITCH-CONTROLLED SPLIT RECEPTACLE, DUPLEX RECEPTACLE (SPLIT RECEPTACLE AT START OF RUN)

Use this variation of circuit map 7 where it is more practical to locate a switch-controlled receptacle at the start of a cable run. Only the bottom half of the first receptacle is controlled by the wall switch; the top half of the receptacle, and all other receptacles on the circuit, are always hot. Requires two-wire and three-wire cables. Some electricians help people identify switched receptacles by installing them upside down.

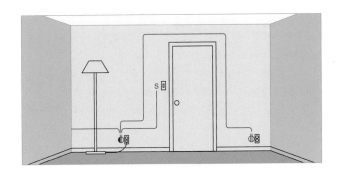

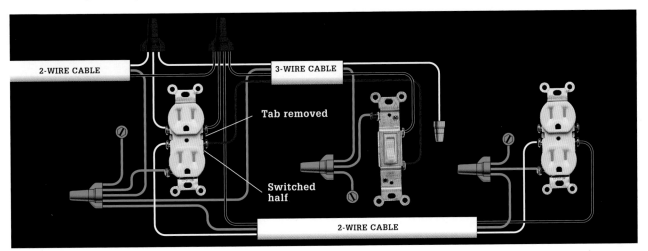

11. DOUBLE RECEPTACLE CIRCUIT WITH SHARED NEUTRAL WIRE (RECEPTACLES ALTERNATE CIRCUITS)

This layout features two 120-volt circuits wired with one three-wire cable connected to a double-pole circuit breaker. The black hot wire powers one circuit; the red wire powers the other. The white wire is a shared neutral that serves both circuits. When wired with 12/2 and 12/3 cable and receptacles rated for 20 amps, this layout can be used for the two small-appliance circuits required in a kitchen. Remember to use a GFCI circuit breaker if you use this circuit for kitchen counter top receptacles.

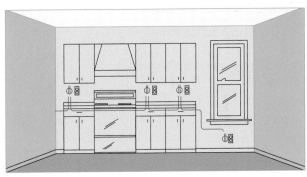

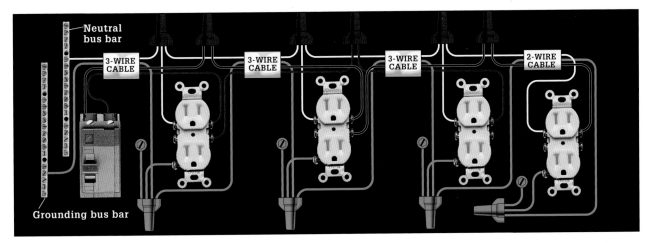

12. DOUBLE RECEPTACLE SMALL-APPLIANCE CIRCUIT WITH GFCIs & SHARED NEUTRAL WIRE

Use this layout variation of circuit map 10 to wire a double receptacle circuit when code requires that some of the receptacles be GFCIs. The GFCIs should be wired for single-location protection (see circuit map 2). Requires three-wire and two-wire cables.

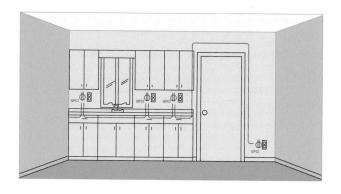

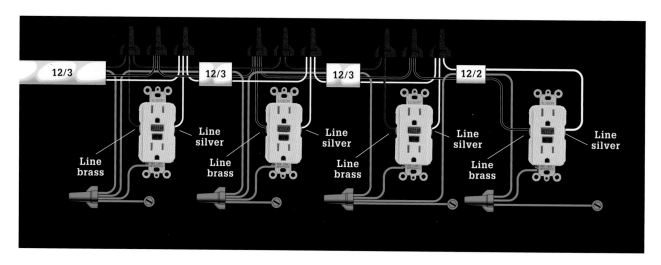

13. DOUBLE RECEPTACLE SMALL APPLIANCE CIRCUIT WITH GFCIs & SEPARATE NEUTRAL WIRES

If the room layout or local codes do not allow for a shared neutral wire, use this layout instead. The GFCIs should be wired for single-location protection (see circuit map 2). Requires two-wire cable.

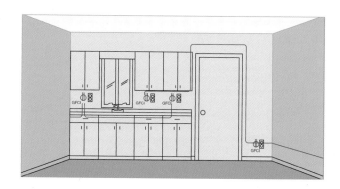

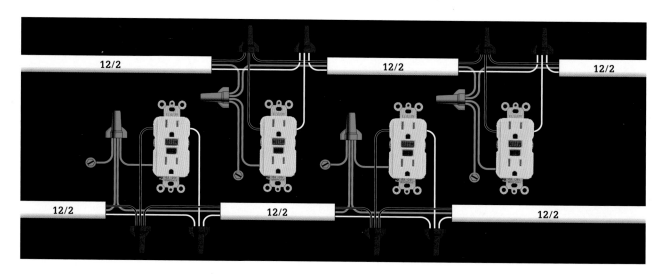

14. 120/240-VOLT RANGE RECEPTACLE

This layout is for a 40- or 50-amp, 120/240-volt dedicated appliance circuit wired with 8/3 or 6/3 cable, as required by code for a large kitchen range. The black and red circuit wires, connected to a double-pole circuit breaker in the circuit breaker panel, each bring 120 volts of power to the setscrew terminals on the receptacle. The white circuit wire attached to the neutral bus bar in the circuit breaker panel is connected to the neutral setscrew terminal on the receptacle.

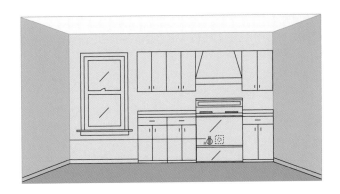

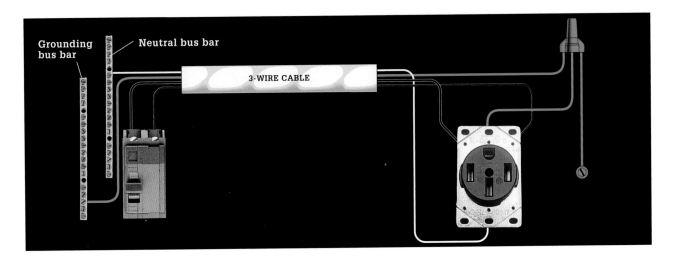

15. 240-VOLT BASEBOARD HEATERS, THERMOSTAT

This layout is typical for a series of 240-volt baseboard heaters controlled by a wall thermostat. Except for the last heater in the circuit, all heaters are wired as shown below. The last heater is connected to only one cable. The sizes of the circuit and cables are determined by finding the total wattage of all heaters. Requires two-wire cable.

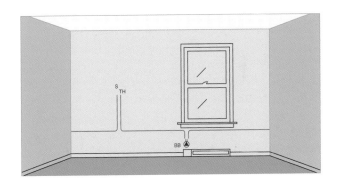

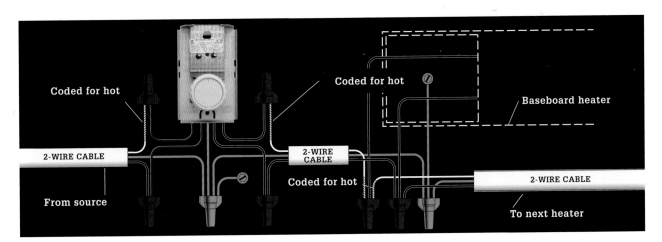

16. DEDICATED 120-VOLT COMPUTER CIRCUIT, ISOLATED-GROUND RECEPTACLE

This 15-amp isolated-ground circuit provides extra protection against surges and interference that can harm electronics. It uses 14/3 cable with the red wire serving as an extra grounding conductor. The red wire is tagged with green tape for identification. It is connected to the grounding screw on an isolated-ground receptacle and runs back to the grounding bus bar in the circuit breaker panel without touching any other house wiring.

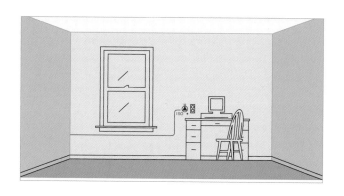

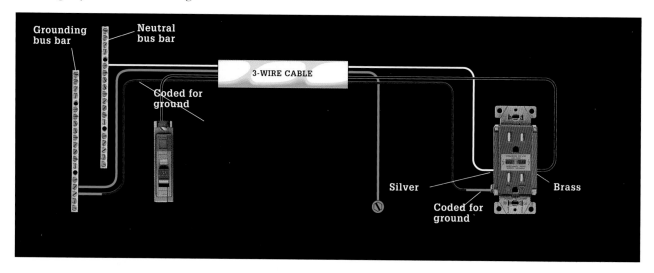

17. 240-VOLT APPLIANCE RECEPTACLE

This layout represents a 20-amp, 240-volt dedicated appliance circuit wired with 12/2 cable, as required by code for a large window air conditioner. Receptacles are available in both singleplex (shown) and duplex styles. The black and the white circuit wires connected to a double-pole breaker each bring 120 volts of power to the receptacle (combined, they bring 240 volts). The white wire is tagged with black tape to indicate it is hot.

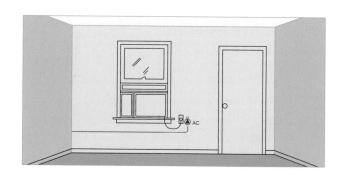

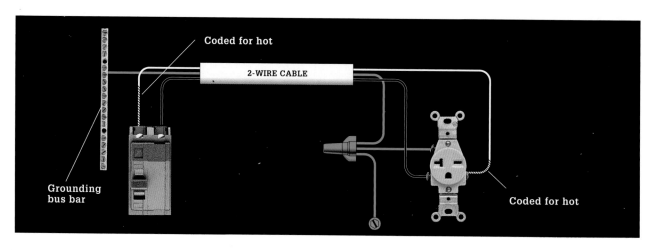

18. GANGED SINGLE-POLE SWITCHES CONTROLLING SEPARATE LIGHT FIXTURES

This layout lets you place two switches controlled by the same 120-volt circuit in one double-gang electrical box. A single-feed cable provides power to both switches. A similar layout with two feed cables can be used to place switches from different circuits in the same box. Requires two-wire cable.

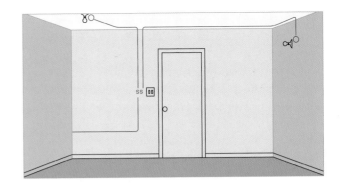

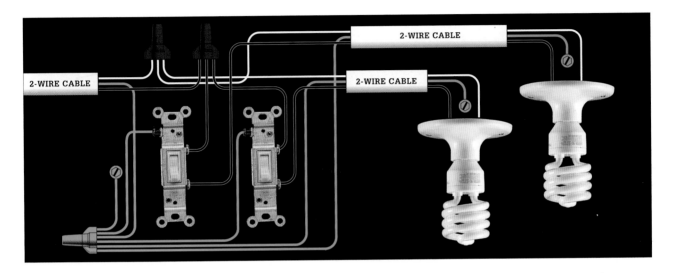

19. GANGED SWITCHES CONTROLLING A LIGHT FIXTURE AND A VENT FAN

This layout lets you place two switches controlled by the same 120-volt circuit in one double-gang electrical box. A single-feed cable provides power to both switches. A standard switch controls the light fixture, and a time-delay switch controls the vent fan.

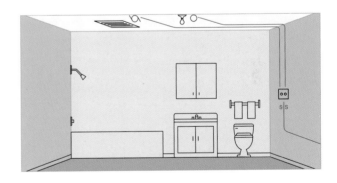

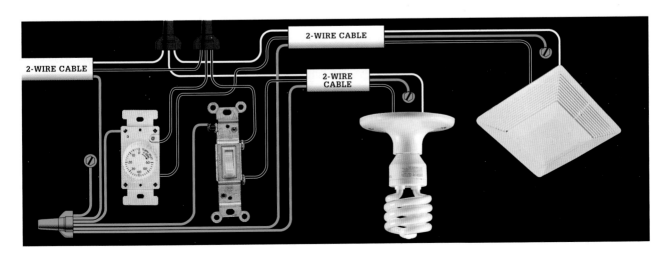

20. THREE-WAY SWITCHES & LIGHT FIXTURE (FIXTURE BETWEEN SWITCHES)

This layout for three-way switches lets you control a light fixture from two locations. Each switch has one common screw terminal and two traveler screws. Circuit wires attached to the traveler screws run between the two switches, and hot wires attached to the common screws bring current from the power source and carry it to the light fixture. Requires parallel runs of 2-wire cable.

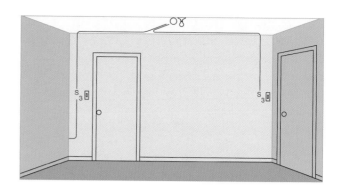

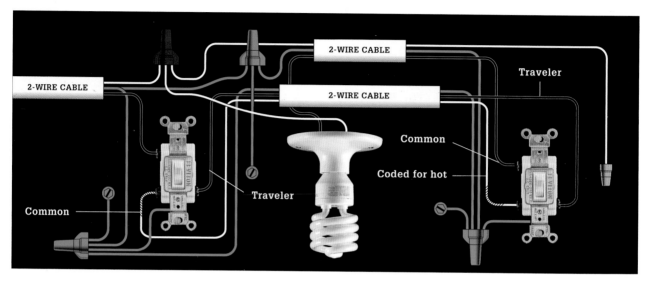

21. THREE-WAY SWITCHES & LIGHT FIXTURE (FIXTURE AT START OF CABLE RUN)

Use this layout variation of circuit map 19 where it is more convenient to locate the fixture ahead of the three-way switches in the cable run. Requires two-wire and three-wire cables.

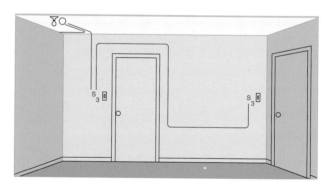

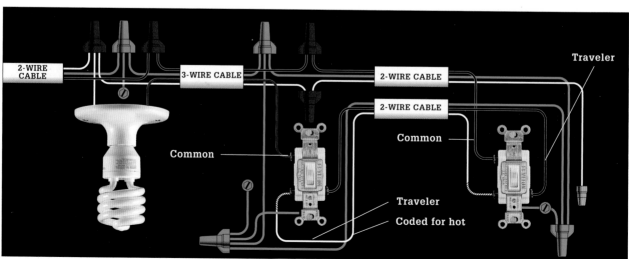

22. THREE-WAY SWITCHES & LIGHT FIXTURE (FIXTURE AT END OF CABLE RUN)

This variation of the three-way switch layout (circuit map 20) is used where it is more practical to locate the fixture at the end of the cable run. Requires two-wire and three-wire cables.

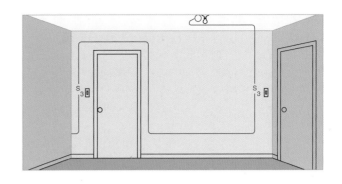

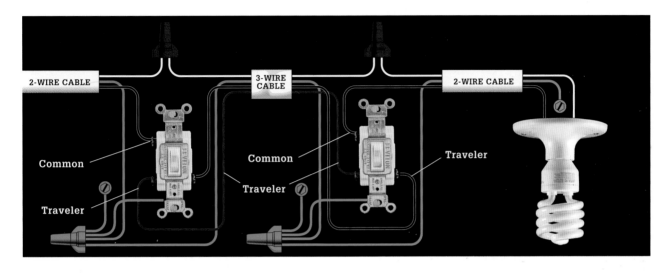

23. THREE-WAY SWITCHES & LIGHT FIXTURE WITH DUPLEX RECEPTACLE

Use this layout to add a receptacle to a three-way switch configuration (circuit map 21). Requires two-wire and parallel runs of two-wire cables.

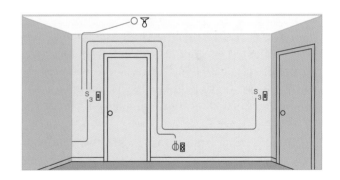

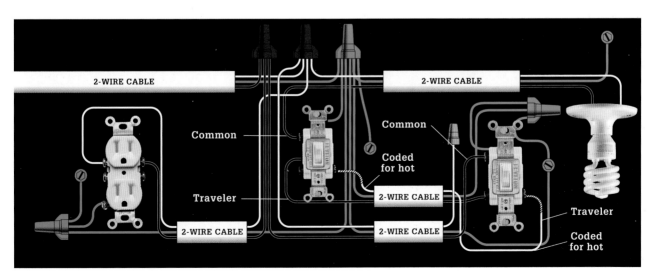

24. THREE-WAY SWITCHES & MULTIPLE LIGHT FIXTURES (FIXTURES BETWEEN SWITCHES)

This is a variation of circuit map 20. Use it to place multiple light fixtures between two three-way switches where power comes in at one of the switches. Requires two- and three-wire cable.

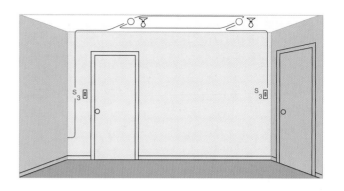

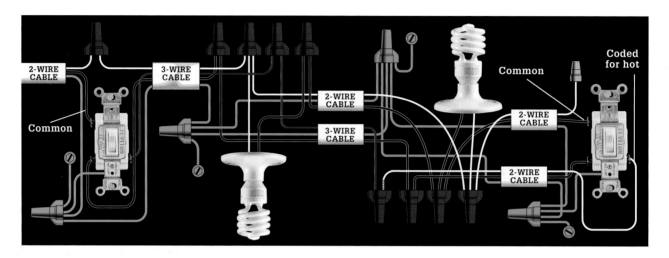

25. THREE-WAY SWITCHES & MULTIPLE LIGHT FIXTURES (FIXTURES AT BEGINNING OF RUN)

This is a variation of circuit map 21. Use it to place multiple light fixtures at the beginning of a run controlled by two three-way switches. Power comes in at the first fixture. Requires two- and three-wire cable.

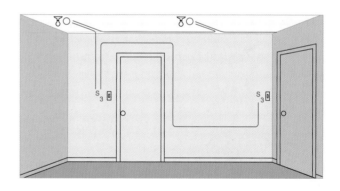

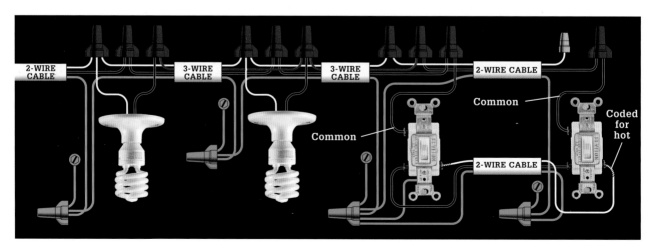

26. FOUR-WAY SWITCH & LIGHT FIXTURE (FIXTURE AT START OF CABLE RUN)

This layout lets you control a light fixture from three locations. The end switches are three-way, and the middle is four-way. A pair of three-wire cables enter the box of the four-way switch. The white and red wires from one cable attach to the top pair of screw terminals (line 1), and the white and red wires from the other cable attach to the bottom screw terminals (line 2). Requires two three-way switches and one four-way switch and two-wire and three-wire cables.

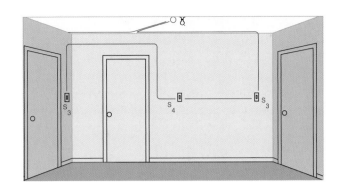

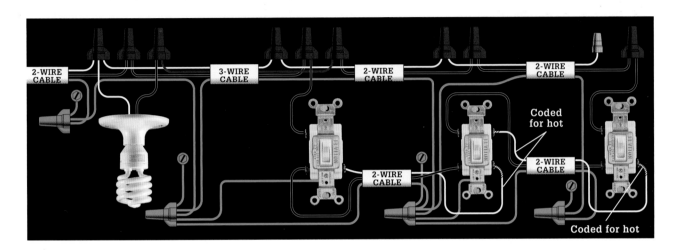

27. FOUR-WAY SWITCH & LIGHT FIXTURE (FIXTURE AT END OF CABLE RUN)

Use this layout variation of circuit map 26 where it is more practical to locate the fixture at the end of the cable run. Requires two three-way switches and one four-way switch and two-wire and three-wire cables.

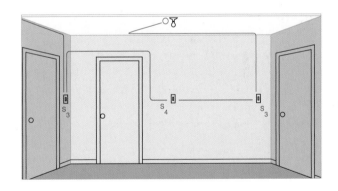

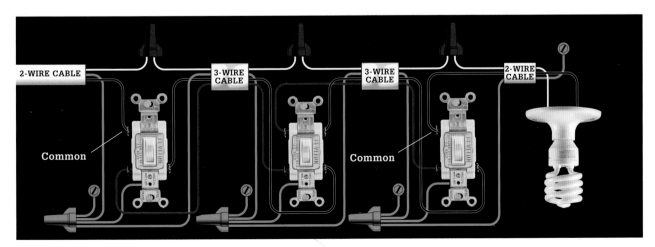

28. MULTIPLE FOUR-WAY SWITCHES CONTROLLING A LIGHT FIXTURE

This alternate variation of the four-way switch layout (circuit map 27) is used where three or more switches will control a single fixture. The outer switches are three-way, and the middle are four-way. Requires two three-way switches and two four-way switches and two-wire and three-wire cables.

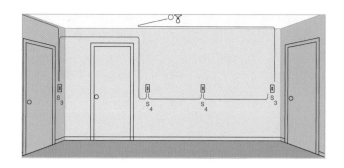

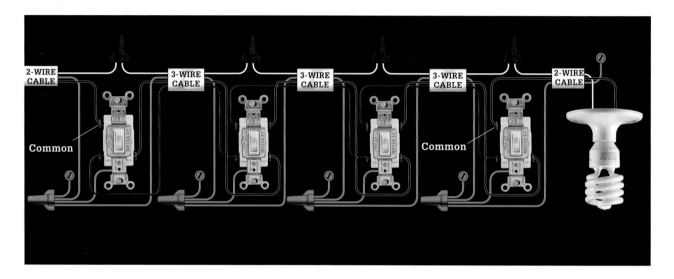

29. FOUR-WAY SWITCHES & MULTIPLE LIGHT FIXTURES

This variation of the four-way switch layout (circuit map 26) is used where two or more fixtures will be controlled from multiple locations in a room. Outer switches are three-way, and the middle switch is a four-way. Requires two three-way switches and one four-way switch and two-wire and three-wire cables.

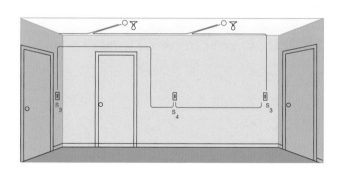

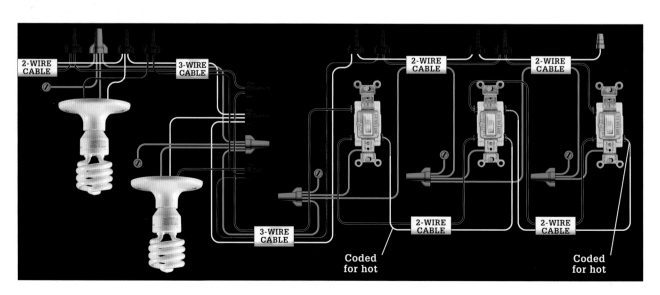

30. CEILING FAN/LIGHT FIXTURE CONTROLLED BY GANGED SWITCHES (FAN AT END OF CABLE RUN)

This layout is for a combination ceiling fan/light fixture controlled by a speed-control switch and dimmer in a double-gang switch box. Requires two-wire and three-wire cables.

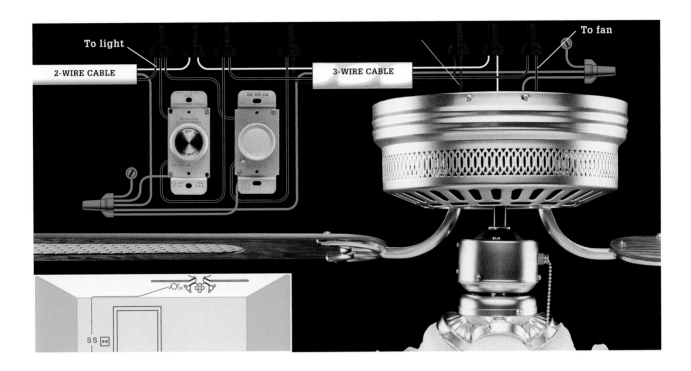

31. CEILING FAN/LIGHT FIXTURE CONTROLLED BY GANGED SWITCHES (SWITCHES AT END OF CABLE RUN)

Use this switch loop layout variation when it is more practical to install the ganged speed control and dimmer switches for the ceiling fan at the end of the cable run. Requires two-wire and parallel runs of two-wire cables.

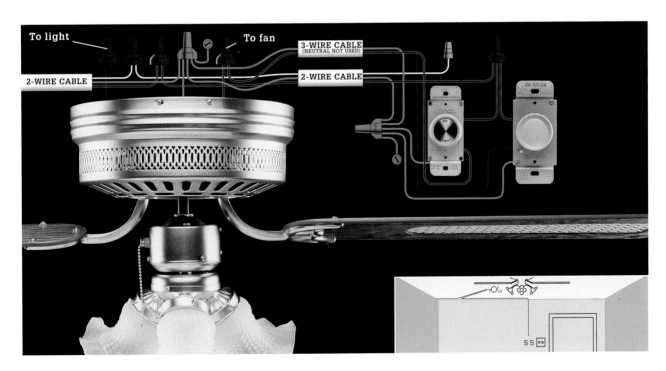

Common Wiring Projects

The instructions that follow show you how to accomplish the most popular home wiring projects. Refer to pertinent sections elsewhere in the book to find background information on tools and skills needed to get the job done.

In this chapter:

- GFCI & AFCI Breakers
- Whole-House Surge Arrestors
- Service Panels
- Grounding & Bonding a Wiring System
- Subpanels
- 120/240-Volt Dryer Receptacles
- 120/240-Volt Range Receptacles
- Ceiling Lights
- Recessed Ceiling Lights
- Track Lights
- Undercabinet Lights
- Vanity Lights
- Low-Voltage Cable Lights
- Hard-Wired Smoke & CO Alarms
- Landscape Lights
- Doorbells
- Programmable Thermostats
- Wireless Switches
- Baseboard Heaters
- Wall Heaters
- Underfloor Radiant Heat Systems
- Ceiling Fans
- Remote-Control Ceiling Fan Retrofit
- Bathroom Exhaust Fans
- Range Hoods
- Backup Power Supply
- Installing a Transfer Switch
- Outbuildings
- Motion-Sensing Floodlights
- Standalone Solar Lighting System

GFCI & AFCI Breakers

Understanding the difference between GFCI (ground-fault circuit interrupter) and AFCI (arc fault circuit interrupter) is tricky for most homeowners. Essentially it comes down to this: Arc-fault interrupters keep your house from burning down; ground-fault interrupters keep people from being electrocuted.

The National Electric Code (NEC) requires that an AFCI breaker be installed on most branch circuits that supply outlets or fixtures in newly constructed homes. The NEC also requires adding AFCI protection to these circuits when you add new circuits and modify or extend existing circuits. They're a prudent precaution in any home, especially if it has older wiring. AFCI breakers will not interfere with the operation of GFCI receptacles, so it is safe to install an AFCI breaker on a circuit that contains GFCI receptacles.

GROUND-FAULT CIRCUIT-INTERRUPTERS

A GFCI is an important safety device that disconnects a circuit in the event of a ground fault (when current takes a path other than the neutral back to the panel).

On new construction, GFCI protection is required for receptacles in these locations: kitchen counter tops, bathrooms, garages, unfinished basements, crawlspaces, outdoors, within six feet of sinks, and in unfinished accessory buildings such as storage and work sheds. In general it is a good practice to protect all receptacle and fixture locations that could encounter damp or wet circumstances.

Tools & Materials ▸

Insulated
  screwdriver
Circuit tester

Combination tool
AFCI or
  GFCI breaker

ARC-FAULT CIRCUIT INTERRUPTERS

AFCIs detect arcing (sparks) that can cause fires between and along damaged wires. AFCI protection is required for 15- and 20-amp, 120-volt circuits that serve living rooms, family rooms, dens, parlors, libraries, dining rooms, bedrooms, sun rooms, kitchens, laundry areas, closets, and hallways. AFCI protection is not required for circuits serving bathrooms, garages, the exterior of the home, appliances such as furnaces and air handlers.

The easiest way to provide AFCI protection for a circuit is to install an AFCI circuit breaker labeled as a "combination" device in the electrical panel. The 2014 NEC allows several alternate methods of providing AFCI protection, but you should consult an electrician before using these alternate methods. You should install combination AFCI circuit breakers when installing new circuits that require AFCI protection. You should install either combination AFCI circuit breakers or AFCI receptacles when you modify, replace, or extend an existing circuit that requires AFCI protection.

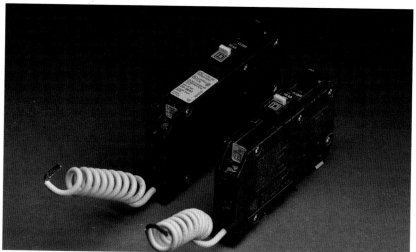

AFCI breakers (left) are similar in appearance to GFCI breakers (right), but they function differently. AFCI breakers trip when they sense an arc fault. GFCI breakers trip when they sense fault between the hot wire and the ground.

An AFCI-protected receptacle

How to Install an AFCI or GFCI Breaker

Locate the breaker for the circuit you'd like to protect. Turn off the main circuit breaker. Remove the cover from the panel, and test to ensure that power is off (see page 80). Remove the breaker you want to replace from the panel. Remove the black wire from the LOAD terminal of the breaker.

Find the white wire on the circuit you want to protect, and remove it from the neutral bus bar.

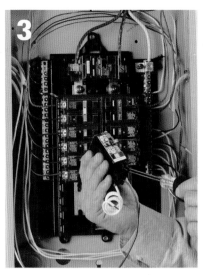

Flip the handle of the new AFCI or GFCI breaker to OFF. Loosen both of the breaker's terminal screws. Connect the white circuit wire to the breaker terminal labeled PANEL NEUTRAL. Connect the black circuit wire to the breaker terminal labeled LOAD POWER.

Connect the new breaker's coiled white wire to the neutral bus bar on the service panel.

Make sure all the connections are tight. Snap the new breaker into the bus bar.

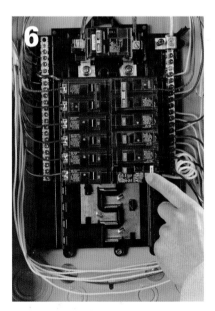

Turn the main breaker on. Turn off and unplug all fixtures and appliances on the AFCI or GFCI breaker circuit. Turn the AFCI or GFCI breaker on. Press the test button. If the breaker is wired correctly, the breaker trips open. If it doesn't trip, check all connections or consult an electrician. Replace the panel cover.

Whole-House Surge Arrestors

Electrical surges caused by lighting or utility malfunctions can destroy or seriously damage sensitive electronics. Many homes contain tens of thousands of dollars worth of computers and home entertainment equipment protected by no more than a $10 plug-in surge suppressor. While these devices do afford a modest level of protection, they are no match for the voltage a lightning strike will push through a system. And they offer no protection for the wiring itself. Whole-house surge arrestors provide comprehensive protection for the wiring and devices attached to it.

Whole-house surge arrestors are available in two basic types. One type is wired on the utility side of the panel, normally at the meter. When installed by a licensed electrician, these devices provide the highest level of protection, shielding the panel and all electrical devices in the house. The other type wires directly into the panel and protects all circuits originating at that panel. Manufacturers offer units that are housed in separate boxes (these look like a small subpanel) as well as models that are designed to replace a double-pole breaker in the panel itself. These install like standard breakers. Both types provide protection for the whole house. Freestanding models are also available with separate protection for phone, data, and cable-television lines—a wise addition if you need to protect networked computers or cable-TV receivers.

Whatever style you choose, look for models with the Underwriters Laboratories 1449 rating and indicator lights showing that the system is protected. Most manufacturers also include a warranty against defect that covers a certain amount of property damage.

A whole-house surge arrestor is an inexpensive defense against expensive damage from high-voltage shocks caused by lightning strikes and power surges. Most models install next to the main panel.

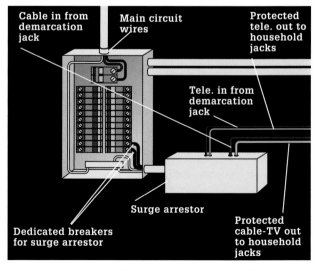

A surge arrestor installed at the panel protects all downstream connected devices and wires.

Tools & Materials ▸

Hammer	Conduit nipple
Combination tool	and locknuts
Screwdrivers	Two 15- or
Cable ripper	20-amp single-
Linesman's pliers	pole breakers
Circuit tester	Coaxial cable
Crimping tools	and terminators
Whole-house	UTP cable
surge arrestor	and terminators

How to Install a Whole-House Surge Arrestor

Turn off power at the main breaker. Remove the cover, and test to make sure the power is off. Mount the arrestor near the service panel following the manufacturer's instructions. Typically the arrestor mounts on one side of the panel so its knockout lines up with a lower knockout on the panel. Remove the knockout on the panel. Install a conduit nipple on the arrestor, and thread the wires from the arrestor through the nipple and into the panel. Slip the other end of the nipple through the opening in the panel, and tighten the locknut. Secure the box to the wall with screws as directed.

Connect the two black wires to two dedicated 15- or 20-amp breakers. Trim the wires as short as possible without making sharp bends. Connect the white neutral wire to the neutral bar and the green grounding wire to the grounding bar. Keep wire lengths as short as possible. Snap the new breakers into the bus bar. Restore the power and carefully test that the voltage between the two black arrestor leads is 240 volts. Replace the panel cover and the arrestor cover. If the arrestor has indicator lights, they should glow, showing that the system is now protected.

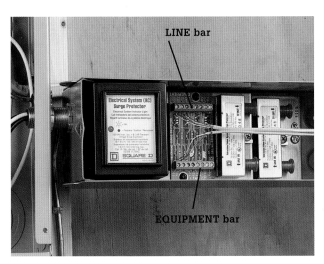

LINE bar

EQUIPMENT bar

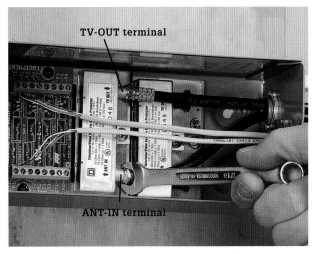

TV-OUT terminal

ANT-IN terminal

Variation: If the arrestor has separate protection for the telephone circuits, remove the cable that runs from the phone demarcation jack to the junction box. Then remove a knockout in the arrestor and route a new UTP cable from the demarcation jack to the arrestor. Strip insulation from the wires and connect them to the terminals on the LINE bar (labeled IN on some models) on the phone protection module in the arrestor. Run a UTP cable from the EQUIPMENT bar (labeled OUT on some models) to the junction box. Strip and connect the wires from this cable to the appropriate terminals in the arrestor and the junction box.

Variation: If the arrestor has separate protection for a cable television circuit, remove the appropriate knockout from the arrestor and run a coaxial cable to the arrestor from the cable-TV demarcation jack. Connect the coaxial cable to the ANT-IN terminal on the cable-TV protection module. Run another coaxial cable from the TV-OUT terminal to the cable TV junction box or the distribution panel. Do not overtighten the connections.

Service Panels

Only a generation ago, fuse boxes were commonplace. But as our demands for power increased, homeowners replaced the 60-amp boxes with larger, safer, and more reliable circuit breaker panels. Typical new homes were built with perfectly adequate 100-amp load centers. But today, as average home size has risen to more than 2,500 sq. ft. and the number of home electronics has risen exponentially, 100 amps is often inadequate service. As a result, many homeowners have upgraded to 200-amp service, and new single-family homes often include 250 amps or even 400 amp service.

Upgrading your electrical service panel from 100 amps to 200 amps is an ambitious project that requires a lot of forethought. The first step is to obtain a permit. When you are ready to begin, you will need to have your utility company disconnect your house from electrical service at the transformer that feeds your house. When you schedule this, talk to your utility company about the size of your service drop or lateral. That may need to be upgraded too. Not only does this involve working them into your schedule, it means you will have no power during the project. You can rent a portable generator to provide a circuit or two, or you can run a couple extension cords from a friendly neighbor. But unless you are a very fast worker, plan on being without power for at least one to two days while the project is in process.

Also check with your utility company to make sure you know what equipment is theirs and what belongs to you. In most cases, the electric meter and everything on the street side belongs to the power company, and the meter base and everything on the house side is yours. Be aware that if you tamper with the sealed meter in any way, you likely will be fined. Utility companies will not re-energize your system without approval from your inspecting agency.

Upgrading a service panel is a major project. Do not hesitate to call for help at any point if you're unsure what to do.

Tools & Materials ▸

200-amp load center (service panel)	Weatherhead
	Service cable
200-amp bypass meter base	Circuit wires
	Plywood backer board
Circuit breakers (AFCI if required by local code)	Screwdrivers
	Drill/driver
	Tape
Schedule 80 or RMC conduit and fittings	Allen wrench
	Circuit tester
	Multimeter

After

Before

Modern homeowners consume more power than our forebears, and it is often necessary to upgrade the electrical service to keep pace. While homeowners are not allowed to make the final electrical service connections, removing the old panel and installing the new panel and meter base yourself can save you hundreds or even thousands of dollars.

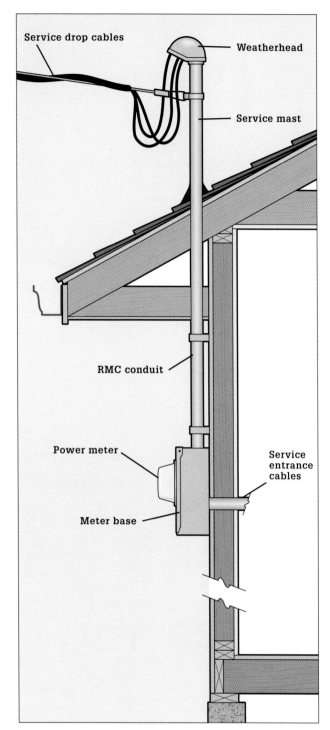

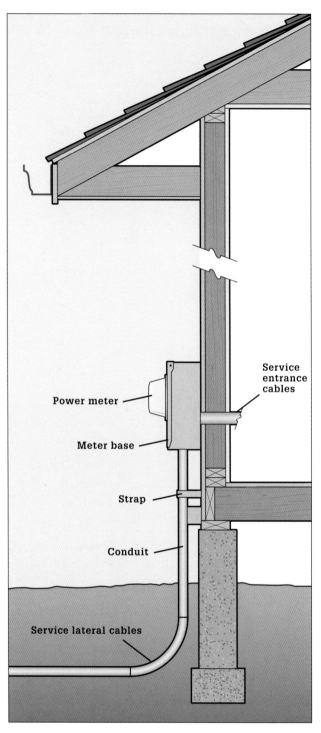

Aboveground service drop. In this common configuration, the service cables from the closest transformer (called the service drop) connect to service entrance wires near the weatherhead. This connection is called the service point and is where your property usually begins. The service entrance wires from the weatherhead are routed to a power meter that's owned by your utility company but is housed in a base that's considered your property. From the meter the service entrance wires enter your house through the wall and are routed to the main service panel, where they are connected to the main circuit breaker.

Underground service lateral. Increasingly, homebuilders are choosing to have power supplied to their new homes underground instead of an overhead service drop. Running the cables in the ground eliminates problems with power outages caused by ice accumulation or fallen trees, but it entails a completely different set of cable and conduit requirements. For the homeowner, however, the differences are minimal, because the hookups are identical once the power service reaches the meter.

Locating Your New Panel ▸

Local codes dictate where the main service panel may be placed relative to other parts of your home. Although the codes vary (and always take precedence), national codes stipulate that a service panel (or any other distribution panel) may not be located near flammable materials, in a bathroom, clothes closet or other area designated for storage, above stairway steps, or directly above a workbench or other permanent work station or appliance. The panel also can't be located in a crawl space. If you are installing a new service entry hookup, there are many regulations regarding height of the service drop and the meter. Contact your local inspections office for specific regulations.

All the equipment you'll need to upgrade your main panel is sold at most larger building centers. It includes (A) a new 200-amp panel; (B) a 200-amp bypass meter base (also called a socket); (C) individual circuit breakers (if your new panel is the same brand as your old one you may be able to reuse the old breakers); (D) new, THW, THHW, THWN-2. RHW, RHW-2, XHHW (2/0 copper seen here); (E) 2" dia. rigid metallic conduit; (F) weatherhead shroud for mast.

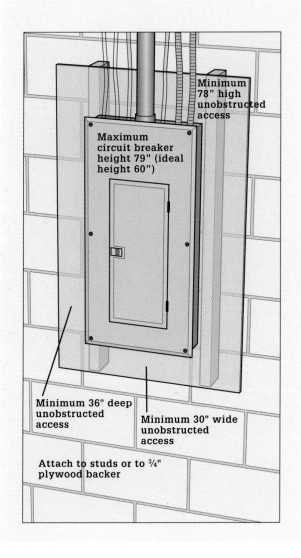

Minimum 78" high unobstructed access

Maximum circuit breaker height 79" (ideal height 60")

Minimum 36" deep unobstructed access

Minimum 30" wide unobstructed access

Attach to studs or to ¾" plywood backer

Meter

Shutoff switch

The main circuit breaker (called the service equipment) may need to be located outside next to the electric meter if your main panel is too far away from the point where the service cable enters your house. The maximum distance allowed varies widely, from as little as 3 ft. to more than 10 ft. Wiring the service cable through the shutoff has the effect of transforming your main panel into a subpanel, which will impact how the neutral and ground wires are attached (see Subpanels, pages 186 to 189).

How to Replace a Main Panel

Shut off power to the house at the transformer. This must be done by a technician who is certified by your utility company. Also have the utility worker remove the old meter from the base. It is against the law for a homeowner to break the seal on the meter.

Label all incoming circuit wires before disconnecting them. Labels should be written clearly on tape that is attached to the cables outside of the existing service panel. Test the circuits before starting to make sure they are labeled correctly.

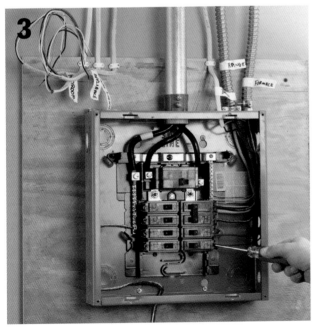

Disconnect incoming circuit wires from breakers, grounding bar, and neutral bus bar. Also disconnect cable clamps at the knockouts on the panel box. Retract all circuit wires from the service panel and coil it up neatly, with the labels clearly visible.

Unscrew the lugs securing the service entry cables at the top of the panel. For 240-volt service you will find two heavy-gauge SE cables, probably with black sheathing. Each cable carries 120 volts of electricity. A neutral service cable, usually of smaller gauge than the SE cables, will be attached to the neutral bus bar. This cable returns current to the source.

(continued)

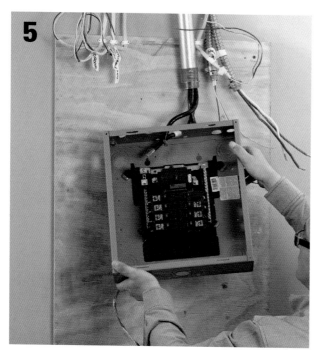

5

Remove the old service panel box. Boxes are rated for a maximum current capacity; and if you are upgrading, the components in the old box will be undersized for the new service levels. The new box will have a greater number of circuit slots as well.

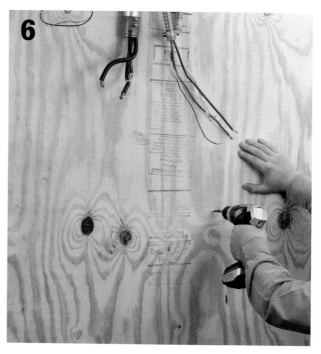

6

Replace the old panel backer board with a larger board in the installation area (see sidebar, page 174). A piece of ¾" plywood is typical. Make sure the board is well secured at wall framing members.

7

Attach the new service panel box to the backer board, making sure that at least two screws are driven through the backer and into wall studs. Drill clearance holes in the back of the box at stud locations if necessary. Use roundhead screws that do not have tapered shanks so the screwhead seats flat against the panel.

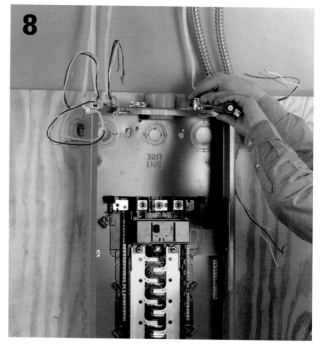

8

Attach properly sized cable clamps to the box at the knockout holes. Install one cable per knockout in this type of installation and plan carefully to avoid removing knockouts that you do not need to remove (if you do make a mistake, you can fill the knockout hole with a plug).

Splicing in the Box ▸

Some wiring codes allow you to make splices inside the panel box if the circuit wire is too short. Use the correct wire cap and wind electrical tape over the conductors where they enter the cap. If your municipality does not allow splices in the panel box, you'll have to rectify a short cable by splicing it in a junction box before it reaches the panel and then replacing the cable with a longer section for the end of the run. Make sure each circuit line has at least 12" of slack.

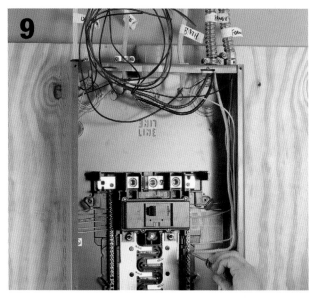

Attach the white neutral from each circuit cable to the neutral bus bar. Most panels have a preinstalled neutral bus bar, but in some cases you may need to purchase the bar separately and attach it to the panel back. The panel should also have a separate grounding bar that you also may need to purchase separately. Attach the grounds as well.

Attach the hot lead wire to the terminal on the circuit breaker, and then snap the breaker into an empty slot. When loading slots, start at the top of the panel and work your way downward. It is important that you balance the circuits as you go to equalize the amperage. For example, do not install all the 15-amp circuits on one side and all the 20-amp circuits on the other.

Create an accurate circuit index and affix it to the inside of the service panel door. List all loads that are on the circuit as well as the amperage. Once you have restored power to the new service panel (see step 18), test out each circuit to make sure you don't have any surprises. With the main breakers on, shut off all individual circuit breakers, and then flip each one on by itself. Walk through your house and test every switch and receptacle to confirm the loads on that circuit.

(continued)

12

Install grounding conductors (see pages 180 to 185). Local codes are very specific about how the grounding and bonding needs to be accomplished. For example, some require multiple rods driven at least 6 ft. apart. Discuss your grounding requirements thoroughly with your inspector or an electrician before making your plan.

13

Replace the old meter base (have the utility company remove the meter when they shut off power to the house, step 1). Remove the old meter base, also called a socket, and install a new base that's rated for the amperage of your new power service. Here, a 200-amp bypass meter base is being installed.

14

Update the conduit that runs from your house to the bottom of the meter base. This should be 2" rigid conduit in good repair. Attach the conduit to the base and wall with the correct fittings. Rigid metal conduit is a good option, but Schedule 80 PVC is probably the best choice for housing the service entrance wires.

15

Install new service entrance wires. Each wire carries 120 volts from the meter to the service wire lugs at the top of your service panel. Code is very specific about how these connections are made. In most cases, you'll need to tighten the terminal nuts with a specific amount of torque that requires a torque wrench to measure. Also attach the sheathed neutral wire to the neutral/grounding lug.

16

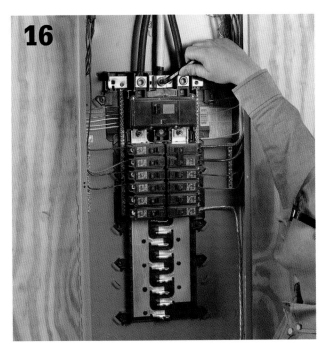

Attach the SE wires to the lugs connected to the main breakers at the top of your service entry panel. Do not remove too much insulation on the wires—leaving the wires exposed is a safety hazard. The neutral service entry wire is attached either directly to the neutral bus bar or to a metal bridge that is connected to the neutral bonding bus bar. Install the green grounding screw provided with the panel.

17

Install service entrance wires from the meter to the weatherhead, where the connections to the service drop wires are made. Only an agent for your public utility company may make the hookup at the weatherhead.

Tall Mast, Short Roof ▸

The service drop must occur at least 10 ft. above ground level, and as much as 14 ft. in some cases. Occasionally, this means that you must run the conduit for the service mast up through the eave of your roof and seal the roof penetration with a boot.

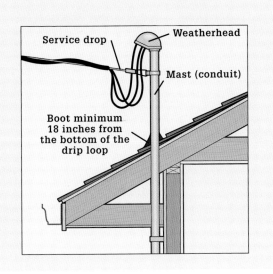

18

Have the panel and all connections inspected and approved by your local building department, and then contact the public utility company to make the connections at the power drop. Once the connections are made, turn the main breakers on and test all circuits.

Grounding & Bonding a Wiring System

All home electrical systems must be bonded and grounded according to code standards. This entails two tasks: the metal water and gas pipes must be connected electrically to create a continuous low resistance path back to the main electrical panel; and the main electrical panel must be grounded to a grounding electrode such as a ground rod or rods driven into the earth near the foundation of your house. Although the piping system is bonded to the ground through your main electrical service panel, the panel grounding and the piping bonding are unrelated when it comes to function. The grounding wire that runs from your electrical panel to grounding electrode helps even out voltage increases that often occur because of lightning and other causes. The wires that bond your metal piping are preventative, and they only become important in the unlikely event that an electrical conductor energizes the pipe. In that case, correct bonding of the piping system will ensure that the current does not remain in the system, where it could electrocute anyone who touches a part of the system, such as a faucet handle. Bonding is done relatively efficiently at the water heater, as the gas piping and water piping generally there.

Gas pipe in older homes is usually steel or copper. The bonding connection point for these pipes can be at any accessible location, such as at the water heater or at the gas meter. Gas pipe in some new homes is a flexible material called corrugated stainless steel tubing (CSST). The bonding point for CSST must be at the first piece of steel or copper pipe where the gas service enters the home. This is because lightning can blow holes in CSST, causing a gas leak.

A pair of 8-ft.-long metal ground rods are driven into the earth next to your house to provide a path to ground for your home wiring system.

Tools & Materials ▸

Hammer	3 pipe
Straight edge	ground clamps
screwdriver	Eye and ear
Drill	protection
½" drill bit	Work gloves
A length of	Grounding rods
ground wire	5-lb. maul
Some wire staples	Caulk

How to Bond Metallic Piping

Determine the amperage rating of your electrical service by looking at your main breakers. The system amperage (usually 100 or 200 amps) determines the required gauge of the bonding wire you need. #4 copper wire is sufficient for service not exceeding 200 amps. Smaller, less expensive copper wire is allowed for services between 100 and 175 amps. Check with your electrical inspector if you want to use wire smaller than #4.

Run the bonding wire from a point near your water heater (a convenient spot if you have a gas-fueled water heater) to an exit point where the wire can be bonded to the grounding wire that leads to the exterior grounding electrodes. This is frequently done at the service panel. Run this wire as you would any other cable, leaving approximately 6 to 8 ft. of wire at the water heater. If you are running this wire through the ceiling joists, drill a ½" hole as close to the center as possible to not weaken the joist. Staple the wire every 2 ft. if running it parallel to the joists.

Install pipe ground clamps on each pipe (hot water supply, cold water supply, gas), roughly a foot above the water heater. Do not install clamps near a union or elbow because the tightening of the clamps could break or weaken soldered joints. Also make sure the pipes are free and clear of any paint, rust, or any other contaminant that may inhibit a good clean connection. Do not overtighten the clamps. Use clamps that are compatible with the pipe so that corrosion will not occur. Use copper or brass clamps on copper pipe. Use brass or steel clamps on steel pipe.

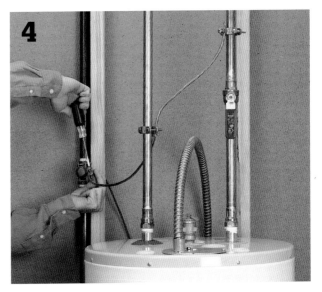

Route the ground wire through each clamp wire hole and then tighten the clamps onto the wire. Do not cut or splice the wire: The same wire should run through all clamps.

(continued)

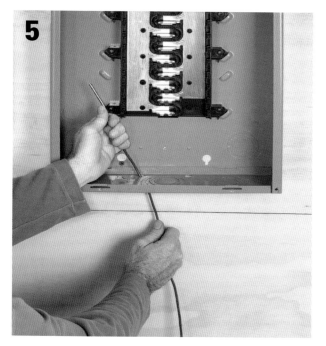

5

At the panel, turn off the main breaker. Open the cover by removing the screws, and set the cover aside. Route the ground wire through a small ⅜" hole provided towards the rear of the panel on the top or bottom. You will usually have to knock the plug out of this hole by placing a screwdriver on it from the outside and tapping with a hammer. Make sure the ground wire will not come into contact with the bus bars in the middle of the panel or any of the load terminals on the breakers.

6

Locate an open hole on your ground and neutral bus and insert the ground wire. These holes are large enough to accommodate up to a #4 awg wire, but it may be difficult at times. If you're having trouble pushing the wire in, trim a little wire off the end and try with a clean cut piece. Secure the set screw at the lug. Replace the panel cover and turn the main breaker back on.

Tips for Grounding the Main Service Panel

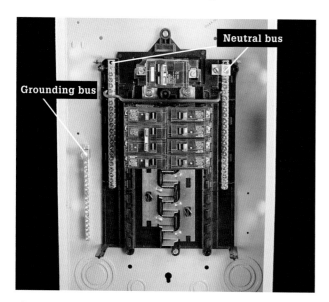

Neutral bus

Grounding bus

The neutral and grounding wires should not be connected to the same bus in most subpanels. The grounding bus should be bonded to the subpanel cabinet. The neutral bus should not be bonded to the subpanel cabinet.

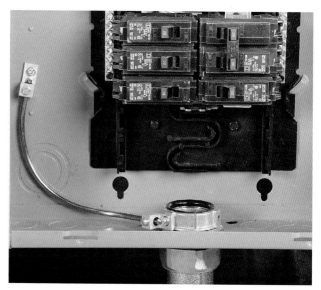

Metallic conduit must be physically and electrically connected to panel cabinets. A bonding bushing may be required in some cases, where not all of a knockout is removed.

Ground Rod Installation

The ground rod is an essential part of the grounding system. Its primary function is to create a path to ground for electrical current, such as lightning, line surges, and unintentional contact with high voltage lines. If you upgrade your electrical service you likely will need to upgrade your grounding wire and rods to meet code.

Note: Different municipalities have different requirements for grounding, so be sure to check with the AHJ (Authority Having Jurisdiction) first before attempting to do this yourself.

Call before you dig! Make sure the area where you will be installing the ground rods is free and clear from any underground utilities.

Exercise Your Breakers ▸

Your breakers (including the main) should be "exercised" once a year to ensure proper mechanical function. Simply turn them off and then back on. A convenient time to perform the exercise is at daylight savings time, when you'll need to reset all of your clocks anyway.

How to Install a Grounding Electrode System

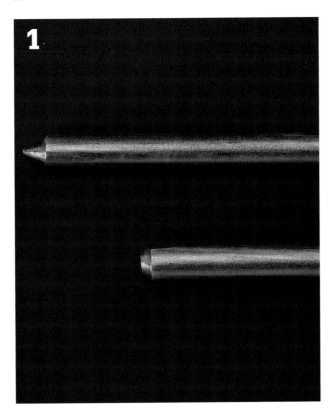

1

Begin by purchasing two copper-coated steel ground rods ⅝" diameter by 8' long. Grounding rods have a driving point on one end and a striking face on the other end.

2

Drill a 5/16" hole in the rim joist of your house, as close as practical to the main service panel to the outside of the house above the ground level at least 6".

(continued)

7

Dig out a few inches around each rod to create clearance for the five-pound maul. Creating a shallow trench beneath the grounding wire between the rods is also a good idea. Drive each rod with the maul until the top of the rod is a few inches below grade.

8

Inject caulk into the hole in the rim joist on both the interior and exterior side.

Tips for Grounding

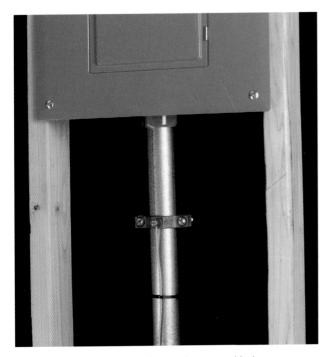

A listed metal strap may be used to ground indoor communication wires such as telephone and cable TV if an intersystem bonding terminal is not available.

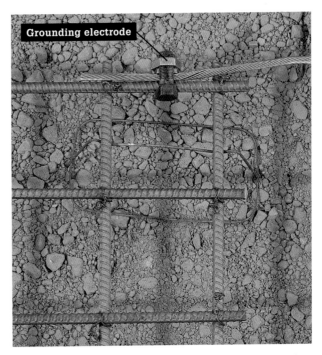

Grounding electrode

A piece of reinforcing bar encased in a concrete footing is a common grounding electrode in new construction. Called an ufer, the electrode must be No. 4 or larger rebar and at least 20 ft. long. (Shown prior to pouring concrete.)

Subpanels

Install circuit breaker subpanels if the main circuit breaker panel does not have enough open breaker slots for the new circuits you are planning. Subpanels serve as a second distribution center for connecting circuits. They receive power from a double-pole circuit breaker you install in the main circuit breaker panel.

If the main service panel is so full that there is no room for the double-pole subpanel breaker, you can reconnect some of the existing 120-volt circuits to special slimline breakers (photos below).

Plan your subpanel installation carefully, making sure your electrical service supplies enough power to support the extra load of the new subpanel circuits. Assuming your main service is adequate, consider installing an oversized subpanel breaker in the main panel to provide enough extra amps to meet the needs of future wiring projects.

Also consider the physical size of the subpanel, and choose one that has enough extra slots to hold circuits you may want to install later. The smallest panels have room for up to six single-pole breakers

(or three double-pole breakers), while the largest models can hold 20 single-pole breakers or more.

Subpanels often are mounted near the main circuit breaker panel. Or, for convenience, they can be installed close to the areas they serve, such as in a new room addition or a garage. In a finished room, a subpanel can be painted or housed in a decorative cabinet so it is less of a visual distraction. If it is covered, make sure the subpanel is easily accessible and clearly identified.

Tools & Materials ▸

Hammer	Cable clamps
Screwdriver	Three-wire NM cable
Circuit tester	Cable staples
Cable ripper	Double-pole circuit breaker
Combination tool	Circuit breaker subpanel
Screws	Slimline circuit breakers

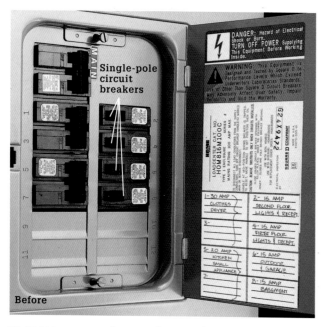
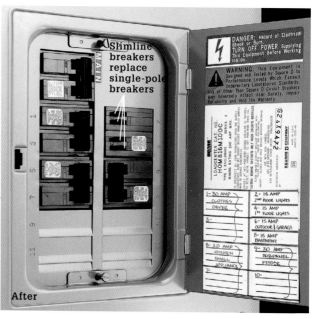

To conserve space in a service panel, you can replace single-pole breakers with slimline breakers. Slimline breakers take up half the space of standard breakers, allowing you to fit two circuits into one single slot on the service panel. In the service panel shown above, four single-pole 120-volt breakers were replaced with slimline breakers to provide the double opening needed for a 30-amp, 240-volt subpanel feeder breaker. Use slimline breakers (if your municipality allows them) with the same amp rating as the standard single-pole breakers you are removing, and make sure they are approved for use in your panel. If your municipality and panel allow slimline breakers, there may be restrictions on the quantity and location where they may be installed on the panel.

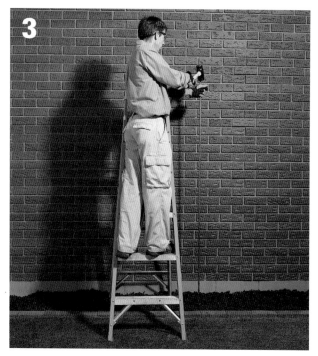

About a foot from the foundation of the house, pound one ground rod into the earth with a five-pound maul. If you encounter a rock or other obstruction, you can pound the ground rod at an angle as long as it does not exceed 45°. Drive until only 3" or 4" of the rod is above ground. Measure at least 6 ft. from the first ground rod and pound in another one.

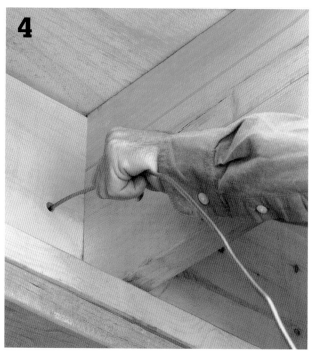

Run uninsulated #4 copper wire from the ground bus in your main service panel through the hole in the rim joist and to the exterior of the house, leaving enough wire to connect the two ground rods together.

Using a brass clamp commonly referred to as an acorn, connect the wire to the first ground rod, pulling the wire taut so no slack exists. Continue pulling the wire to reach the second grounding rod, creating a continuous connection.

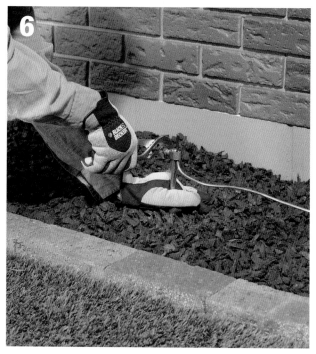

Connect the second ground rod with another acorn to the uncut grounding wire previously pulled through the first acorn. Trim the excess wire.

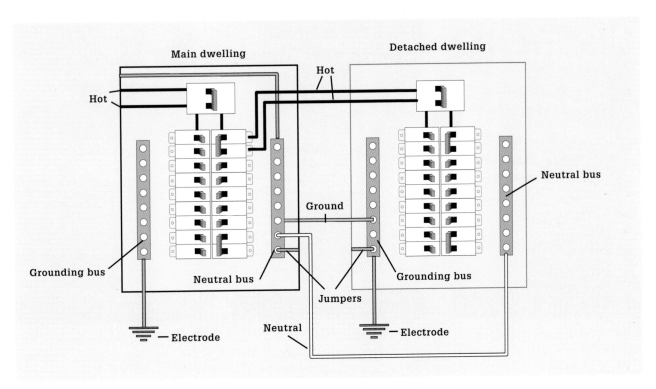

Wiring diagram for wiring a feeder from the main service panel to a subpanel in a separate building.

How to Install a Subpanel

Subpanels are subject to the same installation and clearance rules as service panels. The subpanel can be mounted to the sides of studs or to plywood attached between two studs. The panel shown here extends ½" past the face of studs so it will be flush with the finished wall surface.

Open a knockout in the subpanel using a screwdriver and hammer. Run the feeder cable from the main circuit breaker panel to the subpanel, leaving about 2 ft. of excess cable at each end. See page 40 if you need to run the cable through finished walls.

Attach a cable clamp to the knockout in the subpanel. Insert the cable into the subpanel, and then anchor it to framing members within 8" of each panel and every 54" thereafter.

(continued)

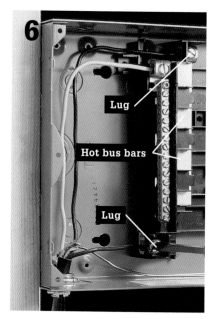

Strip away outer sheathing from the feeder cable using a cable ripper. Leave at least ¼" of sheathing extending into the subpanel. Tighten the cable clamp screws so the cable is held securely, but not so tightly that the wire sheathing is crushed.

Strip ½" of insulation from the white neutral feeder wire, and attach it to the main lug on the subpanel neutral bus bar. Connect the grounding wire to a setscrew terminal on the grounding bus bar. Fold excess wire around the inside edge of the subpanel.

Strip away ½" of insulation from the red and the black feeder wires. Attach one wire to the main lug on each of the hot bus bars. Fold excess wire around the inside edge of the subpanel.

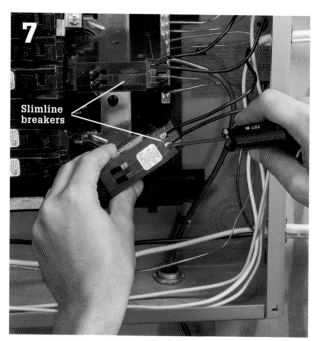

At the main circuit breaker panel, shut off the main circuit breaker, and then remove the coverplate and test for power (page 80). If necessary, make room for the double-pole feeder breaker by removing single-pole breakers and reconnecting the wires to slimline circuit breakers. Open a knockout for the feeder cable using a hammer and screwdriver. Note: some panels do not allow slimline breakers and some restrict where slimline breakers can be installed. Read the instructions on the panel cover.

Strip away the outer sheathing from the feeder cable so that at least ¼" of sheathing will reach into the main service panel. Attach a cable clamp to the cable, and then insert the cable into the knockout, and anchor it by threading a locknut onto the clamp. Tighten the locknut by driving a screwdriver against the lugs. Tighten the clamp screws so the cable is held securely, but not so tightly that the cable sheathing is crushed.

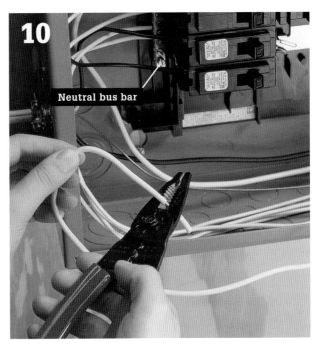

Bend the bare copper wire from the feeder cable around the inside edge of the main circuit breaker panel, and connect it to one of the setscrew terminals on the grounding bus bar.

Strip away ½" of insulation from the white feeder wire. Attach the wire to one of the setscrew terminals on the neutral bus bar. Fold excess wire around the inside edge of the service panel.

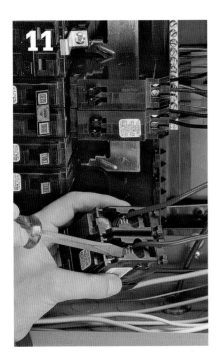

Strip ½" of insulation from the red and the black feeder wires. Attach one wire to each of the setscrew terminals on the double-pole feeder breaker. *Note: If your subpanel arrived with a preinstalled grounding screw in the panel back, remove and discard it.*

Hook the end of the feeder circuit breaker over the guide hooks on the panel, and then push the other end forward until the breaker snaps onto the hot bus bars (follow manufacturer's directions). Fold excess wire around the inside edge of the circuit breaker panel.

If necessary, open two tabs where the double-pole feeder breaker will fit, and then reattach the cover plate. Label the feeder breaker on the circuit index. Turn the main breaker on, but leave the feeder breaker off until all subpanel circuits have been connected and inspected.

120/240-Volt Dryer Receptacles

Many dryers require both 120- and 240-volt power. If you are installing this type of electric dryer, you will need to install a 30-amp, 120/240-volt receptacle that feeds from a dedicated 30-amp double-pole breaker in your service panel. Verify your dryer's electric requirements before wiring a new receptacle.

Begin the installation by identifying a location for the dryer receptacle. Run 10/3 NM cable from the service panel to the new receptacle. If you are mounting the dryer receptacle box on an unfinished masonry wall, run the THNN wire in conduit and secure the box and conduit with masonry screws. If you are mounting the receptacle box in finished drywall, cut a hole, fish the cable through, and mount the receptacle in the wall opening.

Tools & Materials ▸

Combination tool
Drill
Circuit tester
Hammer
Screwdriver
30-amp double-
   pole breaker

30-amp 120/240-volt
   dryer receptacle
10/3 NM cable or 10-gauge
   THHN/THWN
Receptacle box
Conduit
   (for masonry walls)

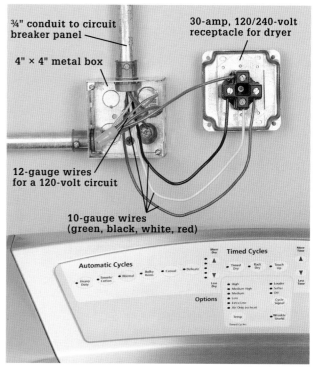

¾" conduit to circuit breaker panel

4" × 4" metal box

30-amp, 120/240-volt receptacle for dryer

12-gauge wires for a 120-volt circuit

10-gauge wires (green, black, white, red)

A 240-volt installation is no more complicated than wiring a single-pole breaker and outlet. The main difference is that the dryer circuit's double-pole breaker is designed to contact both 120-volt bus bars in the service panel. Together these two 120-volt circuits serve the dryer's heating elements with 240 volts of power. The timer, switches, and other dryer electronics utilize the circuit's 120-volt power.

How to Install a 120/240-Volt Dryer Receptacle

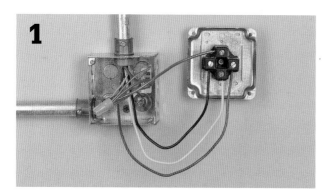

1

Connect the white neutral wire to the silver neutral screw terminal. Connect each of the black and the red wires to either of the brass screw terminals (the terminals are interchangeable). Connect the green ground wire to the receptacle grounding screw. Attach the cover plate.

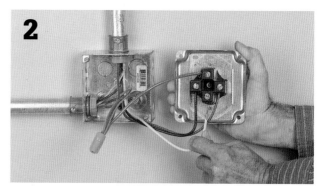

2

With the service panel main breaker shut off, connect the dryer cable to a dedicated 30-amp double-pole breaker. Connect the ground wire to the panel grounding bar. Connect the white neutral wire to the neutral bar. Connect the red and the black wires to the two brass screw terminals on the breaker. Snap the breaker into the bus bar. Attach the panel cover. Turn the breakers on, and test the circuit.

120/240-Volt Range Receptacles

Many electric ranges require both 120- and 240-volt power. If you are installing this type of electric range, you will need to install a 40- or 50-amp 120/240-volt receptacle that feeds from a dedicated 40- or 50-amp breaker in the service panel. Breaker amperage depends on the amount of current the range draws. Verify requirements before wiring a receptacle.

A range receptacle and breaker installation is no more complicated than wiring a single-pole breaker and outlet. The main difference is that the range circuit's double-pole breaker is designed to contact both 120-volt bus bars in the service panel. Together these two 120-volt circuits serve the range's heating elements with 240 volts of power. The timer, switches, and other range electronics utilize the circuit's 120-volt power.

Modern range receptacles accept a four-prong plug configuration. The cable required is four-conductor cable, containing three insulated wires and one ground. The two hot wires might be black and red (shown below) or black and black with a red stripe. The neutral wire is generally white or gray. The grounding wire is green or bare. The size used for a kitchen range is usually 6/3 grounded NM copper cable. The receptacle itself is generally surface mounted for easier installation (shown below), though flush-mounted units are also available.

Tools & Materials ▸

Combination tool	Surface-mounted
Circuit tester	range receptacle
Drill	6/3 grounded
Hammer	NM cable
Screwdriver	40- or 50-amp
Drywall saw	double-pole
Fish tape	circuit breaker

How to Install a Kitchen Range Receptacle

Turn power off. Identify a location for the surface-mounted range receptacle. Cut a small hole in the wall. Fish the cable from the service panel into the wall opening. Thread the cable into a surface-mounted receptacle and clamp it. Strip insulation from the individual wires.

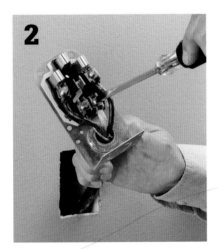

Wire the receptacle. Connect the bare copper ground wire to the receptacle grounding screw. Connect the white neutral wire to the silver neutral screw terminal. Connect each of the hot (black and red) wires to either of the brass screw terminals (the terminals are interchangeable). Mount the housing on the wall and attach the cover plate.

Wire the cable to a 40- or 50-amp breaker. With the main breaker off, remove the panel cover. Remove a knockout from the panel and feed the cable into the panel. Connect the ground to the grounding bar. Connect the neutral wire from the cable to the neutral bar. Connect the red and the black wires to the two brass screw terminals on the breaker. Snap it into the bus bar. Attach the panel cover. Turn the breakers on and test the circuit.

Ceiling Lights

Ceiling fixtures don't have any moving parts, and their wiring is very simple, so, other than changing bulbs, you're likely to get decades of trouble-free service from a fixture. This sounds like a good thing, but it also means that the fixture probably won't fail and give you an excuse to update a room's look with a new one. Fortunately you don't need an excuse. Upgrading a fixture is easy and can make a dramatic impact on a room. You can substantially increase the light in a room by replacing a globe-style fixture with one with separate spot lights, or you can simply install a new fixture that matches the room's décor. Check the weight rating of the box to which you will attach your fixture. Older boxes may not handle a heavy fixture.

Tools & Materials ▸

Replacement light fixture
Wire stripper
Voltage sensor
Insulated screwdrivers
Wire connectors
Eye protection

If you are unsure how much weight the existing box can handle, consider changing the box. New light fixture boxes should handle fixtures up to 50 pounds. Support the fixture independently from the box if the fixture weighs more than 50 pounds.

Installing a new ceiling fixture can provide more light to a space, not to mention an aesthetic lift. It's one of the easiest upgrades you can do.

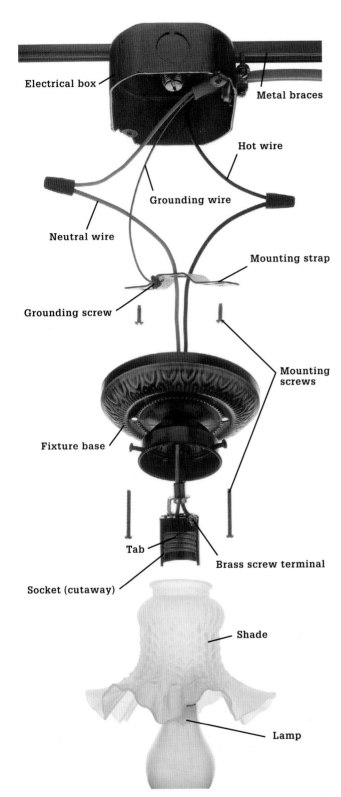

Electrical box

Metal braces

Hot wire

Grounding wire

Neutral wire

Mounting strap

Grounding screw

Mounting screws

Fixture base

Tab

Brass screw terminal

Socket (cutaway)

Shade

Lamp

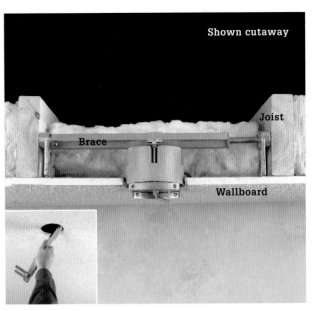

Shown cutaway

Joist

Brace

Wallboard

If the new fixture is much heavier than the original fixture, it will require additional bracing in the ceiling to support the electrical box and the fixture. The manufacturer's instructions should specify the size and type of box. If the ceiling is finished and there is no access from above, you can remove the old box and use an adjustable remodeling brace appropriate for your fixture (shown). The brace fits into a small hole in the ceiling (inset). Once the bracing is in place, install a new electrical box specified for the new fixture.

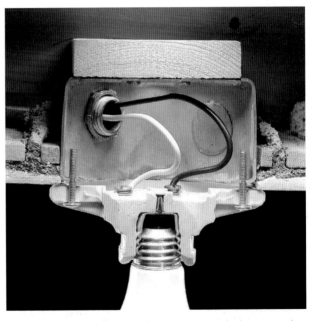

No matter what a ceiling light fixture looks like on the outside, they all attach in basically the same way. An electrical box in the ceiling is fitted with a mounting strap, which holds the fixture in place. The bare wire from the ceiling typically connects to the mounting strap. The two wires coming from the fixture connect to the black and the white wires from the ceiling.

Inexpensive light fixtures have screw terminals mounted directly to the backside of the fixture plate. Often, as seen here, they have no grounding terminal. Some codes do not allow this type of fixture, but even if your hometown does approve them, it is a good idea to replace them with a better quality, safer fixture that is UL-approved.

How to Replace a Ceiling Light

Shut off power to the ceiling light, and remove the shade or diffuser. Loosen the mounting screws and carefully lower the fixture, supporting it as you work (do not let light fixtures hang by their electrical wires alone). Test with a voltage sensor to make sure no power is reaching the connections.

Remove the twist connectors from the fixture wires or unscrew the screw terminals and remove the white neutral wire and the black lead wire (inset).

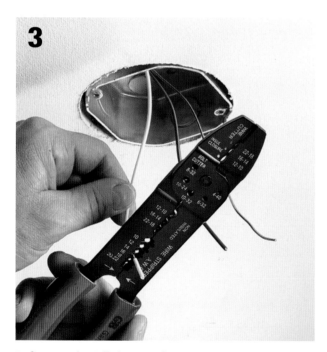

Before you install the new fixture, check the ends of the wires coming from the ceiling electrical box. They should be clean and free of nicks or scorch marks. If they're dirty or worn, clip off the stripped portion with your combination tool. Then strip away about ¾" of insulation from the end of each wire.

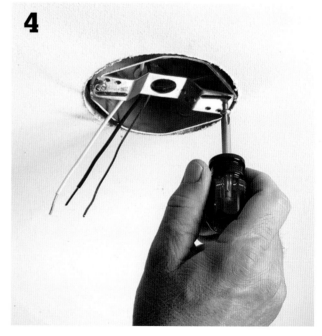

Attach a mounting strap to the ceiling fixture box if there is not one already present. Your new light may come equipped with a strap; otherwise you can find one for purchase at any hardware store.

5

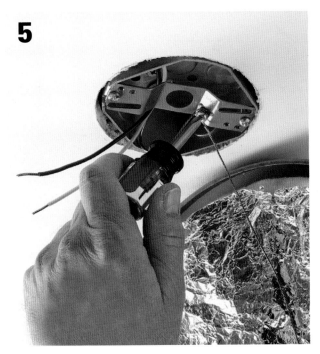

Lift the new fixture up to the ceiling (you may want a helper for this), and attach the bare copper ground wire from the power supply cable to the grounding screw or clip on the mounting strap. Also attach the ground wire from the fixture to the screw or clip.

6

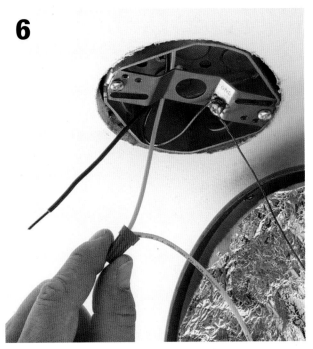

With the fixture supported by a ladder or a helper, join the white wire lead and the white fixture wire with a wire connector (often supplied with the fixture).

7

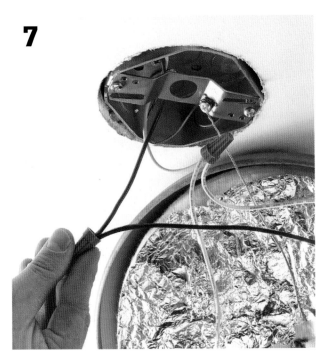

Connect the black power supply wire to the black fixture wire with a wire connector.

8

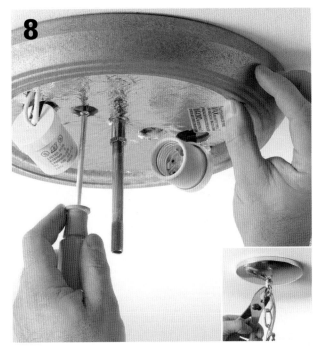

Position the new fixture mounting plate over the box so the mounting screw holes align. Drive the screws until the fixture is secure against the ceiling. *Note: Some fixtures are supported by a threaded rod or nipple in the center that screws into a female threaded opening in the mounting strap (inset).*

Recessed Ceiling Lights

Recessed lights are versatile fixtures suited for a variety of situations. Fixtures rated for outdoor use can also be installed in roof soffits and overhangs for accent and security lighting. Recessed fixtures can also be installed over showers or tubs. Be sure to use fixture cans and trims rated for bathroom use.

There are recessed lighting cans in all shapes and sizes for almost every type of ceiling or cabinet. Cans are sold for unfinished ceilings (new construction) or for finished ceilings (retrofit installation). Cans are also rated as insulation compatible or for uninsulated ceilings. Be sure to use the correct one for your ceiling to prevent creating a fire hazard. The 2012 International Residential Code requires that recessed lights installed in unconditioned spaces (such as attics) be insulation contact (IC) rated, air tight, and sealed to the drywall.

Choose the proper type of recessed light fixture for your project. There are two types of fixtures: those rated for installation within insulation (left), and those which must be kept at least 3" from insulation (right). Self-contained thermal switches shut off power if the unit gets too hot for its rating. A recessed light fixture must be installed at least ½" from combustible materials.

Tools & Materials ▸

Recessed-lighting can for new construction or remodeling and trim
Circuit tester

Cable ripper
Combination tool
Pliers

Fish tape
Hack saw
Drywall saw

NM cable
Work gloves
Eye protection

Recessed ceiling lights often are installed in series to provide exacting control over the amount and direction of light. Spacing the canisters in every other ceiling joist bay is a common practice.

Recessed Materials

Recessed ceiling light housings come in many sizes and styles for various purposes and budgets. Some are sold with trim kits (below) included. Some common types are: new construction recessed housing (sold in economical multipacks) (A); airtight recessed housings (for heated rooms below unheated ceilings) (B); shallow recessed housings (for rooms with 2" × 6" ceiling joists) (C); small aperture recessed housing (D); recessed slope ceiling housing (for vaulted ceilings) (E).

Trim kits for recessed ceiling lights may be sold separately. Common types include: open trim with reflective baffle (A); eyeball trim (B); baffle trim (black) (C); shower light trim (D); open trim (E); baffle trim (full reflective) (F).

How to Install Recessed Ceiling Lights

Mark the location for the light canister. If you are installing multiple lights, measure out from the wall at the start and end of the run, and connect them with a chalkline snapped parallel to the wall. If the ceiling is finished with a surface (wallboard), see next page.

Install the housing for the recessed fixture. Housings for new construction (or remodeling installations where the installation area is fully accessible from either above or below) have integral hanger bars that you attach to each joist in the joist bay.

Run electric cable from the switch to each canister location. Multiple lights are generally installed in series so there is no need to make pigtail connections in the individual boxes. Make sure to leave enough extra cable at each location to feed the wire into the housing and make the connection.

Run the feeder cables into the electrical boxes attached to the canister housings. You'll need to remove knockouts first and make sure to secure the cable with a wire staple within 8" of the entry point to the box.

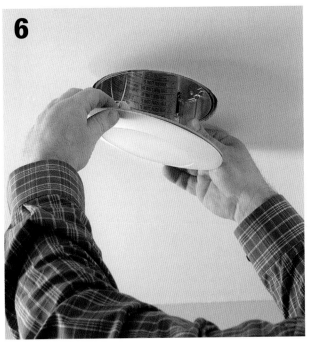

Connect the feeder wires to the fixture wires inside the junction box. Twist the hot lead together with the black fixture wire, as well as the black lead to other fixtures further downline. Also connect the neutral white wires. Join the ground wires and pigtail them to the grounding screw or clip in the box. Finish the ceiling, as desired.

Attach your trim kit of choice. Normally these are hung with torsion spring clips from notches or hooks inside the canister. This should be done after the ceiling is installed and finished for new construction projects. With certain types of trim kits, such as eyeball trim, you'll need to install the light bulb before the trim kit.

How to Connect a Recessed Fixture Can in a Finished Ceiling

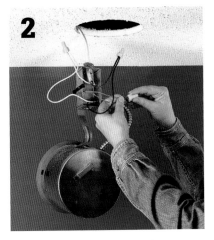

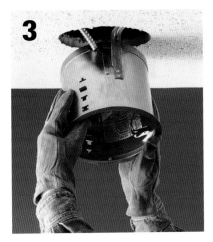

Make the hole for the can. Most fixtures will include a template for sizing the hole. Fish 14/2 cable from the switch location to the hole. Pull about 16" of cable out of the hole for making the connection.

Remove a knockout from the electrical box attached to the can. Thread the cable into the box; secure it with a cable clamp. Remove sheathing insulation. Connect the black fixture wire to the black circuit wire, the white fixture wire to the white circuit wire, and then connect the ground wire to the grounding screw or grounding wire attached to the box.

Retrofit cans secure themselves in the hole with spring-loaded clips. Install the can in the ceiling by depressing the mounting clips so the can will fit into the hole. Insert the can so that its edge is tight to the ceiling. Push the mounting clips back out so they grip the drywall and hold the fixture in place. Install the trim piece.

Track Lights

Track lighting offers a beautiful and functional way to increase the amount of light in a room or simply to update its look. A variety of fixture and lamp options let you control the shape, color, and intensity of the light. Installing track lighting in place of an existing ceiling-mounted light fixture involves basic wiring and hand-tool skills, but the connections are even easier to make than with traditional light fixtures. Once installed, the system is very easy to upgrade or expand in the future.

Tools & Materials ▸

Drill/driver and bits
Wire stripper
Screwdriver
Voltage sensor
Toggle bolts
Track light heads

Prewired track
    and fittings
Wire connector
Ceiling box
Eye protection

If you currently have a ceiling-mounted light fixture that is not meeting your lighting needs, it's simple to replace it with a track-lighting fixture. With track lighting you can easily change the type and number of lights, their position on the track, and the direction they aim. These fixtures come in many different styles, including short 3-ft. track systems with just one or two lights up to 12-ft. systems with five or more lights.

How to Install Track Lighting

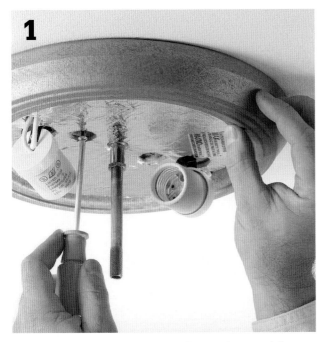

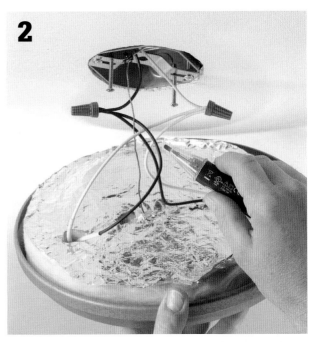

Disconnect the old ceiling light fixture (for remodeling projects) after shutting off power to the circuit at the main service panel. The globe or diffuser and the lamps should be removed before the fixture mounting mechanism is detached.

Test the fixture wires with a voltage sensor to make sure the circuit is dead. Support the fixture from below while you work—never allow a light fixture to hang by its electrical wires alone. Remove the wire connectors and pull the wires apart. Remove the old light fixture.

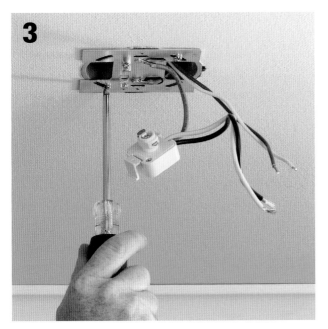

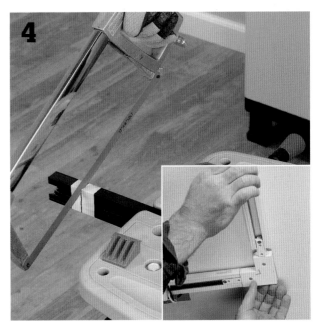

Attach the mounting strap for the new track light to the old ceiling box. If the mounting strap has a hole in the center, thread the circuit wires through the hole before screwing the strap to the box. The green or bare copper ground from the circuit should be attached to the grounding screw or clip on the strap or box.

Cut the track section to length, if necessary, using a hack saw. Deburr the cut end with a metal file. If you are installing multiple sections of track, assemble the sections with the correct connector fittings (sold separately from your kit). You can also purchase T-fittings or L-fittings (inset photo) if you wish to install tracks in either of these configurations.

(continued)

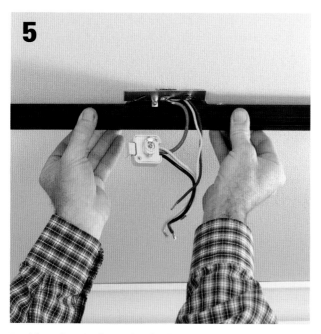

5

Position the track section in the mounting saddle on the mounting strap and hold it temporarily in place in the location where it will be installed. The track section will have predrilled mounting holes in the back. Draw a marking point on the ceiling at each of these locations. If your track does not have predrilled mounting holes, remove it and drill a ³⁄₁₆" hole in the back every 16".

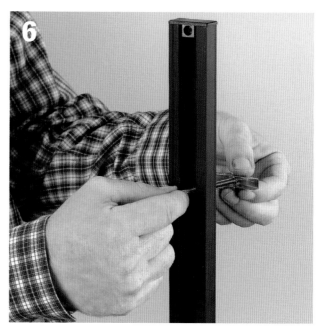

6

Insert the bolt from a toggle bolt or molly bolt into each predrilled screw location and twist the toggle or molly back onto the free end. These types of hardware have greater holding power than anchor sleeves. Drill a ⅝" dia. access hole in the ceiling at each of the mounting hole locations you marked on the ceiling in step 5.

7

Insert the toggle or molly into the access hole far enough so it clears the top of the hole and the wings snap outward. Then tighten each bolt so the track is snug against the ceiling. If the mounting hole happens to fall over a ceiling joint, simply drive a wallboard screw at that hole location.

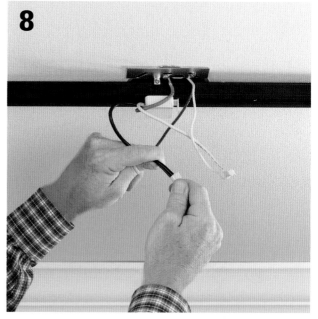

8

Hook up wires from the track's power supply fitting to the circuit wires. Connect black to black and white to white. The grounding wire from the power supply fitting can either be pigtailed to the circuit ground wire and connected to the grounding screw or clip, or it can be twisted together with the circuit grounding wire at the grounding terminal. Snap the fitting into the track if you have not already done so.

9

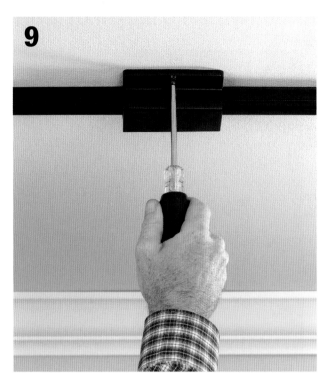

Attach the protective cover that came with your kit to conceal the ceiling box and the electrical connections. Some covers simply snap in place, others require a mounting screw.

10

Dead end

Cap the open ends of the track with a dead end cap fitting. These also may require a mounting screw. Leaving track ends open is a safety violation.

11

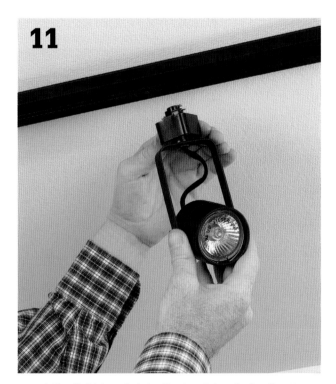

Insert the light heads into the track by slipping the stem into the track slot and then twisting it so the electrical contact points on the head press against the electrified inner rails of the track slot. Tug lightly on the head to make sure it is secure before releasing it.

12

Arrange the track light heads so their light falls in the manner you choose, and then depress the locking tab on each fixture to secure it in position. Restore power, and test the lights.

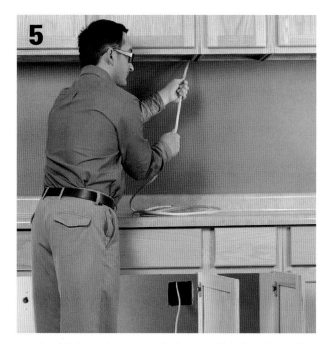

Feed cable into the access hole at the light location until the end reaches the access hole below. Don't cut the cable yet. Reach into the access hole and feel around for the free cable end, and then pull it out through the access hole once you've found it. Cut the cable, making sure to leave plenty of extra on both ends.

String the cable into a piece of flexible conduit that's long enough to reach between the two access holes in the base cabinets. Attach a connector to each end of the conduit to protect the cable sheathing from the sharp edges of the cut metal. *Tip: To make patching the cabinet back easier, drill a new access hole for the cable near the square access hole.*

Hang the conduit with hanger straps attached to the base cabinet frame or back panel, drilling holes in the side walls of the cabinet where necessary to thread the conduit through. On back panels, use small screws to hang the straps instead of brads or nails. Support the conduit near both the entrance and the exit holes (the conduit should extend past the back panels by a couple of inches).

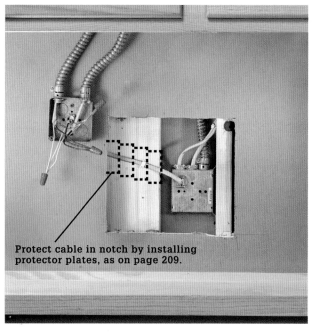

Protect cable in notch by installing protector plates, as on page 209.

Variation: If you are installing more than one undercabinet light, run cable down from each installation point as you did for the first light. Mount an electrical junction box to the cabinet back near the receptacle providing the power. Run the power cables from each light through flexible conduit and make connections inside the junction box. Be sure to attach the junction box cover once the connections are made.

9

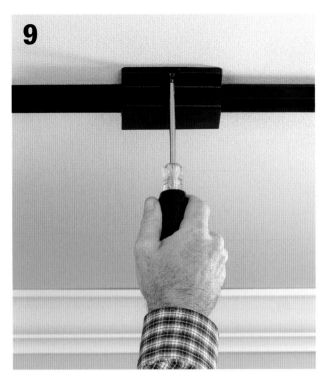

Attach the protective cover that came with your kit to conceal the ceiling box and the electrical connections. Some covers simply snap in place, others require a mounting screw.

10

Dead end

Cap the open ends of the track with a dead end cap fitting. These also may require a mounting screw. Leaving track ends open is a safety violation.

11

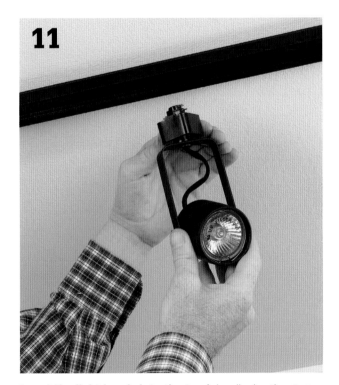

Insert the light heads into the track by slipping the stem into the track slot and then twisting it so the electrical contact points on the head press against the electrified inner rails of the track slot. Tug lightly on the head to make sure it is secure before releasing it.

12

Arrange the track light heads so their light falls in the manner you choose, and then depress the locking tab on each fixture to secure it in position. Restore power, and test the lights.

Undercabinet Lights

Hardwired undercabinet lights illuminate the kitchen countertop and sink areas that fall in the shadow of ceiling lights. Most of these light fixtures, which are often called strip lights, utilize fluorescent, halogen, or xenon bulbs that emit very low levels of heat and are therefore very efficient.

If you are doing a kitchen remodel with all-new cabinets, run the new light circuit wiring before the cabinets are installed. For a retrofit, you'll need to find an available power source to tie into. Options for this do not include the dedicated 20-amp small-appliance receptacle circuits that are required in kitchens. The best bet is to run new circuit wire from a close-by ceiling light switch box, but this will mean cutting into the walls to run cable. Another option is to locate a receptacle that's on the opposite side of a shared wall, preferably next to a location where a base cabinet is installed in the kitchen. This room should not be a breakfast room, dining, room, pantry, or similar area, because these rooms are also served by the small appliance receptacle circuits. By cutting an access hole in the cabinet back you can tie into the receptacle box and run cable through the wall behind the cabinets, up to the upper cabinet location, and out the wall to supply the fixture that's mounted to the underside of the upper cabinet.

You can purchase undercabinet lights that are controlled by a wall switch, but most products have an integral on/off button so you can control lights individually.

Tools & Materials ▸

Circuit tester	Undercabinet lighting kit
Utility knife	14/2 NM cable
Wallboard saw	Wire connectors
Hammer	Switch box
Screwdriver	Switch
Drill and hole saw	Eye protection
Jigsaw	Hardboard panel
Wire stripper	adhesive

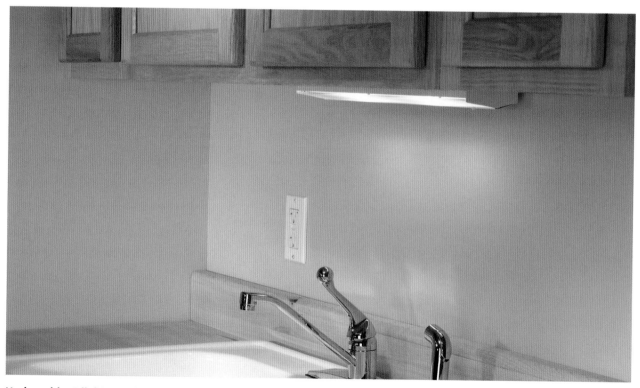

Undercabinet lights provide directed task lighting that bring sinks and countertop work surfaces out from the shadows. Hardwired lights may be controlled either by a wall switch or an onboard on/off switch located on the fixture. *Note: Do not supply power for lights from the small-appliance circuit.*

How to Install a Hardwired Undercabinet Light

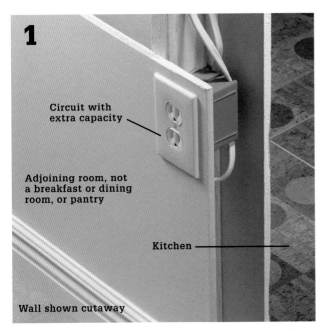

1

Circuit with extra capacity

Adjoining room, not a breakfast or dining room, or pantry

Kitchen

Wall shown cutaway

Look in the adjoining room for a usable power source in the form of a receptacle that has a box located in the wall behind your base cabinets. Unlike the small-appliance circuit with outlets in your backsplash area, these typically are not dedicated circuits (which can't be expanded). Make sure that the receptacle's circuit has enough capacity to support another load. Shut the power to the receptacle off at the main service panel and test for power.

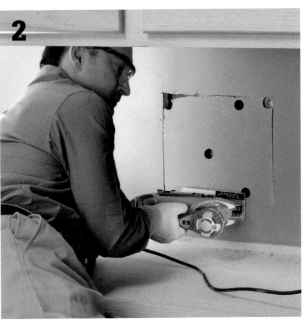

2

Cut a hole in the base cabinet back panel to get access to the wall behind it in roughly the area where you know the next-door receptacle to be. Use a keyhole saw or drywall saw and make very shallow cuts until you have positively identified the locations of the electrical box and cables. Then finish the cuts with a jigsaw.

3

Drill an access hole into the kitchen wall for the cable that will feed the undercabinet light. A ½" dia. hole should be about the right size if you are using 12-ga. or 14-ga. sheathed NM cable.

4

Cut a small access hole (4" × 4" or so) in the back panel of the base cabinet directly below the undercabinet light location.

(continued)

5

Feed cable into the access hole at the light location until the end reaches the access hole below. Don't cut the cable yet. Reach into the access hole and feel around for the free cable end, and then pull it out through the access hole once you've found it. Cut the cable, making sure to leave plenty of extra on both ends.

6

String the cable into a piece of flexible conduit that's long enough to reach between the two access holes in the base cabinets. Attach a connector to each end of the conduit to protect the cable sheathing from the sharp edges of the cut metal. *Tip: To make patching the cabinet back easier, drill a new access hole for the cable near the square access hole.*

7

Hang the conduit with hanger straps attached to the base cabinet frame or back panel, drilling holes in the side walls of the cabinet where necessary to thread the conduit through. On back panels, use small screws to hang the straps instead of brads or nails. Support the conduit near both the entrance and the exit holes (the conduit should extend past the back panels by a couple of inches).

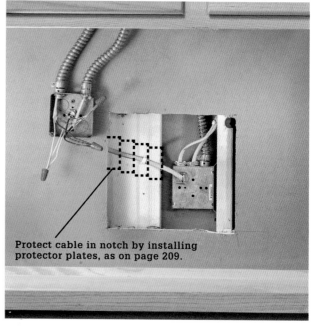

Protect cable in notch by installing protector plates, as on page 209.

Variation: If you are installing more than one undercabinet light, run cable down from each installation point as you did for the first light. Mount an electrical junction box to the cabinet back near the receptacle providing the power. Run the power cables from each light through flexible conduit and make connections inside the junction box. Be sure to attach the junction box cover once the connections are made.

Remove the receptacle from the box you are tying into and insert the new circuit cable into one of the knockouts using a cable clamp. Check a wire capacity chart (see page 26) to make sure the box is big enough for the new conductors. Replace it with a larger box if necessary. Reinstall the receptacle once the connections are made.

Install the undercabinet light. Some models have a removable diffuser that allows access to the fixture wires, and these should be screwed to the upper cabinet prior to making your wiring hookups. Other models need to be connected to the circuit wires before installation. Check your manufacturer's installations.

Connect wires inside the light fixture according to the light manufacturer's directions. Make sure the incoming cable is stapled just before it enters the light box and that a cable clamp is used at the knockout in the box to protect the cable. Restore power, and test the light.

Cut patches of hardboard and fit them over the access holes, overlapping the edges of the cutouts. Adhere them to the cabinet backs with panel adhesive.

Vanity Lights

Many bathrooms have a single fixture positioned above the vanity, but a light source in this position casts shadows on the face and makes grooming more difficult. Light fixtures on either side of the mirror is a better arrangement.

For a remodel, mark the mirror location, run cable, and position boxes before drywall installation. You can also retrofit by installing new boxes and drawing power from the existing fixture.

The light sources should be at eye level; 66" is typical. The size of your mirror and its location on the wall may affect how far apart you can place the sconces, but 36" to 40" apart is a good guideline.

Tools & Materials ▸

Drywall saw	Electrical boxes
Drill	and braces
Combination tool	Vanity light fixtures
Circuit tester	NM cable
Screwdrivers	Wire connectors
Hammer	Eye protection

Vanity lights on the sides of the mirror provide good lighting.

How to Replace Vanity Lights in a Finished Bathroom

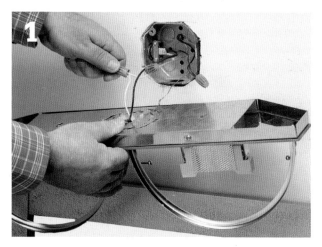

Turn off the power at the service panel. Remove the old fixture from the wall, and test to make sure that the power is off. Then remove a strip of drywall from around the old fixture to the first studs beyond the approximate location of the new fixtures. Make the opening large enough that you have room to route cable from the existing fixture to the boxes.

Mark the location for the fixtures, and install new boxes. Install the boxes about 66" above the floor and 18" to 20" from the centerline of the mirror (the mounting base of some fixtures is above or below the bulb, so adjust the height of the bracing accordingly). If the correct location is on or next to a stud, you can attach the box directly to the stud; otherwise you'll need to install blocking or use boxes with adjustable braces (shown).

3

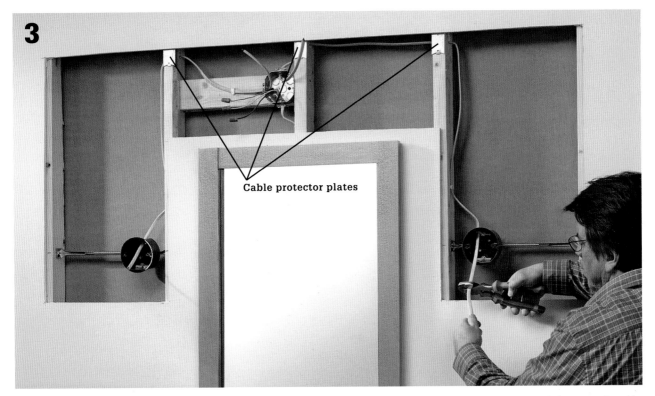

Cable protector plates

Open the side knockouts on the electrical box above the vanity. Then drill ⅝" holes in the centers of any studs between the old fixture and the new ones. Run two NM cables from the new boxes for the fixtures to the box above the vanity. Protect the cable with metal protector plates. Secure the cables with cable clamps, leaving 11" of extra cable for making the connection to the new fixtures. Remove sheathing, and strip insulation from the ends of the wires.

4

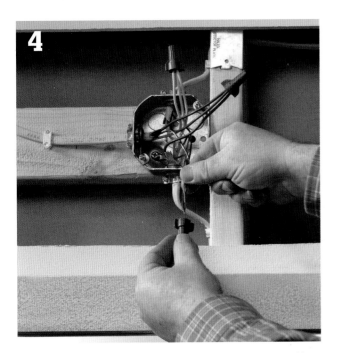

Connect the white wires from the new cables to the white wire from the old cable, and connect the black wires from the new cables to the black wire from the old cable. Connect the ground wires. Cover all open boxes, and then replace the drywall, leaving openings for the fixture and the old box. (Cover the old box with a solid junction box cover plate.)

5

Install the fixture mounting braces on the boxes. Attach the fixtures by connecting the black circuit wire to the black fixture wire and connecting the white circuit wire to the white fixture wire. Connect the ground wires. Position each fixture over each box, and attach with the mounting screws. Restore power, and test the circuit.

Low-Voltage Cable Lights

This unique fixture system is a mainstay of retail and commercial lighting and is now becoming common in homes. Low-voltage cable systems use two parallel cables to suspend and provide electricity to fixtures mounted anywhere on the cables. A 12-volt transformer feeds low-voltage power to the cables.

The system's ease of installation, flexibility, and the wide variety of individual lights available make it perfect for all kinds of spaces. Low-voltage cable light systems are ideal for retrofits and for situations where surface-mounted track is undesirable or impossible to install.

Low-voltage Cable Lighting Kit ▸

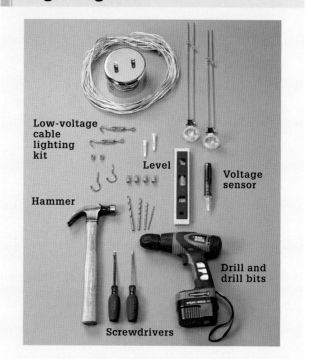

Low-voltage cable lighting kit | Level | Voltage sensor | Hammer | Drill and drill bits | Screwdrivers

Tools & Materials ▸

Combination tool
Screwdriver
Drill
Fish tape
Low-voltage cable
   light kit

Switch
Electrical boxes
NM cable
Level
Eye protection

Low-voltage cable lights are low profile and easy to install, but they provide a surprising amount of light.

How to Install Low-Voltage Cable Lighting

Cable Light Kits ▶

Low-voltage cable lights typically are sold in kits that contain the hanging lights, the low-voltage cable, and a decorative transformer that can be ceiling mounted or wall mounted.

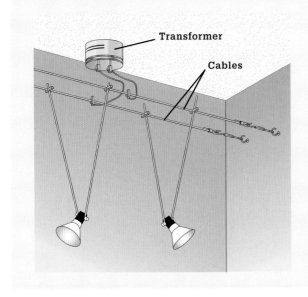

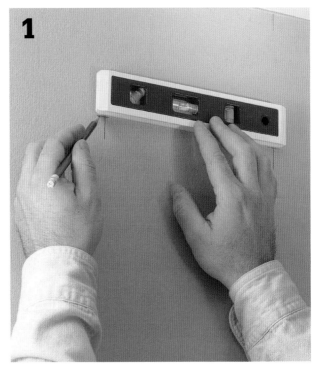

1

Lay out locations for the screw eyes that are used to suspend the cables, which should be in a parallel line. The path should lead the cables within a foot of the existing ceiling fixture box that you are using to provide power.

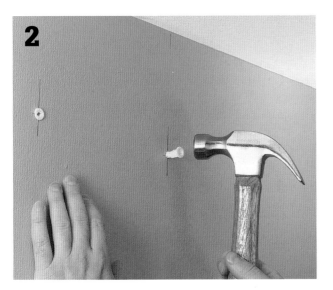

2

Install wall anchors at the appointed locations for the screw eyes that will suspend the cables. Plastic sleeve anchors are adequate in most cases. Drive the anchors into guide holes with a hammer.

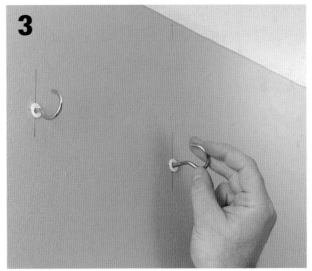

3

Twist the screw eyes into the wall anchor sleeves, taking care to make sure they are driven in equal amounts and are not overdriven. Install a set of screw eyes the same distance apart on each facing wall in the installation area. Cut two pieces of low-voltage cable to span between screw eyes on facing walls. Recommendations may vary— for the project shown here the cable is cut 12" shorter than the distance between the screw eyes.

(continued)

4

Use the crimping hardware in your kit to form small loops at the ends of each cable. Slip the loops over the screw eyes on one end, and attach them to turnbuckles at the opposite ends. Slide the turnbuckles over the screw eyes and tighten them until the cables are taut.

5

Attach the transformer crossbar to the electrical box containing the circuit leads. Shut off the power at the main service panel and test for power, and then remove the old fixture, if you have not already done so.

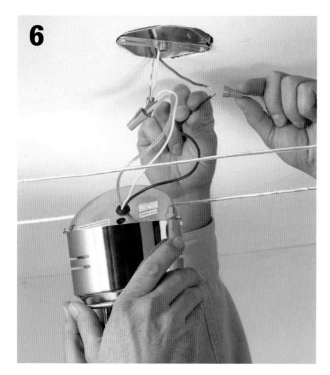

6

Make wiring connections for the transformer inside the electrical box. Make sure the transformer is supported while you join the wires. Be sure to attach the grounding wires to the grounding screw or clip in the box.

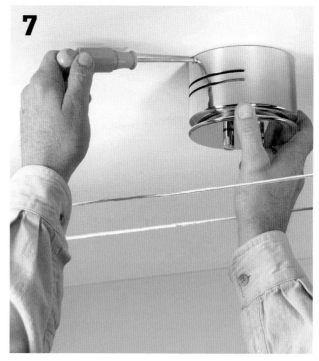

7

Mount the transformer onto the electrical box according to the manufacturer's instructions. The model shown here has a separate chrome cover that is secured with a setscrew after the transformer is mounted to the crossbar.

8

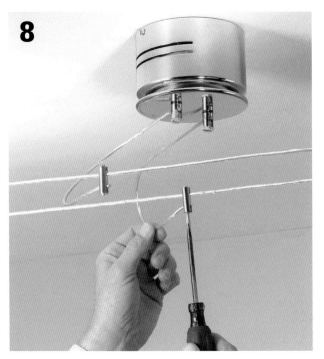

Thread short lengths of cable into the openings on the screw terminals on the transformer. Tighten the screws until the pointed probe in each terminal pierces the cable sheathing and makes contact with the wire inside. Do the same with the other ends of the jumper cables using the provided connector hardware.

Wall-Mount It ▸

Install the transformer in a wall location if there is a more convenient power source or if you simply prefer the appearance of the wall location.

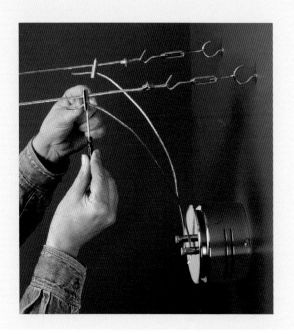

9

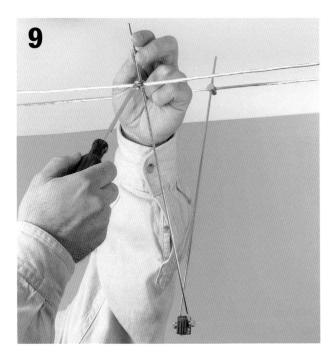

Hang the light fixture holders from the cables, tightening the screws in the hanger ends until their probes pierce the cable sheathing and make contact. It's a good idea to hang all of the fixtures and arrange them to your liking before you begin tightening the screws and piercing the sheathing.

10

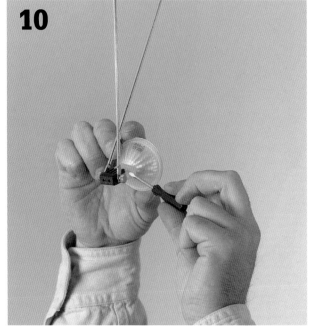

Insert the special low-voltage bulbs into the fixture holders and secure them as instructed (here, we are tightening a setscrew). Turn on the power and test the lights, adjusting the angles and directions of the bulbs.

Hard-Wired Smoke & CO Alarms

Smoke and carbon monoxide (CO) alarms are an essential safety component of any living facility. All national fire protection codes require that new homes have a hard-wired smoke alarm in every sleeping room and on every level of a residence, including basements and habitable attics.

Three types of alarms exist that can alert you to a fire. Photoelectric alarms are better at detecting fires with lots of flames. Ionization alarms are slightly better at detecting smoldering fires. Heat alarms detect high temperature created by a fire.

Many experts recommend installing photoelectric alarms instead of the more common ionization alarms, or as an alternative, installing some of each type. Heat alarms may be installed in addition to smoke alarms but may not be substituted for them.

Smoke alarms have a limited service life of about ten years. You should replace smoke alarms after ten years regardless of whether the alarm sounds when you press the test button. The test button, especially on older alarms, may only test the sounding device, not the smoke detection system.

Hard-wired alarms operate on your household electrical current but have battery backups in case of a power outage. On new homes, all smoke alarms must be wired in a series so that every alarm sounds regardless of the fire's location. When wiring a series of alarms, be sure to use alarms of the same brand to

Tools & Materials ▸

Screwdriver
Combination tool
Fish tape
Drywall saw
Wall or ceiling
   outlet boxes
Cable clamps
   (if boxes are not
   self-clamping)

Two- and three-wire
   14-gauge
   NM cable
Alarms
Wire connectors
15-amp single-pole
   AFCI breaker
Eye protection

ensure compatibility. Always check local codes before starting the job.

Smoke alarms installed on the ceiling should be at least 4" from the wall. Smoke alarms installed on the wall should be at least 4" and not more than 12" from the ceiling. As always, read and follow the manufacturer's instructions.

Smoke and CO alarms are considered such important safety devices that national codes require updating these alarms to current code requirements during some types of remodeling projects. Enforcement of this requirement varies by jurisdiction, so check with your building department about their policies when adding a bedroom and before major remodeling.

Smoke alarms and carbon monoxide (CO) alarms are required in new construction. Hard-wired CO alarms (A) are triggered by the presence of carbon monoxide gas. Smoke alarms are available in photoelectric and ionizing models. In ionizing detectors (B), a small amount of current flows in an ionization chamber. When smoke enters the chamber, it interrupts the current, triggering the alarm. Photoelectric alarms (C) rely on a beam of light, which when interrupted by smoke triggers an alarm. Heat alarms (D) sound an alarm when they detect areas of high heat in the room.

How to Connect a Series of Hard-Wired Smoke Alarms

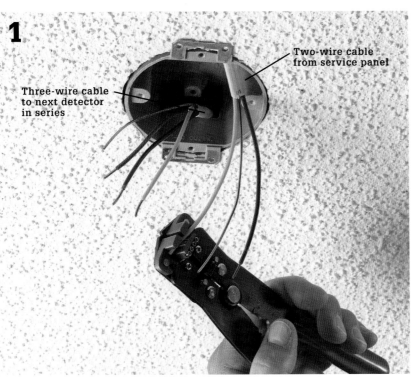

1

Three-wire cable to next detector in series

Two-wire cable from service panel

Pull 14/2 NM cable from the panel into the first ceiling electrical box in the smoke alarm series. Pull 14/3 NM cable between the remaining alarm outlet boxes. Use cable clamps to secure the cable in each outlet box. Remove sheathing, and strip insulation from wires.

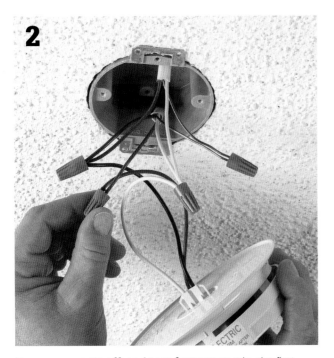

2

Ensure power is off, and test for power. Wire the first alarm in the series. Use a wire connector to connect the ground wires. Splice the black circuit wire with the alarm's black lead and the black wire going to the next alarm in the series. Splice the white circuit wire with the alarm's white wire and the white (neutral) wire going to the next alarm in the series. Splice the red traveler wire with the odd-colored alarm wire (in this case, also a red wire).

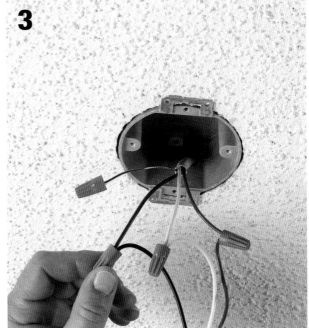

3

Wire the remaining alarms in the series by connecting the like-colored wires in each outlet box. Always connect the red traveler wire to the odd-colored (in this case, red) alarm wire. This red traveler wire connects all the alarms together so that when one alarm sounds, all the alarms sound. If the alarm doesn't have a grounding wire, cap the ground with a wire connector. When all alarms are wired, install and connect the new 15-amp AFCI breaker.

Landscape Lights

Some landscape lighting manufacturers pitch their systems as security products. If you keep the outside of your house well lit, the reasoning goes, the thieves will turn elsewhere to find easier pickings. It's possible that the companies are right about this. But probably the stronger arguments are for improved safety and appearance.

It can't be surprising that adding some light to the dark makes going places safer. This idea has been around for a long time—a very long time. But the notion that you can improve the look of your house by adding some nightlights is more recent. In fact, decorating with exterior lights became widespread only in the last 25 years, when low-voltage landscape lighting showed up.

Low-voltage lights are powered by a transformer that steps 120-volt current down to a safe 12 volts. Choosing the location for the transformer is an important part of planning. You have two options:

inside the house and outside the house. The outside installation is a little easier, but the inside one is a little better, especially from a security standpoint. Also take some time to review your light placement. Once you are happy with the plan, drive a small stake where you want each light to go.

Tools & Materials ▸

Drill/driver & bits
Hammer
Screwdrivers
Hacksaw
Spade
Low-voltage fixture

Wires
Transformer
Stakes
Hacksaw
Eye protection

Low-voltage lights are safe to install and use to beautify your outdoor spaces. Unlike solar landscape lights, they are powered by good old reliable electricity, so they really can stay on all night if you wish them to.

Parts of a Landscape Light System

Landscape lighting can be ordered in kit form or as individual pieces. Kits include a few light heads, some wire, and a transformer that changes standard house current into low-voltage power. If you want half a dozen lights along the front walk, for example, then the kit is a good idea. It's cheaper, very easy to install, and will last a long time unless the lights get run over by a lawnmower.

Typical low-voltage outdoor lighting systems consist of: lens cap (A), lens cap posts (B), upper reflector (C), lens (D), base/stake/cable connector assembly (contains lower reflector) (E), low-voltage cable (F), lens hood (G), 7-watt 12-volt bulbs (H), cable connector caps (I), control box containing transformer and timer (J), and light sensor (K).

How To Modify Landscape Lights for Deck Installation

Specialty lights can cost a lot more than the standard plastic spike-base lamps. Because of this, many people modify the cheaper units to serve other purposes. To do this, first cut off the spike-base with a hacksaw.

To install a modified light on a deck, bore a wire-clearance hole through a deck board. Then feed the low-voltage wire through this hole, and attach the base to the deck with screws. The same technique can be used to install modified units on planters or railings.

How to Install Low-Voltage Landscape Lights

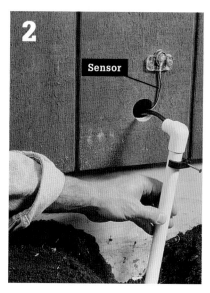

Install the transformers. In a garage, mount one on a wall within 24" of a GFCI receptacle and at least 12" off the floor. On an outdoor receptacle on a wall or a post, mount the transformer on the same post or an adjacent post at least 12" off the ground and not more than 24" from the receptacle.

Drill a hole through the wall or rim joist for the low-voltage cable and any sensors to pass through. If a circuit begins in a high-traffic area, protect the cable by running it through a short piece of PVC pipe or conduit, and then into the shallow trench.

Attach the end of the low-voltage wire to the terminals on the transformer. Make sure that both strands of wire are held tightly by their terminal screws.

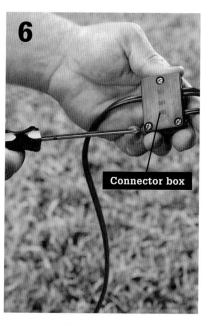

Transformers usually have a simple mechanism that allows you to set times for the lights to come ON and go OFF automatically. Set these times before hanging the transformer.

Many low-voltage light fixtures are modular, consisting of a spiked base, a riser tube, and a lamp. On these units, feed the wires and the wire connector from the light section down through the riser tube and into the base.

Take apart the connector box and insert the ends of the fixture wire and the low-voltage landscape cable into it. Puncture the wire ends with the connector box leads. Reassemble the connector box.

7

Feed the wire connector back into the light base, and attach it to the lampholder according to directions. Install the low-voltage light bulb.

8

Assemble the fixture parts that cover the bulb, including the lens cap and reflector or the cap.

9

Lay out the lights, with the wires attached, in the pattern you have chosen. Then cut the sod between fixtures with a spade. Push the blade at least 6" deep and pry open a seam by rocking the blade back and forth.

10

Gently force the cable into the slot formed by the spade; don't tear the wire insulation. A paint stick (or a cedar shingle) is a good tool for this job. Push the wire to the bottom of the slot.

11

Firmly push the light into the slot in the sod. If the lamp doesn't seat properly, pull it out and cut another slot at a right angle to the first, and try again.

12

Once the lamp is stabilized, tuck any extra wire into the slot using the paint stick. No part of the wire should be exposed when you are done with the job.

Doorbells

Most doorbell problems are caused by loose wire connections or worn-out switches. Reconnecting loose wires or replacing a switch requires only a few minutes. Doorbell problems also can occur if the chime unit becomes dirty or worn or if the low-voltage transformer burns out. Both parts are easy to replace. Because doorbells operate at low voltage, the switches and the chime unit can be serviced without turning off power to the system. However, when replacing a transformer, always turn off the power at the main service panel.

Some older houses have other low-voltage transformers in addition to the doorbell transformer. These transformers control heating and air-conditioning thermostats (see page 224 to 227) or other low-voltage systems. When testing and repairing a doorbell system, it is important to identify the correct transformer. A doorbell transformer has a rating of 24 volts or less. This rating is printed on the face of the transformer. The location of your doorbell transformer is based on local custom and the age of your home. It may be near or attached to the service panel. It may be in the attic, basement, crawlspace, or garage.

In most modern heating and air-conditioning systems, the transformer serving the system is inside the furnace cabinet. In older systems, it may be located near the furnace.

Occasionally, a doorbell problem is caused by a broken low-voltage wire somewhere in the system. You can test for wire breaks with a battery-operated multitester. If the test indicates a break, new low-voltage wires must be installed between the transformer and the switches or between the switches and chime unit. Replacing low-voltage wires is not a difficult job, but it can be time-consuming. You may choose to have an electrician do this work.

Tools & Materials ▸

Continuity tester
Screwdriver
Multimeter
Needlenose pliers
Cotton swab
Rubbing alcohol

Replacement
doorbell switch
(if needed)
Masking tape
Replacement chime
unit (if needed)

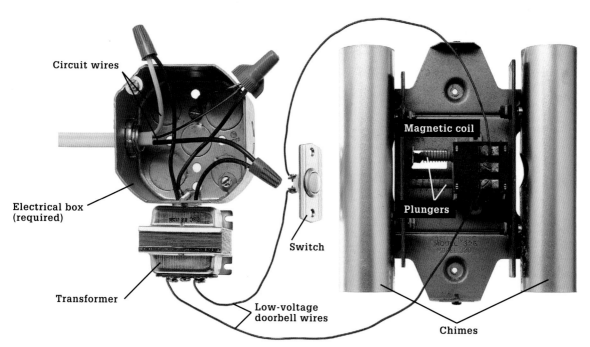

Circuit wires

Electrical box (required)

Transformer

Switch

Low-voltage doorbell wires

Magnetic coil

Plungers

Chimes

A home doorbell system is powered by a transformer that reduces 120-volts to 24 volts or less. Current flows from the transformer to one or more push-button switches. When pushed, the switch activates a magnetic coil inside the chime unit, causing a plunger to strike a musical tuning bar.

How to Test a Nonfunctional Doorbell System

1

Remove the mounting screws holding the doorbell switch to the siding.

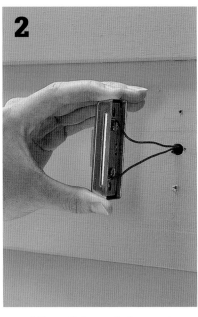

2

Carefully pull the switch away from the wall.

3

Inspect wire connections on the switch. If wires are loose, reconnect them to the screw terminals. Test the doorbell by pressing the button. If the doorbell still does not work, disconnect the switch and test it with a continuity tester.

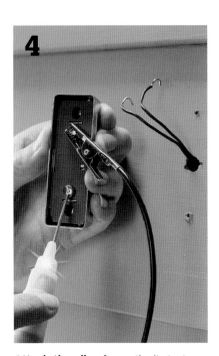

4

Attach the clip of a continuity tester to one screw terminal and touch the probe to the other screw terminal. Press the switch button. The tester should glow. If not, then the switch is faulty and must be replaced.

5

Twist the doorbell switch wires together temporarily to test the other parts of the doorbell system.

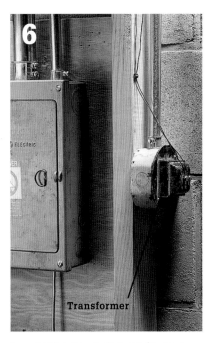

6

Transformer

Locate the doorbell transformer. If it's not near the service panel, look in the garage, crawlspace, and attic.

(continued)

7

Identify the doorbell transformer by reading its voltage rating. Doorbell transformers have a voltage rating of 24 volts or less. Turn off power to the transformer at the main service panel. Remove the cover on the electrical box, and test wires for power. Reconnect any loose wires. Replace taped connections with wire connectors.

8

Reattach the cover plate. Inspect the low-voltage wire connections, and reconnect any loose wires using needlenose pliers or a screwdriver. Turn on power to the transformer at the main service panel.

9

Touch the probes of the multitester to the low-voltage screw terminals on the transformer. If the transformer is operating properly, the meter will detect power within 2 volts of the transformer's rating. If not, the transformer is faulty and must be replaced.

10

Test the chime unit. Remove the cover plate on the doorbell chime unit. Inspect the low-voltage wire connections, and reconnect any loose wires.

11

Test that the chime unit is receiving current. Touch probes of a multimeter to screw terminals. If the multimeter detects power within 2 volts of the transformer rating, then the unit is receiving proper current. If it detects no power or very low power, there is a break in the low-voltage wiring, and new wires must be installed.

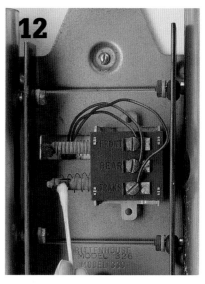

12

Clean the chime plungers (some models) with a cotton swab dipped in rubbing alcohol. Reassemble doorbell switches, and then test the system by pushing one of the switches. If the doorbell still does not work, then the chime unit is faulty and must be replaced (see page 223).

How to Replace a Doorbell Switch

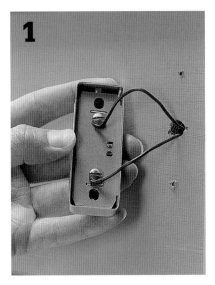

Remove the doorbell switch mounting screws, and carefully pull the switch away from the wall.

Disconnect wires from the switch. Tape wires to the wall to prevent them from slipping into the wall cavity.

Purchase a new doorbell switch, and connect the wires to the screw terminals on the new switch. (Wires are interchangeable and can be connected to either terminal.) Anchor the switch to the wall.

How to Replace a Doorbell Chime Unit

Turn off power to the doorbell at the main panel. Remove the cover plate from the old chime. Label the low-voltage wires FRONT, REAR, or TRANS to identify their screw terminal locations. Disconnect the wires. Remove the old chime unit.

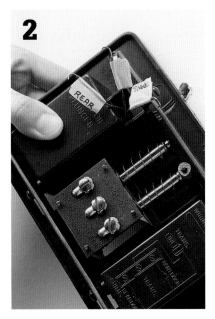

Purchase a new chime unit that matches the voltage rating of the old unit. Thread the low-voltage wires through the base of the new chime unit. Attach the chime unit to the wall using the mounting screws included with the installation kit.

Connect the low-voltage wires to the screw terminals on the new chime unit. Attach the cover plate, and turn on the power at the main service panel.

Programmable Thermostats

A thermostat is a temperature-sensitive switch that automatically controls home heating and air-conditioning systems. There are two types of thermostats. Low-voltage thermostats control whole-house heating and air conditioning from one central location. Line-voltage thermostats are used in zone heating systems, where each room has its own heating unit and thermostat.

A low-voltage thermostat is powered by a transformer (usually located inside the furnace) that reduces 120-volt current to about 24 volts. A low-voltage thermostat is very durable, but failures can occur if wire connections become loose or dirty, if thermostat parts become corroded, or if a transformer wears out. Some thermostat systems have two transformers. One transformer controls the heating unit, and the other controls the air-conditioning unit.

Line-voltage thermostats are powered by the same circuit as the heating unit, usually a 240-volt circuit. Always make sure to turn off the power before servicing a line-voltage thermostat (typically, these are found in electric heaters).

A thermostat can be replaced in about one hour. Many homeowners choose to replace standard low-voltage or line-voltage thermostats with programmable setback thermostats. These programmable thermostats can cut energy use by up to 35 percent.

When buying a new thermostat, make sure the new unit is compatible with your heating/air-conditioning system. For example, a thermostat intended for a furnace and air conditioner may not work with a heat pump. For reference, take along the brand name and model number of the old thermostat and of your heating/air-conditioning units. When buying a new low-voltage transformer, choose a replacement with voltage and amperage ratings that match the old thermostat.

Tools & Materials ▸

Screwdriver   New thermostat
Masking tape

A programmable thermostat allows you to significantly reduce your energy consumption by taking greater control over your heating and cooling system.

Traditional Low-Voltage Thermostats

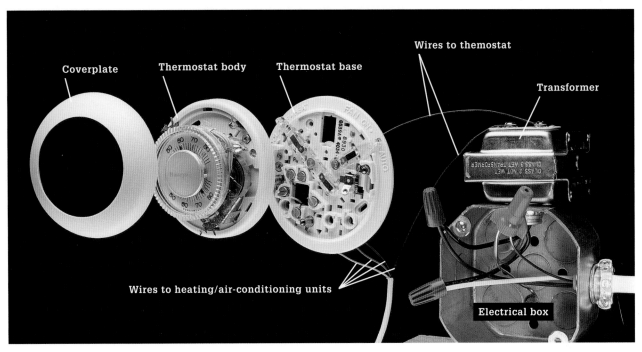

Coverplate

Thermostat body

Thermostat base

Wires to thermostat

Transformer

Wires to heating/air-conditioning units

Electrical box

Low-voltage thermostat systems have a transformer that is either connected to an electrical junction box or mounted inside a furnace access panel. Very thin wires (18 to 22 gauge) send current to the thermostat. The thermostat constantly monitors room temperatures and sends electrical signals to the heating/cooling unit through additional wires. The number of wires connected to the thermostat varies from two to six, depending on the type of heating/air-conditioning system. In the common four-wire system shown above, power is supplied to the thermostat through a single wire attached to screw terminal R. Wires attached to other screw terminals relay signals to the furnace heating unit, the air-conditioning unit, and the blower unit. Before removing a thermostat, make sure to label each wire to identify its screw terminal location.

Programmable Thermostats

Programmable thermostats contain sophisticated circuitry that allows you to set the heating and cooling systems in your house to adjust automatically at set times of the day. Replacing a manual thermostat with a programmable model is a relatively simple job that can have big payback on heating and cooling energy savings.

How to Upgrade to a Programmable Thermostat

1

Start by removing the existing thermostat. Turn off the power to the furnace at the main service panel, and test for power. Then remove the thermostat cover.

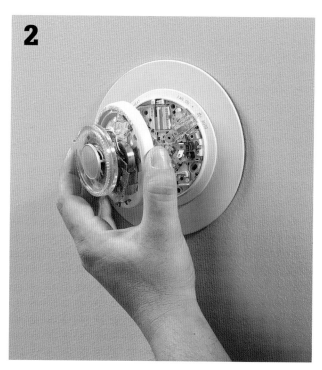

2

The body of the thermostat is held to a wall plate with screws. Remove these screws, and pull the body away from the wall plate. Set the body aside.

3

The low-voltage wires that power the thermostat are held by screw terminals to the mounting plate. Do not remove the wires until you label them with tape according to the letter printed on the terminal to which each wire is attached.

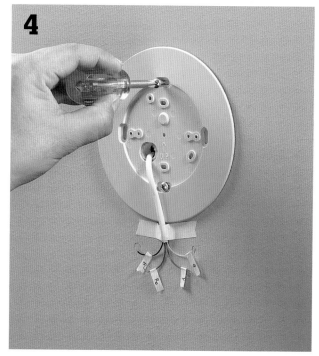

4

Once all the wires are labeled and removed from the mounting plate, tape the cable that holds these wires to the wall to keep it from falling back into the wall. Then unscrew the mounting plate and set it aside.

5

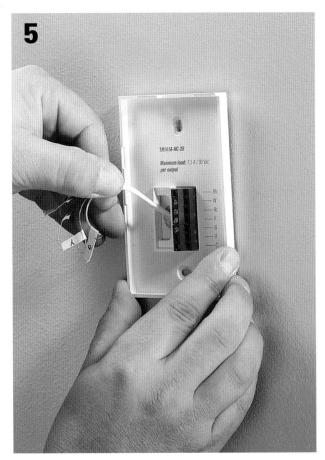

Position the new thermostat base on the wall, and guide the wires through the central opening. Screw the base to the wall using wall anchors if necessary.

6

Check the manufacturer's instructions to establish the correct terminal for each low-voltage wire. Then connect the wires to these terminals, making sure each screw is secure.

7

Programmable thermostats require batteries to store the programs so they won't disappear if the power goes out in a storm. Make sure to install batteries before you snap the thermostat cover in place. Program the new unit to fit your needs, and then turn on the power to the furnace.

Mercury Thermostats ▸

Older model thermostats (and even a few still being made today) often contained one or more small vials of mercury totaling 3 to 4 grams in weight. Because mercury is a highly toxic metal that can cause nerve damage in humans, along with other environmental problems, DO NOT dispose of an old mercury thermostat with your household waste. Instead, bring it to a hazardous waste disposal site or a mercury recycling site if your area has one (check with your local solid waste disposal agency). The best way to determine if your old thermostat contains mercury is simply to remove the cover and look for the small glass vials or ampules containing the silverfish mercury substance. If you are unsure, it is always better to be safe and keep the device in question out of the normal waste stream.

Wireless Switches

Sometimes a light switch is just in the wrong place, or it would be more convenient to have two switches controlling a single fixture. Adding a second switch the conventional way generally requires hours of work and big holes in walls. (Electricians call this a three-way switch installation.) Fortunately wireless switch kits are available to perform basically the same function for a fraction of the cost and effort. There is a bit of real wiring involved here, but it's not nearly as complicated as the traditional method of adding a three-way switch installation.

The kits work by replacing a conventional switch with a unit that has a built-in radio frequency receiver that will read a remote device mounted within a 50-ft. radius. The kits come with a remote, battery-powered switch (it looks like a standard light switch) that you can attach to a wall with double-sided tape.

Two other similar types of wireless switch kits are also available. One allows you to control a plugged-in lamp or appliance with a remote light switch. The second type allows you to control a conventional light fixture remotely, but instead of replacing the switch, the receiver screws in below the light bulb. This is particularly useful if you want to control a pull-chain light from a wall switch.

Tools & Materials ▸

Voltage sensor
Screwdrivers
Wire connectors

Wireless switch
transmitter &
receiver/switch

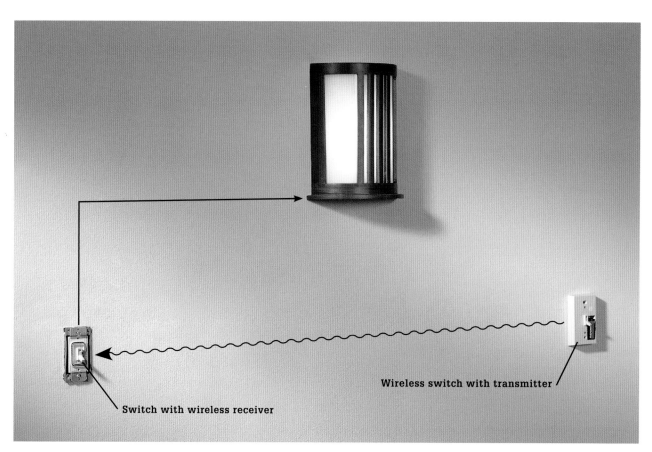

Wireless switch with transmitter

Switch with wireless receiver

A wireless switch is a two-part switching system: a wireless switch with a battery-powered transmitter can be attached to any wall surface; an existing switch is then replaced with a new switch containing a receiver that is triggered by signals from the wireless transmitter, effectively creating a three-way switch condition.

Wireless Switch Products ▸

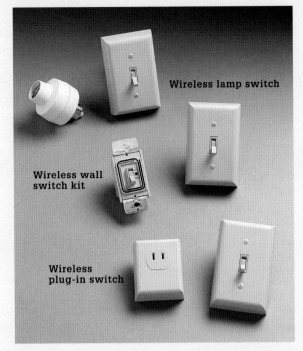

Wireless kits are available to let you switch lights on and off remotely in a variety of ways: at the switch, at the plug, or at the bulb socket.

The remote switch is a wireless transmitter that requires a battery. The transmitter switch attaches to the wall with adhesive tape or velcro strips.

A receiver with a receptacle can be plugged into any receptacle to give it wireless functionality. The switch is operated with a remote control transmitter.

A radio-controlled light fixture can be threaded into the socket of any existing light fixture so it can be turned on and off with a remote control device.

How To Install a Wireless Wall Switch

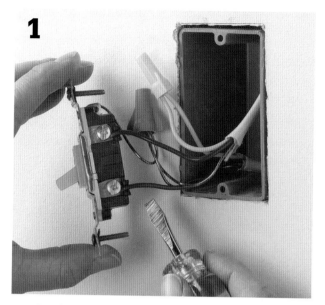

Get rid of the old switch. Shut off power to the switch circuit, and then disconnect and remove the old switch.

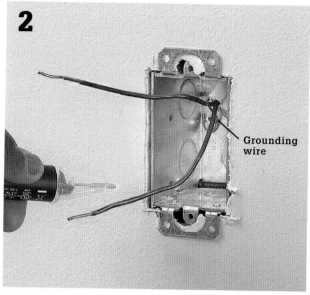

Grounding wire

Identify the lead wire. Carefully separate the power supply wires (any color but white or green) in the switch box so they are not contacting each other or any other surface. Restore power and test each lead wire with a sensor to identify which wire carries the power (the LINE) and which is headed for the fixture the switch controls (the LOAD). Shut power back off, and then label the wires.

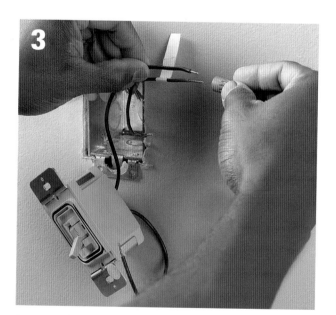

Connect the LINE wire to the LINE terminal or wire on the switch. Connect the LOAD wire (or wires) to the LOAD terminal or wire. The neutral whites (if present) and green grounding wires should be twisted together with a connector. The greens should be grounded to the grounding clip or terminal in the box. *Note: Some switch boxes, such as the one above, are wired with NM2 cable that has two blacks and a green wire and no white.*

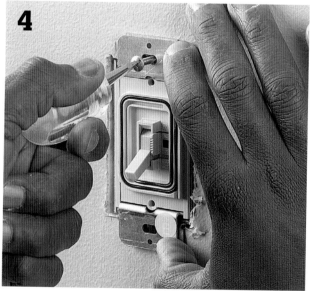

Once the wires are firmly connected, you can attach the switch to the box. Tuck the new switch and wires neatly back into the box. Then drive the two long screws that are attached to the new switch into the two holes in the electrical box.

5

Attach the cover plate to the new wireless switch. Turn the power service back on, and test to make sure the switch operates normally.

6

Remove the backing from the adhesive pads on the back of the wireless switch transmitter box. Install a new 9-volt battery (or other type as required) in the box, and connect it to the switch transmitter terminals.

7

Stick the transmitter box to the wall at the desired location. The box should be no more than 50 ft. from the receiver switch (see manufacturer's suggestions). The box should be at the same height (usually 48") as the other switch boxes.

8

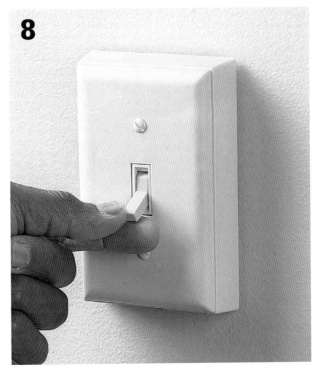

Test the operation of both switches. Each switch should successfully turn the light fixture on and off. You've just successfully created a three-way switch installation without running any new wires.

Baseboard Heaters

Baseboard heaters are a popular way to provide additional heating for an existing room or primary heat to a converted attic or basement.

Heaters are generally wired on a dedicated 240-volt circuit controlled by a thermostat. Several heaters can be wired in parallel and controlled by a single thermostat (see circuit map 15, page 157).

Baseboard heaters are generally surface-mounted without boxes, so in a remodeling situation, you only need to run cables before installing wallboard. Be sure to mark cable locations on the floor before installing drywall. Retrofit installations are also not difficult. You can remove existing baseboard and run new cable in the space behind. Baseboard heaters (and other heating equipment) get very hot and can ignite nearby combustible materials. Maintain the manufacturers recommended distance between the heater and materials such as curtains, blinds, and wood.

Tools & Materials ▸

Drill/driver
Wire stripper
Cable ripper
Wallboard saw
Baseboard heater or heaters
240-thermostat (in-heater or in-wall)
12/2 NM cable
Electrical tape
Basic wiring supplies

Baseboard heaters can provide primary or supplemental heat for existing rooms or additions. Install heaters with clear space between the heater and the floor.

Baseboard Thermostats

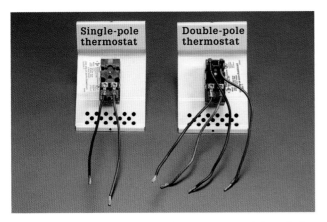

Single-pole and double-pole thermostats work in a similar manner, but double-pole models are safer. The single-pole model will open the circuit (causing shutoff) in only one leg of the power service. Double-pole models have two sets of wires to open both legs, lessening the chance that a person servicing the heater will contact a live wire.

In-heater and wall-mount are the two types of baseboard thermostats you can choose from. If you are installing multiple heaters, a single wall-mount thermostat is more convenient. Individual in-heater thermostats give you more zone control, which can result in energy savings.

How Much Heater Do You Need? ▸

If you don't mind doing a little math, determining how many lineal feet of baseboard heater a room requires is not hard.

1. Measure the area of the room in square feet (length × width): _____
2. Multiply the area by 10 to get the baseline minimum wattage: _____
3. Add 5% for each newer window or 10% for each older window: _____
4. Add 10% for each exterior wall in the room: _____
5. Add 10% for each exterior door: _____
6. Add 10% if the space below is not insulated: _____

7. Add 20% if the space above is not well insulated: _____
8. Add 10% if ceiling is more than 8 ft. high: _____
9. Total of the baseline wattage plus all additions: _____
10. Divide this number by 250 (the wattage produced per foot of standard baseboard heater): _____
11. Round up to a whole number. This is the minimum number of feet of heater you need. _____

Note: It is much better to have more feet of heater than is required than fewer. Having more footage of heater does not consume more energy; it does allow the heaters to work more efficiently.

Planning Tips for Baseboard Heaters ▸

- Baseboard heaters require a dedicated circuit. A 20-amp, 240-volt circuit of 12-gauge copper wire will power up to 16 ft. of heater.
- Do not install a heater beneath a wall receptacle. Cords hanging down from the receptacle are a fire hazard.

- Do not mount heaters directly on the floor. You should maintain at least 1" of clear space between the baseboard heater and the floor covering.
- Installing heaters directly beneath windows is a good practice.
- Locate wall thermostats on interior walls only, and do not install directly above a heat source.

How to Install a 240-Volt Baseboard Heater

1

At the heater locations, cut a small hole in the drywall 3" to 4" above the floor. Pull 12/2 NM cables through the first hole: one from the thermostat, the other to the next heater. Pull all the cables for subsequent heaters. Middle-of-run heaters will have two cables, while end-of-run heaters have only one cable. (See also circuit map 15, page 157.)

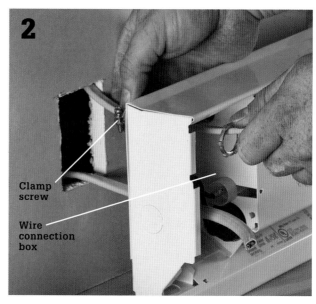

2

Clamp screw

Wire connection box

Remove the cover on the wire connection box. Open a knockout for each cable that will enter the box, and then feed the cables through the cable clamps and into the wire connection box. Attach the clamps to the wire connection box, and tighten the clamp screws until the cables are gripped firmly.

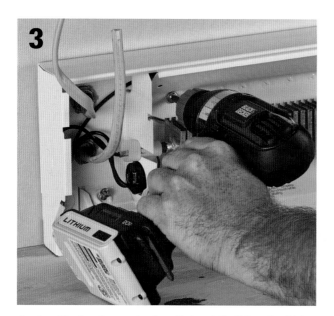

3

Anchor the heater against wall about 1" off floor by driving flathead screws through the back of the housing and into studs. Strip away cable sheathing so at least ½" of sheathing extends into the heater. Strip ¾" of insulation from each wire using a combination tool.

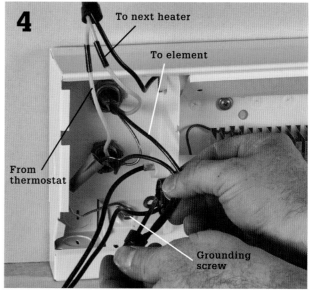

4

To next heater

To element

From thermostat

Grounding screw

Make connections to the heating element if the power wires are coming from a thermostat or another heater controlled by a thermostat. See the next page for other wiring schemes. Connect the white circuit wires to one of the wire leads on the heater. Tag white wires with black tape to indicate they are hot. Connect the black circuit wires to the other wire lead. Connect a grounding pigtail to the green grounding screw in the box, and then join all grounding wires with a wire connector. Reattach the cover.

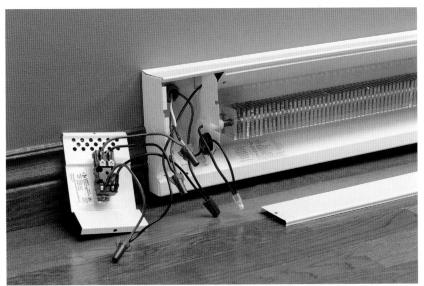

One heater with end-cap thermostat.
Run both power leads (black plus tagged neutral) into the connection box at either end of the heater. If installing a single-pole thermostat, connect one power lead to one thermostat wire and connect the other thermostat wire, to one of the heater leads. Connect the other hot LINE wire to the other heater lead. If you are installing a double-pole thermostat, make connections with both legs of the power supply.

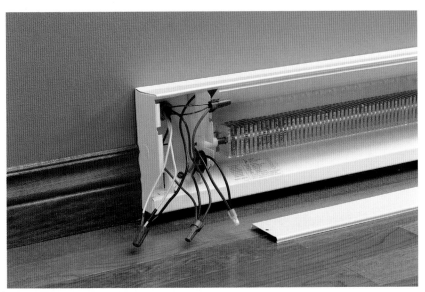

Multiple heaters. At the first heater, join both hot wires from the thermostat to the wires leading to the second heater in line. Be sure to tag all white neutrals hot. Twist copper ground wires together and pigtail them to the grounding screw in the baseboard heater junction box. This parallel wiring configuration ensures that power flow will not be interrupted to the downstream heaters if an upstream heater fails.

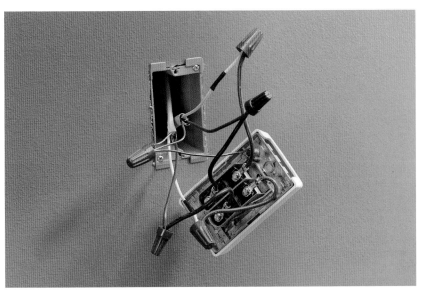

Wall-mounted thermostat. If installing a wall-mounted thermostat, the power leads should enter the thermostat first and then be wired to the individual heaters singly or in series. Hookups at the heater are made as shown in step 4. Be sure to tag the white neutral as hot in the thermostat box as well as in the heater box.

Wall Heaters

Installing a wall heater is an easy way to provide supplemental heat to a converted attic or basement without expanding an existing HVAC system.

Wall heaters are easy to install during a remodel (most have a separate can assembly that you attach to the framing before the drywall is installed). They can also be retrofitted.

Most models available at home centers use 120-volt current (shown below), but 240-volt models are also available.

Tools & Materials ▸

Drywall saw
Drill
Fish tape
Combination tool
Screwdrivers
12/2 NM cable
Wire connectors
Wall heater
Thermostat
(optional)
Wallboard saw

Wall heaters are an easy-to-install way to provide supplemental heat. Some models have built-in thermostats, while others can be controlled by a remote thermostat.

How to Install a Wall Heater in a Finished Wall

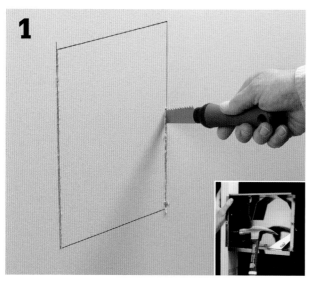

Make an opening in the wall for the heater. Use a stud finder to locate a stud in the area where you want to install the heater. Mark the opening for the heater according to the manufacturer's guidelines so that one side of the heater sits flush with a stud. Pay attention to clearance requirements. Cut the opening with a wallboard saw. If the wall is open, install the heater can before hanging drywall (inset).

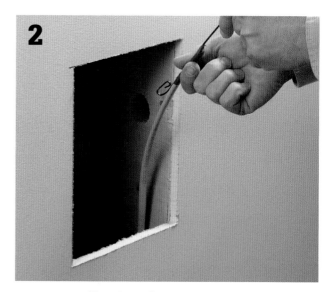

Turn power off, and test for power. Pull 12/2 NM cable from the main panel to the wall opening. If the heater is controlled by a separate thermostat, pull cable to the thermostat, and then run another cable from the thermostat to the heater location.

3

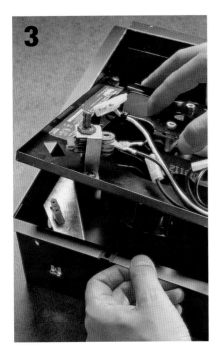

Disconnect and remove the motor unit from the heater can. Remove a knockout from the can, and route the cable into the can.

4

Install the can in the opening. Secure the cable with a clamp, leaving 8" to 12" of cable exposed. Attach the can to the framing as directed by the manufacturer.

5

Wire the heater. Connect the black circuit wire to one of the black heater leads. Connect the white circuit wire to the other lead. Connect the grounds.

6

Secure the heater unit in the can as directed by the manufacturer. Reconnect the motor if necessary. Attach the grill and thermostat knob as directed. Connect the new circuit breaker at the main panel.

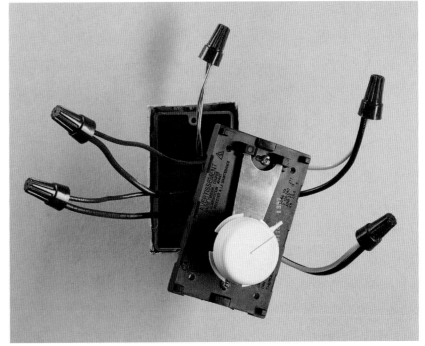

Variation: Connect a thermostat to control a wall heater. Some wall heaters do not use built-in thermostats. Install a thermostat in the heater circuit before the wall heater. Connect the black and the white wires coming from the main panel to the red leads on the thermostat. Connect the wires going to the heater to the black leads on the thermostat. Connect the grounds.

Underfloor Radiant Heat Systems

Floor-warming systems require very little energy to run and are designed to heat ceramic tile floors only; they generally are not used as sole heat sources for rooms.

A typical floor-warming system consists of one or more thin mats containing electric resistance wires that heat up when energized, like an electric blanket. The mats are installed beneath the tile and are hardwired to a 120-volt GFCI circuit. A thermostat controls the temperature, and a timer turns the system off automatically.

The system shown in this project includes two plastic mesh mats, each with its own power lead that is wired directly to the thermostat. Radiant mats may be installed over a plywood subfloor, but if you plan to install floor tile you should put down a base of cementboard first, and then install the mats on top of the cementboard.

A crucial part of installing this system is to use a multimeter to perform several resistance checks to make sure the heating wires have not been damaged during shipping or installation.

Electrical service required for a floor-warming system is based on size. A smaller system may connect to an existing circuit, but a larger one will need a dedicated circuit; follow the manufacturer's requirements. These systems should be on a GFCI-protected circuit.

To order a floor-warming system, contact the manufacturer or dealer (see Resources, page 331). In most cases, you can send them plans and they'll custom-fit a system for your project area.

Tools & Materials ▸

Vacuum cleaner	Trowel or rubber float
Multimeter	Conduit
Tape measure	Thinset mortar
Scissors	Thermostat with sensor
Router/rotary tool	Junction box(es)
Marker	Tile or stone
Electric wire fault	floorcovering
indicator (optional)	Drill
Hot glue gun	Double-sided
Radiant floor mats	carpet tape
12/2 NM cable	Cable clamps

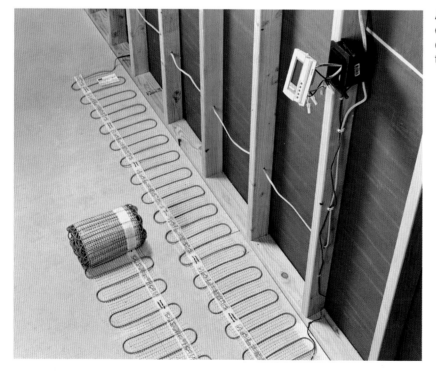

A radiant floor-warming system employs electric heating mats that are covered with floor tile to create a floor that's cozy underfoot.

Installation Tips ▸

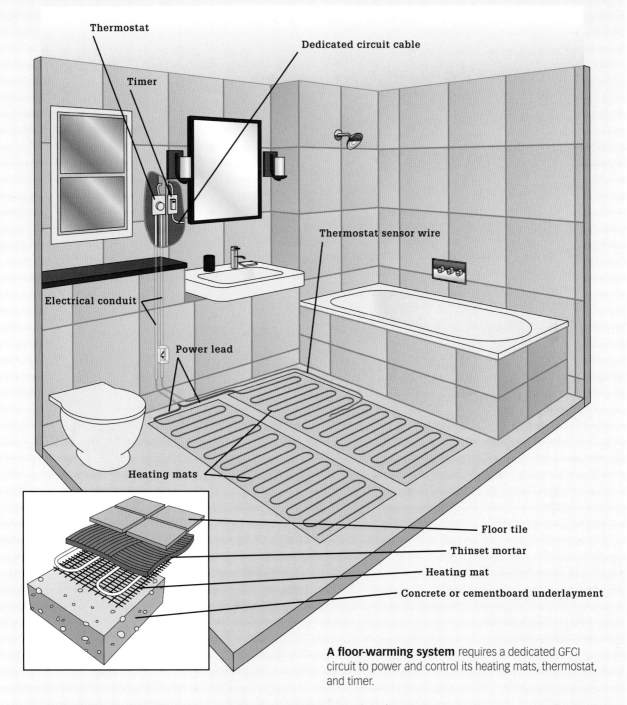

Thermostat

Timer

Dedicated circuit cable

Thermostat sensor wire

Electrical conduit

Power lead

Heating mats

Floor tile

Thinset mortar

Heating mat

Concrete or cementboard underlayment

A floor-warming system requires a dedicated GFCI circuit to power and control its heating mats, thermostat, and timer.

- Each radiant mat must have a direct connection to the power lead from the thermostat, with the connection made in a junction box in the wall cavity. Do not install mats in series.
- Do not install radiant floor mats under shower areas.
- Do not overlap mats or let them touch.
- Do not cut heating wire or damage heating wire insulation.
- The distance between wires in adjoining mats should equal the distance between wire loops measured center to center.

Installing a Radiant Floor-Warming System

Floor-warming systems must be installed on a circuit with adequate amperage and a GFCI breaker. Smaller systems may tie into an existing circuit, but larger ones need a dedicated circuit. Follow local building and electrical codes that apply to your project.

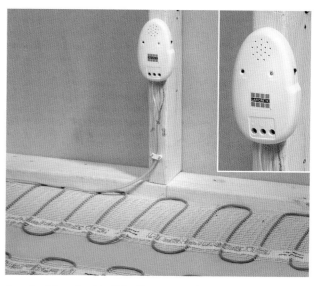

An electric wire fault indicator monitors each floor mat for continuity during the installation process. If there is a break in continuity (for example, if a wire is cut) an alarm sounds. If you choose not to use an installation tool to monitor the mat, test for continuity frequently using a multimeter.

How To Install a Radiant Floor-Warming System

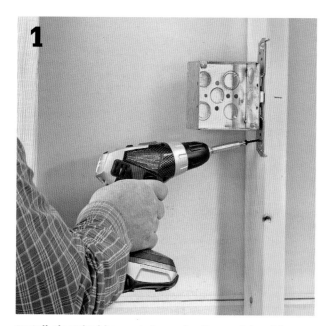

1

Install electrical boxes to house the thermostat and timer. In most cases, the box should be located 60" above floor level. Use a 4"-deep × 4"-wide double-gang box for the thermostat/timer control if your kit has an integral model. If your timer and thermostat are separate, install a separate single box for the timer.

2

Drill access holes in the sole plate for the power leads that are preattached to the mats (they should be over 10 ft. long). The leads should be connected to a supply wire from the thermostat in a junction box located in a wall near the floor and below the thermostat box. The access hole for each mat should be located directly beneath the knockout for that cable in the thermostat box. Drill through the sill plate vertically and horizontally so the holes meet in an L-shape.

3

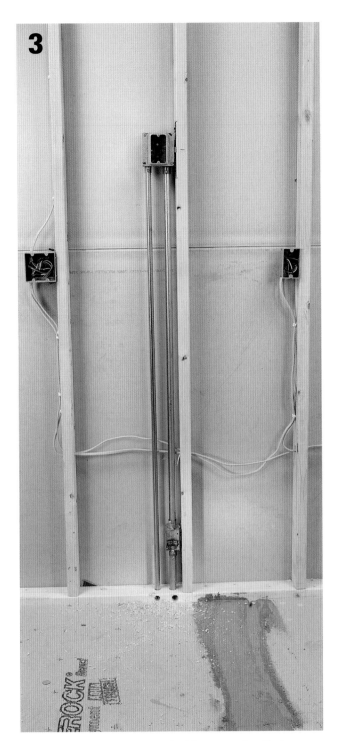

Run conduit from the electrical boxes to the sill plate. The line for the supply cable should be ¾" conduit. If you are installing multiple mats, the supply conduit should feed into a junction box about 6" above the sill plate and then continue into the ¾" hole you drilled for the supply leads. The sensor wire needs only ½" conduit that runs straight from the thermostat box via the thermostat. The mats should be powered by a dedicated 20-amp GFCI circuit of 12/2 NM cable run from your main service panel to the electrical box (this is for 120-volt mats—check your instruction manual for specific circuit recommendations).

4

Clean the floor surface thoroughly to get rid of any debris that could potentially damage the wire mats. A vacuum cleaner generally does a more effective job than a broom.

5

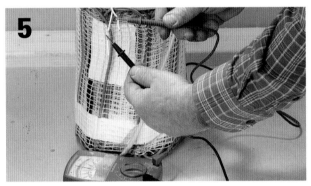

Test for resistance using a multimeter set to measure ohms. This is a test you should make frequently during the installation, along with checking for continuity. If the resistance is off by more than 10% from the theoretical resistance listing (see manufacturer's chart in installation instructions), contact a technical support operator for the kit manufacturer. For example, the theoretical resistance for the 1 × 50 ft. mat seen here is 19, so the ohms reading should be between 17 and 21.

6

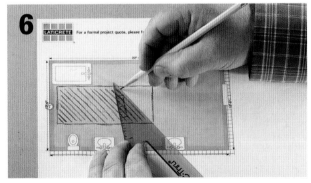

Finalize your mat layout plan. Most radiant floor warming mat manufacturers will provide a layout plan for you at the time of purchase, or they will give you access to an online design tool so you can come up with your own plan. This is an important step to the success of your project, and the assistance is free.

(continued)

7

Unroll the radiant mat or mats and allow them to settle. Arrange the mat or mats according to the plan you created. It's okay to cut the plastic mesh so you can make curves or switchbacks, but do not cut the heating wire under any circumstances, even to shorten it.

8

Finalize the mat layout, and then test the resistance again using a multimeter. Also check for continuity in several different spots. If there is a problem with any of the mats, you should identify it and correct it before proceeding with the mortar installation.

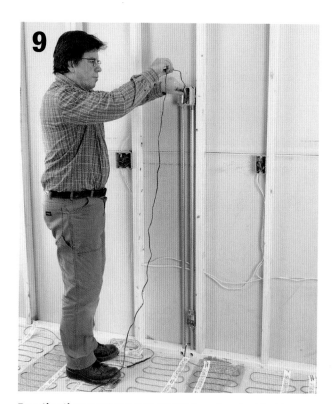

9

Run the thermostat sensor wire from the electrical box down the ½" conduit raceway and out the access hole in the sill plate. Select the best location for the thermostat sensor, and mark the location onto the flooring. Also mark the locations of the wires that connect to and lead from the sensor.

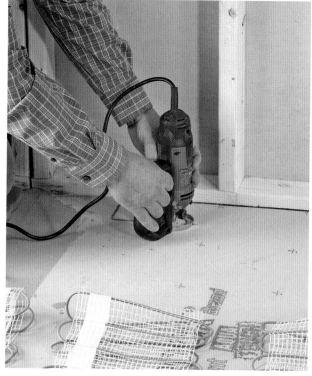

Variation: If your local codes require it, roll the mats out of the way, and cut a channel for the sensor and the sensor wires into the floor or floor underlayment. For most floor materials, a spiral cutting tool does a quick and neat job of this task. Remove any debris.

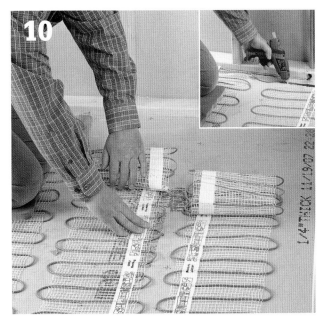

Bond the mats to the floor. If the mats in your system have adhesive strips, peel off the adhesive backing and roll out the mats in the correct position, pressing them against the floor to set the adhesive. If your mats have no adhesive, bind them with strips of double-sided carpet tape. The thermostat sensor and the power supply leads should be attached with hot glue (inset photo) and run up into their respective holes in the sill plate if you have not done this already. Test all mats for resistance and continuity.

Cover the floor installation areas with a layer of thinset mortar that is thick enough to fully encapsulate all the wires and mats (usually around ¼" in thickness). Check the wires for continuity and resistance regularly, and stop working immediately if there is a drop in resistance or a failure of continuity. Allow the mortar to dry overnight.

Connect the power supply leads from the mat or mats to the NM cable coming from the thermostat inside the junction box near the sill. Power must be turned off. The power leads should be cut so about 8" of wire feeds into the box. Be sure to use cable clamps to protect the wires.

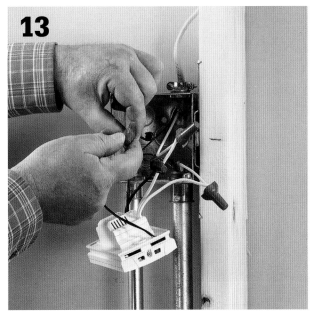

Connect the sensor wire and the power supply lead (from the junction box) to the thermostat/timer according to the manufacturer's directions. Attach the device to the electrical box, restore power, and test the system to make sure it works. Once you are convinced that it is operating properly, install floor tiles and repair the wall surfaces.

Ceiling Fans

Ceiling fans are installed and wired like ceiling fixtures. They always require heavy-duty bracing and electrical boxes rated for ceiling fans.

Most standard ceiling fans work with a wall switch functioning as master power for the unit. Pull chains attached to the unit control the fan and lights. In these installations, it's fairly simple to replace an existing ceiling fixture with a fan and light.

If you will be installing a new circuit for the fan, use three-wire cable so both the light and the motor can be controlled by wall switches (see circuit maps 30 and 31, page 165).

Because ceiling fans generally weigh more than ceiling lights and the motion of the blade creates more stress, it is very important that the ceiling box is securely mounted and is rated for ceiling fans. Ceiling boxes rated for ceiling fans are marked with the phrase "For ceiling fan support." If your existing ceiling box is not fan-rated, replace it with one that is. And be sure to inspect the manner in which the box is mounted to make sure it is strong enough (see page 246).

Installation varies from fan to fan, so be sure to follow the manufacturer's instructions.

Tools & Materials ▸

Screwdriver	2 × 4 lumber or
Combination tool	adjustable ceiling
Pliers or	fan crossbrace
adjustable wrench	1½" and 3" coarse-
Circuit tester	thread screws
Hammer	Eye protection
Ceiling fan light kit	Downrod (if needed)

A ceiling fan helps keep living spaces cooler in the summer and warmer in the winter. Replacing an overhead light with a fan/light is an easy project with big payback.

Ceiling Fan Types

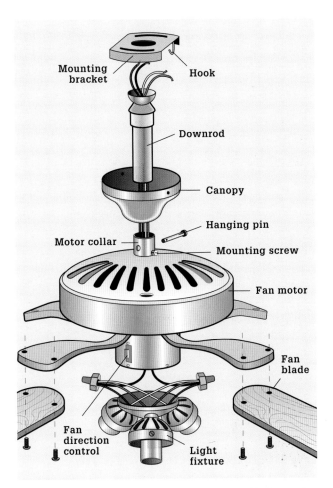

Bracket-mounted ceiling fans are hung directly from a mounting bracket that is attached to the ceiling box. A canopy conceals the motor and the connections.

Downrod mounted ceiling fans are supported by a metal rod that's hung from the ceiling mounting bracket. The length of the rod determines the height of the fan. Downrod fans are used in rooms with ceilings 8 ft. high or higher. You may need to buy a longer downrod if you have a very high ceiling.

Fans That Heat ▸

The first generation of ceiling fans did one job: they spun and moved air. As the technology advanced, light kits were added to replace the light source that is lost when a fan-only appliance is installed. Now, some ceiling fans are manufactured with electric heating elements that can produce up to 5,000 BTUs of heat, comparable to a small space heater. Located in the fan canopy, the ceramic heat elements direct heat out the vents and force it down to the living level in the room, along with the heated air that naturally rises.

Fan-mounted heaters are relatively light duty, so they generally do not require a dedicated circuit. In most cases, you can supply power to the heater/fan with any 15-amp room light circuit that has extra capacity.

Supporting Ceiling Boxes

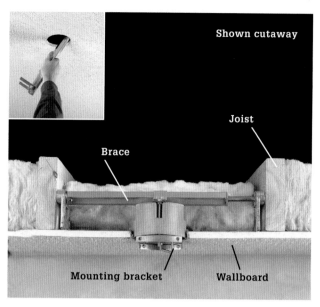

Add a wood brace above the ceiling box if you have access from above (as in an attic). Cut a 24" brace to fit and nail it between the ceiling joists. Drive a couple of deck screws through the ceiling box and into the brace. If the box is not fan-rated, replace it with one that is.

Install an adjustable fan brace if the ceiling is closed and you don't want to remove the wallcoverings. Remove the old light and the electrical box, and then insert the fan brace into the box opening (inset photo). Twist the brace housing to cause it to telescope outward. The brace should be centered over the opening and at the right height so the ceiling box is flush with the ceiling surface once it is hung from the brace.

Bracket-Mounted Fans

Direct-mount fan units have a motor housing with a mounting tab that fits directly into a slot on the mounting bracket. Fans with this mounting approach are secure and easy to install but difficult to adjust.

Ball-and-socket fan units have a downrod, but instead of threading into the mounting bracket, the downrod has an attached ball that fits into a hanger "socket" in the mounting bracket. This installation allows the fan to move in the socket and find its own level for quiet operation.

How to Install Downrod Ceiling Fans

1

Shut off the power to the circuit at the panel. Unscrew the existing fixture and carefully pull it away from the ceiling. Test for power by inserting the probes of a tester into the wire connectors on the black and the white wires. Disconnect and remove the old fixture.

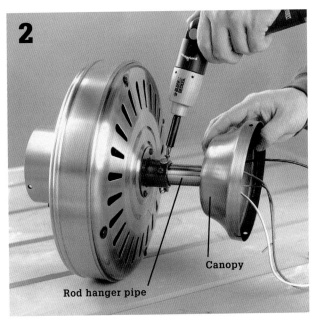

2

Canopy

Rod hanger pipe

Run the wires from the top of the fan motor through the canopy and then through the rod hanger pipe. Slide the rod hanger pipe through the canopy and attach the pipe to the motor collar using the included hanging pin. Tighten the mounting screws firmly.

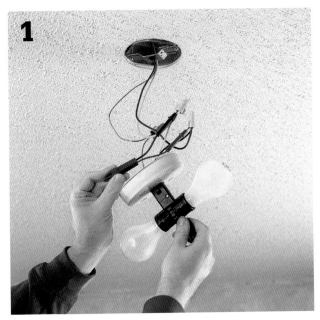

3

Hanging pin

Hang the motor assembly by the hook on the mounting bracket. Connect the wires according to manufacturer's directions, using wire connectors to join the fixture wires to the circuit wires in the box. Gather the wires together and tuck them inside the fan canopy. Lift the canopy and attach it to the mounting bracket.

4

Fan housing

Attach the fan blades with the included hardware. Connect the wiring for the fan's light fixture according to the manufacturer's directions. Tuck all wires into the switch housing, and attach the fixture. Install light bulbs. Restore power, and test the fan.

Remote-Control Ceiling Fan Retrofit

Ceiling fan remote control switches offer an easy way of controlling both the lighting and fan function of your ceiling fan. They are commonly used when there are only a hot and neutral at the fan location or where the ability to switch two different functions is not present in the wiring. The remote can save you the need to install another switch and/or the need to pull another wire to your ceiling fan. Many different remotes on the market can be used with different manufacturer ceiling fans, so you are not limited to the brand of fan you are using.

Tools & Materials ▸

Ceiling fan remote kit
Wire connectors
Screwdrivers
Pliers
Needle nose pliers
Wire strippers
Circuit tester
Eye protection

A retrofit remote control kit lets you take the hassle (and the pull chains) out of operating just about any ceiling fan and light.

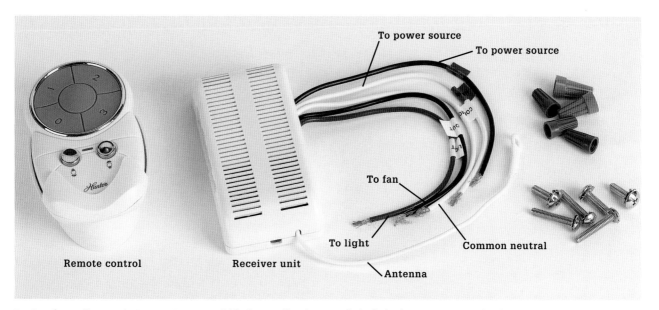

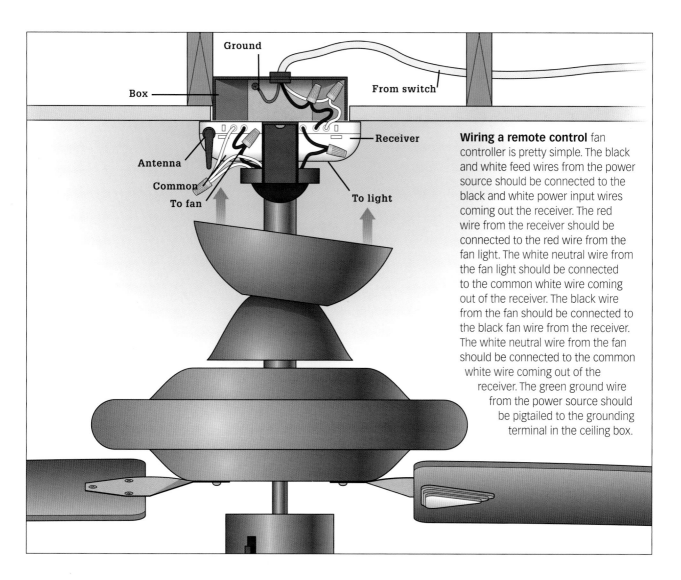

Parts of an aftermarket remote control kit for a ceiling fan usually include the remote control unit (some come with a cradle) and the receiver unit. Your unit may come with color-coded wire connectors and mounting hardware as well.

Wiring a remote control fan controller is pretty simple. The black and white feed wires from the power source should be connected to the black and white power input wires coming out the receiver. The red wire from the receiver should be connected to the red wire from the fan light. The white neutral wire from the fan light should be connected to the common white wire coming out of the receiver. The black wire from the fan should be connected to the black fan wire from the receiver. The white neutral wire from the fan should be connected to the common white wire coming out of the receiver. The green ground wire from the power source should be pigtailed to the grounding terminal in the ceiling box.

How to Retrofit a Remote Control to a Ceiling Fan

Turn your fan on high speed and turn the lights on. Then, at the main service panel, shut off the power to the circuit that supplies your ceiling fan.

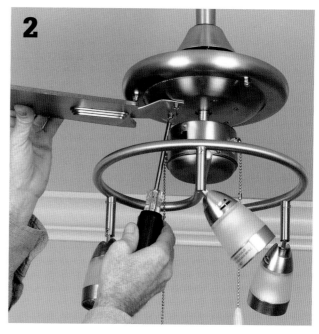

Remove the fan blades, one at a time on opposite sides of one another, so as to not overweight a certain side, which could bend the shaft and create a wobble. There are generally two vertically installed Phillips head #10 screws that hold the blade bracket to the motor housing.

If a light kit was installed on the fan, remove it as well. First, remove the bulbs and any glass diffusers, and then remove the light kit itself. Usually you'll find three horizontally installed #6 Phillips head screws attached to the pan directly below the motor housing. Unplug the light kit from the fan wires and set aside.

If your fan has a downrod between the motor housing and the ceiling, remove the canopy on the top of the pipe connected to the mounting plate on the ceiling. You should find two to four horizontally installed #6 screws near the base of the canopy. Remove the screws, and slide the canopy down to expose the wiring.

5

Check all wires with a circuit tester to verify there is no power present.

6

Disconnect the black, red or blue, and white wires from the electrical box wires.

7

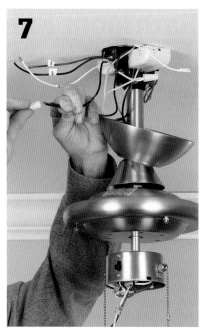

Install the receiving unit of the remote fan kit. Connect the black and white wires from the receiving unit input to the black and the white wires coming from the electrical box in the ceiling. If a red wire was used originally to feed the light portion of the fan, cap this wire with a wire nut and fold it into the box.

8

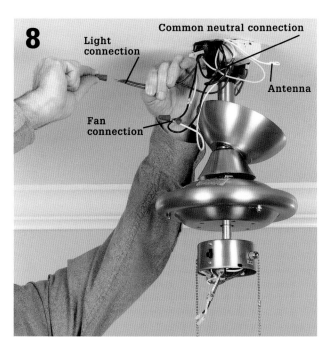

Light connection

Common neutral connection

Antenna

Fan connection

Connect the output of the receiving unit to the fan's associated wiring: black wire to black wire, white wire to white wire, and blue wire to blue wire (or red to red, or red to blue). If a downrod was used to hang the fan, place the receiving unit above the ball and flange portion of the mounting bracket.

9

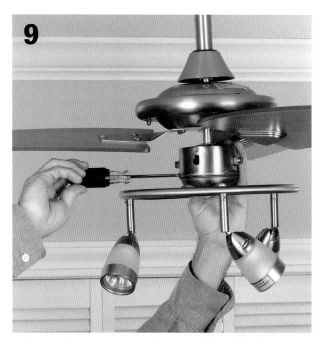

Reinstall the canopy, fan blades, and light kit. Restore power. Install the batteries into the remote control sending unit, and test to make sure the fan is spinning on all three modes: Low, Medium, and High. Test the light switch to verify the light switch works as well. Disconnect and remove the pullchains.

Mark the exit location in the roof next to a rafter for the exhaust duct. Drill a pilot hole, and then saw through the sheathing and roofing material with a reciprocating saw to make the cutout for the exhaust tailpiece.

Remove a section of shingles from around the cutout, leaving the roofing paper intact. Remove enough shingles to create an exposed area that is at least the size of the exhaust termination flange.

Exhaust termination flange

Exhaust tailpiece

Attach a hose clamp to the rafter next to the roof cutout about 1" below the roof sheathing (top). Insert the exhaust tailpiece into the cutout and through the hose clamp, and then tighten the clamp screw (bottom).

Slide one end of the exhaust duct over the tailpiece, and slide the other end over the outlet on the fan unit. Slip hose clamps or straps around each end of the duct, and tighten the clamps.

Wrap the exhaust duct with pipe insulation. Insulation prevents moist air inside the hose from condensing and dripping down into the fan motor.

Apply roofing cement to the bottom of the exhaust termination flange, and then slide the termination over the tailpiece. Nail the termination flange in place with self-sealing roofing nails, and then patch in shingles around the cover.

5

Check all wires with a circuit tester to verify there is no power present.

6

Disconnect the black, red or blue, and white wires from the electrical box wires.

7

Install the receiving unit of the remote fan kit. Connect the black and white wires from the receiving unit input to the black and the white wires coming from the electrical box in the ceiling. If a red wire was used originally to feed the light portion of the fan, cap this wire with a wire nut and fold it into the box.

8

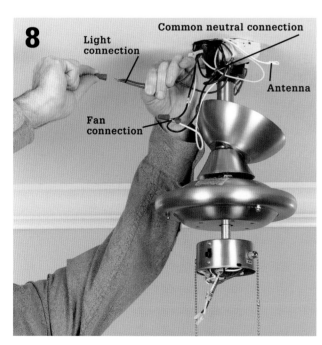

Common neutral connection

Light connection

Antenna

Fan connection

Connect the output of the receiving unit to the fan's associated wiring: black wire to black wire, white wire to white wire, and blue wire to blue wire (or red to red, or red to blue). If a downrod was used to hang the fan, place the receiving unit above the ball and flange portion of the mounting bracket.

9

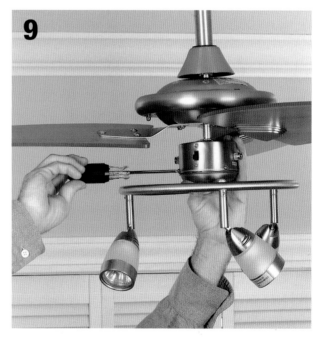

Reinstall the canopy, fan blades, and light kit. Restore power. Install the batteries into the remote control sending unit, and test to make sure the fan is spinning on all three modes: Low, Medium, and High. Test the light switch to verify the light switch works as well. Disconnect and remove the pullchains.

Bathroom Exhaust Fans

Most exhaust fans are installed in the center of the bathroom ceiling or over the toilet area. A fan installed over the tub or shower area must be rated for use in wet areas. You can usually wire a fan that just has a light fixture into a main bathroom lighting circuit. Units with built-in heat lamps or blowers require separate circuits.

If the fan you choose doesn't come with a mounting kit, purchase one separately. A mounting kit should include an exhaust hose (duct), a vent tailpiece, and an exterior terminal.

The most common exhaust options are a roof exhaust and a soffit exhaust. Sometimes the exhaust can be directed out a sidewall. The instructions in this book are for a shingle roof covering. You should have a roofer install the exhaust termination if you have any other roof covering material or if you are not comfortable walking on your roof.

A soffit exhaust involves routing the duct to a soffit (roof overhang) where it is connected to a terminal that directs the exhaust outside. While soffit exhausts are allowed, they are not recommended, because the moisture can be drawn back into the attic through the soffit vents. Check with the exhaust fan manufacturer for instructions about how to run and terminate the exhaust duct.

Tools & Materials ▸

Drill
Jigsaw
Combination tool
Screwdrivers
Caulk gun
Reciprocating saw
Pry bar
Screws
Double-gang retrofit electrical box

NM cable (14/2, 14/3)
Cable clamp
Hose clamps
Pipe insulation
Roofing cement
Self-sealing roofing nails
Shingles
Wire connectors
Switch and timer
Eye protection

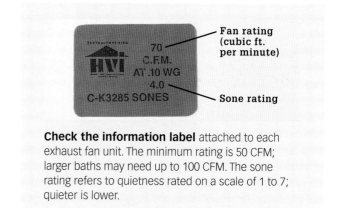

Check the information label attached to each exhaust fan unit. The minimum rating is 50 CFM; larger baths may need up to 100 CFM. The sone rating refers to quietness rated on a scale of 1 to 7; quieter is lower.

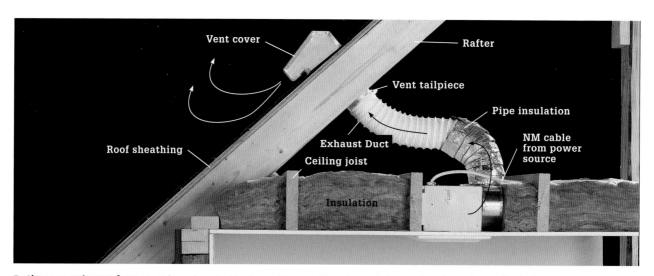

Bathroom exhaust fans must be exhausted to the outdoors, either through the roof or through a wall. Flexible ductwork is allowed for bath exhaust fans (but not for clothes dryers).

How to Install a Bathroom Exhaust Fan

Position the fan unit against a ceiling joist. Outline the fan onto the ceiling surface. Remove the unit, drill pilot holes at the corners of the outline, and cut out the area with a jigsaw or drywall saw.

Remove the grille from the fan unit, and then position the unit against the joist with the edge recessed ¼" from the finished surface of the ceiling (so the grille can be flush mounted). Attach the unit to the joist using drywall screws.

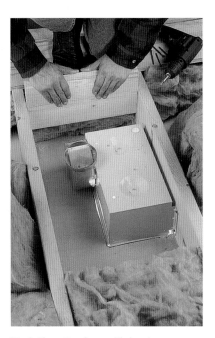

Variation: For fans with heaters or light fixtures, some manufacturers recommend using 2× lumber to build dams between the ceiling joists to keep the insulation at least 6" away from the fan unit.

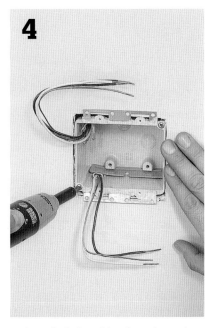

Switch box location

Mark and cut an opening for a double-gang box on the wall next to the latch side of the bathroom door, and then run a 14/3 NM cable from the switch cutout to the fan unit. Run a 14/2 NM cable from the power source to the cutout.

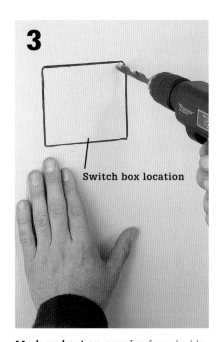

Strip 10" of sheathing from the ends of the cables, and then feed the cables into a double-gang retrofit switch box so at least ½" of sheathing extends into the box. Clamp the cables in place. Tighten the mounting screws until the box is secure.

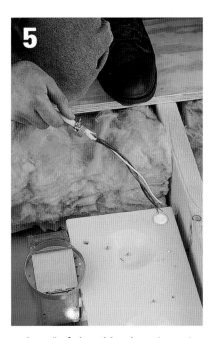

Strip 10" of sheathing from the end of the cable at the unit, and then attach a cable clamp to the cable. Insert the cable into the fan unit. From the inside of the unit, screw a locknut onto the threaded end of the clamp.

(continued)

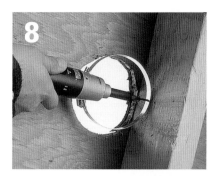

Exhaust tailpiece

Mark the exit location in the roof next to a rafter for the exhaust duct. Drill a pilot hole, and then saw through the sheathing and roofing material with a reciprocating saw to make the cutout for the exhaust tailpiece.

Remove a section of shingles from around the cutout, leaving the roofing paper intact. Remove enough shingles to create an exposed area that is at least the size of the exhaust termination flange.

Exhaust termination flange

Attach a hose clamp to the rafter next to the roof cutout about 1" below the roof sheathing (top). Insert the exhaust tailpiece into the cutout and through the hose clamp, and then tighten the clamp screw (bottom).

Slide one end of the exhaust duct over the tailpiece, and slide the other end over the outlet on the fan unit. Slip hose clamps or straps around each end of the duct, and tighten the clamps.

Wrap the exhaust duct with pipe insulation. Insulation prevents moist air inside the hose from condensing and dripping down into the fan motor.

Apply roofing cement to the bottom of the exhaust termination flange, and then slide the termination over the tailpiece. Nail the termination flange in place with self-sealing roofing nails, and then patch in shingles around the cover.

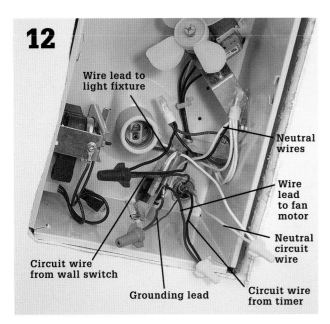

12

Wire lead to light fixture

Neutral wires

Wire lead to fan motor

Neutral circuit wire

Circuit wire from wall switch

Grounding lead

Circuit wire from timer

Turn power off, and test for power. Make the following wire connections at the fan unit: the black circuit wire from the timer to the wire lead for the fan motor; the red circuit wire from the single-pole switch (see step 14) to the wire lead for the light fixture in the unit; the white neutral circuit wire to the neutral wire lead; the circuit grounding wire to the grounding lead on the fan unit. Make all connections with wire connectors. Attach the cover plate over the unit when the wiring is completed.

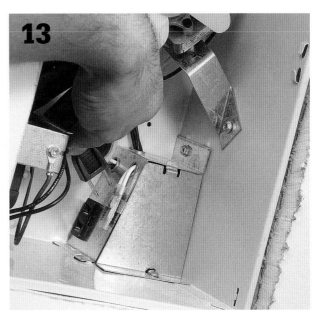

13

Connect the fan motor plug to the built-in receptacle on the wire connection box, and attach the fan grille to the frame using the mounting clips included with the fan kit. *Note: If you removed the wall and ceiling surfaces for the installation, install new surfaces before completing this step.*

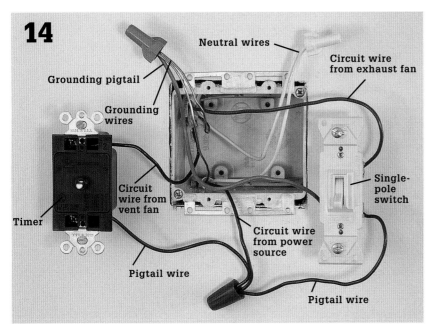

14

Neutral wires

Circuit wire from exhaust fan

Grounding pigtail

Grounding wires

Circuit wire from vent fan

Circuit wire from power source

Single-pole switch

Timer

Pigtail wire

Pigtail wire

Turn power off, and test for power. At the switch box, add black pigtail wires to one screw terminal on the timer and to one screw terminal on the single-pole switch; add a green grounding pigtail to the groundling screw on the switch. Make the following wire connections: the black circuit wire from the power source to the black pigtail wires; the black circuit wire from the vent fan to the remaining screw on the timer; the red circuit wire from the vent fan to the remaining screw on the switch. Join the white wires with a wire connector. Join the grounding wires with a green wire connector.

15

Tuck the wires into the switch box, and then attach the switch and timer to the box. Attach the cover plate and timer dial. Turn on the power.

Range Hoods

Range hoods do more than just get rid of cooking odors. Their most important job is to reduce the amount of water vapor in the air that's generated by routine cooking. The pot of water that boils for 30 minutes before you remember to drop in the pasta adds a lot of water vapor into your house. Usually the results are innocent enough. But prolonged periods of high moisture can lead to mildew and other molds that can stain your walls and ceilings and possibly make family members sick.

The hardest part of adding a range hood is installing the ductwork between the hood and the outside of your house. Always use galvanized steel, copper, or stainless steel ducts. Never use flexible duct, including flexible metal duct. If the range is located on an outside wall, the best choice is to run the duct from the back of the hood straight through the wall. If you have wood siding, this job is not difficult. But if you have brick or stone, plan on spending several hours to cut this hole.

If the range is on an interior wall, the preferred route is usually from the top of the hood through the roof. It's also possible to put the duct into the attic, then across the ceiling (between two rafters or trusses) and out through an overhanging soffit. Follow the hood manufacturer's instructions about the size and length of the duct. A duct that is too long or too small will not work well and may be a grease fire hazard.

National codes require that a dedicated 20-amp, 120-circuit serve a range hood. You may not draw power from existing circuits. If your range hood includes a microwave oven, be sure to read the installation instructions, preferably before you buy the microwave. You may need a different cabinet above the range. Inspectors may not approve microwaves that are too close to the range.

Tools & Materials ▸

Hammer	Rangehood
Jigsaw	Galvanized sheet metal
Screwdrivers	ducts and fittings
Drill/driver & bits	Wire connectors
Utility knife	Sheet metal screws
Circular saw	Foil tape
Caulk gun	Plastic roof cement
Exhaust exterior	Caulk
termination	Eye protection

A range hood captures steam and airborne food particles and draws them directly out of your house through an exhaust duct. For slide-in ranges, the hood usually is installed under a short cabinet that contains the ductwork connection.

Range Hoods

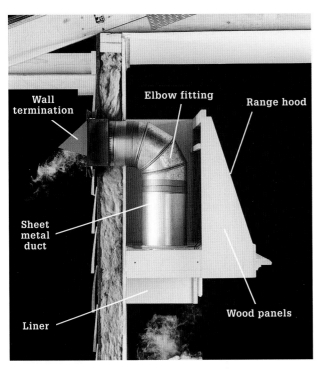

Cabinet-mounted range hoods draw steam upward and out of the house through a wall-mounted or roof-mounted termination.

Labels: Wall termination, Elbow fitting, Range hood, Sheet metal duct, Wood panels, Liner

Wall-mounted range hoods function in the same manner as cabinet mounted, but they are not integrated into the kitchen cabinet system.

Downdraft exhaust pulls steam downward and exhausts it out through a wall exhaust. While leaving the space above the stovetop uncluttered, these exhausts are much less efficient (in large part because steam naturally rises).

Label: Blower unit

Island exhausts hang down from ceiling-mounted ductwork and draw steam and odors up from stovetops that are installed in kitchen islands. They typically have a very contemporary appearance.

How to Install a Range Hood

Install the sheet metal duct in the wall first, and then cut a hole in the back of the range hood cabinet and mount the cabinet over the duct. Cut a hole in the bottom of the cabinet to match the opening on the top of the hood. The range hood often comes with templates to help you cut holes in the right place.

Make sure the circuit power is turned off at the service panel, and test for power. Then join the power cable wires to the lead wires inside the range hood. Use wire connectors for this job.

Get someone to help lift the range hood into place and hold it there while you attach it. Drive two screws through both sides and into the adjacent cabinets. If the hood is slightly small for the opening, slip a shim between the hood and the walls, trying to keep the gaps even.

Run ductwork from the cabinet to the exhaust exit point. Use two 45° adjustable elbows to join the duct in the wall to the top of the range hood. Use sheet metal screws and foil tape to hold all parts together and keep them from moving. Connect the duct securely to the fan outlet, and connect all sections so they do not leak. A leaky connection can allow grease-laden air to collect on the wood and start a fire.

Exhaust Termination Locations

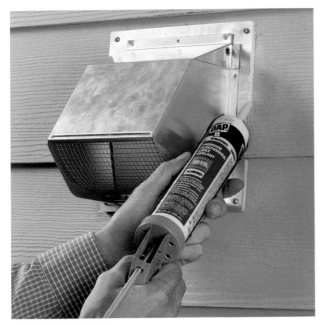

Wall termination: If the duct comes out through the sidewall of the house, install a vertical termination hood. Make sure to seal around the perimeter of the hood with exterior caulk. Don't locate the termination too close to a window, or the fumes will circulate back into the home.

Masonry wall termination: You can run ductwork out through an exterior wall made of brick or stucco, but it is a lot of work. You need to cut an opening in the wall with a masonry saw or chip one with a cold chisel, and then attach the termination hood with masonry nails.

Soffit termination: If the duct goes through an overhang soffit, you'll need a transition fitting to connect the round duct to a short piece of rectangular duct. Once these parts are installed, add a protective grille to keep animals and insects from getting into the duct. Don't locate the termination near a soffit ventilation opening; the fumes and moisture will be drawn back into the attic.

Roof termination: For ducts that pass through the roof, cut an access hole through the roofing and sheathing, and then install a weatherproof cap on top of the duct and under the roofing shingles. Make a waterproof seal by caulking the cap with plastic roof cement. If you don't have much roofing experience, consult a roofing manual for some more information on this step. Have a roofer do this is you have a roof covering other than shingles or if your roof is steep or high. Also see page 254.

Backup Power Supply

Installing a backup generator is an invaluable way to prepare your family for emergencies. The simplest backup power system is a portable gas-powered generator and an extension cord or two. A big benefit of this approach is that you can run a refrigerator and a few worklights during a power outage with a tool that can also be transported to remote job sites or on camping trips when it's not doing emergency backup duty. This is also the least expensive way to provide some backup power for your home. You can purchase a generator at most home centers and be up and running in a matter of hours. If you take this approach, it is critically important that you make certain any loads being run by your generator are disconnected from the utility power source.

The next step up is to incorporate a manual transfer switch for your portable generator. Transfer switches are permanently hardwired to your service panel. They are mounted on either the interior or the exterior of your house between the generator and the service panel. You provide a power feed from the generator into the switch. The switch is wired to selected essential circuits in your house, allowing you to power lights, furnace blowers, and other loads that can't easily be run with an extension cord. But perhaps the most important job a transfer switch performs is to disconnect the utility power. If the inactive utility power line is attached to the service panel, "backfeed" of power from your generator to the utility line can occur when the generator kicks in. This condition could be fatal to line workers who are trying to restore power. The potential for backfeed is the main reason many municipalities insist that only a licensed electrician hook up a transfer switch. Using a transfer switch not installed by a professional may also void the warranty of the switch and the generator.

Automatic transfer switches turn on the generator and switch off the utility supply when they detect a significant drop in line voltage. They may be installed with portable generators, provided the generator is equipped with an electric starter.

Large standby generators that resemble central air conditioners are the top of the line in backup power supply systems. Often fueled by home natural gas lines or propane tanks that offer a bottomless fuel source, standby generators are made in sizes with as much as 20 to 40 kilowatts of output—enough to supply all of the power needs of a 5,000-sq.-ft. home.

Generators have a range of uses.
Large hard-wired models can provide instant emergency power for a whole house. Smaller models (below) are convenient for occasional short-term backup as well as job sites or camping trips.

Choosing a Backup Generator

A 2,000- to 5,000-watt gas-powered generator and a few extension cords can power lamps and an appliance or two during shorter-term power outages. Appliances must not be connected to household wiring and the generator simultaneously. Never plug a generator into an outlet. Never operate a generator indoors. Run extension cords through a garage door.

A permanent transfer switch patches electricity from a large portable generator through to selected household circuits via an inlet at your service panel (inset), allowing you to power hardwired fixtures and appliances with the generator.

For full, on-demand backup service, install a large standby generator wired through to an automatic transfer panel. In the event of a power outage, the household system instantly switches to the generator.

A Typical Backup System

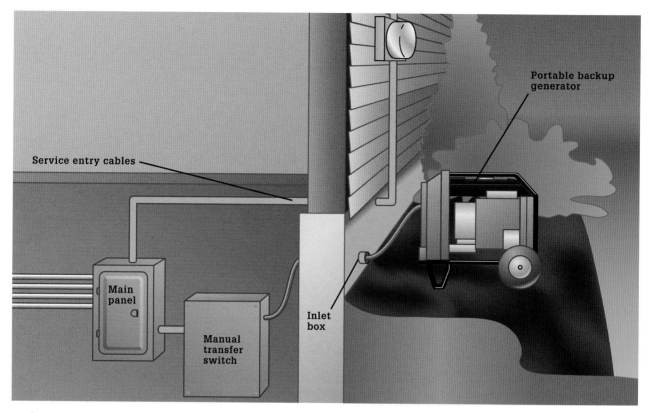

Backup generators supply power to a manual transfer switch, which disconnects the house from the main service wires and routes power from the generator through selected household circuits.

Choosing a Generator

Choosing a generator for your home's needs requires a few calculations. The chart below gives an estimate of the size of generator typically recommended for a house of a certain size. You can get a more accurate number by adding up the power consumption (the watts) of all the circuits or devices to be powered by a generator. It's also important to keep in mind that, for most electrical appliances, the amount of power required at the moment you flip the ON switch is greater than the number of watts required to keep the device running. For instance, though an air conditioner may run on 15,000 watts of power, it will require a surge of 30,000 watts at startup (the power range required to operate an appliance is usually listed somewhere on the device itself). These two numbers are called run watts and surge watts. Generators are typically sold according to run watts (a 5,000-watt generator can sustain 5,000 watts). They are also rated for a certain number of surge watts (a 5,000-watt generator may be able to produce a surge of

10,000 watts). If the surge watts aren't listed, ask, or check the manual. Some generators can't develop many more surge watts than run watts; others can produce twice as much surge as run wattage.

It's not necessary to buy a generator large enough to match the surge potential of all your circuits (you won't be turning everything on simultaneously), but surge watts should factor in your purchasing decision. If you will be operating the generator at or near capacity, it is also a wise practice to stagger startups for appliances.

SIZE OF HOUSE (IN SQUARE FEET)	RECOMMENDED GENERATOR SIZE (IN KILOWATTS)
Up to 2,700	5–11
2,701–3,700	14–16
3,701–4,700	20
4,701–7,000	42–47

Types of Transfer Switches

Cord-connected transfer switches (shown above) are hard-wired to the service panel (in some cases they're installed after the service panel and operate only selected circuits). These switches contain a male receptacle for a power supply cord connected to the generator. Automatic transfer switches (not shown) detect voltage drop-off in the main power line and switch over to the emergency power source.

When using a cord-connected switch, consider mounting an inlet box to the exterior wall. This will allow you to connect a generator without running a cord into the house.

Generator Tips ▸

If you'll need to run sensitive electronics such as computers or home theater equipment, look for a generator with power inverter technology that dispenses "clean power" with a stable sine wave pattern.

A generator that will output 240-volt service is required to run most central air conditioners. If your generator has variable output (120/240) make sure the switch is set to the correct output voltage.

Running & Maintaining a Backup System

Even with a fully automatic standby generator system fueled by natural gas or propane, you will need to conduct some regular maintenance and testing to make sure all systems are ready in the event of power loss. If you're depending on a portable generator and extension cords or a standby generator with a manual transfer switch, you'll also need to know the correct sequence of steps to follow in a power emergency. Switches and panels also need to be tested on a regular basis, as directed in your owner's manual. And be sure that all switches (both interior and exterior) are housed in an approved enclosure box.

Pull-cord starter

Smaller portable generators often use pull-cords instead of electric starters.

ANATOMY OF A PORTABLE BACKUP GENERATOR

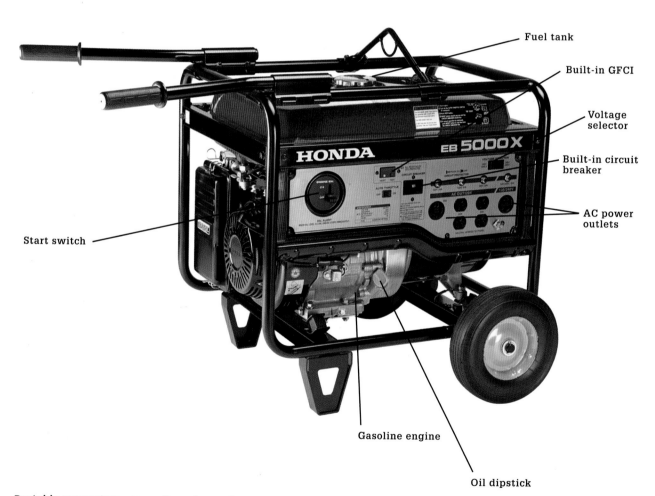

Fuel tank

Built-in GFCI

Voltage selector

Built-in circuit breaker

AC power outlets

Start switch

Gasoline engine

Oil dipstick

Portable generators use small gasoline engines to generate power. A built-in electronics panel sets current to AC or DC and the correct voltage. Most models will also include a built-in circuit breaker to protect the generator from damage in the event it is connected to too many loads. Better models include features like built-in GFCI protection. Larger portable generators may also feature electric starter motors and batteries for push-button starts.

Operating a Manual System During an Outage

Plug the generator in at the inlet box. Make sure the other end of the generator's outlet cord is plugged into the appropriate outlet on the generator (120-volt or 120/240-volt AC) and the generator is switched to the appropriate voltage setting.

Start the generator with the pull-cord or electric starter (if your generator has one). Let the generator run for several minutes before flipping the transfer switch.

Flip the manual transfer switch. Begin turning on loads one at a time by flipping breakers on, starting with the ones that power essential equipment. Do not overload the generator or the switch, and do not run the generator at or near full capacity for more than 30 minutes at a time.

Maintaining & Operating an Automatic Standby Generator

If you choose to spend the money and install a dedicated standby generator of 10,000 watts or more and operate it through an automatic transfer switch or panel, you won't need to lift a hand when your utility power goes out. The system kicks in by itself. However, you should follow the manufacturer's instructions for testing the system, changing the oil, and running the motor periodically.

Installing a Transfer Switch

A transfer switch is installed next to the main service panel to override the normal electrical service with power from a backup generator during a power outage. Manual transfer switches require an operator to change the power source, while automatic switches detect the loss of power, start the back-up generator, and switch over to the backup power feed. Because the amount of electricity created by a backup generator is not adequate to power all of the electrical circuits in your house, you'll need to designate a few selected circuits to get backup current (see page267).

A manual transfer switch connects emergency circuits in your main panel to a standby generator.

Tools & Materials ▸

Circuit tester
Drill/driver
Screwdrivers
Hammer
Wire cutters
Cable ripper
Wire strippers

Level
Manual transfer switch
Screws
Wire connectors
   (yellow)
Standby power
   generator

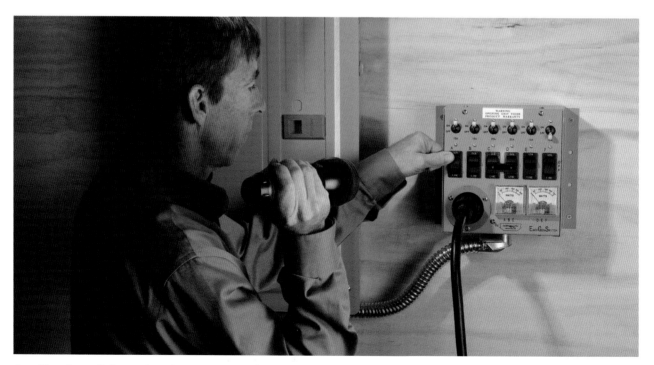

One flip of a switch reassigns the power source for each critical circuit so your backup generator can keep your refrigerator, freezer, and important lights running during an outage of utility power.

Selecting Backup Circuits ▸

Before you purchase a backup generator, determine which loads you will want to power from your generator in the event of a power loss. Generally you will want to power your refrigerator, freezer, and maybe a few lights. Add up the running wattage ratings of the appliances you will power up to determine how large your backup generator needs to be. Because the startup wattage of many appliances is higher than the running wattage, avoid starting all circuits at the same time—it can cause an overload situation with your generator. Here are some approximate running wattage guidelines (see page 132 to 137 for more information on calculating electrical loads):

- Refrigerator: 750 watts
- Forced air furnace: 1,100 to 1,500 watts
- Incandescent lights: 60 watts per bulb (CFL and LED lights use less wattage)
- Sump pump: 800 to 1,000 watts
- Garage door opener: 550 to 1,100 watts
- Television: 300 watts

Add the wattage values of all the loads you want to power, and multiply the sum by 1.25. This will give you the minimum wattage your generator must produce. Portable standby generators typically output 5,000 to 7,500 watts. Most larger, stationary generators can output 10,000 to 20,000 watts (10 to 20 kilowatts).

How to Install a Manual Transfer Switch

1

Turn off the main power breaker in your electrical service panel. CAUTION: The terminals where power enters the main breakers will still be energized.

2

Determine which household circuits are critical for emergency usage during a power outage. Typically this will include the refrigerator, freezer, furnace, and at least one light or small appliance circuit.

(continued)

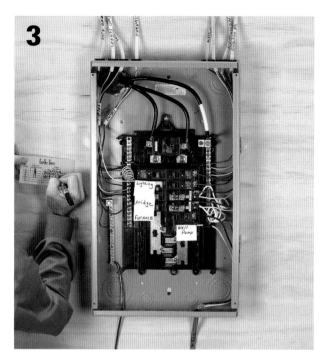

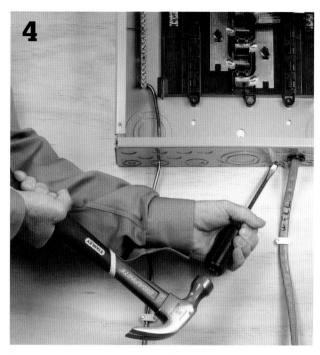

Match your critical circuits with circuit inlet on your pre-wired transfer switch. Try to balance the load as best you can in the transfer switch: For example, if your refrigerator is on the leftmost switch circuit, connect your freezer to the circuit farthest to the right. Double-pole (240-volt) circuits will require two 120-volt circuit connections. Also make sure that 15-amp and 20-amp circuits are not mismatched with one another.

Select and remove a knockout at the bottom of the main service panel box. Make sure to choose a knockout that is sized to match the connector on the flexible conduit coming from the transfer switch.

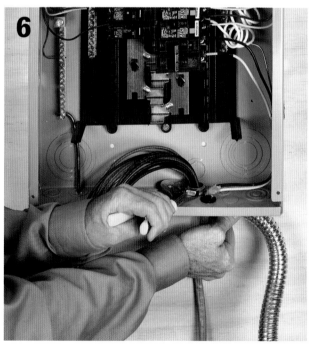

Feed the wires from the transfer switch into the knockout hole, taking care not to damage the insulation. You will note that each wire is labeled according to which circuit in the switch box it feeds.

Secure the flexible conduit from the switch box to the main service panel using a locknut and a bushing where required.

Attach the transfer switch box to the wall so the closer edge is about 18" away from the center of the main service panel. Use whichever connectors make sense for your wall type.

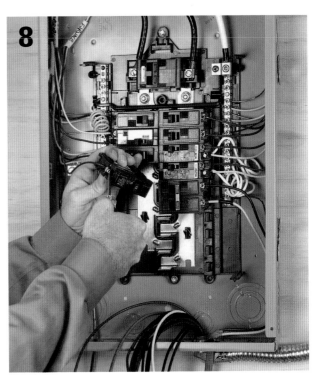

Remove the breaker for the first critical circuit from the main service panel box, and disconnect the hot wire lead from the lug on the breaker.

Locate the red wire for the switch box circuit that corresponds to the circuit you've disconnected. Attach the red wire to the breaker you've just removed, and then reinstall the breaker.

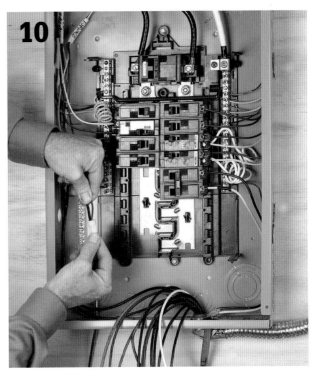

Locate the black wire from the same transfer switch circuit, and twist it together with the old feed wire, using a yellow wire connector. Tuck the wires neatly out of the way at the edges of the box. Proceed to the next circuit, and repeat the process.

(continued)

11

If any of your critical circuits are 240-volt circuits, attach the red leads from the two transfer switch circuits to the double-pole breaker. The two circuits originating in the transfer switch should be next to one another, and their switches should be connected with a handle tie. If you have no 240-volt circuits you may remove the preattached handle tie and use the circuits individually.

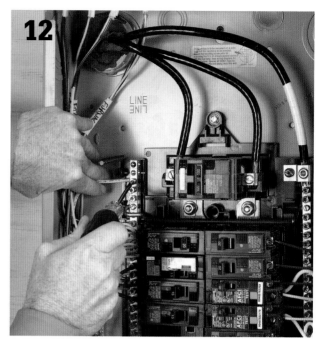

12

Once you have made all circuit connections, attach the white neutral wire from the transfer switch to an opening in the neutral bus bar of the main service panel.

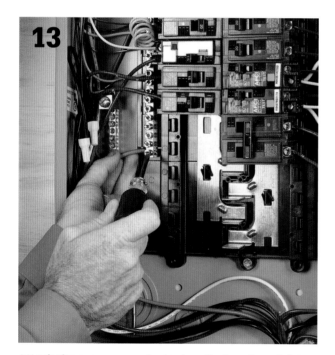

13

Attach the green ground wire from the transfer switch to an open port on the grounding bar in your main service panel. This should complete the installation of the transfer switch. Replace the cover on the service panel box, and make sure to fill in the circuit map on your switch box.

14

Begin testing the transfer switch by making sure all of the switches on it are set to the LINE setting. The power should still be OFF at the main panel breakers.

Make sure your standby generator is operating properly and has been installed professionally. See page 262 for information on choosing a generator that is sized appropriately for your needs.

15

Before turning your generator on, attach the power cord from the generator to the switch box. Never attach or detach a generator cord with the generator running. Turn your standby power generator on, and let it run for a minute or two.

16

Flip each circuit switch on the transfer switch box to GEN, one at a time. Try to maintain balance by moving back and forth from circuits on the left and right side. Do not turn all circuits on at the same time. Observe the onboard wattage meters as you engage each circuit, and try to keep the wattage levels in balance. When you have completed testing the switch, turn the switches back to LINE, and then shut off your generator.

Outbuildings

Nothing improves the convenience and usefulness of an outbuilding more than electrifying it. Running a new underground circuit from your house to an outbuilding lets you add receptacles and light fixtures both inside the outbuilding and on its exterior. If you run power to an outbuilding, you are required to install at least one receptacle.

Adding one or two 120-volt circuits is not complicated, but every aspect of the project is strictly governed by local building codes. Therefore, once you've mapped out the job and have a good idea of what's involved, visit your local building department to discuss your plans and obtain a permit for the work.

This project demonstrates standard techniques for running a circuit cable from the house exterior to a shed, plus the wiring and installation of devices inside the shed. To add a new breaker and make the final circuit connections to your home's main service panel, see page 174. If you run power to an outbuilding, you are required to install at least one receptacle.

First, determine how much current you will need. For basic electrical needs, such as powering a standard light fixture and small appliances or power tools, a 120-volt, 15-amp circuit should be sufficient. A small workshop may require one or two 120-volt, 20-amp circuits. If you need any 240-volt circuits or more than two 120-volt, 20-amp circuits, you will need to install at least a 60-amp subpanel with appropriate feeder wires. Installing a subpanel in an outbuilding is similar to installing one inside your home, but there are some important differences.

You may use #14 copper wire for one 120-volt, 15-amp circuit or #12 copper wire for one 120-volt, 20-amp circuit. Use #10 copper wire for two 120-volt, 20 amp circuits. Also, if the shed is more than 150 ft. away from the house, you may need heavier-gauge cable to account for voltage drop.

Most importantly, don't forget to call before you dig. Have all utility and service lines on your property marked even before you make serious project plans. This is critical for your safety of course, and it may affect where you can run the circuit cable.

Adding an electrical circuit to an outbuilding such as this shed greatly expands the activities the building will support and is also a great benefit for home security.

Tools & Materials ▸

Spray paint
Trenching shovel
(4" wide blade)
4" metal junction box
Metal L-fittings (2)
and conduit nipple
for conduit
Wood screws
Conduit with
watertight
threaded and
compression fittings
Wrenches

Hacksaw
90° sweeps for
conduit (2)
Plastic conduit
bushings (2)
Pipe straps
Silicone caulk
and caulk gun
Double-gang
boxes, metal (2)
One exterior
receptacle box
(with cover)

Single-pole switches (2)
Interior ceiling light
fixture and metal
fixture box
Exterior motion-
detector fixture and
plastic fixture box
EMT metal conduit
and fittings for
inside the shed
Utility knife
UF two-wire cable
(12 gauge)

THNN wire
(12 gauge)
20-amp GFCI-
protected circuit
breaker
Wire stripper
Pliers
Screwdrivers
Wire connectors
Hand tamper
Schedule 80 conduit
Eye protection

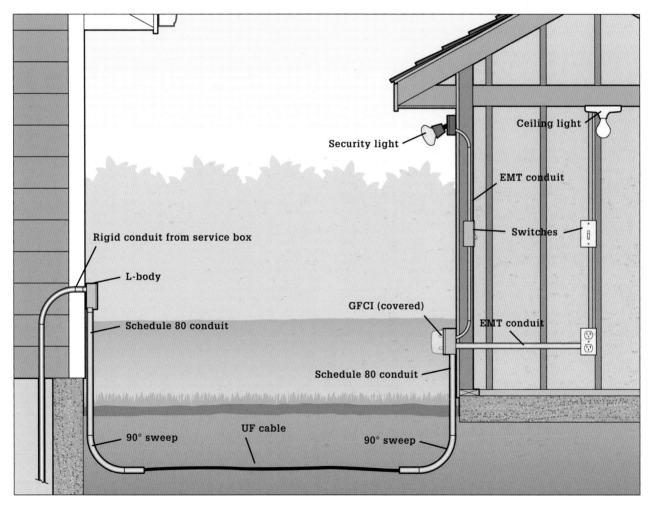

A basic outdoor circuit starts with a waterproof fitting at the house wall connected to a junction box inside. The underground circuit cable—rated UF (underground feeder)—runs in a 24"-deep trench and is protected from exposure at both ends by metal or PVC conduit. Inside the shed, standard NM cable runs through metal conduit to protect it from damage (not necessary if you will be adding interior wallcoverings). All receptacles in the shed must be GFCI protected.

How to Wire an Outbuilding

Identify the circuit's exit point at the house and entry point at the shed and mark them. Mark the path of the trench between the exit and entry points using spray paint. Make the route as direct as possible. Dig the trench to the depth required by local code (24") using a narrow trenching shovel.

From outside, drill a hole through the exterior wall and the rim joist at the exit point for the cable (you'll probably need to install a bit extender or an extra-long bit in your drill). Make the hole just large enough to accommodate the L-body conduit fitting and conduit nipple.

Assemble the conduit and junction box fittings that will penetrate the wall. Here, we attached a 12" piece of ¾" IMC (intermediate metallic conduit) and a sweep to a metal junction box with a compression fitting and then inserted the conduit into the hole drilled in the rim joist. The junction box is attached to the floor joist.

From outside, seal the hole around the conduit with expandable spray foam or caulk, and then attach the free end of the conduit to the back of a waterproof L-body fitting. Mount the L-body fitting to the house exterior with the open end facing downward.

Cut a length of IMC to extend from the L-fitting down into the trench using a hacksaw. Deburr the cut edges of the conduit. Secure the conduit to the L-fitting, and then attach a 90° sweep to the bottom end of the conduit using compression fittings. Add a bushing to the end of the sweep to protect the circuit cable. Anchor the conduit to the wall with a corrosion-resistant pipe strap.

Inside the shed, drill a ¾" dia. hole in the shed wall. On the interior of the shed, mount a junction box with a knock-out removed to allow the cable to enter through the hole. On the exterior side directly above the end of the UF trench, mount an exterior-rated receptacle box with cover. The plan (and your plan may differ) is to bring power into the shed through the hole in the wall behind the exterior receptacle.

Run conduit from the exterior box down into the trench. Fasten the conduit to the building with a strap. Add a 90° sweep and bushing, as before. Secure the conduit to the box with an offset fitting. Anchor the conduit with pipe straps, and seal the entry hole with caulk.

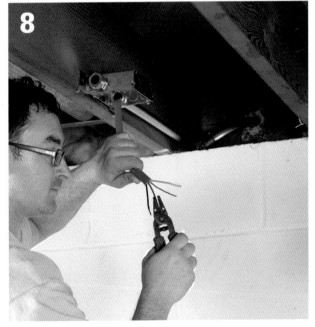

Run UF cable from the house to the outbuilding. Feed one end of the UF circuit cable up through the sweep and conduit and into the L-fitting at the house (the back or side of the fitting is removable to facilitate cabling). Run the cable through the wall and into the junction box, leaving at least 12" of extra cable at the end.

(continued)

Lay the UF cable into the trench, making sure it is not twisted and will not contact any sharp objects. Roll out the cable, and then feed the other end of the cable up through the conduit and into the receptacle box in the shed, leaving 12" of slack.

Inside the outbuilding, install the remaining boxes for the other switches, receptacles, and lights. With the exception of plastic receptacle boxes for exterior exposure, use metal boxes if you will be connecting the boxes with metal conduit.

Connect the electrical boxes with conduit and fittings. Inside the outbuilding, you may use inexpensive EMT to connect receptacle, switch, and fixture boxes. Once you've planned your circuit routes, start by attaching couplings to all of the boxes.

Cut a length of conduit to fit between the coupling and the next box or fitting in the run. If necessary, drill holes for the conduit through the centers of the wall studs. Attach the conduit to the fitting that you attached to the first box.

13

If you are surface-mounting the conduit or running it up or down next to wall studs, secure it with straps no more than 3 ft. apart. Use elbow fittings for 90° turns and setscrew couplings for joining straight lengths as needed. Make holes through the wall studs only as large as necessary to feed the conduit through.

14

THNN wire

Measure to find how much wire you'll need for each run, and cut pieces that are a foot or two longer. Before making L-turns with the conduit, feed the wire through the first conduit run.

15

Feed the other ends of the wires into the next box or fitting in line. It is much easier to feed wire into 45° and 90° elbows if they have not been attached to the conduit yet. Continue feeding wire into the conduit and fitting until you have reached the next box in line.

16

LIGHT

RF

Once you've reached the next box in line, coil the ends of the wires and repeat the process with new wire for the next run. Keep working until all of the wire is run and all of the conduit and fittings are installed and secured. If you are running multiple feed wires into a single box, write the origin or destination on a piece of masking tape and stick it to each wire end.

(continued)

17

Note: Your Code may require an in-use rated receptacle box cover (see page 62).

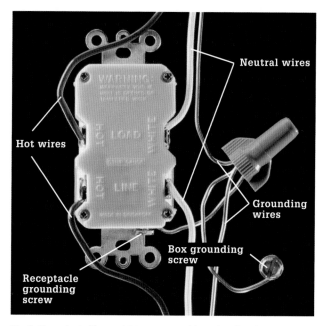

Neutral wires

Hot wires

Grounding wires

Box grounding screw

Receptacle grounding screw

Make the wiring connections at the receptacles. Strip ¾" of insulation from the circuit wires using a wire stripper. Connect the white (neutral) wire and black (hot) wire of the UF cable to the LINE screw terminals on the receptacle. Connect the white (neutral) and black (hot) wires from the NM cable to the LOAD terminals. Pigtail the bare copper ground wires and connect them to the receptacle ground terminal and the metal box. Install the receptacle and cover plate.

Variation: Installing a GFCI-protected breaker for the new circuit at the main service panel is the best way to protect the circuit and allows you to use regular receptacles in the building, but an alternative that is allowed in many areas is to run the service into a GFCI-protected receptacle and then wire the other devices on the circuit in series. If you use this approach, only the initial receptacle needs to be a GFCI receptacle.

18

19

Continue installing receptacles in the circuit run, and then run service from the last receptacle to the switch box for the light fixture or fixtures. (If you anticipate a lot of load on the circuit, you should probably run a separate circuit for the lights). Twist the white neutral leads and grounding leads together and cap them. Attach the black wires to the appropriate switches. Install the switches and cover plate.

Install the light fixtures. For this shed, we installed a caged ceiling light inside the shed and a motion-detector security light on the exterior side (see pages 280 to 283).

Run NM cable from the electrical box in the house at the start of the new circuit to the main service panel. Use cable staples if you are running the cable in floor joist cavities. If the cable is mounted to the bottom of the floor joists or will be exposed, run it through conduit.

At the service panel, feed the NM cable in through a cable clamp. Arrange for your final electrical inspection before you install the breaker. Then attach the wires to a new circuit breaker, and install the breaker in an empty slot. Label the new circuit on the circuit map.

Turn on the new circuit, and test all of the receptacles and fixtures. Depress the Test button and then the Reset button if you installed a GFCI receptacle. If any of the fixtures or receptacles is not getting power, check the connections first, and then test the receptacle or switch for continuity with a multimeter. Backfill the trench.

Motion-Sensing Floodlights

M ost houses and garages have floodlights on their exteriors. You can easily upgrade these fixtures so that they provide additional security by replacing them with motion-sensing floodlights. Motion-sensing floods can be set up to detect motion in a specific area—like a walkway or driveway—and then cast light into that area. And there are few things intruders like less than the spotlight. These lights typically have timers that allow you to control how long the light stays on and photosensors that prevent the light from coming on during the day.

A motion-sensing light fixture provides inexpensive and effective protection against intruders. It has an infrared eye that triggers the light fixture when a moving object crosses its path. Choose a light fixture with a photo cell to prevent the light from turning on in daylight; an adjustable timer to control how long the light stays on; and range control to adjust the reach of the motion-sensor eye.

Tools & Materials ▸

Circuit tester
Jigsaw
Fish tape
Screwdrivers
Wire cutter
Cable ripper
Wire stripper

Caulk gun
Motion-sensing
  floodlight fixture
Electrical box
NM cable
Wire connectors
Eye Protection

An exterior floodlight with a motion sensor is an effective security measure. Keep the motion sensor adjusted to cover only the area you wish to secure—if the coverage area is too large, the light will turn on frequently.

How to Install a New Exterior Fixture Box

On the outside of the house, make the cutout for the motion-sensor light fixture. Outline the light fixture box on the wall, drill a pilot hole, and complete the cutout with a wallboard saw or jigsaw.

Estimate the distance between the indoor switch box and the outdoor motion-sensor box, and cut a length of NM cable about 2 ft. longer than this distance. Use a fish tape to pull the cable from the switch box to the motion-sensor box. See pages 41 and 42 for tips on running cable through finished walls.

Mounting bracket

Retrofit box

Strip about 10" of outer insulation from the end of the cable using a cable ripper. Open a knockout in the retrofit light fixture box with a screwdriver. Insert the cable into the box so that at least ¼" of outer sheathing reaches into the box. Apply a heavy bead of silicone or polyurethane caulk to the flange of the electrical box before attaching it to the wall.

Mounting screws

Insert the box into the cutout opening, and tighten the mounting screws until the brackets draw the outside flange firmly against the siding.

How to Replace a Floodlight with a Motion-Sensor Light

1

Turn off power to the old fixture. To remove it, unscrew the mounting screws on the part of the fixture attached to the wall. There will probably be four of them. Carefully pull the fixture away from the wall, exposing the wires. Don't touch the wires yet.

2

Before you touch any wires, use a voltage sensor to verify that the circuit is dead. With the light switch turned on, insert the sensor's probe into the electrical box and hold the probe within ½" of the wires inside to confirm that there is no voltage. Disconnect the wire connectors, and remove the old fixture.

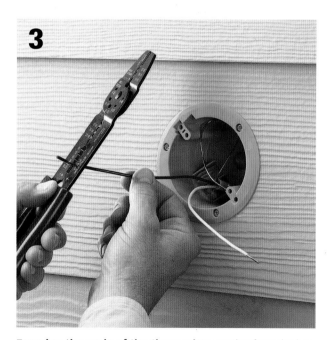

3

Examine the ends of the three wires coming from the box (one white, one black, and one bare copper). They should be clean and free of corrosion. If the ends are in poor condition, clip them off and then strip ¾" of wire insulation with a combination tool.

4   Grounding clip

If the electrical box is nonmetallic and does not have a metal grounding clip, install a grounding clip or replace the box with one that does have a clip, and make sure the ground wire is attached to it securely. Some light fixtures have a grounding terminal on the base. If yours has one, attach the grounding wire from the house directly to the terminal.

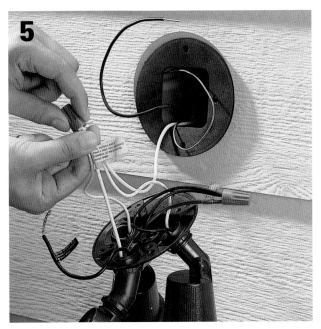

Now you can attach the new fixture. Begin by sliding a rubber or foam gasket (usually provided with the fixture) over the wires and onto the flange of the electrical box. Set the new fixture on top of a ladder or have a helper hold it while you make the wiring connections. There may be as many as three white wires coming from the fixture. Join all white wires, including the feed wire from the house, using a wire connector.

Next, join the black wire from the box and the single black wire from the fixture with a wire connector. You may see a couple of black wires and a red wire already joined on the fixture. You can ignore these in your installation.

Neatly tuck all the wires into the box so they are behind the gasket. Align the holes in the gasket with the holes in the box, and then position the fixture over the gasket so its mounting holes are also aligned with the gasket. Press the fixture against the gasket, and drive the four mounting screws into the box. Install floodlights (exterior rated) and restore power.

Test the fixture. You will still be able to turn it on and off with the light switch inside. Flip the switch on and pass your hand in front of the motion sensor. The light should come on. Adjust the motion sensor to cover the traffic areas, and pivot the light head to illuminate the intended area.

Standalone Solar Lighting System

A self-contained electrical circuit with dedicated loads, usually 12-volt light fixtures, is one of the most useful solar amenities you can install. A standalone system is not tied into your power grid, which greatly reduces the danger of installing the components yourself. Plus, the fact that your light fixtures are independent of the main power source means that even during a power outage you will have functioning emergency and security lights.

Installing a single solar-powered circuit is relatively simple, but don't take the dangers for granted. Your work will require permits and inspections in most jurisdictions, and you can't expect to pass if the work is not done to the exact specifications required.

Solar panels that convert the sun's energy into electricity are called photovoltaic (PV) panels, and they produce direct current (DC) power. PV solar panel systems can be small and designed to accomplish a specific task, or they can be large enough to provide power or supplementary power to an entire house. Before you make the leap into a large system, it's a good idea to familiarize yourself with the mechanics of solar power. The small system demonstrated in this project is relatively simple and is a great first step into the world of solar. The fact that the collector, battery, and lights are a standalone system makes this a very easy project to accomplish. By contrast, installing panels that provide direct supplementary power through your main electrical service panel is a difficult wiring job that should be done by professional electricians only.

This 60-watt solar panel is mounted on a garage roof and powers a self-contained home security lighting system. Not only does this save energy costs, it keeps the security lights working even during power outages.

Schematic Diagram for an Off-the-Grid Solar Lighting System

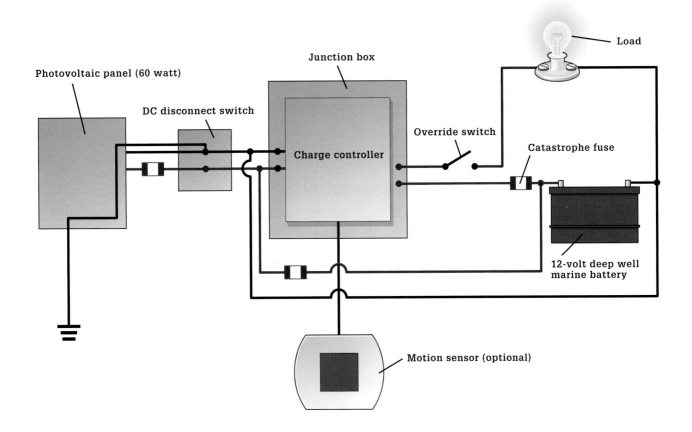

Photovoltaic panel (60 watt)

DC disconnect switch

Junction box

Charge controller

Override switch

Load

Catastrophe fuse

12-volt deep well marine battery

Motion sensor (optional)

Tools & Materials ▸

Tape measure
Drill/driver with bits
Caulk gun
Crimping tool
Wiring tools
Metal-cutting saw
Photovoltaic panel
  (50 to 80 watts)
Charge controller
Catastrophe fuse
Battery sized for
  3 day autonomy
Battery case
Battery cables
12-volt LED lights
  including motion-
  sensor light
Additional 12-volt light
  fixtures as desired

20 ft. Unistrut 1⅞"
  thick U-channel (See
  Resources, page 331)
(4) 45° Unistrut
  connectors
(2) 90° Unistrut
  angle brackets
(4) Unistrut hold
  down clamps
(12) ⅜" spring nuts
(12) ⅜"-dia. × 1"-long
  hex-head bolts
  with washers
DC-rated disconnect
  or double throw
  snap switch
6" length of ½"-dia.
  liquid-tight flexible
  metallic conduit

(2) ½" liquid
  tight connectors
(2) Lay-in
  grounding lugs
(2) Insulated terminal
  bars to accept one
  2-gauge wire and
  4 12-gauge wires
(2) Cord cap
  connectors for
  ½"-dia. cable
½" ground rod
  and clamp
Copper wire
  (6, 12-gauge)
Green ground screws
½" Flexible metallic
  conduit or
  Greenfield

½" Greenfield
  connectors
(4) ¹¹⁄₁₆" junction boxes
  with covers
(4) square boxes
  with covers
PVC 6"× 6" junction
  box with cover
14/2 UF wire
¼" × 20 nuts and
  bolts with lock
  washers
Roof flashing boot
Roof cement
Silicon caulk
Eye protection

Mounting PV Panels

The mounting stand for the PV panel is constructed from metal U-channel (a product called Unistrut is seen here. See Resources page 331) and pre-bent fasteners. Position the solar panel where it will receive the greatest amount of sunlight for the longest period of time each day—typically the south-facing side of a roof or wall. For a circuit with a battery reserve that powers two to four 12-volt lights, a collection panel rated between 40 and 80 watts of output should suffice. These panels can range from $200 to $600 in price, depending on the output and the overall quality.

The stand components are held together with bolts and spring-loaded fasteners. The 45° and 90° connectors are manufactured specifically for use with this Unistrut system.

Connections for the feed wires that carry current from the collector are made inside an electrical box mounted on the back of the collector panel.

An EPDM rubber boot seals off the opening where the PVC conduit carrying the feed wires penetrates the roof.

How to Wire a DC Lighting Circuit

Mount a junction box inside the building where the conduit and wiring enter from the power source. Secure the box to the conduit with appropriate connectors. Run two #14 awg wires through the conduit and connect them to the positive and negative terminals on the panel (see previous page).

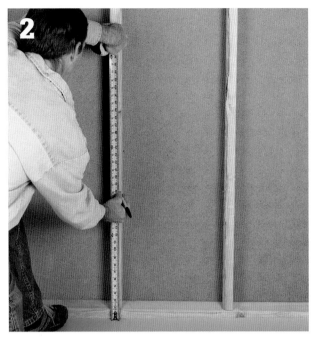

Plan the system layout. Determine the placement of the battery, and then decide where you will position the charge controller and DC disconnect. The battery should be placed at least 18" off the floor, in a well-ventilated area where it won't be agitated by everyday activity. Mark locations directly on the wall.

Attach a junction box for enclosing the DC disconnect, which is a heavy-duty switch, to a wall stud near the battery and charge controller location. Use a metal single-gang box with mounting flanges.

Run flexible metal conduit from the entry point at the power source to the junction box for the DC disconnect box. Use hangers rated for flexible conduit.

(continued)

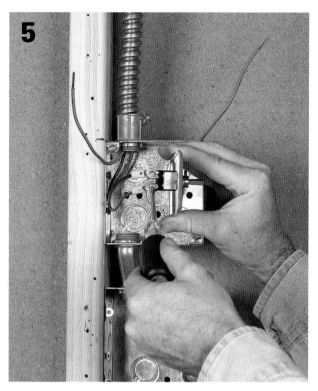

Attach the DC disconnect switch to the wire leads from the power source.

Attach a double gang metal junction box to the building's frame beneath the DC disconnect box to enclose the charge controller.

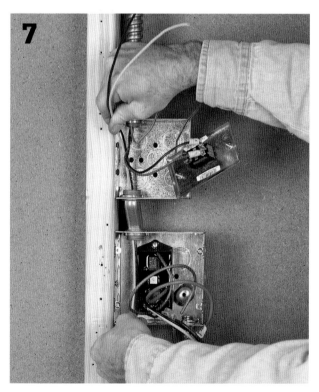

Install the charge controller inside the box. Run flexible conduit with connectors and conductors from the disconnect box and to the charge controller box.

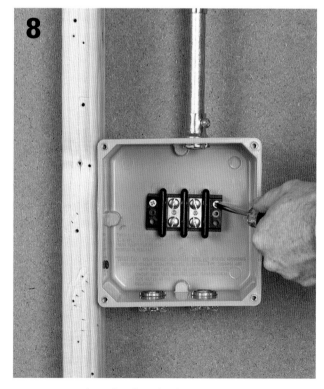

Mount a PVC junction box for the battery controller about 2 ft. above the battery location, and install two insulated terminal bars within the box.

Build a support shelf for the battery using 2 × 4s. The shelf should be at least 18" above ground. Set the battery on the shelf in a sturdy plastic case.

Set up grounding protection. Pound an 8-ft. long, ½"-dia. ground rod into the ground outside the building, about 1 ft. from the wall on the opposite side of the charge controller. Leave about 2" of the rod sticking out of the ground. Attach a ground rod clamp to the top of the rod. Drill a ⁵⁄₁₆" hole through the garage wall (underneath a shake or siding piece) and run the #6-gauge THWN wire to the ground rod. This ground will facilitate lightning protection. See pages 180 to 185 for more information on grounding the system.

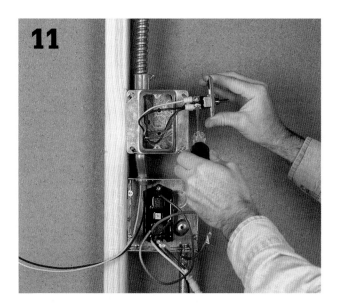

Wire the DC disconnect. Attach the two #14-gauge wires to the two terminals labeled "line" on the top of the DC disconnect switch.

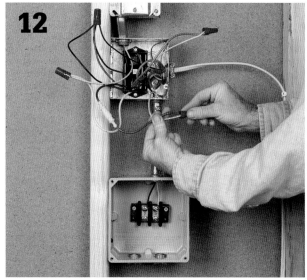

Wire the charge controller. Route two more #14-gauge wires from the bottom of the DC disconnect terminals into the 4" × ¹¹⁄₁₆" junction box and connect to the "Solar Panel In" terminals on the charge controller. The black wire should connect to the negative terminal in the PVC box and the red to the positive lead on the charge controller. Finish wiring of the charge controller according to the line diagram provided with the type of controller purchased. Generally the load wires connect to the orange lead, and the red wire gets tied to the battery through a fuse.

(continued)

OPTION: Attach a motion sensor. Some charge controllers come equipped with a motion sensor to maximize the efficiency of your lighting system—these are especially effective when used with security lighting. The motion sensor is typically mounted to a bell box outside and wired directly to the charge controller with an 18-gauge × 3-conductor insulated cable. A system like this can support up to three motion sensors. Follow the manufacturer's directions for installing and wiring the motion sensor.

Run wiring to the loads (exterior DC lighting fixtures in this case) from the charge controller. DC light fixtures (12-volt) with LED bulbs can be purchased at marine and RV stores if you can't find them in your home center or electrical supply store. For more information on wiring exterior light fixtures, see pages 280 to 283.

Install the battery. Here, a deep-cell 12-volt marine battery is used. First, cut and strip each of the two battery cables at one end and install into the battery control junction box through cord cap connectors. Terminate these wires on two separate, firmly mounted insulated terminal blocks.

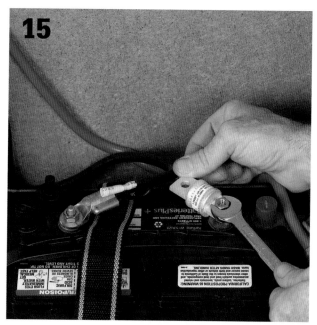

Install the catastrophe fuse onto the positive terminal using nuts and bolts provided with the battery cables. Connect the battery cables to the battery while paying close attention to the polarity (red to positive and black to negative). Make sure all connections have been made and double checked.

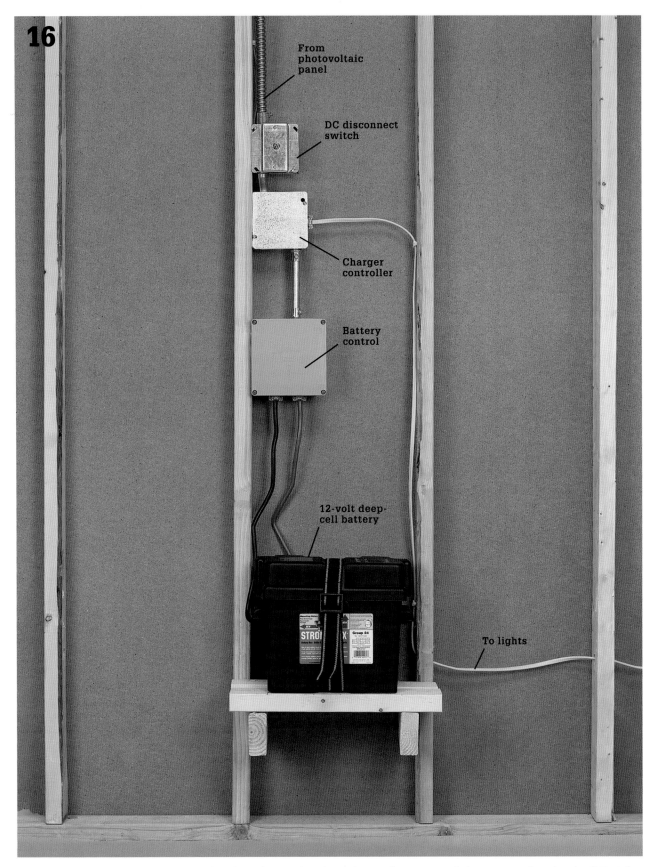

16

From
photovoltaic
panel

DC disconnect
switch

Charger
controller

Battery
control

12-volt deep-
cell battery

To lights

Cover all junction boxes, remove the bag from the panel, and turn the DC disconnect switch on to complete the circuit. Test the lights, and adjust the time to desired setting.

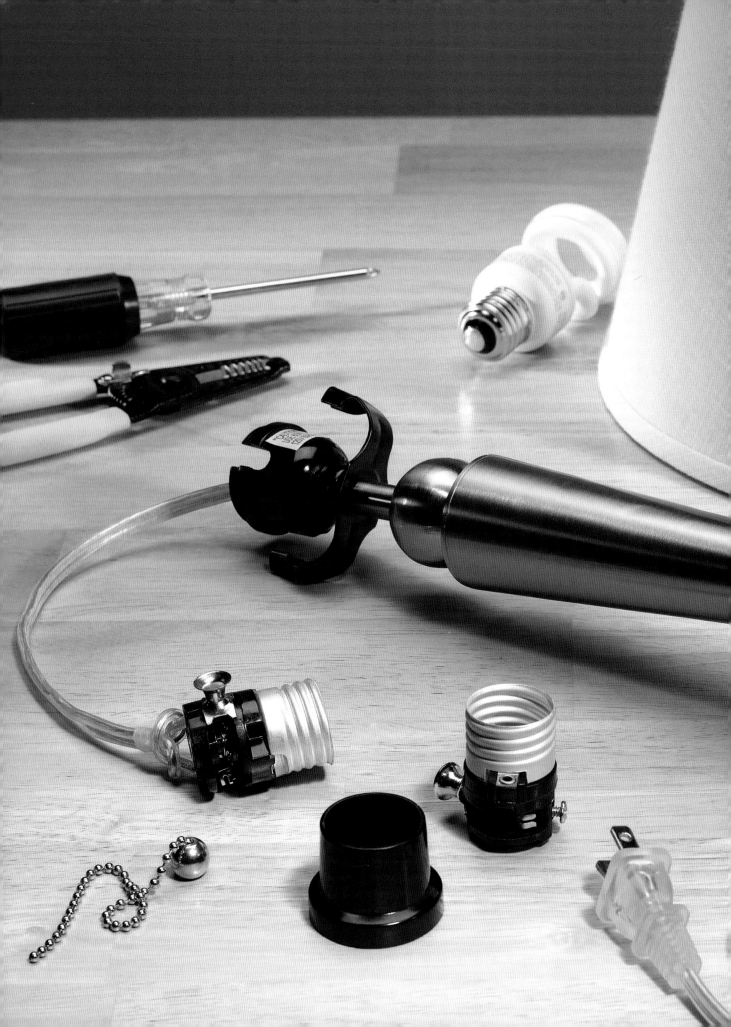

Repair Projects

"Repair" and "wiring" are two words you don't see together too much anymore. In most cases of an electrical failure, the repair is to replace the failed device. But it may also be reconnected to a bad splice or a loose connection.

The electrical items that most frequently require actual repairs are light fixtures. If you include lamps and cords in this category, you've pretty much covered it. Most electrical failures result from poorly made connections in the original installation. Exceptions are switches, which tend to wear out over time and require replacement, and ceiling fans. Ceiling fans are unique in that, like switches, they contain moving parts—and rapidly moving parts at that. Catching a switch pull chain on a moving blade is the cause of many ceiling fan problems, along with blades that have fallen out of balance and have begun to wobble.

When replacing part of an electrical fixture, the rule of thumb for finding the replacement part is to remove the broken part and bring it with you to a lighting or electrical supply store. Failing that, take down the make and serial number of the fixture so the clerk can look up part information for you.

In this chapter:

- Repairing Light Fixtures
- Repairing Chandeliers
- Repairing Ceiling Fans
- Repairing Fluorescent Lights
- Replacing Plugs & Cords
- Replacing a Lamp Socket

Repairing Light Fixtures

Light fixtures are attached permanently to ceilings or walls. They include wall-hung sconces, ceiling-hung globe fixtures, recessed light fixtures, and chandeliers. Most light fixtures are easy to repair using basic tools and inexpensive parts.

If a light fixture fails, always make sure the light bulb is screwed in tightly and is not burned out. A faulty light bulb is the most common cause of light fixture failure. If the light fixture is controlled by a wall switch, also check the switch as a possible source of problems.

Light fixtures can fail because the sockets or built-in switches wear out. Some fixtures have sockets and switches that can be removed for minor repairs. These parts are held to the base of the fixture with mounting screws or clips. Other fixtures have sockets and switches that are joined permanently to the base. If this type of fixture fails, purchase and install a new light fixture.

Damage to light fixtures often occurs because homeowners install light bulbs with wattage ratings that are too high. Prevent overheating and light fixture failures by using only light bulbs that match the wattage ratings printed on the fixtures.

Techniques for repairing fluorescent lights are different from those for incandescent lights. Refer to pages 304 to 309 to repair or replace a fluorescent light fixture.

Tools & Materials ▶

Circuit tester
Screwdriver
Continuity tester

Combination tool
Replacement parts,
  as needed

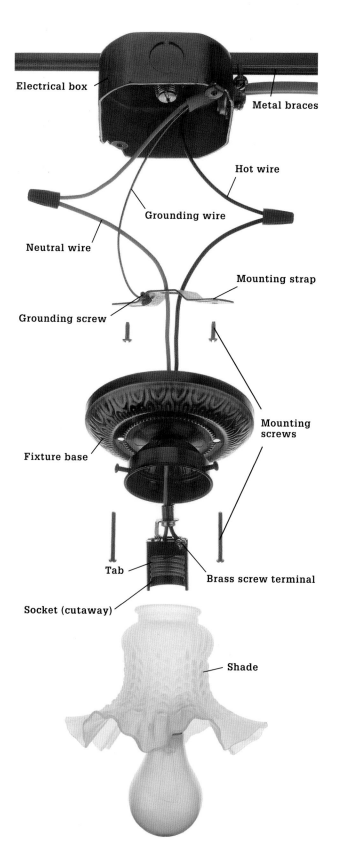

In a typical incandescent light fixture, a black hot wire is connected to a brass screw terminal on the socket. Power flows to a small tab at the bottom of the metal socket and through a metal filament inside the bulb. The power heats the filament and causes it to glow. The current then flows through the threaded portion of the socket and through the white neutral wire back to the main service panel.

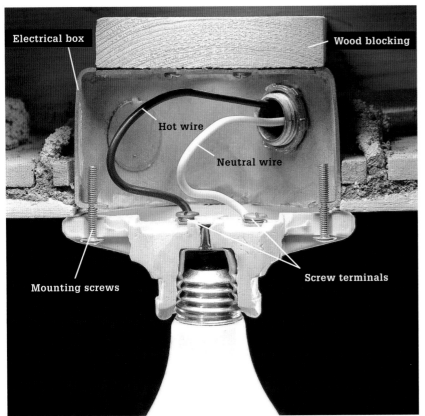

Electrical box

Wood blocking

Hot wire

Neutral wire

Mounting screws

Screw terminals

Before 1959, incandescent light fixtures (shown cutaway) often were mounted directly to an electrical box or to plaster lath. Electrical codes now require that fixtures be attached to mounting straps that are anchored to the electrical boxes. If you have a light fixture attached to plaster lath, install an approved electrical box with a mounting strap to support the fixture.

PROBLEM	REPAIR
Wall- or ceiling-mounted fixture flickers or does not light.	1. Check for faulty light bulb. 2. Check wall switch and replace, if needed. 3. Check for loose wire connections in electrical box. 4. Test socket and replace, if needed (pages 314 to 315). 5. Replace light fixture.
Built-in switch on fixture does not work.	1. Check for faulty light bulb. 2. Check for loose wire connections on switch. 3. Replace switch. 4. Replace light fixture.
Chandelier flickers or does not light.	1. Check for faulty light bulb. 2. Check wall switch and replace, if needed. 3. Check for loose wire connections in electrical box. 4. Test sockets and fixture wires, and replace, if needed.
Recessed fixture flickers or does not light.	1. Check for faulty light bulb. 2. Check wall switch, and replace, if needed. 3. Check for loose wire connections in electrical box. 4. Test fixture, and replace, if needed.

How to Remove a Light Fixture & Test a Socket

1

Turn off the power to the light fixture at the main panel. Remove the light bulb and any shade or globe, then remove the mounting screws holding the fixture base and the electrical box or mounting strap. Carefully pull the fixture base away from the box.

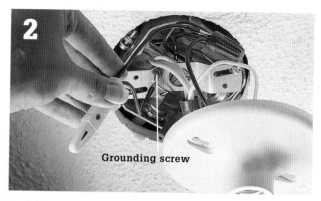

2

Grounding screw

Test for power with a circuit tester. The tester should not glow. If it does, there is still power entering the box. Return to the panel and turn off power to the correct circuit.

3

Disconnect the light fixture base by loosening the screw terminals. If the fixture has wire leads instead of screw terminals, remove the light fixture base by unscrewing the wire connectors.

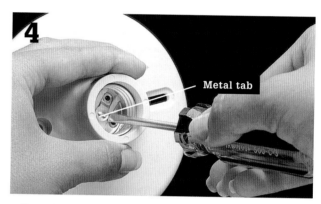

4

Metal tab

Adjust the metal tab at the bottom of the fixture socket by prying it up slightly with a small screwdriver. This adjustment will improve the contact between the socket and the light bulb.

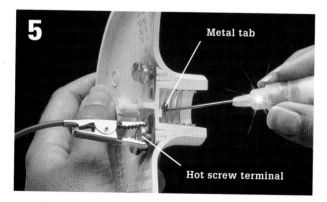

5

Metal tab

Hot screw terminal

Test the socket (shown cutaway) by attaching the clip of a continuity tester to the hot screw terminal (or black wire lead) and touching probe of the tester to the metal tab in the bottom of the socket. The tester should glow. If not, the socket is faulty and must be replaced.

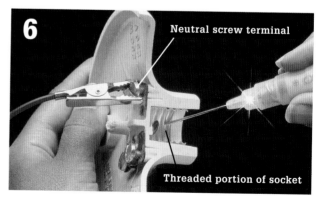

6

Neutral screw terminal

Threaded portion of socket

Attach the tester clip to the neutral screw terminal (or white wire lead), and touch the probe to the threaded portion of the socket. The tester should glow. If not, the socket is faulty and must be replaced. If the socket is permanently attached, replace the fixture.

How to Replace a Socket

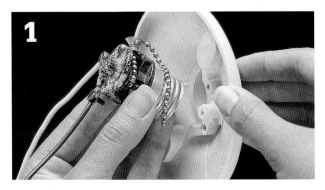

Remove the old light fixture. Remove the socket from the fixture. The socket may be held by a screw, clip, or retaining ring. Disconnect wires attached to the socket.

Purchase an identical replacement socket. Connect the white wire to the silver screw terminal on the socket, and connect the black wire to the brass screw terminal. Attach the socket to the fixture base, and reinstall the fixture.

How to Test & Replace a Built-in Light Switch

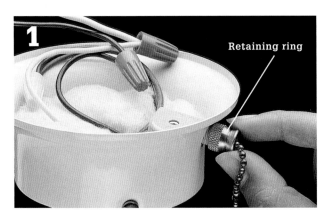

Retaining ring

Remove the light fixture. Unscrew the retaining ring holding the switch.

Switch leads

Label the wires connected to the switch leads. Disconnect the switch leads, and remove the switch.

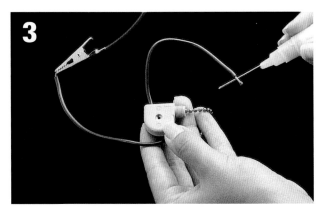

Test the switch by attaching the clip of the continuity tester to one of the switch leads and holding the tester probe to the other lead. Operate the switch control. If the switch is good, the tester will glow when the switch is in one position but not both.

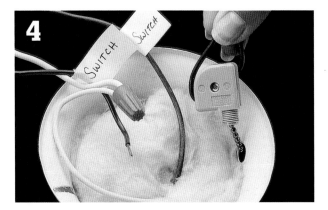

If the switch is faulty, purchase and install a duplicate switch. Remount the light fixture, and turn on the power at the main service panel.

Repairing Chandeliers

Repairing a chandelier requires special care. Because chandeliers are heavy, it is a good idea to work with a helper when removing a chandelier. Support the fixture to prevent its weight from pulling against the wires.

Chandeliers have two fixture wires that are threaded through the support chain from the electrical box to the hollow base of the chandelier. The socket wires connect to the fixture wires inside this base.

Fixture wires are identified as hot and neutral. Look closely for a raised stripe on one of the wires. This is the neutral wire that is connected to the white circuit wire and white socket wire. The other smooth fixture wire is hot and is connected to the black wires.

If you have a new chandelier, it may have a grounding wire that runs through the support chain to the electrical box. If this wire is present, make sure it is connected to the grounding wires in the electrical box.

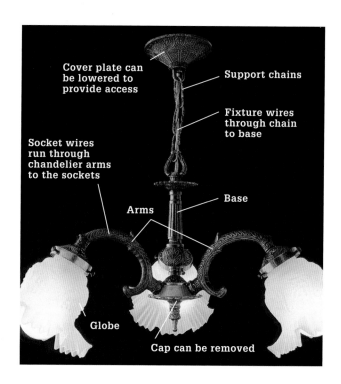

Cover plate can be lowered to provide access

Support chains

Fixture wires through chain to base

Socket wires run through chandelier arms to the sockets

Base

Arms

Globe

Cap can be removed

How to Repair a Chandelier

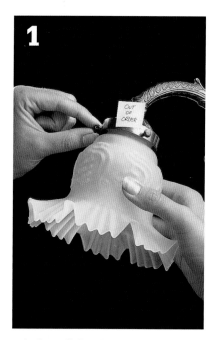

Label any lights that are not working using masking tape. Turn off power to the fixture at the main service panel. Remove light bulbs and all shades or globes.

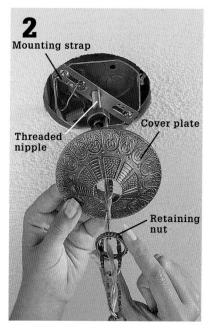

Mounting strap

Threaded nipple

Cover plate

Retaining nut

Unscrew the retaining nut, and lower the decorative coverplate away from the electrical box. Most chandeliers are supported by a threaded nipple attached to a mounting strap.

Mounting strap

Mounting bolt

Bolt cap nut

Mounting variation: Some chandeliers are supported only by the cover plate that is bolted to the electrical box mounting strap. These types do not have a threaded nipple.

3

Grounding screw

Test for power with a circuit tester. The tester should not glow. If it does, turn off power to the correct circuit at the panel.

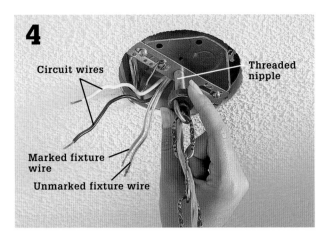

4

Circuit wires

Threaded nipple

Marked fixture wire

Unmarked fixture wire

Disconnect fixture wires by removing the wire connectors. Unscrew the threaded nipple and carefully place the chandelier on a flat surface.

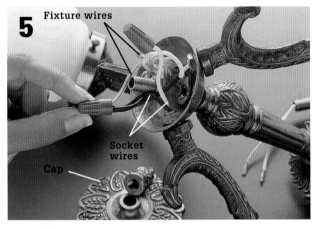

5

Fixture wires

Socket wires

Cap

Remove the cap from the bottom of the chandelier, exposing the wire connections inside the hollow base. Disconnect the socket wires and fixture wires.

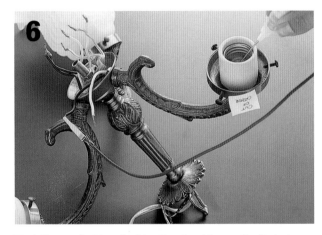

6

Test the socket by attaching the clip of the continuity tester to the black socket wire and touching the probe to the tab in the socket. Repeat with the socket threads and the white socket wire. If the tester does not glow, the socket must be replaced.

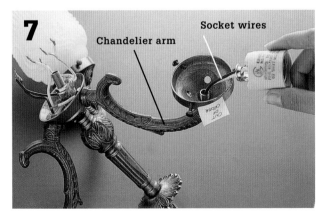

7

Chandelier arm

Socket wires

Remove a faulty socket by loosening any mounting screws or clips and pulling the socket and socket wires out of the fixture arm. Purchase and install a new chandelier socket, threading the socket wires through the fixture arm.

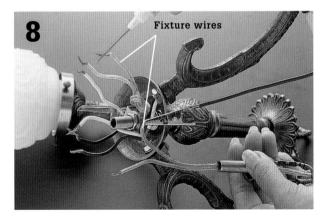

8

Fixture wires

Test each fixture wire by attaching the clip of the continuity tester to one end of the wire and touching the probe to other end. If the tester does not glow, the wire must be replaced. Install new wires, if needed, then reassemble and rehang the chandelier.

Repairing Ceiling Fans

Ceiling fans contain rapidly moving parts, making them more susceptible to trouble than many other electrical fixtures. Installation is a relatively simple matter, but repairing a ceiling fan can be very frustrating. The most common problems you'll encounter are balance and noise issues and switch failure, usually precipitated by the pull chain breaking. In most cases, both problems can be corrected without removing the fan from the ceiling. But if you have difficulty on ladders or simply don't care to work overhead, consider removing the fan when replacing the switch.

Ceiling fans are subject to a great deal of vibration and stress, so it's not uncommon for switches and motors to fail. Minimize wear and tear by making sure blades are in balance so the fan doesn't wobble.

Tools & Materials ▸

Screwdriver
Combination tool

Replacement switch
Voltage sensor

How to Troubleshoot Blade Wobble

1

Start by checking and tightening all hardware used to attach the blades to the mounting arms and the mounting arms to the motor. Hardware tends to loosen over time, and this is frequently the cause of wobble.

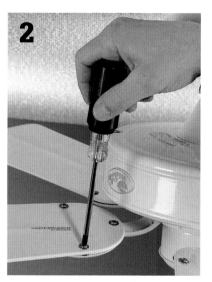

2

If wobble persists, try switching around two of the blades. Often this is all it takes to get the fan back into balance. If a blade is damaged or warped, replace it.

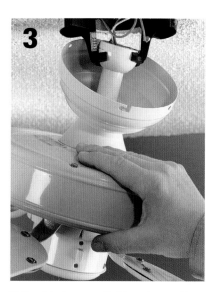

3

If the blades are tight and you still have wobble, turn the power off at the panel, remove the fan canopy, and inspect the mounting brace and the connection between the mounting pole and the fan motor. If any connections are loose, tighten them, and then replace the canopy.

How to Fix a Loose Wire Connection

1

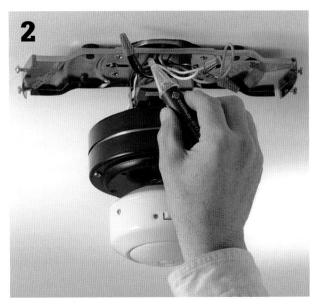

2

A leading cause of fan failure is loose wire connections. To inspect these connections, first shut off the power to the fan. Remove the fan blades to gain access, and then remove the canopy that covers the ceiling box and fan mounting bracket. Most canopies are secured with screws on the outside shell. Have a helper hold the fan body while you remove the screws so it won't fall.

Once the canopy is lowered, you'll see black, white, green, copper, and possibly blue wires. Hold a voltage sensor within ½" of these wires with the wall switch that controls the fan in the ON position. The black and blue wires should cause the sensor to beep if power is present.

3

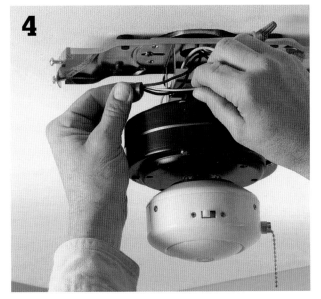

4

Shut off power, and test the wires by placing a voltage sensor within ½" of the wires. If the sensor beeps or lights up, then the circuit is still live and is not safe to work on. When the sensor does not beep or light up, the circuit is dead and may be worked upon.

When you have confirmed that there is no power, check all the wire connections to make certain each is tight and making good contact. You may be able to see that a connection has come apart and needs to be remade. But even if you see one bad connection, check them all by gently tugging on the wire connectors. If the wires pull out of the wire connector or the connection feels loose, unscrew the wire connector from the wires. Turn the power back on and see if the problem has been solved.

How to Replace a Ceiling Fan Pull-Chain Switch

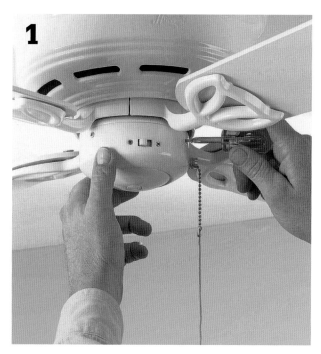

1

Turn off the power at the panel. Use a screwdriver to remove the three to four screws that secure the bottom cap on the fan switch housing. Lower the cap to expose the wires that supply power to the pull-chain switch.

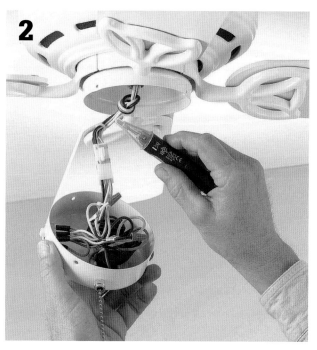

2

Test the wires by placing a voltage sensor within ½" of the wires. If the sensor beeps or lights up, then the circuit is still live and is not safe to work on. When the sensor does not beep or light up, the circuit is dead and may be worked upon.

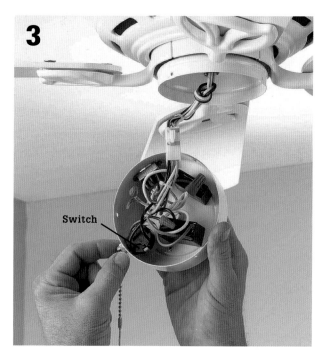

3

Switch

Locate the switch unit (the part that the pull chain used to be attached to if it broke off); it's probably made of plastic. You'll need to replace the whole switch. Fan switches are connected with three to eight wires, depending on the number of speed settings.

4

Attach a small piece of tape to each wire that enters the switch, and write an identifying number on the tape. Start at one side of the switch, and label the wires in the order they're attached.

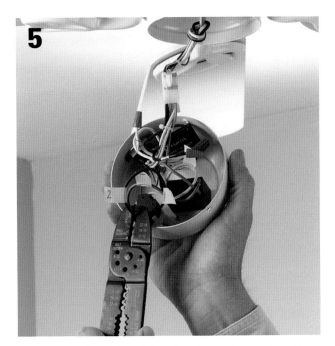

5

Disconnect the old switch wires, in most cases by cutting the wires off as close to the old switch as possible. Unscrew the retaining nut that secures the switch to the switch housing.

Buyer's Tip ▶

Here's how to buy a new switch. Bring the old switch to the hardware store or home center, and find an identical new switch—one with the same number and color of wires. It should also attach to the fan motor wires in the same way (slots or screw terminals or with integral wires and wire connectors) and attach to the fan in the same way. If you are unable to locate an identical switch, find the owners manual for your ceiling fan and contact the manufacturer. Or, find the brand and model number of the fan and order a switch from a ceiling fan dealer or electronics supply store.

6

Remove the switch. There may be one or two screws that hold it in place or it may be secured to the outside of the fan with a small knurled nut, which you can loosen with needlenose pliers. Purchase an identical new switch.

7

Connect the new switch using the same wiring configuration as on the old model. To make connections, first use a wire stripper to strip ¾" of insulation from the ends of each of the wires coming from the fan motor (the ones you cut in step 5). Attach the wires to the new switch in the same order and configuraion as they were attached to the old switch. Secure the new switch in the housing, and make sure all wires are tucked neatly inside. Reattach the bottom cap. Restore power to the fan. Test all the fan's speeds to make sure all the connections are good.

Repairing Fluorescent Lights

Fluorescent lights are relatively trouble free and use less energy than incandescent lights. A typical fluorescent tube lasts about three years and produces two to four times as much light per watt as a standard incandescent light bulb.

The most frequent problem with a fluorescent light fixture is a worn-out tube. If a fluorescent light fixture begins to flicker or does not light fully, remove and examine the tube. If the tube has bent or broken pins or black discoloration near the ends, replace it. Light gray discoloration is normal in working fluorescent tubes. When replacing an old tube, read the wattage rating and the color temperature rating printed on the tube, and buy a new tube with matching ratings. The color temperature rating is a measure of the color of the light produced by the tube. Most people prefer a "warm" light in the 2,700K range. Never dispose of old tubes by breaking them. Fluorescent tubes contain a small amount of hazardous mercury. Check with your local environmental control agency or health department for disposal guidelines.

Fluorescent light fixtures also can malfunction if the sockets are cracked or worn. Inexpensive replacement sockets are available at any hardware store and can be installed in a few minutes.

If a fixture does not work even after the tube and sockets have been serviced, the ballast probably is defective. Faulty ballasts may leak a black, oily substance and can cause a fluorescent light fixture to make a loud humming sound. Although ballasts can be replaced, always check prices before buying a new ballast. It may be cheaper to purchase and install a new fluorescent fixture rather than to replace the ballast in an old fluorescent light fixture.

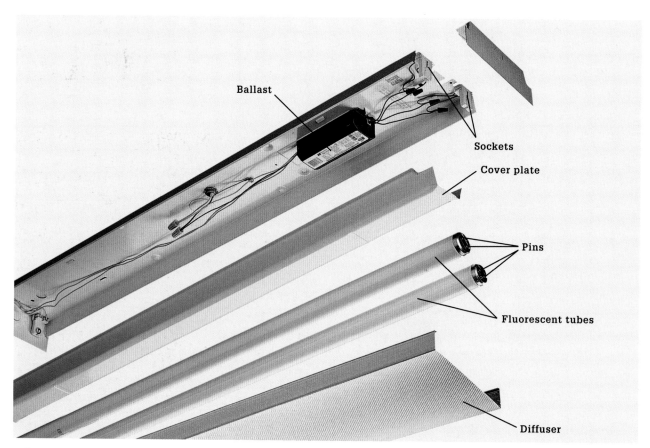

A fluorescent light works by directing electrical current through a special gas-filled tube that glows when energized. A white translucent diffuser protects the fluorescent tube and softens the light. A cover plate protects a special transformer, called a ballast. The ballast regulates the flow of 120-volt household current to the sockets. The sockets transfer power to metal pins that extend into the tube.

PROBLEM	REPAIR
Tube flickers, or lights partially.	1. Rotate tube to make sure it is seated properly in the sockets. 2. Replace tube and the starter (where present) if tube is discolored or if pins are bent or broken. 3. Replace the ballast if replacement cost is reasonable. Otherwise, replace the entire fixture.
Tube does not light.	1. Check wall switch and replace, if needed. 2. Rotate the tube to make sure it is seated properly in sockets. 3. Replace tube and the starter (where present) if tube is discolored or if pins are bent or broken. 4. Replace sockets if they are chipped or if tube does not seat properly. 5. Replace the ballast or the entire fixture.
Noticeable black substance around ballast.	Replace ballast if replacement cost is reasonable. Otherwise, replace the entire fixture.
Fixture hums.	Replace ballast if replacement cost is reasonable. Otherwise, replace the entire fixture.

Tools & Materials ▸

Screwdriver
Ratchet wrench
Combination tool
Circuit tester
Replacement tubes
Starters, or ballast
   (if needed)
Replacement fluorescent light fixture
   (if needed)

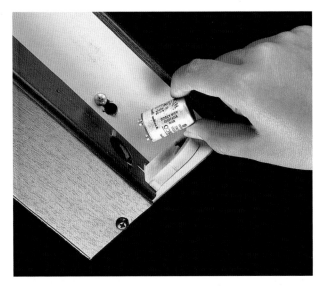

Older fluorescent lights may have a small cylindrical device, called a starter, located near one of the sockets. When a tube begins to flicker, replace both the tube and the starter. Turn off the power, and then remove the starter by pushing it slightly and turning it counterclockwise. Install a replacement that matches the old starter.

How to Replace a Fluorescent Tube

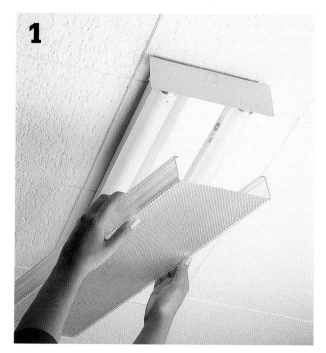

1

Turn off power to the light fixture at the switch. Remove the diffuser to expose the fluorescent tube.

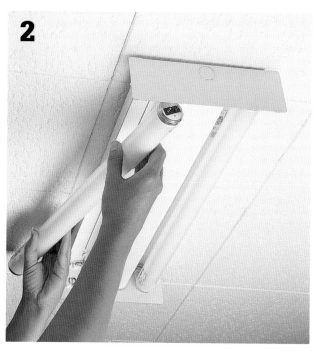

2

Remove the fluorescent tube by rotating it ¼ turn in either direction and sliding the tube out of the sockets. Inspect the pins at the end of the tube. Tubes with bent or broken pins should be replaced.

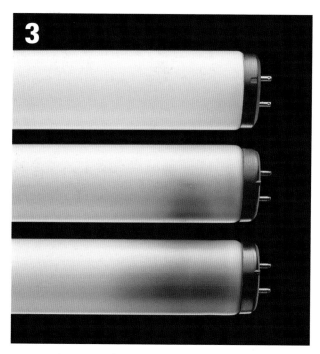

3

Inspect the ends of the fluorescent tube for discoloration. The new tube in good working order (top) shows no discoloration. The normal, working tube (middle) may have gray color. A worn-out tube (bottom) shows black discoloration.

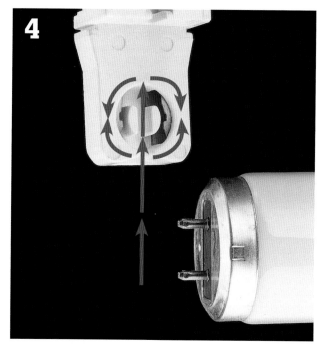

4

Install a new tube with the same wattage rating as the old tube. Insert the tube so that pins slide fully into sockets, and then twist tube ¼ turn in either direction until it is locked securely. Reattach the diffuser, and turn on the power at the switch.

How to Replace a Socket

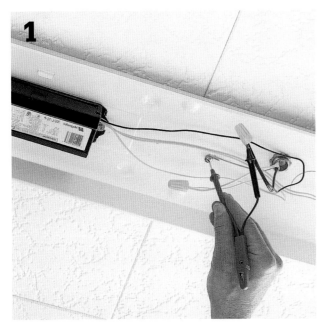

1

Turn off the power at the switch. Remove the diffuser, fluorescent tube, and the cover plate. Test for power by touching one probe of a neon circuit tester to the grounding screw and inserting the other probe into the hot wire connector. If the tester glows, return to the panel and turn off the correct circuit.

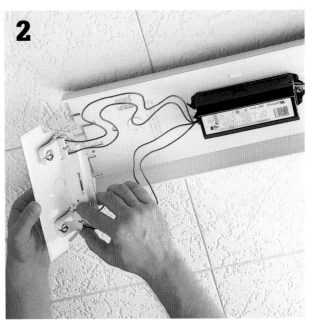

2

Remove the faulty socket from the fixture housing. Some sockets slide out, while others must be unscrewed.

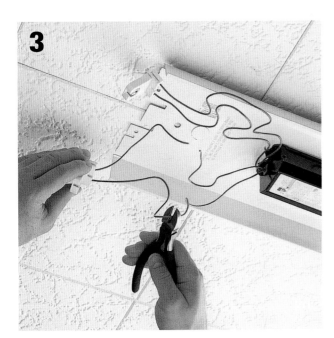

3

Disconnect wires attached to the socket. For push-in fittings (above) remove the wires by inserting a small screwdriver into the release openings. Some sockets have screw terminal connections, while others have preattached wires that must be cut before the socket can be removed.

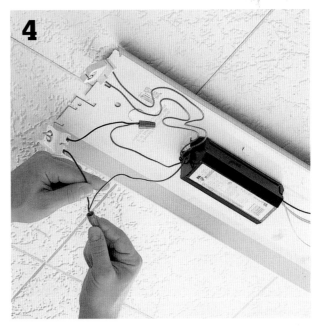

4

Purchase and install a new socket. If the socket has preattached wire leads, connect the leads to the ballast wires using wire connectors. Replace the cover plate and then the fluorescent tube, making sure that it seats properly. Replace the diffuser. Restore power to the fixture at the panel, and test.

How to Replace a Ballast

1

Turn off the power at the panel, and then remove the diffuser, fluorescent tube, and cover plate. Test for power using a circuit tester (page 302, step 3).

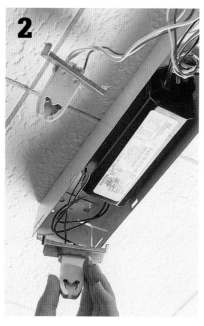

2

Remove the sockets from the fixture housing by sliding them out or by removing the mounting screws and lifting the sockets out.

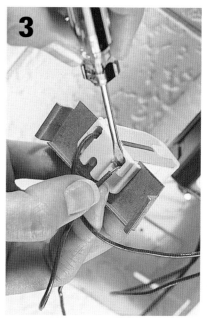

3

Disconnect the wires attached to the sockets by pushing a small screwdriver into the release openings (above), by loosening the screw terminals, or by cutting wires to within 2" of sockets.

4

Remove the old ballast using a ratchet wrench or screwdriver. Make sure to support the ballast so it does not fall.

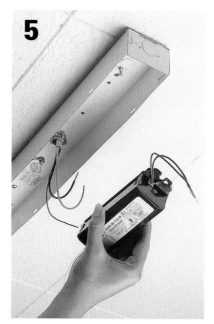

5

Install a new ballast that has the same ratings as the old ballast.

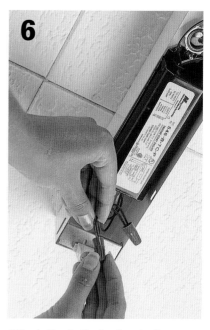

6

Attach the ballast wires to the socket wires using wire connectors, screw terminal connections, or push-in fittings. Reinstall the cover plate, fluorescent tube, and diffuser. Turn on power to the light fixture at the panel.

How to Replace a Fluorescent Light Fixture

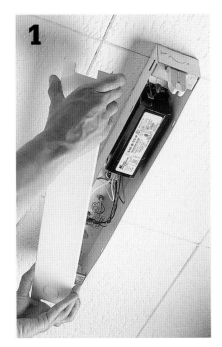

1

Turn off power to the light fixture at the panel. Remove the diffuser, tube, and cover plate. Test for power using a circuit tester.

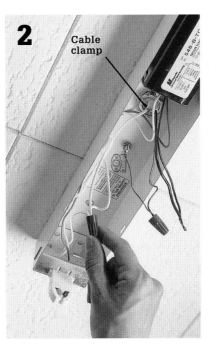

2

Cable clamp

Disconnect the insulated circuit wires and the bare copper grounding wire from the light fixture. Loosen the cable clamp holding the circuit wires.

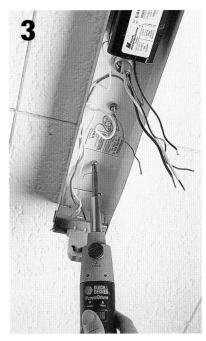

3

Unscrew the fixture from the wall or ceiling and carefully remove it. Make sure to support the fixture so it does not fall.

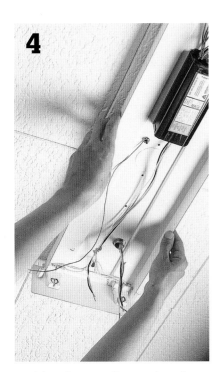

4

Position the new fixture, threading the circuit wires through the knockout opening in the back of the fixture. Screw the fixture in place so it is firmly anchored to framing members.

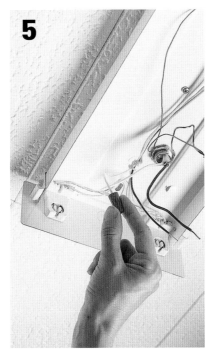

5

Connect the circuit wires to the fixture wires using wire connectors. Follow the wiring diagram included with the new fixture. Tighten the cable clamp holding the circuit wires.

6

Attach the fixture cover plate, and then install the fluorescent tubes and attach the diffuser. Turn on power to the fixture at the panel, and test.

Replacing Plugs & Cords

Replace an electrical plug whenever you notice bent or loose prongs, a cracked or damaged casing, or a missing insulating faceplate. A damaged plug poses a shock and fire hazard.

Replacement plugs are available in different styles to match common appliance cords. Always choose a replacement that is similar to the original plug. Flat-cord and quick-connect plugs are used with light-duty appliances, such as lamps and radios. Round-cord plugs are used with larger appliances, including those that have three-prong grounding plugs.

Some tools and appliances use polarized plugs. A polarized plug has one wide prong and one narrow prong, corresponding to the hot and neutral slots found in a standard receptacle.

If there is room in the plug body, tie the individual wires in an underwriter's knot to secure the plug to the cord (see photo, right).

Tools & Materials ▸

Combination tool
Needlenose pliers
Screwdriver
Replacement plug

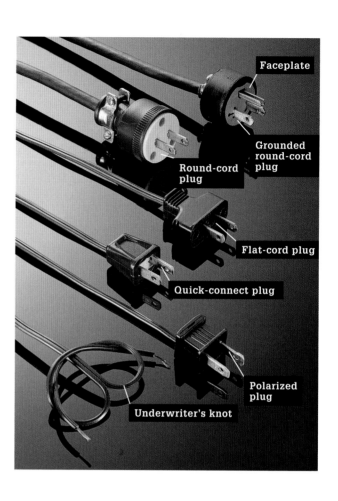

Faceplate
Grounded round-cord plug
Round-cord plug
Flat-cord plug
Quick-connect plug
Polarized plug
Underwriter's knot

How to Install a Quick-Connect Plug

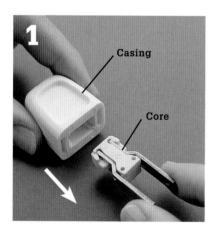

1 Casing / Core

Squeeze the prongs of the new quick-connect plug together slightly, and pull the plug core from the casing. Cut the old plug from the flat-cord wire with a combination tool, leaving a clean cut end.

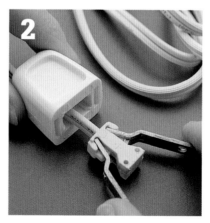

2

Feed unstripped wire through the rear of the plug casing. Spread the prongs, and then insert the wire into the opening in the rear of the core. Squeeze the prongs together; spikes inside the core penetrate the cord. Slide the casing over the core until it snaps into place.

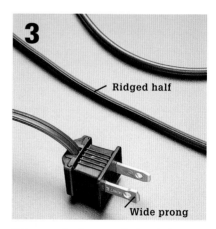

3 Ridged half / Wide prong

When replacing a polarized plug, make sure that the ridged half of the cord lines up with the wider (neutral) prong of the plug.

How to Replace a Round-Cord Plug

Cut off the round cord near the old plug using a combination tool. Remove the insulating faceplate on the new plug and feed the cord through the rear of the plug. Strip about 3" of outer insulation from the round cord. Strip ¾" insulation from the individual wires.

Underwriter's knot

Tie an underwriter's knot with the black and the white wires. Make sure the knot is located close to the edge of the stripped outer insulation. Pull the cord so that the knot slides into the plug body.

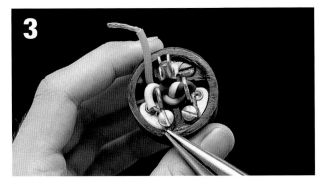

Hook the end of the black wire clockwise around the brass screw and the white wire around the silver screw. On a three-prong plug, attach the third wire to the grounding screw. If necessary, excess grounding wire can be cut away.

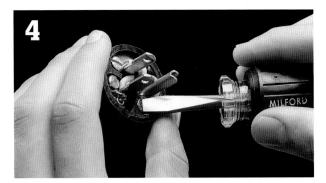

Tighten the screws securely, making sure the copper wires do not touch each other. Replace the insulating faceplate.

How to Replace a Flat-Cord Plug

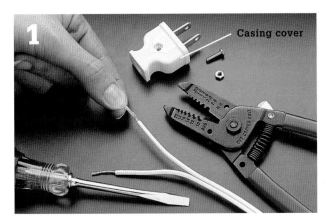

Casing cover

Cut the old plug from cord using a combination tool. Pull apart the two halves of the flat cord so that about 2" of wire are separated. Strip ¾" insulation from each half. Remove the casing cover on the new plug.

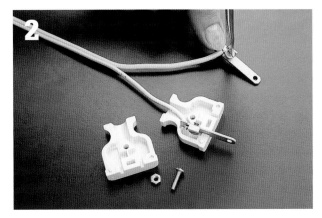

Hook the ends of the wires clockwise around the screw terminals, and tighten the screw terminals securely. Reassemble the plug casing. Some plugs may have an insulating faceplate that must be installed.

How to Replace a Lamp Cord

With the lamp unplugged, the shade off, and the bulb out, you can remove the socket. Squeeze the outer shell of the socket just above the base, and pull the shell out of the base. The shell is often marked "Press" at some point along its perimeter. Press there, and then pull.

Under the outer shell there is a cardboard insulating sleeve. Pull this off and you'll reveal the socket attached to the end of the cord.

With the shell and insulation set aside, pull the socket away from the lamp (it will still be connected to the cord). Unscrew the two screws to completely disconnect the socket from the cord. Set the socket aside with its shell (you'll need them to reassemble the lamp).

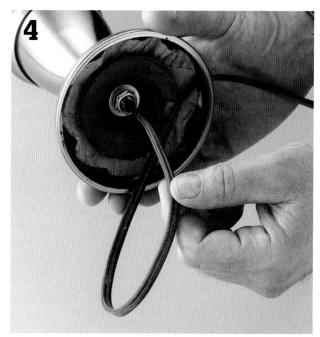

Remove the old cord from the lamp by grasping the cord near the base and pulling the cord through the lamp.

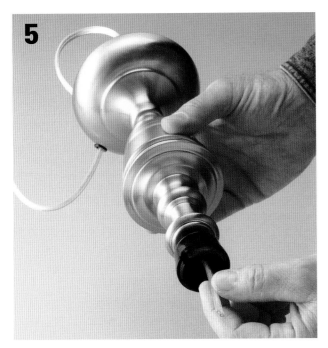

5

Bring your damaged cord to a hardware store or home center and purchase a similar cord set. (A cord set is simply a replacement cord with a plug already attached.) Snake the end of the cord up from the base of the lamp through the top so that about 3" of cord is visible above the top.

6

Carefully separate the two halves of the cord. If the halves won't pull apart, you can carefully make a cut in the middle with a knife. Strip away about ¾" of insulation from the end of each wire.

7

Connect the ends of the new cord to the two screws on the side of the socket (one of which will be silver in color, the other brass-colored). One half of the cord will have ribbing or markings along its length; wrap that wire clockwise around the silver screw, and tighten the screw. The other half of the cord will be smooth; wrap it around the copper screw, and tighten the screw.

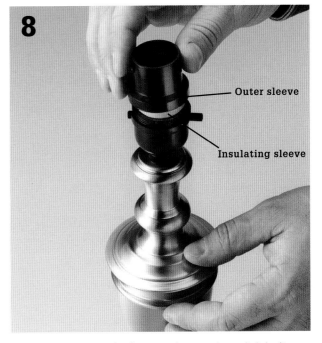

8

Outer sleeve

Insulating sleeve

Set the socket on the base. Make sure the switch isn't blocked by the harp—the part that holds the shade on some lamps. Slide the cardboard insulating sleeve over the socket so the sleeve's notch aligns with the switch. Now slide the outer sleeve over the socket, aligning the notch with the switch. It should snap into the base securely. Screw in a light bulb, plug the lamp in, and test it.

Replacing a Lamp Socket

Next to the cord plug, the most common source of trouble in a lamp is a worn lightbulb socket. When a lamp socket assembly fails, the problem is usually with the socket-switch unit, although replacement sockets may include other parts you do not need.

Lamp failure is not always caused by a bad socket. You can avoid unnecessary repairs by checking the lamp cord, plug, and light bulb before replacing the socket.

Tools & Materials ▸

Replacement socket
Continuity tester
Screwdriver

Socket-mounted switch types are usually interchangeable: choose a replacement you prefer. Clockwise from top left: twist knob, remote switch, pull chain, push lever.

Tip ▸

When replacing a lamp socket, you can improve a standard ON-OFF lamp by installing a three-way socket.

How to Repair or Replace a Lamp Socket

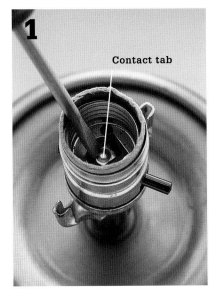

1

Contact tab

2

Outer shell

Insulating sleeve

3

Unplug the lamp. Remove the shade, light bulb, and harp (shade bracket). Scrape the contact tab clean with a small screwdriver. Pry the contact tab up slightly if flattened inside the socket. Replace the bulb, plug in the lamp, and test. If the lamp does not work, unplug, remove the bulb, and continue with the next step.

Squeeze the outer shell of the socket near the "Press" marking, and lift it off. On older lamps, the socket may be held by screws found at the base of the screw socket. Slip off the cardboard insulating sleeve. If the sleeve is damaged, replace the entire socket.

Check for loose wire connections on the screw terminals. Refasten any loose connections, and then reassemble the lamp, and test. If connections are not loose, remove the wires, lift out the socket, and continue with the next step.

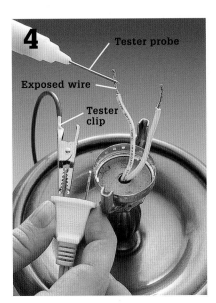

4

Tester probe

Exposed wire

Tester clip

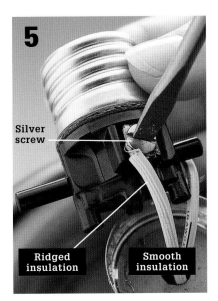

5

Silver screw

Ridged insulation

Smooth insulation

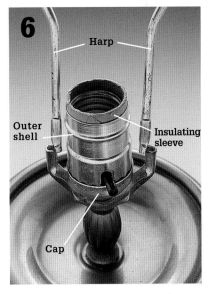

6

Harp

Outer shell

Insulating sleeve

Cap

Test for lamp cord problems with a continuity tester. Place the clip of the tester on one prong of the plug. Touch the probe to one exposed wire, and then to the other wire. Repeat the test with the other prong of the plug. If the tester fails to light for either prong, then replace the cord and plug. Retest the lamp.

If cord and plug are functional, then choose a replacement socket marked with the same amp and volt ratings as the old socket. One half of flat-cord lamp wire is covered by insulation that is ridged or marked: attach this wire to the silver screw terminal. Connect the other wire to the brass screw.

Slide the insulating sleeve and outer shell over the socket so that the socket and screw terminals are fully covered and the switch fits into the sleeve slot. Press the socket assembly down into the cap until the socket locks into place. Replace the harp, light bulb, and shade.

APPENDIX: Common Mistakes

An electrical inspector visiting your home might identify a number of situations that are not up to code. These situations may not be immediate problems. In fact, it is possible that the wiring in your home has remained trouble free for many years.

Nevertheless, any wiring or device that is not up to code carries the potential for problems, often at risk to your home and your family. In addition, you may have trouble selling your home if it is not wired according to accepted methods.

Most local electrical codes are based on the National Electrical Code (NEC), a book updated and published every three years by the National Fire Protection Agency. This code book contains rules and regulations for the proper installation of electrical wiring and devices. Most public libraries carry reference copies of the NEC.

All electrical inspectors are required to be well versed in the NEC. Their job is to know the NEC regulations and to make sure these rules are followed in order to prevent fires and ensure safety. If you have questions regarding your home wiring system, your local inspector will be happy to answer them.

While a book cannot possibly identify all potential wiring problems in your house, we have identified some of the most common wiring defects here and will show you how to correct them. When working on home wiring repair or replacement projects, refer to this section to help identify any conditions that may be hazardous.

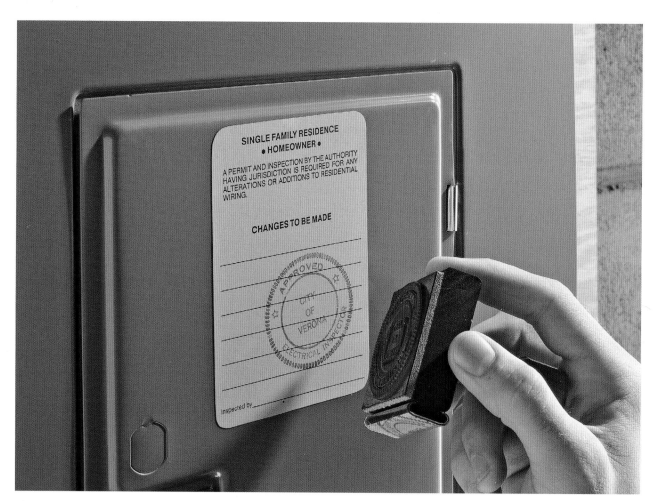

Electrical inspectors are on the lookout for common mistakes. The following pages detail problems to avoid so you will pass inspection on the first try.

Service Panel Inspection

Problem: Rust stains are found inside the main service panel. This problem occurs because water seeps into the service head outside the house and drips down into the service panel.

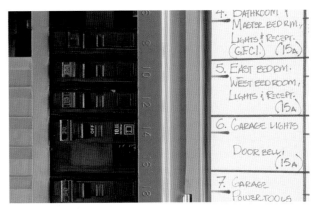

Solution: Have an electrician examine the service mast, weather head, service entrance cables, and the main panel. If the panel or service wires have been damaged, new electrical service must be installed.

Problem: This problem is actually a very old and very dangerous solution. A penny or a knockout behind a fuse effectively bypasses the fuse, preventing an overloaded circuit from blowing the fuse. This is very dangerous and can lead to overheated wiring.

Solution: Remove the penny and replace the fuse. Have a licensed electrician examine the panel and circuit wiring. If the fuse has been bypassed for years, wiring may be dangerously compromised, and the circuit may need to be replaced. In addition, if you have the old Edison fuse socket, replace it with a new S-type fuse socket. This eliminates the related problem of installing the wrong-size fuse in the panel.

Problem: Two wires connected to one single-pole breaker is a sign of an overcrowded panel and also a dangerous code violation unless the breaker is approved for such a connection.

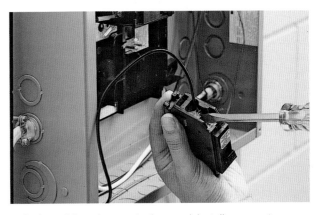

Solution: If there is room in the panel, install a separate breaker for the extra wire. If the panel is overcrowded, have an electrician upgrade the panel or install a subpanel.

Other Common Panel Problems

Problem: Too much bare wire exposed at the breaker connection. This presents a short-circuit hazard. **Solution:** With power off, trim the feed wire so no more than ½" of bare wire is exposed, and then reconnect.

Problem: There is no handle tie (or there is an improper handle tie) on breaker pair controlling a 240-volt circuit. **Solution:** Install a handle tie approved by the circuit breaker manufacturer.

Problem: Conductor too small for breaker size. The #14 copper wires seen here are rated for 15 amp circuits. The 30-amp breaker allows too much current in the wires and could cause a fire. **Solution:** Replace the wires with wires approved for the circuit breaker size.

Problem: There is more than one neutral in a buss terminal. Sharing slots is fine for grounding wires, but each neutral wire should have its own terminal. **Solution:** Remove one of the wires and find an open terminal for it.

Problem: Arc-fault protection (AFCI) circuit breakers may fail, especially if they are tripped with some frequency. **Solution:** Test each breaker as recommended by the manufacturer by depressing the "Test" button. If the breaker is functioning correctly it will trip when the button is pushed.

Problem: GFCI circuit breakers may fail, especially if they are tripped with some frequency. **Solution:** Test each breaker as recommended by the manufacturer by depressing the "Test" button. If the breaker is functioning correctly it will trip when the button is pushed.

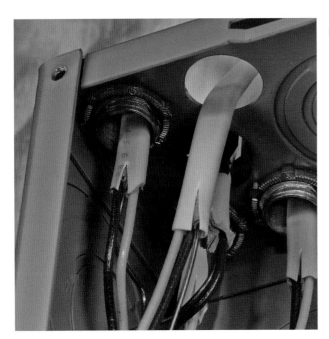

Problem: There is a missing cable clamp at panel box. All NM cable entering a service panel (or any other box) needs protection from sharp edges that can cut sheathing. **Solution:** Disconnect the cable in the box, and retract and reinstall it with cable clamps.

Problem: The shared hot terminal on the breaker is not wired correctly. The example above is correct: the conductors should be positioned on opposite sides of the terminal and held securely in the separate grooves by the terminal screw.

Common Cable Problems

Problem: Cable running across joists or studs is attached to the edge of framing members. Electrical codes forbid this type of installation in exposed areas such as unfinished basements and crawl spaces.

Solution: Protect cable by drilling holes in framing members at least 2" from exposed edges and threading the cable through the holes.

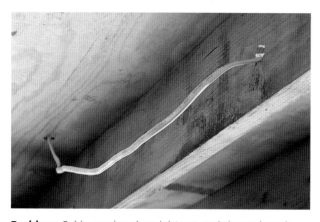

Problem: Cable running along joists or studs hangs loosely. Loose cables can be pulled accidentally, causing damage to wires.

Solution: Anchor the cable to the side of the framing members at least 1¼" from the edge using plastic staples. NM cable should be stapled every 4½ ft. and within 8" of each electrical box.

Cable shown cutaway

Problem: Cable threaded through studs or joists lies close to the edge of the framing members. NM cable (shown cutaway) can be damaged easily if nails or screws are driven into the framing members during remodeling projects.

Solution: Install metal nail guards to protect cable from damage. Nail guards are available at hardware stores and home centers.

Problem: Unclamped cable enters a metal electrical box. Edges of the knockout can rub against the cable sheathing and damage the wires. *Note: With smaller plastic boxes, clamps are not required if cables are anchored to framing members within 8" of the box.*

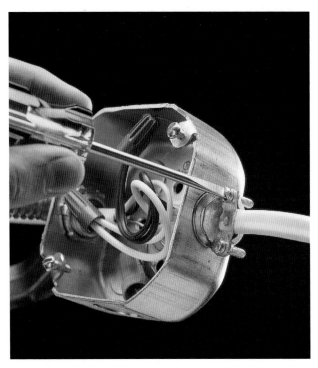

Solution: Anchor the cable to the electrical box with a cable clamp. Several types of cable clamps are available at hardware stores and home centers.

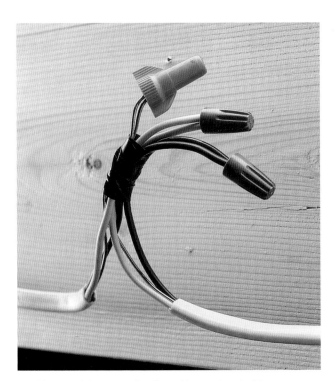

Problem: Cables are spliced outside an electrical box. Exposed splices can spark and create a risk of shock or fire.

Solution: Bring installation up to code by enclosing the splice inside a metal or plastic electrical box. Make sure the box is large enough to accommodate the number of wires it contains.

Checking Wire Connections

Problem: Two or more wires are attached to a single-screw terminal. This type of connection is seen in older wiring but is now prohibited by the NEC.

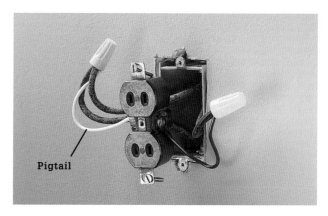

Pigtail

Solution: Disconnect the wires from the screw terminal, and then join them to a short length of wire (called a pigtail) using a wire connector. Connect the other end of the pigtail to the screw terminal.

Exposed wire

Problem: Bare wire extends past a screw terminal. Exposed wire can cause a short circuit if it touches the metal box or another circuit wire.

Solution: Clip the wire and reconnect it to the screw terminal. In a proper connection, the bare wire wraps completely around the screw terminal, and the plastic insulation just touches the screw head.

Problem: Wires are connected with electrical tape. Electrical tape was used frequently in older installations, but it can deteriorate over time, leaving bare wires exposed inside the electrical box.

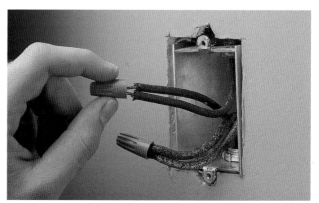

Solution: Replace electrical tape with wire connectors. You may need to clip away a small portion of the wire so the bare end will be covered completely by the connector.

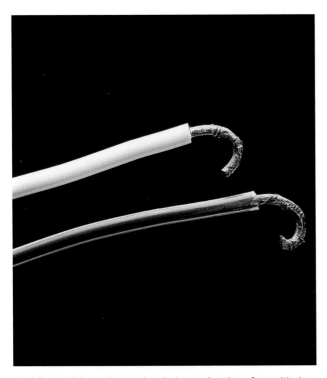

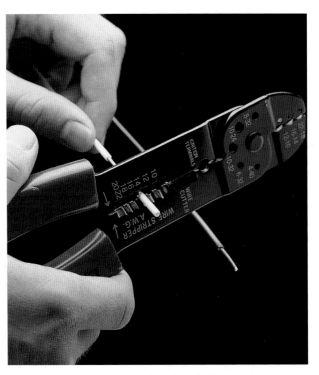

Problem: Nicks and scratches in bare wires interfere with the flow of current. This can cause the wires to overheat.

Solution: Clip away damaged portion of wire, restrip about ¾" of insulation, and reconnect the wire to the screw terminal.

Electrical Box Inspection

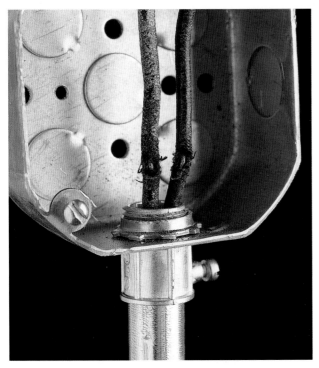

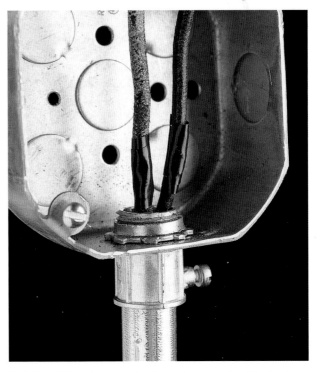

Problem: Insulation on wires is cracked or damaged. If damaged insulation exposes bare wire, a short circuit can occur, posing a shock hazard and fire risk.

Solution: Wrap damaged insulation temporarily with plastic electrical tape. Damaged circuit wires should be replaced by an electrician.

(continued)

Problem: Open electrical boxes create a fire hazard if a short circuit causes sparks (arcing) inside the box.

Solution: Cover an open metal box with a solid metal cover plate. Cover an open plastic box with a plastic cover plate. Cover plates are available at any hardware store. Electrical boxes must remain accessible and cannot be sealed inside ceilings or walls.

Problem: Short wires are difficult to handle. The NEC requires that each wire in an electrical box have at least 3" of workable length from the front of the box.

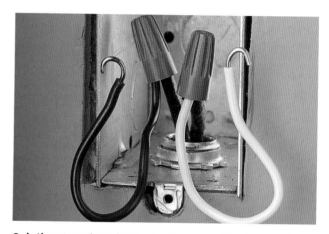

Solution: Lengthen circuit wires by connecting them to short pigtail wires using wire connectors. Pigtails can be cut from scrap wire but should be the same gauge and color as the circuit wires and at least 3" long.

Problem: A recessed electrical box is hazardous, especially if the wall or ceiling surface is made from a flammable material, such as wood paneling. The NEC prohibits this type of installation.

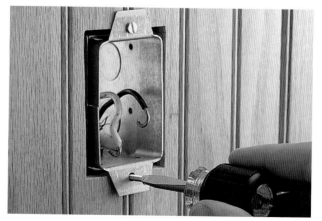

Solution: Add an extension ring to bring the face of the electrical box flush with the surface. Extension rings come in several sizes and are available at hardware stores.

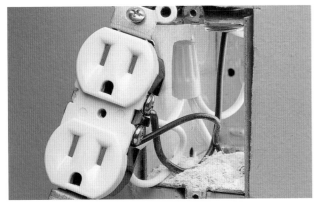

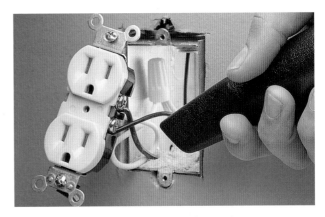

Problem: Open electrical boxes create a fire hazard if a short circuit causes sparks (dust and dirt in an electrical box can cause hazardous high-resistance short circuits). When making routine electrical repairs, always check the electrical boxes for dust and dirt buildup.

Solution: Vacuum the electrical box clean using a narrow nozzle attachment. Make sure power to the box is turned off at the panel before vacuuming.

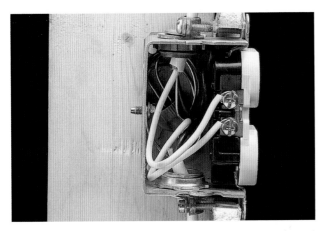

Problem: A crowded electrical box (shown cutaway) makes electrical repairs difficult. This type of installation is prohibited, because the heat in the box can damage the wire or device and cause a fire.

Solution: Replace the electrical box with a deeper electrical box.

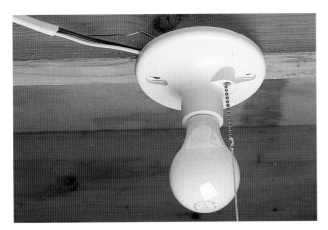

Problem: A light fixture is installed without an electrical box. This installation exposes the wiring connections and provides no support for the light fixture.

Solution: Install an approved electrical box to enclose the wire connections and support the light fixture.

Common Electrical Cord Problems

Problem: A lamp or appliance cord runs underneath a rug. Foot traffic can wear off insulation, creating a short circuit that can cause fire or shock.

Solution: Reposition the lamp or appliance so that the cord is visible. Replace worn cords.

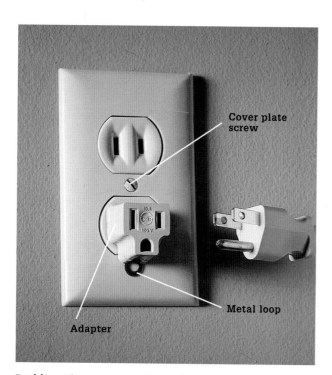

Cover plate screw

Metal loop

Adapter

GFCI receptacle

Problem: Three-prong appliance plugs do not fit a two-slot receptacle. Do not use three-prong adapters unless the metal loop on the adapter is tightly connected to the cover plate screw on receptacle.

Solution: Install a three-prong grounded receptacle if a means of grounding exists at the box. Install a GFCI receptacle in kitchens and bathrooms or if the electrical box is not grounded. Label the receptacle: "No Equipment Ground".

Problem: A lamp or appliance plug is cracked, or an electrical cord is frayed near the plug. Worn cords and plugs create a fire and shock hazard.

Solution: Cut away damaged portions of wire, and install a new plug (see pages 310 to 311). Replacement plugs are available at appliance stores and home centers.

Problem: An extension cord is too small for the power load drawn by a tool or appliance. Undersized extension cords can overheat, melting the insulation and leaving bare wires exposed.

Solution: Use an extension cord with wattage and amperage ratings that meet or exceed the rating of the tool or appliance. Extension cords are for temporary use only. Never use an extension cord for a permanent installation.

Inspecting Receptacles & Switches

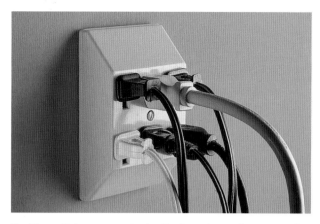

Problem: Octopus receptacle attachments used permanently can overload a circuit and cause overheating of the receptacle.

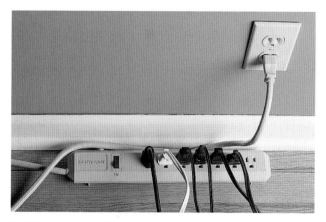

Solution: Use a multi-receptacle power strip with built-in overload protection. This is for temporary use only. If the need for extra receptacles is frequent, upgrade the wiring system.

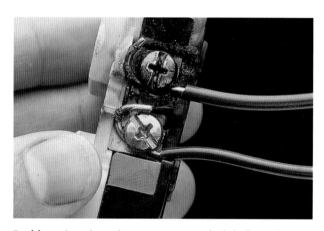

Problem: Scorch marks near screw terminals indicate that electrical arcing has occurred. Arcing usually is caused by loose wire connections.

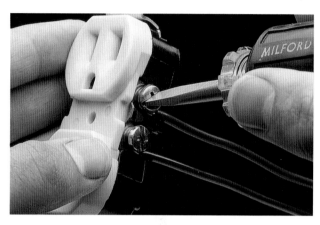

Solution: If the insulation is damaged, cut the wires back to intact insulation. Otherwise, clean the wires with fine grit sandpaper or steel wool. Replace the receptacle. Make sure wires are connected securely to screw terminals.

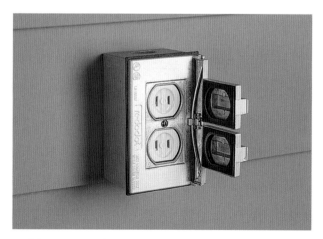

Problem: An exterior receptacle box allows water to enter the box when receptacle slots are in use.

Solution: Replace the old receptacle box (no longer code compliant) with an in-use box that has a bubble cover to protect plugs from water while they are in the slots.

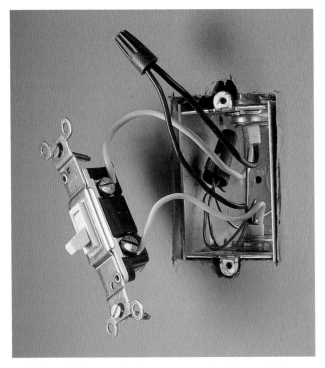

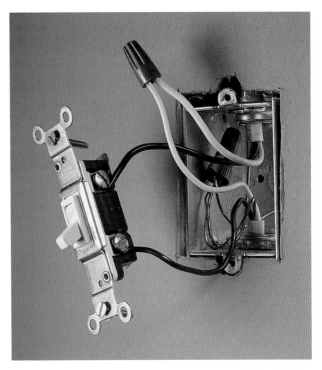

Problem: White neutral wires are connected to a switch. Although the switch appears to work correctly in this installation, it is dangerous because the light fixture carries voltage when the switch is off.

Solution: Connect the black hot wires to the switch, and join the white wires together with a wire connector.

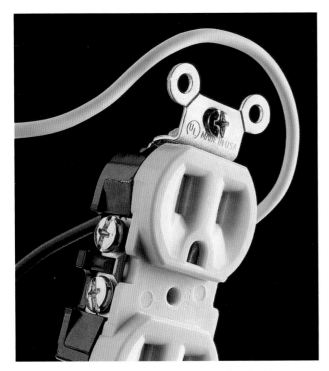

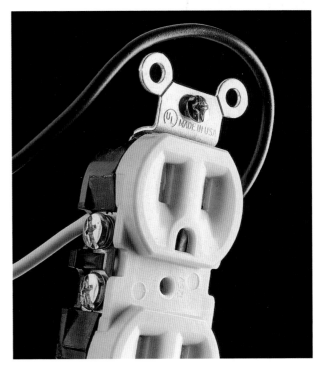

Problem: White neutral wires are connected to the brass screw terminals on the receptacle, and black hot wires are attached to silver screw terminals. This installation is hazardous because live voltage flows into the long neutral slot on the receptacle.

Solution: Reverse the wire connections so that the black hot wires are attached to brass screw terminals and white neutral wires are attached to silver screw terminals. Live voltage now flows into the short slot on the receptacle.

Conversions

Metric Equivalent

Inches (in.)	1/64	1/32	1/25	1/16	1/8	1/4	3/8	2/5	1/2	5/8	3/4	7/8	1	2	3	4	5	6	7	8	9	10	11	12	36	39.4
Feet (ft.)																								1	3	3 1/12
Yards (yd.)																									1	1 1/12
Millimeters (mm)	0.40	0.79	1		1.59	3.18	6.35	9.53	10	12.7	15.9	19.1	22.2	25.4	50.8	76.2	101.6	127	152	178	203	229	254	279	305	914	1,000
Centimeters (cm)				0.95	1	1.27	1.59	1.91	2.22	2.54	5.08	7.62	10.16	12.7	15.2	17.8	20.3	22.9	25.4	27.9	30.5	91.4	100
Meters (m)																					.30	.91	1.00

Converting Measurements

TO CONVERT:	TO:	MULTIPLY BY:
Inches	Millimeters	25.4
Inches	Centimeters	2.54
Feet	Meters	0.305
Yards	Meters	0.914
Miles	Kilometers	1.609
Square inches	Square centimeters	6.45
Square feet	Square meters	0.093
Square yards	Square meters	0.836
Cubic inches	Cubic centimeters	16.4
Cubic feet	Cubic meters	0.0283
Cubic yards	Cubic meters	0.765
Pints (U.S.)	Liters	0.473 (Imp. 0.568)
Quarts (U.S.)	Liters	0.946 (Imp. 1.136)
Gallons (U.S.)	Liters	3.785 (Imp. 4.546)
Ounces	Grams	28.4
Pounds	Kilograms	0.454
Tons	Metric tons	0.907

TO CONVERT:	TO:	MULTIPLY BY:
Millimeters	Inches	0.039
Centimeters	Inches	0.394
Meters	Feet	3.28
Meters	Yards	1.09
Kilometers	Miles	0.621
Square centimeters	Square inches	0.155
Square meters	Square feet	10.8
Square meters	Square yards	1.2
Cubic centimeters	Cubic inches	0.061
Cubic meters	Cubic feet	35.3
Cubic meters	Cubic yards	1.31
Liters	Pints (U.S.)	2.114 (Imp. 1.76)
Liters	Quarts (U.S.)	1.057 (Imp. 0.88)
Liters	Gallons (U.S.)	0.264 (Imp. 0.22)
Grams	Ounces	0.035
Kilograms	Pounds	2.2
Metric tons	Tons	1.1

Converting Temperatures

Convert degrees Fahrenheit (F) to degrees Celsius (C) by following this simple formula: Subtract 32 from the Fahrenheit temperature reading. Then mulitply that number by $\frac{5}{9}$. For example, 77°F - 32 = 45. 45 × $\frac{5}{9}$ = 25°C.

To convert degrees Celsius to degrees Fahrenheit, multiply the Celsius temperature reading by $\frac{9}{5}$, then add 32. For example, 25°C × $\frac{9}{5}$ = 45. 45 + 32 = 77°F.

Fahrenheit   Celsius

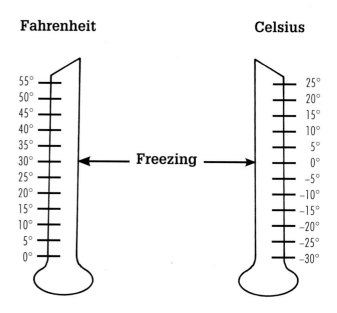

Resources

Applied Energy Innovations
Solar, wind, geothermal installations
612 532 0384
www.appliedenergyinnovations.org

Black & Decker
Portable power tools and more
www.blackandddecker.com

Broan-NuTone, LLC
Vent fans
800 558 1711
www.broan.com

Generac Power Systems
Standby generators and switches
888 436 3722
www.generac.com

**Honda Power Equipment/
American Honda Motor Company, Inc.**
Standby generators
770 497 6400
www.hondapowerequipment.com

Kohler
Standby generators
800 544 2444
www.kohlergenerators.com

Pass & Seymour Legrand
Home automation products
877 295 3472
www.passandseymour.com

Red Wing Shoes Co.
Work shoes and boots shown throughout book
800 733 9464
www.redwingshoes.com

Unistrut Metal Framing
Solar panel mounts
www.unistrut.com

Westinghouse
Ceiling fans, decorative lighting, solar outdoor
   lighting, & other lighting fixtures and bulbs
866 442 7873
Purchase here: www.budgetlighting.com
www.westinghouse.com

Photo Credits

p. 175 photo © Mike Clarke / www.istock.com
p. 192 photo © George Peters / www.istock.com
p. 196 photo courtesy of Broan NuTone
p. 208 photo (top right) courtesy of Kohler
p. 210 photo courtesy of Ikea
p. 244 photo © George Peters / www.istock.com
p. 245 photo © David Ross / www.istock.com

p. 257 (top right) photo © Steve Harmon / istock.com,
   (lower right) photo courtesy of SieMatic
p. 260 photo © Jeff Chevrier / www.istock.com
p. 261 photos (top right & lower) courtesy of Generac
   Power Systems, Inc.
p. 272 photo courtesy of Cabin Fever, featuring McMaster
   Carr vapor-tight light fixtures

Index

AFCI breakers
    common inspection mistakes, 319
    installation, 169
    NEC requirements, 7, 168
    vs. GFCI, 168
air conditioners, central
    wattage of, 135
        See also heating and air
    conditioning
air conditioners, window
    circuits for, 158
    wattage of, 135
        See also heating and air
    conditioning
alarms, smoke/CO, 214–215
ampacity (of wires), 10, 29
amperage
    of circuit breakers, 78
    evaluating loads and, 132
    of fuses, 78
    of service panels, 75
ampere (amp), defined, 14
appliances
    circuits for high-wattage, 11,
        157–158
    circuits from small, 156
    NEC requirements, 125
    powering high voltage, 11
Arc Fault Circuit Interruption (AFCI)
    breakers. See AFCI
armored cables, 14, 19, 27

backup power supply
    transfer switch types, 263
    types of, 260–261
    typical system layout, 262
        See also generators
ballasts, fluorescent light, 308
baseboard heaters
    calculating heating needs, 233
    circuits for, 157, 232, 233
    installation, 240-volt, 234–235
    thermostats for, 233
bathrooms
    circuits for, 150, 159
    exhaust fans, 252–255
    NEC requirements, 125, 126, 129
    vanity lights, 208–209
bedrooms
    AFCI protection, 7
    NEC requirements for, 129
bell-hanger's bits, 40
bonding wiring systems, 180–185
boxes. See electrical boxes
breakers. See circuit breakers
BX cables, 14

cables
    about, 26
    coaxial, 28
    common inspection mistakes, 320
    defined, 14
    electrical box connections and, 63
    NEC requirements, 126, 128
    rubber insulation and, 26
    SE (service entrance), 28
    staples and, 28, 31
    for telephones, 28
    UF (underground feeder) cable,
        27, 28
        See also NM (non-metallic)
    cables
carbon monoxide (CO) alarms,
    214–215
cartridge fuses, 78, 79. See also   fuses
ceiling fans
    about, 244

bracket-mounted installation, 246
    circuits for, 165
    downrod installation, 247
    heating and, 245
    NEC requirements, 127
    repairs
        blade wobble, 300
        loose wire connection, 301
        pull-switch replacement,
            302–303
    retrofit remote control kits,
        248–251
    supporting boxes for, 246
    types of, 245
ceilings
    electrical box support, 246
    light fixtures
        attachment of, 193
        bracing electrical boxes, 70
        in circuit maps, 165
        electrical box installation, 68,
            70
        grounding and, 193
        NEC requirements, 127
        replacing, 194–195
        track lighting installation,
            200–203
    NM cable installation in finished,
        41
    recessed lighting
        about, 196
        in finished ceiling, 199
            installation, 198–199
            trims kits, 197
            types of, 197
    shutting off power for work in, 23
        See also ceiling fans
central air conditioners, wattage of,
    135
chandelier repair, 298–299
circuit breaker panels
    about, 76–77
    NEC requirements, 127, 128
    safety and, 77
        See also service panels
circuit breakers
    AFCI
        common inspection mistakes,
            319
        installation, 169
        NEC requirements, 7, 168
        vs. GFCI, 168
    common inspection problems,
        317–318
    compatibility, 23
    connecting, 80–81
    defined, 14
    exercising, 183
    GFCI
        common inspection mistakes,
            319
        installing, 169
        radiant heat systems and,
            239–240
        vs. AFCI, 169
    installing additional, 77
    NM cable installation and, 35–36
    resetting, 79
    role in electrical system, 11
    safety and, 74
    slimline breakers, 186
    types of, 78
circuit indexes, 22, 177
circuit maps, 150–165
circuits
    about, 16–17
    AFCI protection and, 7

bathroom exhaust fans, 252
    defined, 14
    evaluating loads on, 123, 132–135,
        136, 137
    floor-warming systems and,
        239–240
    generators and backup, 267
    high-wattage appliances and, 11
    maps for, 150–165
    NEC requirements for, 125
    sample circuit evaluation, 136
    sample kitchen project, 144–147
    sample room addition, 140–143
closets, NEC requirements, 127
clothes dryers
    installing 120/240-Volt
        receptacles for, 190
    powering, 11
    receptacles for, 106
    wattage of, 135
CO (carbon monoxide) alarms, 214–215
coaxial cables, 28
computers, 158
concrete walls, installing conduit/ wires on, 46
conductor, defined, 14
conduit
    about, 42–43
    concrete wall installation, 46
    connecting nonmetallic, 45
    defined, 14
    EMT (electrical metallic tubing),
        43, 44
    fill capacity of, 43
    fittings for, 42–43, 44
    installing grounding wires in
        metal, 42
    Intermediate metallic conduit
        (IMC), 43
    LB, 43
    LFC (liquid-tight flexible), 44
    metal, 27
    plastic PVC, 43
    RNC (rigid nonmetallic conduit),
        44
    types of, 42–43
continuity, defined, 14
continuity testers, 98
cords
    common problems with, 326–327
    replacement of lamp, 312–313
crawl spaces, 126
current, defined, 14
current ground faults, 18
    normal pathway for, 18

dimmer switches, 96–97
dining rooms, 129
dishwashers, 134
doorbell systems
    chime unit replacement, 223
    components, 220
    doorbell switch replacement, 223
    testing of non-functional, 221–222
duplex receptacles. See receptacles

Edison adapters, 78
Edison fuses, 317
electrical boxes
    ceiling, support for, 246
    common inspection mistakes,
        321, 323–325
    defined, 14
    exterior fixture box installation,
        281
    fill chart for, 60
    fixtures with built-in, 66
    grounding of metal, 63

inspections and, 130–131
junction box installation, 70–71
light fixture box installation, 68
locating, 69
NEC requirements, 13, 60, 128
NM cable installation and, 36–38
nonmetallic
  types/sizes, 64
  working with, 65
pop-in box installation, 72–73
receptacle box installation, 67
replacing, 72–73
specifications for, 63
switch box installation, 68
types of, 61–62
wallcovering thickness and, 69
electrical circuits. See circuits
electrical loads
  evaluating, 123, 132–133
  locating wattage information,
    134–135
  typical wattage information, 136
  worksheet for evaluating, 137
electrical panels. See service panels
electrical symbols, 139
electrical systems
  components, 12–13, 15
  delivery systems to, 11
  glossary, 14
  tools for, 20–21
electrician's tape, 32
electric meters
  about, 11, 12
  defined, 14
  service panel upgrades/replacements,
    178–179
electric ranges
  in circuit maps, 157
  hoods for, 256–259
  installing 120/240-Volt
    receptacles for, 191
  receptacles for, 106
  wattage of, 134
exhaust fans, bathroom, 252–255
extension cords, 23

fish tape, 21, 39
flexible metal conduit (FMC), 14
floor-warming systems, 238–243
fluorescent lights
  about, 304
  ballast replacement, 308
  replacing fluorescent fixture, 309
  socket replacement, 307
  starter replacement, 305
  troubleshooting, 305
  tube replacement, 306
food disposers, 134
forced-air furnaces, wattage of, 135
framing
  common inspection mistakes, 320
  framing member chart for hole/
    notch size, 34
  NM cable installation, 34–38
freezers, 135
fuse panels, 75. See also service panels
fuses
  about, 78
  common inspection mistakes, 317
  compatibility, 23
  defined, 14
  replacing/identifying blown, 79
  role in electrical system, 11
  safety and, 74
  types of, 78

garages, NEC requirements, 126

garbage disposals, 134
gas pipes, metal, bonding, 180, 181–182
generators
  automatic standby, 265, 271
  choosing, 262, 263
  manual transfer switch
    installation, 266–270
  outage operation of portable, 265
  portable backup maintenance,
    164
  selecting backup circuits, 267
  types of, 260–261
  typical system layout, 262
GFCI breakers
  common inspection mistakes, 319
  installation, 169
  radiant heat systems and,
    239–240
  vs. AFCI, 168
Greenfield conduit, 14
grounded wires, defined, 14
ground faults, 18
grounding
  about, 18–19
  ceiling light fixtures and, 193
  ground faults, 18
  service panel upgrades/
    replacements, 178
  wiring systems, 180–185
grounding electrode systems, 183–185
grounding rods
  about, 19
  installing, 180, 183–185
grounding wires
  defined, 14
  for electrical system, 12

hallways, NEC requirements, 127, 129
heating and air conditioning, 131
  calculating/chart, 131
  ceiling fans and, 245
  determining need, 131
  evaluation of electrical loads and,
    133
  thermostats
    baseboard heaters, 233
    low-voltage systems, 224–225
    mercury, disposal, 227
    programmable, 224–225
    upgrading to programmable,
      226–227
    underfloor radiant heat systems,
      238–243
    wall heater installation, 236–237
    See also baseboard heaters
hot wires
  defined, 14
  role in electrical system, 10

inspections
  common mistakes, 317-329
  heating and air conditioning and,
    131
  planning electrical projects and,
    123
  preparing for, 7, 130–131
  service panel upgrades and, 179
inspectors, 125
insulator, defined, 14

junction boxes, 70-71. See also
  electrical boxes

kitchens
  circuits for, 150
  NEC requirements, 125, 126, 129
  sample project

circuits for, 144–145
wiring diagrams for, 146–147
undercabinet lights, hardwired,
  204–207
knob and tube wiring, 27

lamps, cord replacement, 312-313.
  See also light fixtures
landscape lights
  about, 216
  deck-use modification, 217
  installation, 218–219
  system components, 217
laundry rooms, 129
light bulbs
  fluorescent, 306
  wattage of, 134
light fixtures
  bathroom vanity lights, 208–209
  built-in switch repair, 297
  chandelier repair, 298–299
  in circuit maps, 151–153, 159–165
  common inspection mistakes, 325
  electrical box installation, 68
  evaluation of electrical loads and,
    133
  landscape lights
    about, 216
    deck-use modification, 217
    installation, 218–219
    system components, 217
  low-voltage cable lights, 210–213
  motion-sensing floodlights
    exterior boxes for, 281
    installing, 280–281
    replacing, 282–283
  NEC requirements, 125, 128
  recessed lighting
    about, 196
    in finished ceiling, 199
    installation, 198–199
    trims kits, 197
    types of, 197
  removing fixture, 296
  replacing fluorescent fixture, 309
  role in electrical system, 10, 12
  socket replacements, 297
  socket testing, 296
  track lighting installation, 200–203
  troubleshooting, 295
  undercabinet lights, hardwired,
    204–207
    See also fluorescent lights
living areas
  NEC requirements for, 125, 126,
    129
  sample room addition
    circuits for, 140–141
    wiring diagrams for, 142–143
local codes, 125
low-voltage cable lights, 210–213
low-voltage landscape lights.
  See landscape lights

main service panels. See service panels
mercury switches, 85
mercury thermostats, disposal, 227
metal clad (MC) cable, 27
meters
  about, 11, 12
  defined, 14
  service panel upgrades/replacements and,
    178–179
microwave ovens
  individual circuits for, 11
  wattage of, 134
motion-sensing floodlights

exterior boxes for, 281
installation, 280–281
replacing, 282–283
motion-sensor switches, 85
multimeters , 21, 118–119

National Electrical Code
   AFCI breakers and, 13
   by area, 129
   bathrooms, 125, 126
   cables and, 126
   ceiling fans/fixtures, 127
   circuit breaker panels, 127
   closets/storage spaces, 127
   electrical boxes, 13, 128
   fixtures, 128
   GFCI receptacles, 126
   grounding, 128, 180
   hallways, 127
   kitchens, 125, 126
   living area requirements, 125, 126
   permanent appliances and, 125
   planning electrical projects and, 122, 125
   receptacles, 125, 128
   service panels, 128
   stairways, 126
   switch requirements, 7, 128
   wires/cables, 128
neutral wires
   defined, 14
   role in electrical system, 10
   in switches, 7
NM (non-metallic) cables
   about, 19, 27, 28
   defined, 14
   framing member chart for holes/notches, 34
   installing
      finished ceilings, 41
      finished walls, 39–40
      unfinished walls, 34–38
   local regulations, 34
   measuring, 34
   reading, 29
   sheathing colors, 28
   sheathing/insulation stripping, 30

octagonal boxes, 60
outbuildings, 272–279
outdoors
   circuits for, 151
   garage receptacles and, 7
   GFCI receptacles and, 114
   landscape lights
      about, 216
      deck-use modification, 217
      installation, 218–219
      system components, 217
   motion-sensing floodlights
      exterior boxes for, 281
      installing, 280–281
      replacing, 282–283
   NEC requirements for, 129
   outbuildings, 272–279
   types of cable for, 42
outlets
   defined, 14
   installing surface mounted system from, 50–57
   See also receptacles
overload, defined, 14

permits, 7, 121, 123
   upgrading service panels and, 172
pigtail wire, defined, 14
planning

evaluating loads, 123, 132–133
   locating wattage information, 134–135
   sample circuit evaluation, 136
   typical wattage information, 136
   worksheet for, 137
examining service panels, 122, 124
   National Electrical Code and, 122
   permits and, 121, 123
   sample kitchen project
      circuits for, 144–145
      wiring diagrams for, 146–147
   sample room addition
      circuits for, 140–141
      wiring diagrams for, 142–143
   wiring diagrams, 123
      drawing, 138–139
      electrical symbol key, 139
plug fuses. See fuses
plug-in testers, 21, 118
plugs
   flat-cord plug replacement, 311
   quick-connect installation, 310
   replacing, 310
   round-cord plug replacement, 311
polarization, 19
polarized receptacles
   about, 19
   defined, 14
pop-in electrical boxes, 72–73
power defined, 14
   production of, 11
   shutting off, 22
   testing receptacles for, 22
programmable thermostats.
   See thermostats

raceway
   cutting metal, 52
   making corners with, 54
   splicing, 55
      See also conduit; surface-mounted wiring
radiant heat systems, 238–243
range hoods
   about, 256
   installation, 258–259
   termination points for, 259
   types of, 257
receptacle adapters, 19, 326
receptacles
   adapters for, 19
   AFCI, 7, 108
   childproofing and, 107
   circuit maps containing, 150–151, 153–158, 161
   for clothes dryers, 190
   common inspection mistakes, 322, 328
   common problems with, 326–327
   defined, 14
   duplex, 108
   electrical box installation for, 67
   for electric ranges, 191
   garages and, 7
   GFCI
      about, 108, 114
      AFCI breakers and, 168
      multiple-location protection installation, 116–117
      NEC requirements, 7, 126
      single-location protection installation, 115
      wiring of, 114
   high voltage, 106

inspections and, 130–131
   installation of new, 112–113
   NEC requirements, 125, 128
   older types, 105
   overloading, 328
   polarized, 14, 19
   recessed wall, 107
   replacement, 7
   replacing, 7
   role in electrical system, 10, 13
   safety and, 22–23
   selecting, 103
   surface-mounted, 106
   for surface-mounted wiring, 49
   switch-controlled split receptacles, 154–155
   switch/receptacles, 93, 101
   tamper resistant three-slot, 19
   testing for power, 22, 118–119
   troubleshooting common problems, 109
   types of, 104
   wiring
      end-of-run vs. middle-of-run, 110
      split-circuit, 110–111
      two-slot, 110–111
Romex cables. See Non-metallic (NM) cables
room heaters, 135

safety
   baseboard heaters and, 232
   basics of, 22–23
   circuit breaker panels, 77
   circuit breakers and fuses and, 74
   need for, 9
   smoke/CO alarms, 214–215
   switches and, 83
screw terminals defined, 14
   wall switches and, 86
SE (service entrance) cable, 28
service drops, 172, 173, 179
service laterals, 172, 173
service masts, 11, 12
   safety and, 23
   short roofs and, 179
service panels
   about, 74–75
   capacity of, 74–75
   common inspection mistakes, 317–319
   defined, 14
   fuse panels, 75
   grounding main, 182
   location of, 174
   NEC requirements, 127, 128
   planning electrical projects and, 122, 124
   replacing main, 175–179
   role in electrical system, 11, 13
   shutting off power to, 75
   splicing in box, 177
   upgrading
      equipment for, 174
      location for new panel, 174
      permits for, 172
      replacing main, 175–179
   whole-house surge arrestors, 170–171
short circuit, defined, 14
smoke alarms, hardwired, 214–215
sockets
   replacement of fluorescent, 307
   replacement/repair of lamp, 314–315
solar light systems. See standalone solar

lighting systems
speed-control switches, 165
stairways, 126, 129
standalone solar lighting systems
  about, 284–285
  DC lighting circuit wiring, 287–291
  PV (photovoltaic) panel
    installation, 286
storage spaces
  NEC requirements, 127
stud finders, 52
subpanels
  about, 74–75, 77, 186
  connecting to main service
    panels, 186
  installation, 187–189
  installation planning worksheet,
    187
surface-mounted wiring
  about, 48
  components of system, 49
  cutting metal raceways, 52
  installing, 50–57
  installing wall anchors, 52
  receptacles for, 49
surge arrestors, whole house. See whole-house
  surge arrestors
surge protectors, 107
switch-controlled split receptacles, 154–155
switches
  about, 83
  built-in switch repair, 297
  in circuit maps, 151–155, 159–165
  common inspection mistakes,
    322, 329
  defined, 14
  dimmer switches
    about, 96
    circuits for, 165
    installation, 97
    types of, 96
  electrical box installation for, 68
  NEC requirements for, 7, 128
  neutral wire requirements, 7
  pilot-light switches, 93, 99
  role in electrical system, 10, 13
  safety and, 83
  speed-control, 165
  switch-controlled split receptacles,
    154–155
  switch/receptacles, 93, 101
  testing, 98–101
  testing manual operation of, 101
  timer switches, 94–95, 100, 101
  wireless switches
    installation, 230–231
    types of, 228–229
  See also wall switches

telephones, cable for, 28
thermostats
  baseboard heaters, 233
  low-voltage systems, 224–225
  mercury, disposal, 227
  programmable, 224–225
  upgrading to programmable,
    226–227
THHN/THWN wire, 28, 49
timer switches
  about, 94–95
  testing, 100, 101
tools
  diagnostic, 21
  double-insulated, 19
  fish tape, 21
  tool belts, 21
  for use with wiring, 20

touchless circuit testers, 21, 118
track lighting, 200–203

UF (underground feeder) cable, 27,
  28
ufers, 185
UL (Underwriters Laboratories), 14,
  22
undercabinet lights, 204–207
underfloor radiant heat, 238–243
Underwriters Laboratories (UL), 14, 22
utility companies, upgrading/replacing service
  panels, 172, 175
utility rooms, 129

vanity lights, bathroom, 208–209
vent fans, circuits for, 158
vents
  bathroom exhaust fans, 252–255
  range hoods, 256–259
  vent fan circuits, 158
voltage (volts), 10–11, 14

wall anchor installation, 52
wall heaters, installing, 236–237
walls
  bathroom vanity lights, 208–209
  installing conduit/wires on concrete,
    46
  installing wall anchors, 52
  NEC receptacle spacing
    requirements, 125
  NM cable installation in finished,
    39–40
  NM cable installation in
    unfinished, 34–38
  recessed receptacles, 107
  shutting off power for work in, 23
wall switches
  in circuit maps, 151–155, 159–165
  double switches, 92, 101
  four-way
    about, 86, 90
    in circuit maps, 163–164
    replacing, 91
    testing, 99
    typical installation, 90
  historical types, 85
  installing, 86
  NEC requirements, 84, 125
  pilot-light switches
    about, 93
    testing, 99
  repairing/replacing, 84
  single-pole
    about, 86, 87
    in circuit maps, 151–153, 159
    testing, 98
    typical installation, 87
  three-way
    about, 86, 87
    in circuit maps, 160–162
    replacing, 88
    testing, 99
    typical installation, 87
water heaters
  bonding/ground wiring systems and,
    180, 181
  powering, 11
  wattage of, 134
water pipes, metal, bonding, 180,
  181–182
wattage (watt)
  of air conditioners, 135
  defined, 14
whole-house surge arrestors
  installation, 171

selecting, 170
  types of, 170
window air conditioners
  circuits for, 158
  wattage of, 135
wire connectors
  coding for, 29
  connecting to screw terminals, 31
  defined, 14
  push-in, 31, 32
  using, 32
wireless switches
  installation, 230–231
  types of, 228–229
wire nuts. See wire connectors
wires
  aluminum, 26
  ampacity and, 29
  color chart, 26
  concrete wall installation, 46
  connecting with wire connectors, 32
  connectors for, 29, 31, 32
  copper, 26
  NEC requirements, 128
  neutral in switches, 7
  pigtailing, 33
  push-in connectors, 31, 32
  reading unsheathed, 29
  rubber insulation and, 26
  size chart, 26
  THHN/THWN, 28
wiring
  common inspection mistakes, 322
  diagrams, 123
  grounding systems of, 180–185
  knob and tube, 27
  of outbuildings, 272–279
  receptacles
    end-of-run vs. middle-of-run, 110
    split-circuit, 110–111
    two-slot, 110–111
  safety basics, 22–23
  tools for, 20–21
  See also surface-mounted wiring;
    wires
wiring plans
  drawing, 138–139
  electrical symbol key for, 139
  for sample kitchen project, 146–147
  for sample room addition, 142–143

Information and Projects for the Self-Sufficient Homeowner

WHOLE HOME NEWS

From the Experts at Cool Springs Press and Voyageur Press

For even more information on improving your own home or homestead, visit **www.wholehomenews.com** today! From raising vegetables to raising roofs, it's the one-stop spot for sharing questions and getting answers about the challenges of self-sufficient living.

- -

Brought to you by two publishing imprints of the Quayside Publishing Group, Voyageur Press and Cool Springs Press, *Whole Home News* is a blog for people interested in the same things we are: self-sufficiency, gardening, home improvement, country living, and sustainability. Our mission is to provide you with information on the latest techniques and trends from industry experts and everyday enthusiasts.

In addition to regular posts written by our volunteer in-house advisory committee, you'll also meet others from the larger enthusiast community dedicated to "doing it for ourselves." Some of these contributors include published authors of bestselling books, magazine and newspaper journalists, freelance writers, media personalities, and industry experts. And you'll also find features from ordinary folks who are equally passionate about these topics.

Join us at **www.wholehomenews.com** to keep the conversation going. You can also shoot us an email at wholehomenews@quaysidepub.com. We look forward to seeing you online, and thanks for reading!

SPECIAL BONUS:
scan this code for access to online
streaming video of over a dozen
common wiring projects.
www.completeguidevideo.com